When Helmuth von Moltke took over as Chief of the Prussian General Staff, the Prussian army had not fought a major war for more than forty years. Yet within a decade and-a-half he had brought it to the point where it was the strongest in Europe. His successes on the battlefield led to his methods being painstakingly analysed by commentators and slavishly imitated by Western armies.

His success was not only due to far-sighted strategic planning, the comprehensive reorganisation of the General Staff and his grasp of new technologies; it was also due to his leadership of a talented, if disparate, group of subordinates, even if some of them sometimes failed to grasp his overall intentions.

This book examines these key relationships. Foremost among these was his collaboration with the able though choleric Karl Leonhard von Blumenthal; their correspondence reflected every aspect of their campaigns. He was also close to the Crown Prince, whose aide de camp he had been. Moltke was Chief of Staff to Prince Frederick Charles in Denmark in 1864; his admiration for the 'Red Prince' was perhaps not maintained when the latter's caution caused problems. Albrecht von Stosch, Intendant General in 1870–1871, proved brilliantly successful when he had the chance to demonstrate his talents in the field. Edwin von Manteuffel, on whose recommendation Moltke was appointed, was at the centre of Prussian politics for a decade and-a-half before becoming a successful army commander in 1866, and 1870–1871. Perhaps the most talented of Moltke's subordinates was August von Goeben, a successful commander in all three wars of German unification. August von Werder never enjoyed Moltke's confidence to the same extent, but was extremely reliable. On the other hand, both Eduard Vogel von Falckenstein and Karl von Steinmetz caused Moltke considerable difficulty by their stubborn disobedience of his explicit orders.

Behind these relationships there existed the vital rapport which Moltke had with their Chiefs of Staff and his own General Staff officers. It was on his ability to rely on these men to execute his intentions that his success ultimately depended. Theophil von Podbielski, Julius Verdy du Vernois and Paul Bronsart von Schellendorf were some of the brilliant individuals who constituted one of the most powerful teams in military history.

Quintin Barry is a solicitor and a retired Employment Judge. He has also held a variety of offices in both the public and private sector, including the NHS and local radio. He is presently Secretary General of an international group of law firms.

Following a lifelong interest in history, he is the author of a number of books on military history. These include an acclaimed two-volume history of the Franco-Prussian War of 1870–1871, a history of the Austro-Prussian War of 1866, and the first modern history of the Russo-Turkish War of 1877–1878.

He has made a particular study of the life and career of Helmuth von Moltke, which has prompted this present book. He has also written a biography of the 17th Earl of Derby, which was published in 2012.

Moltke.

Moltke and his Generals

A Study in Leadership

Quintin Barry

 Helion & Company Limited

Helion & Company Limited
26 Willow Road
Solihull
West Midlands
B91 1UE
England
Tel. 0121 705 3393
Fax 0121 711 4075
Email: info@helion.co.uk
Website: www.helion.co.uk
Twitter: @helionbooks
Visit our blog http://blog.helion.co.uk/

Published by Helion & Company 2015

Designed and typeset by Bookcraft Ltd, Stroud, Gloucestershire
Cover designed by Paul Hewitt, Battlefield Design (www.battlefield-design.co.uk)
Printed by Lightning Source Limited, Milton Keynes, Buckinghamshire

ISBN 978-1-910294-41-3

British Library Cataloguing-in-Publication Data.
A catalogue record for this book is available from the British Library.

For details of other military history titles published by Helion & Company Limited
contact the above address, or visit our website: http://www.helion.co.uk.

We always welcome receiving book proposals from prospective authors.

Contents

List of Illustrations

List of Maps

Acknowledgements

I should begin by expressing my debt to the many historians who have written of the wars of German Unification, whose researches and opinions prompted me to explore Moltke's relationships with his senior commanders. I should also gratefully acknowledge the help of my publisher, Duncan Rogers of Helion, whose help in preparing this book for publication was, as always, invaluable.

I am also especially grateful to Jean Hawkes, who typed the book with impressive speed; and to Tim Readman, who read the book in draft and made valuable suggestions.

I must also record my thanks to George Anderson, who prepared the maps.

In addition, the publishers wish to acknowledge the following:

- The quotation on page 270 is reprinted by permission of the publisher from *Command in War* by Martin van Creveld, p 103, copyright 1985 Harvard University Press, Cambridge Mass. published by the President and Fellows of Harvard College.
- The quotations on pages 137 and 138 are reprinted by permission of the publisher from *Supplying War* by Martin van Creveld, pp 103-104, copyright 1977 published by Cambridge University Press, Shaftesbury Road, Cambridge.
- The quotations on pages 35 and 38 are reprinted by permission of the publisher from *Makers of Modern Strategy* ed. Peter Paret, pp 296-298, copyright 1994 published by Oxford University Press, Walton Street, Oxford.
- The quotation on page 31 is reprinted by permission of the publisher from *The Politics of the Prussian Army* by Gordon Craig, p 213 copyright 1955 published by Oxford University Press, Walton Street, Oxford.

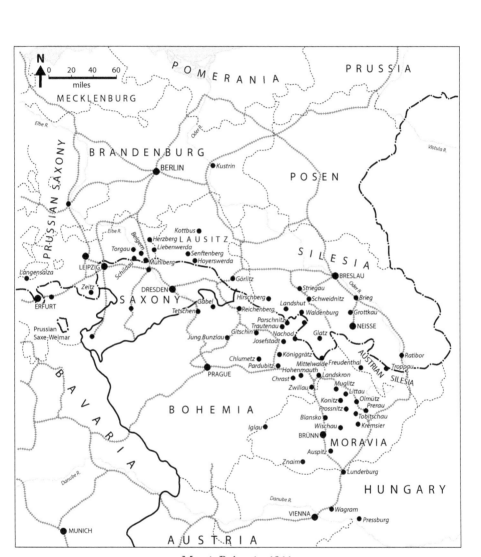

Map 1 Bohemia, 1866.

Map 2 Alsace Lorraine, 1870.

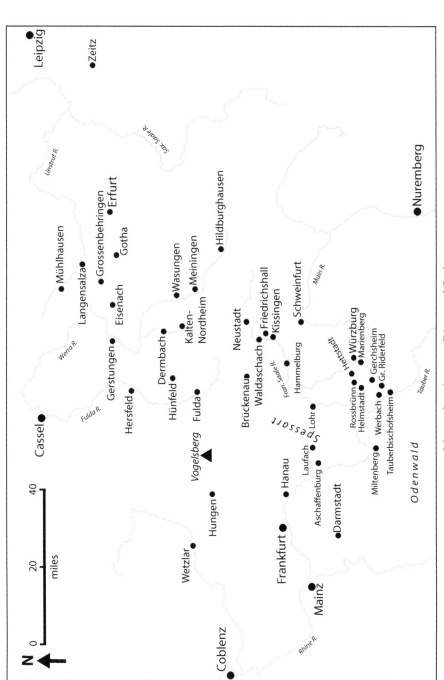

Map 3 Area between Rhine and Saale.

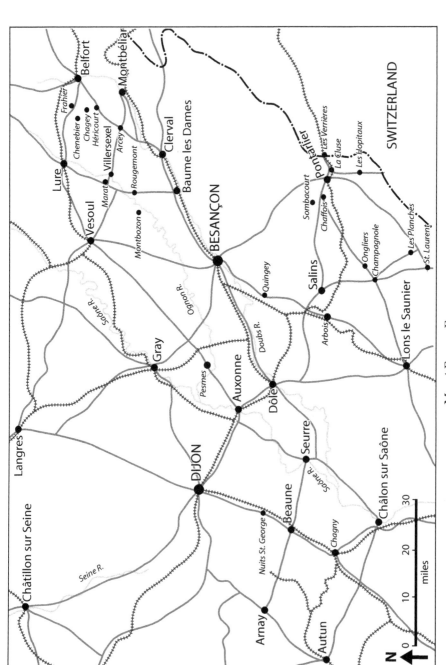

Map 4 Eastern France.

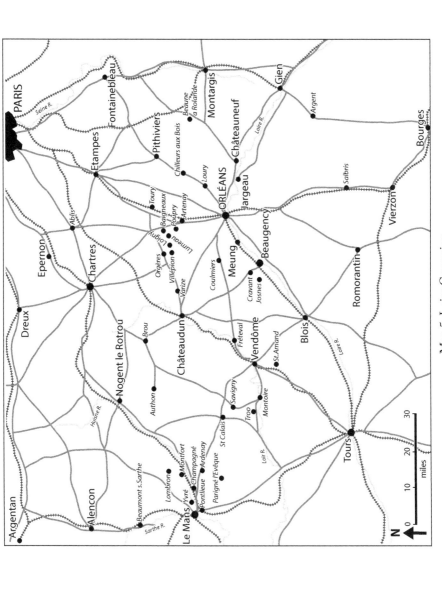

Map 5 Loire Campaign.

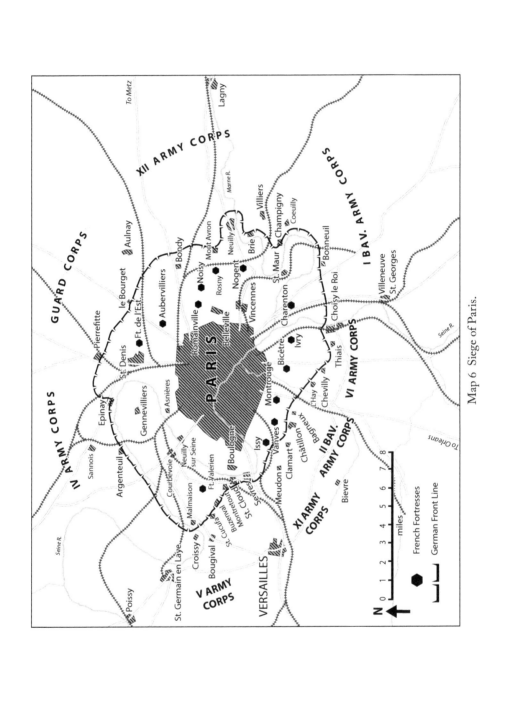

Map 6 Siege of Paris.

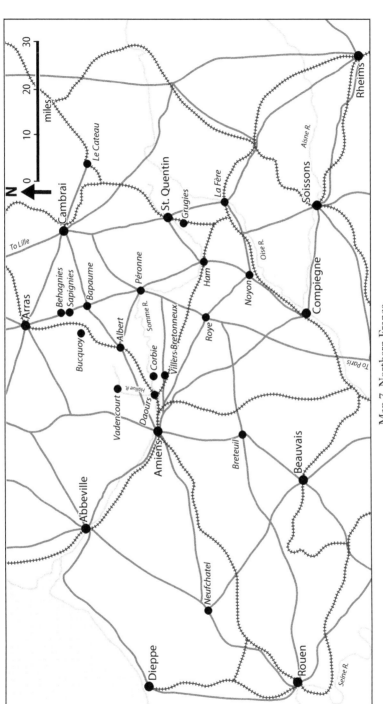

Map 7 Northern France.

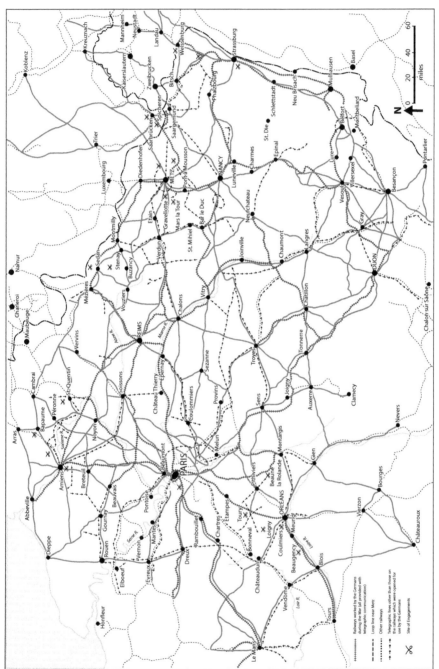

Map 8 Franco–Prussian War, 1870.

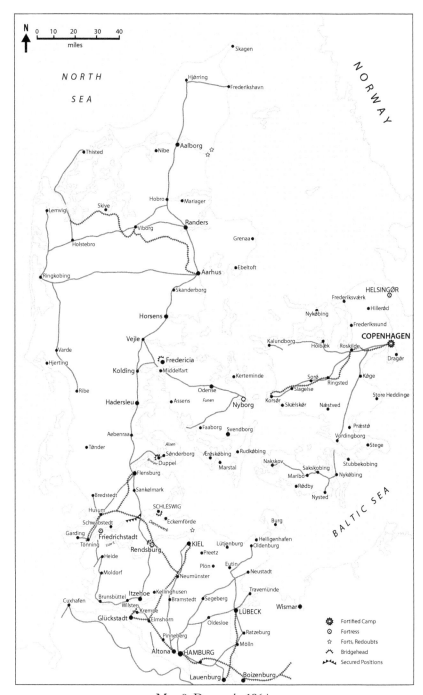

Map 9 Denmark, 1864.

1

Ein Ganz Seltener Mensch

'Das war ein ganz seltener Mensch, ein Mann der systematischen Pflichterfüllung, eine eigenartige Natur, immer fertig und unbedingt zuverlassig, dabei kühl bis ans Herz hinan.' ('He was a very rare kind of man, wholly devoted to duty, an odd character, always prepared and utterly reliable, yet cold to the heart.')[1]

Thus Bismarck, talking in May 1895 about Helmuth von Moltke, four years after the latter's death. In many ways, of course, no one was better qualified than Bismarck to express a view about the personality of the man with whom he worked so closely and to such enormous effect before, during and after the Wars of German Unification. However, in the same conversation he added: 'His was quite a different nature to mine. He never was a runaway.' Certainly, in their public and exterior personalities there was a huge contrast between the outwardly impulsive, passionate and flamboyant statesman and the reserved and careful soldier, and it was to this that Bismarck was referring. But his assessment suggests that he never really got behind Moltke's reticent outward character to understand his real and private personality.

That this was entirely different from the chilly exterior that Bismarck saw appears at once from Moltke's private correspondence. It is impossible to read the tender and loving letters that he wrote to his wife, for instance, throughout their marriage, without being struck by the depth and warmth of affection which they express. His love for Mary was profound, and it was perhaps to her alone that he was able to reveal his capacity for romantic sentiment. Although a shy man, he was extremely self aware and entirely self-confident, as he explained to Mary shortly before they were married:

> The natural friendliness of a kind heart is true courtesy, and the finest polish. In my case a bad bringing up and a youth of privations has often choked this feeling, and still oftener checked its utterance, and so now I have but the acquired coldness of a haughty courtesy, which seldom attracts anyone … My manners are nothing but shyness, varnished over with self confidence and *usage de monde*. The many years of repression in which I grew up have permanently injured my character, suppressed my feelings, and stifled right and noble pride. It was not

until late in life that I began to build up again from within what had not been destroyed.[2]

Moltke was forty one years of age when he wrote these lines to his fiancée, who was not yet sixteen at the time. Although much younger than him, Mary nonetheless understood him very well, writing to him:

> I knew well that all the Moltkes are quiet and reserved. You often show a restraint which some people call *hauteur*. I know that you possess a rich store of gentleness and nobility of heart rarely found in a man. And even among women there are few who possess a warmer heart or deeper sympathy.[3]

One attribute of Moltke's character which Bismarck probably never grasped was his dry sense of humour, which runs through very many of his letters. In the conversation referred to above, Bismarck quoted what he playfully claimed, rather improbably, to be 'the only joke which ever fell from Moltke's lips':

> It was indeed a most critical time: the last few days before our invasion of Bohemia and Saxony. I had received news which made an earlier commencement of the struggle seem advisable, so I begged Moltke to come to me, and asked him if we could start twenty four hours earlier than had been fixed. In reply he asked for paper and pencil, and went into the next room. After about a quarter of an hour he returned and said, 'Yes, it is possible.' To be able to effect this had the same influence on him as a glass of champagne would have on one of us; in other words, the bloodthirsty creature became so joyful that from very light heartedness he made, I believe, the only joke of his life. He had grasped the door knob ready to depart, but turned to me again and said, 'Do you know that the Saxons have blown up the bridge over the Elbe at Dresden?' 'Oh, that is indeed bad news!' said I. 'With water,' added Moltke, and promptly departed. [a play on the words *gesprengt* (blown up) and *besprengt* (watered)][4]

Moltke, who had reached the rank of Major at the time of his marriage in 1842, could look back on a career that had taken an unusual course. He entered the Danish Cadet Academy in Copenhagen at the age of eleven. In old age he observed that it had been a matter of chance that he was thrust into a military career; his own interests and inclination might otherwise have led him into the academic life as a historian or archaeologist.[5]. What he learned as he grew up was the extent to which the power of the intellect dominated everything. It was the breadth of his intellect that, rigorously applied, enabled him to solve the practical problems which he faced; as Professor Bucholz has written he was unique in that 'his wildest ideas were always grounded in the specifics of practical reality'.[6]

Moltke did well in the course of his Danish military education; but in 1821 he resolved to follow his career in an army that offered much greater professional

Bismarck.

opportunities, applying to the King of Prussia for leave to transfer to the Prussian army. It was a decision that cost him four years' seniority, and meant that he must start again to follow a course of education leading to the examinations to become a Prussian officer. In 1822 he qualified for a Prussian commission; thereafter he did well, although his penurious state continued to afflict him; he enjoyed some financial support from his mother, but was never well off, an experience which ensured that he always maintained a frugal attitude to personal expenditure. He graduated from the Prussian War Academy in 1826, and after a brief return to his regiment in Frankfurt an den Oder, served for three years in the General Staff topographical section, where he developed his already impressive skills in drawing and sketching, becoming an extremely accomplished mapmaker.[7]

In March 1832 he was formally appointed as a member of the General Staff, with the rank of First Lieutenant. He was heavily involved in the preparation of military history produced by the staff, working on the campaigns of Frederick the Great. In 1835, with the rank of Captain, he became a company commander in the Kaiser Alexander Guard Grenadier Regiment. This turned out to be the last time he was to serve in a line position in the army. That autumn he participated in the General Staff ride in Silesia, and he followed this by attending combined exercises of the Prussian and Russian armies near Kalisch. After this he was considered for appointment to a post in the Prussian embassy in Paris, but this failed to materialise.[8]

So far, so orthodox; but then, his career at a crossroads, he applied for leave of absence to travel in Turkey and Greece. It was an adventurous decision, and one that was to provide him with some quite unexpected military experience. In Constantinople he and his travelling companion, a Lieutenant von Bergh, were introduced to Chosref Pasha, the Ottoman Commander in Chief. To him they presented a copy of the war game kit used by the Prussian General Staff, and on the following day Moltke gave a demonstration of the game. Chosref, very impressed, invited him to stay on in Constantinople and instruct his officers in the use of the war game. As Moltke later explained, the offer was an attractive one on financial grounds, and he was soon hard at work as a respected adviser of the Ottoman high command. He was still thus engaged in 1837 when three more Prussian officers, Captains von Vincke-Olbendorff, Fischer and von Mühlbach arrived to join him, at a time when the threat from Mehemet Ali in Egypt was growing more and more serious.

Moltke's assignment to the army of Hafiz Pasha gave him the opportunity to put his developing strategic ideas into practice His biographer Eberhard Kessel has reviewed Moltke's written work up to the time he left for Turkey, and found that it adopted much of the teaching of Clausewitz, advocating artillery preparation before the attack, the need to secure defensive positions in retreat, the freedom given by movement and the value of the flank attack.[9] As Arden Bucholz has observed, these were all classic themes. Hafiz was posted on the southern border of Asia Minor in position to block any advance by the Egyptian army under Ibrahim Pasha. By mid May 1839 Hafiz had some 30,000 men at Biradschik in a position on Ibrahim's flank which the latter could not by pass. Mühlbach, who had accompanied Moltke, proposed that bridges be built in the rear of the Turkish position; Moltke and another Prussian officer Friedrich von Laue grimly rejected the suggestion – troops fought better, they argued, when there was no way out.[10]

For a man of his relative youth and limited experience, Moltke certainly did not lack confidence, and he repeatedly offered strong advice to Hafiz as to what he should do; it was advice that Hafiz frequently ignored. When Ibrahim, having found the position at Biradschik too strong for a frontal attack, began a flank march to attack the Turkish rear, Moltke advocated an immediate assault to catch the Egyptians on the march. Hafiz refused. Next, Moltke proposed massing the artillery to protect the Turkish flank. Hafiz, who was acting under the guidance of the mullahs, again refused. Moltke could only watch as his predictions of disaster were fulfilled; on June 24, during the battle at Nisib, the Egyptian army inflicted a decisive defeat on Hafiz, whose army disintegrated, and Moltke and his colleagues escaped only very narrowly indeed.

Moltke returned to Berlin by way of Constantinople, to resume his career as an officer of the General Staff, finding, to his surprise, that he had become a celebrity.

Unusually for one of his rank, he was at this time awarded the order 'Pour le Mérite.' Soon after his return he was posted to the staff of the IV Corps, and it was about this time that he renewed his acquaintance with Marie (or Mary, as Moltke always called her) Burt, the stepdaughter of his sister Augusta, at that time about fourteen years old. He had last seen her at the age of eight, and it was some two years later before they met again; notwithstanding the difference in their ages, it was to be a love match from the start, which brought out the deep affection and warmth in Moltke that was usually masked by his austere professionalism. They were married on April 20 1842.

In 1841 Moltke took a decision that was to be important both professionally and personally, when he joined the promoters of the Berlin Hamburg railway. Dennis Showalter, the author of the seminal 'Railroads and Rifles,' described his recruitment:

> Moltke was initially surprised when he was offered a post on the board of directors. He was not particularly well acquainted with either the men or the idea. He had spent the years from 1835 to 1839 as a military adviser in Turkey, and was out of touch with recent events in Germany. But the promoters knew their man. Moltke had served on the General Staff for twelve years, earning a reputation as a conscientious officer of exceptional talent and an author good enough to supplement his salary by regular contributions to the civilian press. What he did not know about railroads, he could learn. Even more important, the projected Berlin – Hamburg line would have to cross the territory of two other states – Mecklenburg and Danish Lauenburg. A nobleman wearing the crimson stripes of the Prussian General Staff would be a valuable asset in negotiating for concessions in conservative Mecklenburg, and Moltke was Danish by birth, with influential connections in Denmark. It was an ideal combination.[11]

Actually, Moltke was not Danish; but he certainly had family connections there and once engaged to Mary Burt he had a strong personal reason for wanting to see a rapid system of transportation between Hamburg and Berlin.

To Moltke, the military possibilities were obvious; but he also saw in the development of a comprehensive railway system a potential influence for German unity. But although active in the promotion of a private enterprise in which he invested a large part of his savings, he was concerned that commercial considerations might inhibit the construction of a proper network in which less profitable lines were subsidised by those generating more traffic. For this reason he argued for the use of government funds to fill the gaps; state control or state ownership was essential for Prussia to gain to the full the advantages which the railways offered.[12]

Although Moltke himself, because of the pressure of other responsibilities, felt obliged to retire from the board in 1844, his interest in railways and their military potential continued. In the following decade some other influential soldiers began to see clearly the importance of railways for the future – even though, as Showalter noted, this was by no means universal; the engineer corps apparently 'regarded steam engines with indifference or hostility.' On the other hand, Prussian legislation had come into force regulating the construction and regulation of railways, while some prominent officials, notably the future Minister of Commerce August von der Heydt, argued for the nationalisation of the railways.[13]

Moltke also found time in the years immediately following his Turkish years to develop his literary career. He gave a series of successful lectures on his experiences, and wrote a large number of articles. He also published three books; a book of maps, his 'Letters from Turkey' and a history of the Russo-Turkish War of 1828-1829. This last was a major undertaking to which he devoted all the time he could spare; he reported to Mary in August 1843 on the progress he was making:

> I am by this time getting accustomed to my temporary widowhood, and have thrown myself with all my might into my work upon the campaign of 1828. Today I sat for eight hours uninterruptedly, from seven to three o'clock, and wrote a whole section.[14]

That summer he accompanied his corps commander, Prince Charles, a brother of King Frederick William IV, to manoeuvres at Frankfurt an der Oder; the speed of rail travel was still sufficiently novel at the time for him to tell Mary that the journey of fifty six miles took two hours and five minutes. His acquaintance with the Royal family was continuing to develop as he recorded in his letters, not infrequently, for instance, dining with the King. This was to lead in due course to another appointment which exercised a considerable influence on his career.

In 1845 Moltke was appointed aide de camp to Prince Henry, the brother of King Frederick William IV. It was not as surprising an appointment as has been suggested; Moltke was still serving at the time on the staff of the IV Corps, commanded by Prince Charles. The latter would have had every opportunity of judging Moltke's suitability for the post of ADC, and it may be assumed that he was consulted before the appointment was made. Thus began Moltke's career as a courtier, in which he became and always remained extremely close to the Prussian Royal family.

Prince Henry lived in Rome, to which city Moltke and his wife now moved. He enjoyed his time there, and employed his topographical skills to prepare a map of the Eternal City covering ten square miles, which was subsequently published. His stay was not, however, to be prolonged: Prince Henry died in the following year, and Moltke returned to Berlin, uncertain of where his immediate future lay, but apparently open minded about it, writing to Mary on November 8 1846: 'Diest wants me to be aide de camp, but General Krauseneck wishes to keep me on the General Staff, in which there have been great promotions.'[15] As it turned out, he was transferred to the staff of the VIII Corps, based in Coblenz.

Moltke was still serving in Coblenz when the 1848 revolutions exploded all over Europe. During the March Days in Prussia he sent Mary off to Ems, where he judged she would be safer. To Jeanette, his sister-in-law, he wrote:

As to our position here, it is as though we were sitting on a powder barrel ... Generally speaking, it is quite natural that a people who are in the habit of changing their spiritual princes twice in every ten years, should not have a great affection for any one dynasty.'[16]

A day or two later he reflected on the effect that events in Berlin might have, writing to Jeanette on March 29 that he had to pour a good many drops of bitterness into the cup of her fine patriotic feeling:

With reference to what is going on in Germany, I can rejoice in so far as I see in the present state of affairs the only possibility of a united Germany, but not until law and order are restored and some central power comes into existence can any good result ... An attack from outside would be a great blessing at the present moment, but our neighbours to the east and west will wait until we have broken up into parties and destroyed our power ... What a future is Germany throwing away![17]

The proletariat was, he thought, 'the evil spirit which liberalism has conjured up, and which it is no longer able to banish.'

By now, in middle age, Moltke's personality, his private philosophy and his many interests were well settled. They have been exhaustively reviewed by a number of brilliant and perceptive historians, most notably Gerhard Ritter and Rudolf Stadelmann. The former pointed out that it should be understood that Moltke was far more than the typical Prussian soldier:

He might indeed be described as a kind of ideal of German manhood generally, more specifically North German. No Prussian officer was ever less confined within the limits of technical military expertise. In a certain sense, he must be considered the great exception, in any event an absolutely unique figure in the ranks of German generals, an astonishingly talented and versatile man, infinitely curious and open minded ...The study of technical treatises in the military field actually took up very little of his career. As a young General Staff officer he dabbled in languages, attended lectures on literature, read an amazing range of works in several tongues displaying equal interest in fiction, science and the humanities.[18]

As Ritter noted, Moltke's consuming passion was travel, which enabled him to record in elegant prose the penetrating observations which he was able to make of peoples and their countryside, their politics, history and culture, and their social and economic circumstances. Even before his extensive travels in the Near East he had written acutely on the subjects of both Belgium and Poland. His literary style was analysed by Professor Ritter who noted the difference from that of Rühle von Lilienstern and Gneisenau:

It is the difference between a world of ideas rooted primarily in the realms of aesthetics and philosophy and a new approach pointed much more at grasping the realities of history and politics. Moltke too not only carried his copy of Goethe's 'Faust' in his travelling bag but knew the play by heart. He too – especially in his letters to his bride – could revel in poetic images and moods that do not lack the magic of romanticism; and the devout enjoyment of good music was an indispensable element of his life; but Moltke never remained caught in mere sentiment. His style always pressed on beyond rhetoric and effective phraseology to spare and austere objectivity. His understanding of the world moved from the brilliant play of ideas to prompt and practical conclusions.[19]

Moltke's analytical and calculating approach to his profession marked him out as an academic; but that did not in due course prevent him taking decisions in the planning of operations that at first sight were bold in the extreme. It has also been pointed out that his character was not one lacking in ambition, notwithstanding his quiet and reflective exterior. Certainly it is the case that he did not seek fame and adulation – this invariably embarrassed him; but he pursued success in all that he attempted, with a relentless determination, especially once the power to accomplish great results was given to him. Characteristically, however, he wrote to an admirer in 1880:

What some day settles the value of a man's life is not the glamour of success but purity of purpose, loyal adherence to duty … For we ourselves never know how much is due to our own efforts, to others, or to the workings of a higher will. It is wise not to claim too much under the first heading.[20]

His reference to a higher will is unsurprising; it may be taken for granted that he believed in the Christian view of a higher vocation, a belief which he shared with Bismarck. But whereas Bismarck relied on his faith in a divine governance to enable him to bear the responsibilities that fell to him, Moltke had a more realistic view, as Professor Ritter pointed out:

Moltke the humanist possessed a much stronger faith in the power of human reason, in man's capacity to shape the world along rational lines, in the inexorable advance of culture and civilisation. Since God's wisdom ruled the world, using us as its tools, it was merely a matter of everyone doing his job in 'pure endeavour and loyal adherence to duty,' as his vocation dictated. One could not fail then to master unreason and blind chance. The rational optimism and faith in progress rooted in the depth of Moltke's harmonious nature were moderated by the realistic insight of modern empiricism and therefore free of eighteenth century illusions, yet his world concept was also entirely free of tragic and gloomy overtones.[21]

Moltke had a clear view of the world, and his place in it, and of the professional duty that he must discharge. This came before all else. He held, of course, the political views to be expected of his time and class, being conservative, monarchical and anti democratic; but he entirely lacked any political drive. This was something that both Ritter and Stadelmann explored in depth; and both of them, and particularly the former, concluded that in Moltke there was a total absence of any kind of political ambition. Naturally he held and expressed strong opinions at the restless times in which he was to do his job; but they were the thoughtful opinions of a detached observer. From his post as Chief of Staff of the IV Corps, for instance, to which he had been appointed in 1848, he wrote to Mary in strong terms on January 29 1851 indignantly commenting on the humiliating Convention of Olmütz:

> That our whole policy has been so perverted that we must now accept many humiliations, that we must give up everything we have claimed and attempted during the last three years, I quite understand. But that we should muster five hundred thousand men to yield on all points, and help the Austrians over the Elbe on Frederick the Great's birthday, that is difficult to understand.[22]

It was something he felt deeply; he wrote in even stronger terms of outrage to his brother Adolf a few weeks later:

> A more disgraceful peace was never signed. And such an army as we had collected! For twenty four weeks the IV Corps was mobilised and brought out of all the garrisons. And such troops! If only Frederick the Great had had such men! Thirty millions of thalers are gone for a demonstration, and to accept any and every condition. But the worst government cannot ruin this nation. Prussia will yet stand at the head of Germany.[23]

The events of 1850 that had caused Moltke so much distress had seen him at his busiest. In his capacity as Chief of Staff of the IV Corps the diplomatic situation had been deteriorating throughout the year as the political conflict between Austria and Prussia intensified. In October Tsar Nicholas I had purported to decide the dispute in favour of the Austrians, at a meeting in Warsaw attended by the Emperor Franz Joseph and Prince William of Prussia. Following this, Austrian and Bavarian troops advanced through Hesse and threatened Prussian territory. King Frederick William, who had been dithering about whether to order a mobilisation, now decided to do so, and between November 6 and January 31 the Prussian army was mobilised for the first time in 35 years.

Arden Bucholz has described the mobilisation as a disaster from start to finish; and listed six major problems which the process had disclosed.[24] These were the fundamental unwillingness of the Prussian government to go to war, the lack of proper planning, the lack of experience in utilising the railroad system, the lack of any advance warning, poor coordination within the army, and the scale of the management problems involved. Moltke's own corps was mobilised in three weeks, however, and he seems to have considered that it had not gone badly, remarking in his letter to his brother Adolf: 'mobilisation and demobilisation have given me much to do, but the result was satisfactory.'[25] On the other hand, in correspondence with colleagues in other corps, he did insist that in future there should be more advance warning, more coordination and clearer relationships between the standing army, the reserves and the Landwehr.

For the moment Moltke continued to be based at Magdeburg as Chief of Staff of the IV Corps. During this time Reyher, the Chief of the Great General Staff, made a note in Moltke's file which suggested that he was better suited to staff duties than a field command: 'Lastly he lacks the force and vitality without which a troop commander cannot in the long run maintain his authority.' Moltke might not have disagreed with this; he wrote to his brother in 1855: 'Quite possibly I have already reached my full potential, and if I sense the slightest suggestion of a brigade command, I shall withdraw my name.'[26]

Moltke, then, was seen at this stage of his career as lacking the charismatic qualities of a troop leader. Professor Ritter identified the kind of self assurance that he brought to his profession:

> Moltke's on the other hand, was the unshakable calm and assurance of the intellectual, a firmness that never failed to impress his associates on the battle fields of France and Bohemia. It sprang from an insight of incorruptible clarity rather than from iron self discipline. In this uniquely individual identity of rational and ethical character traits, giving rise to an optimism that was reasoned and at once practical, Moltke showed himself, in one aspect of his personality, to be a true heir to the traditions of Frederick the Great.[27]

It was in 1855 that his career was to take a different turn, when the King unexpectedly sent for him. Moltke had hastily to borrow a helmet and sash in order to appear correctly dressed. The King told him that he wished to appoint him as First Adjutant to his nephew Prince Frederick William. It was, Moltke told Mary, an appointment which was opposed by those around the young prince on the basis that it was not required. The selection of Moltke followed an extensive check of his suitability by senior officers. The King recognised that he was asking Moltke to give up a good position: 'The King spoke about the matter with much vivacity and very openly, for quite a quarter of an hour, until I was able to say that I would do my best to be of use to the young prince.'[28]

He was therefore to make a journey to East Prussia, where he was to accompany Frederick William on a short visit to the province, a trip which would enable the parties to see how they got on. In fact they got on very well, and enjoyed the visit, which Moltke fully described in a letter to Adolf soon after his return. Danzig he found to be one of the most beautiful towns he knew, while he was particularly interested to visit the Trakehnen stud farm and the nearby depots for army remounts: 'One rarely sees so many fine horses together; at Trakehnen there are about a thousand mares and foals.'[29] Moltke reported to the King on his return, and in due course his appointment was formally announced; before he took up his duties, however, he was to participate in the annual exercises of the IV Corps.

The new post meant a good deal of travel, which would take him away from Mary for long periods at a time; Moltke made sure, however, that she was kept close to his activities by the stream of affectionate and informative letters that he despatched to her. His first trip was to England and Scotland in September 1855, where Frederick William had already begun a visit to Queen Victoria's court. He and Moltke were there again in the following May, where they attended a prolonged series of Royal engagements, receptions, levées, dinner parties and banquets; these included a visit to the Epsom Derby, and the manoeuvres at Aldershot, held in the presence of Queen Victoria. The burgeoning romance between Frederick William and Princess Victoria, the Princess Royal, would certainly ensure further visits.[30]

That summer Moltke was rewarded for his successful stint as a courtier by his promotion to the rank of Major General; soon after he accompanied Prince Frederick William to Russia, to represent the King at the coronation of Tsar Alexander, from where he wrote another series of letters which were subsequently published in 1877 as 'Letters from Russia.' Quiet and reserved he may have been, but it is apparent from his correspondence that he was thoroughly enjoying the opportunity for travel, not least because he was able to do it in such style. During his visit Moltke was, as always, fascinated by the architecture of the cities, and his letters contained detailed descriptions of the many remarkable buildings which he was taken to see. And, as usual, there were the comprehensive accounts of the spectacular parades, balls, and other court functions which he attended. But, as was his habit, he reflected on the condition of the sixty million people of Russia, the society of which he found paradoxical. He was struck by the contrast between the effect on the upper classes of the importation of the practices of Western Europe by Peter the Great, and on the rest of the people:

> The civilisation of the West so suddenly and violently introduced has never penetrated the lower strata of society. A small number of fashionable Russians in stars and uniforms, educated in the French style, and brought up in the greatest luxury, exist side by side, and without any intermediate steps, with the mass of the strong, bearded, ignorant, but pious and docile people who exceed them in number a hundred fold.[31]

But he also noted the fact that the Russian national character produced highly obedient soldiers:

> The Russian peasants are naturally good humoured and peaceable. I have never seen the people fighting or wrestling. They have no bull-fights or cock-fights. But their feeling for their superiors makes them, much against their inclination it is true, most submissive soldiers.[32]

December 1856 saw Moltke in attendance on his prince on a visit to Paris. He was in spite of himself extremely impressed, and was clearly fascinated by Napoleon III, of whom he wrote:

> I quite thought that Louis Napoleon was taller – he looks better on horseback than on foot. I was struck by the peculiar immobility of his countenance and, I had almost said, the lacklustre look in his eye. He has a good natured kindly smile, which is anything but Napoleonic. He sits generally in a position of quiet repose, with his head slightly on one side, and it is perhaps just this repose which, never forsaking him in a serious emergency, so impresses his excitable subjects. Events have shown that this is no apathy, but the outcome of a thoughtful mind and a firm will. In society he is not imposing, and in conversations he seems even slightly embarrassed. He is all an emperor, but never a king.[33]

Moltke was also very impressed by the Empress Eugénie, and she in her turn took note of him, writing to one of her close friends:

> A general called Moltke or some such name is in attendance on the prince; this general who talks but little is nothing but a dreamer; nevertheless he is always interesting and surprises one by his apt remarks. The Germans are an imposing race. Louis says they are the race of the future. Bah.'[34]

June 1857, and Moltke was back again in London, this time for the formal engagement of Prince Frederick William and Princess Victoria. Again, he wrote a series of letters with the most detailed descriptions of all he had seen, and all of the people he had met. He left out little; but one senses that, as an objective observer, he was faintly amused by the pomp and ceremony which he witnessed. On his return to Berlin, he found a deepening shadow over the Royal family; the King's health was causing growing concern, one effect of which was to delay the wedding of his prince. It meant also that consideration must be given to the appointment of the Prince of Prussia as Prince Regent, which was to lead directly to momentous consequences for the nation.

William became Prince Regent on October 8 1857; on the day before, Reyher, after a short illness, had died, which meant that one of the first acts of the Prince Regent must be to fill a crucially important vacancy. The interregnum at the top of the Prussian army coinciding with the confusion arising from the regency was a matter of the deepest concern, as Moltke, uncertain as to his own situation, wrote to Mary:

> It is quite impossible to foresee what the immediate future may bring forth. The ministers met today, and have come to a resolution how the conduct of state business is meanwhile to be carried on. Military matters especially cannot go on without the supreme head; the prince's second adjutant cannot even be appointed. As soon as that is done, I no doubt, shall be released; till then, here

I must stay. Reitzenstein, from Frankfurt, may be very likely be put in Reyher's place, and it would be a good choice.[35]

On October 29 the Prince Regent made a decision that would change history; he appointed Moltke to be Acting Chief of the Great General Staff to take Reyher's place. In spite of his reference to Reitzenstein's suitability for the post, Moltke cannot have been taken entirely by surprise by his appointment. Moving in the court circles which brought him regularly into contact with the Prince Regent and the Royal family, the possibility of his being appointed must have been openly considered. A key influence in the appointment was that of Edwin von Manteuffel, the Chief of the Military Cabinet, whose advice to Prince William was crucial. Manteuffel had taken up his position early in 1857, and enjoyed the closest rapport with the Prince Regent.

Thus it was that Moltke embarked on his career at the pinnacle of the Prussian army, in a position which, if it began as one of limited power and influence, grew to be decisive in his country's history. That Prussia had the greatest good fortune in this has never been disputed. Nonetheless, the military success of the Prussian army owed much not only to the chief of its General Staff, but also to his relationship with those that were to execute his plans and intentions. Inevitably, they were not always successful in this; but it was part of Moltke's achievement that his relationship with his generals was so effective. To him, especially after 1866, they accorded him immense respect – respect which none could doubt that he deserved. Professor Ritter summed up his capacity for detached intellectual decision making, and his words express precisely the secret of Moltke's success:

> Moltke's attitudes were never purely personal, but always governed by objective considerations; and there has scarcely ever been a general less influenced by passion, more given to ice cold reason. It was precisely this unswerving objectivity that gave him such a lead over more wilful and emotional men.[36]

It was not inconsistent, though, with this analysis that Moltke could occasionally display a wholly blinkered approach to political reality, when he showed an inability to step outside the narrow limits of his professional function. He was, of course, a man of his time and his class; but it is nevertheless disconcerting to encounter instances of this tunnel vision, as for instance when in January 1871, at the height of his bitter dispute with Bismarck, he argued in the Crown Prince's presence for a 'war of extermination.' While this was not a concept to be taken literally, it was nonetheless completely at odds with Bismarck's grasp of the need for a swift and sensible conclusion to the war, and views of this kind meant that the Chancellor was determined to confine Moltke's role in the armistice negotiations to the purely military aspects.

2

Military Philosophy

Moltke never sat down to write a single, comprehensive statement of his military philosophy, but over the years he produced a large number of military writings for various purposes and in different circumstances. Professor Daniel Hughes edited many of these for a collection published as 'Moltke on the Art of War.' He noted that the collected works included eight volumes of memoirs, fourteen volumes of military work, one volume of mobilisation plans, one volume of records of conversations, and a number of smaller items.[1]

Moltke's teaching was always grounded in history, from which he believed strategists had much to learn, provided always that it was studied with a sense of perspective. However, he did not believe that strategy was a science, writing soon after the end of the Franco-Prussian War:

> Strategy is a system of expedients. It is more than a discipline; it is the transfer of knowledge to practical life, the continued development of the original leading thought in accordance with the constantly changing circumstances. It is the art of acting under the pressure of the most difficult conditions.[2]

It was a restatement of the principle set out in his 'Instructions for Large Unit Commanders' of 1869, in which he remarked that 'the teachings of strategy go little beyond the first premises of sound reason.'

Taken together, Moltke's writings became the foundation of the Prusso-German system of military philosophy. His successes on the battlefield meant that all that he wrote was minutely studied, not only in Germany but in every major nation state. In fact his teachings were uncritically accepted to a greater extent outside Germany rather than within, where they were subjected to profound analysis by successive writers who were on occasion prepared to depart from his views. This was especially so when comparisons were made with the teachings of Clausewitz or the system of war practised by Napoleon. As time went by, the contribution of many such writers to the development of strategical science was in its turn severely criticised; Herbert Rosinski described them as 'second-hand, second-rate comparators and commentators

... almost wholly devoid of any original inspirations ... and largely concerned with hair-splitting controversies about the subtleties of Moltke's [and Napoleon's] strategy.'[3]

There were relatively few sources which shaped Moltke's professional thinking. Among the five books which had most influenced him, he listed the works of Homer, the Bible, and Clausewitz's 'On War.' (the other two were the works of the Austrian astronomer Joseph Johann von Littrow, and the German organic chemist Justus von Liebig).[4] Gunther E Rothenberg, who described Moltke as 'the most incisive and important European military writer between the Napoleonic era and the First World War,' considered the sources of his inspiration:

> Like many Prussian soldiers, he attributed some of his ideas to Clausewitz and described himself as his disciple. Yet Clausewitz's actual contribution to Prussian military doctrine and practice is hard to estimate. In Moltke's case there may be some convergence with Clausewitz on the relationship of the state and the army, but much less agreement on organisational and operational matters. Where Clausewitz was ever the philosopher, seeking to discover the universal nature of war and using specific examples primarily as illustrations, Moltke was essentially a grammarian of war who engaged in very little abstract speculation.[5]

As a result of Moltke's disputes with Bismarck during the winter of 1870-1871, one aspect in particular of Clausewitz's teachings has been examined with particular care. Much has been written about Moltke's willingness to accept that political considerations must be taken account of; that war is an instrument of policy, and that the needs of the political situation must at times be allowed to affect strategy. Moltke, writing on the subject in the years following the disputes at Versailles, no doubt had them in mind:

> War is the violent action of nations to attain or maintain purposes of state. It is the most extreme means of carrying out that will and, during its duration, abolishes international treaties between the belligerents. War, as General von Clausewitz says, 'is the continuation of policy with other means.' Thus, and unfortunately, policy cannot be separated from strategy, for politics used war to attain its objectives and has a decisive influence on war's beginning and end. Policy does this in such a manner that it reserves to itself the right to increase its demands during the course of the war or to satisfy itself with minor successes. Given this uncertainty, strategy can direct its endeavours only toward the highest goal attainable with the means at hand. Strategy thus works best in the hands of politics and only for the latter's purposes. But, in its actions, strategy is independent of policy as much as possible. Policy must not be allowed to interfere in operations.[6]

This passage, or rather its source, has provoked academic controversy.

Professor Ritter complained that the phrase 'unfortunately, policy cannot be separated from strategy' is an editorial addition to Moltke's original; while Professor

Hughes, although acknowledging that in some versions the word 'unfortunately' does not appear, considered Ritter's objections to be excessive, and unsupported by archival sources. He observed that Stadelmann, who had had access to the original but now lost archives, had relied on the version set out above.[7] The fact is that the passages from Moltke's writings on the subject can be interpreted either as an acceptance to some extent of Clausewitz, or a departure from it.

General von Caemmerer was satisfied that the passage quoted above showed that in this respect Moltke was not following Clausewitz. He noted that Verdy du Vernois, in his *Studien über den Krieg*, thought that Clausewitz's original proposition to the effect that war under all circumstances was not an independent thing went too far. At the same, however, Verdy had shown that in practice, especially in relation to 1864, the influence of policy on operations was not only important but even sometimes decisive. Caemmerer thought that when Moltke wrote the above passage quoted above, he was 'still not quite free from the ill humour caused by his well known conflict with Bismarck.' As a result Caemmerer concluded that here was 'quite an exceptional case, where this uncommonly unselfish man was not completely free from bias.'[8]

It is not, however, to be supposed that Moltke was blind to the necessity of interaction between political and military leaders; during the dispute over the bombardment of Paris, Moltke accepted that 'even in the course of military operations the command must concede influence on its decisions to political considerations; only adding that 'as free a hand as possible must be given to skilled technical army leadership.'[9] The fact was that the doubts of Moltke and his advisers as to the practicability of the bombardment hardened steadily in the face of Bismarck's gut feeling that he must do all he could to end the war quickly; as is the nature of such debate, neither side participated with an open mind.

Before leaving the subject of policy and its impact on the conduct of war, it is worth noting that it was in wars of coalitions that Moltke regarded the greatest likelihood of political considerations becoming paramount. In coalitions, he wrote, 'the interests of the allies coincide only up to a certain point.' Beyond that, the situation changed:

> In mere coalitions, we cannot demand what is most desirable from a military standpoint, but only that which is advantageous to both allies. Every strategic agreement on the part of allied armies therefore is a sort of compromise in which special interests have to be considered. Such special interests can be silenced only in a unified state.[10]

Moltke's practical experience of this, so far as Prussia was concerned, was the Danish war of 1864; but he must also have had the Franco-Italian campaign against Austria in 1859 in his mind.

If difficult issues could arise between politicians and the military in an autocratic regime, how much worse was it likely to be, Moltke thought, where a democratic government was concerned. He reflected on the Danish situation as it had been in 1864:

Under pressure of public opinion, impassioned speeches in the assembly and partisan furore, a minister responsible to the nation will find it hard to proceed on purely military considerations. Once war is declared the supreme commander must be given full freedom to act by his own discretion. A heavy responsibility weighs on him, before God and his conscience, beside which his responsibility before the tribunal of the nation pales into insignificance. Hence the sovereign is always the proper commander in chief, not accountable in theory, but actually bearing the heaviest responsibility – for who has more at stake when it comes to crown and sceptre?[11]

Moltke's outstanding capacity for originality of thought was nowhere better demonstrated than in his realisation that, in the middle of the nineteenth century, the conduct of war was undergoing a colossal change. Brought about by the technological advances in weaponry and communications, this necessitated a fresh look not only at the tactical consequences, but at strategical doctrine and organisation. He could see clearly that the stopping power of the new rifles and of the rapidly developing artillery might give the tactical defence a considerable advantage. On the other hand, the greatly improved rail and road links, and the ability to communicate promptly with faster moving units gave advantages to the strategic offensive of which Moltke was determined to make use. Indeed, he had to; in 1866 Prussia could not afford a long war and he intended to keep the initiative. Not only this, but, as he wrote after the campaign, 'undoubtedly we will do best in the future to conduct war not in our country but in the enemy's.'[12] One further conclusion could be drawn from this. Prussia's fortresses, which had not been of any actual value in that campaign, offered no direct support but had absorbed 150,000 men who would have been more usefully employed with the field army.

On the other hand, the importance of railways was greatly enhanced where they crossed large rivers, and it was in this context that fortresses became crucial, as Moltke had written as early as 1861:

> Railroads must cross the larger rivers only at fortresses because we must preserve the bridges for our use. Thus, it is necessary to enlarge almost all our fortresses, such as those at Cologne, Coblenz, and Mainz, and to construct new ones at Marienburg and Breslau. Since these are limited by financial means and garrisons, new railroads must cross rivers at existing fortresses. A railroad bridge across a large river outside a fortress is a bridge without regard to military advantages.[13]

Moltke called in particular, for instance, in a paper written in early 1870, for a new bridge at Mainz; in the event of a concentration in the west a huge volume of traffic would have to be handled there; the new bridge should be built below the mouth of the Main, where it would be dominated by the works of the fortress. It was, however, some thirty eight years before Moltke's wish was executed. In the same paper he reached the conclusion that 'only active fighting forces can prevent the opponent using our railroads.' If it became necessary to retreat, he concluded that it was better to take up the rails altogether rather than to rely on breaking the line by destroying a structure.

To achieve the objective of a rapid victory, it was necessary to evolve a new strategic thinking:

> Confronted with the deadlock imposed by new weapons and extended frontages, Moltke ... developed the concept of outflanking the enemy in one continuous strategic-operational sequence combining mobilisation, concentration, movement, and fighting. By seizing the initiative from the outset, he intended to drive his opponent into a partial or complete envelopment, destroying his army in a great and decisive battle of annihilation or encirclement, the *Vernichtungs-* or *Kesselschlacht*.[14]

As experience was to show, not all his subordinates, once on the battlefield, were able to grasp his intentions.

Writing of the campaign of 1866, Schlieffen pointed out the extent to which this proved to be the case:

> The idea of annihilating the enemy, which completely absorbed Moltke, was not fathomed by the subordinate commanders. They understood the problem before them to lie in the junction of the separated armies. In this they agreed with Moltke. But he wished to see the opponent within the circle of the united armies, while they were wiling to leave it to the enemy to concentrate his forces where he desired. Once the armies were concentrated, no matter where, it could then be decided whether to accept battle or not.[15]

Moltke's decision to concentrate his army on the battlefield of Königgrätz marked a departure from the Napoleonic principle that an army should be concentrated well in advance of the battle itself. As Hajo Holborn has pointed out, however, in the period before Königgrätz he had left his options open in this respect; he might have brought his separate armies together before arriving on the battlefield, but it was his judgment to keep them apart until the day of battle. Looking back on this decision, he set down his thinking on the subject, observing that 'every close concentration of large masses is inherently a calamity,' because of the extraordinarily difficult logistic situations that must arise:

> Conditions are more favourable when the fighting forces can be concentrated from different points toward the battlefield on the day of battle, and when operations can be conducted so that a final short march from different directions leads to the enemy's front and flank simultaneously. In that case, strategy has performed its best, and great results should be the result. Of course no foresight

can assure that the operations of separated armies will actually bring about this final success. That is far more dependent not only on the calculable factors of the size of the forces and time, but in many cases on the outcome of minor engagements, and the weather, or on false information. In short, it is dependent on what in the human sense is designated as chance and luck ... But great successes in war cannot be gained without great dangers. The difficult task of an effective high command consists in maintaining the dispersed state of the masses while at the same time preserving the possibility of timely concentration. For that there are no general rules; the problem in each case will be a different one.[16]

Hajo Holborn considered that these observations permitted a glimpse of Moltke's philosophy of war. 'Naturally Moltke was eager to extend the control of reason over warfare as far as possible. But in agreement with Clausewitz he recognised that the political and military problems of war cannot be totally mastered by calculation.'[17] What was possible, however, was to calculate and plan the mobilisation and initial concentration of the army. This was, in Moltke's view, absolutely crucial:

Here, multifarious political, geographic, and national considerations come into question. A mistake in the original assembly of the army can scarcely be rectified in the entire course of the campaign. But these arrangements can be considered long in advance and – assuming the war readiness of the units and the availability of the means of transport – must unfailingly lead to the intended result.[18]

Strategy, however, also included the conduct of the operations themselves. Moltke was careful to emphasise that it was here that would be encountered the independent will of the enemy, which could only be overcome by being prepared and decisive in taking the initiative; and this meant all the uncertainties of combat. Moltke went on, in a famous passage:

The military and moral consequences of every great engagement are of such a far reaching kind that they usually create a fully transformed situation, a new basis for new measures. No plan of operation extends with certainty beyond the first encounter with the enemy's main strength. Only the layman sees in the course of a campaign a consistent execution of a preconceived and highly detailed original concept pursued consistently to the end.[19]

By the time he wrote this essay on strategy in 1871 Moltke was better qualified than anyone alive to discuss the vicissitudes of a great campaign.

The principal lesson to be learned from the study of history was that for a successful commander training and knowledge must be combined with vision and courage. Hajo Holborn has noted the extent to which Moltke's own practice benefited from his historical study and the extent to which he moderated his conclusions in the light of technological and transportation progress. Thus, while Napoleon had occasionally used a detached corps to attack an enemy's flank or rear, he still maintained the value of concentrating one's forces and launching a well timed frontal attack. As Holborn pointed out, notwithstanding the advantages of such a strategy, they had not saved him from ultimate defeat. Moltke drew the conclusion that it would now be possible to plan for concentric movements to a much greater extent than ever before.[20]

Caemmerer examined Moltke's plans for a war against Austria with a view to seeing to what extent Moltke had the essential Napoleonic principle in mind. He noted that a march from Silesia, directly upon Vienna, of ten or twelve days, with six or seven corps, with one left to cover Berlin and one or two for the Rhine provinces, had been found by Moltke as the correct course to follow. Of this, Caemmerer observed:

> This would have been an operation quite in the style of Napoleon, with the massed forces on one line of operation, and if we take into consideration the distribution of the Austrian military forces over the whole empire, it would have become an operation on the inner line. But such a plan of war had to assume that Prussia would make her preparations in all secrecy; that, after the first trainload of troops had started, a clever diplomacy would employ every means of deceiving and delaying the enemy, while at the same time the concentration of the army would be continued with the utmost despatch.[21]

It was, in other words, quite impracticable, bearing in mind that King William's willingness to fight depended on Austria forcing him into a war, and this Moltke well understood. Ironically, however, it was a strategy that Blumenthal, as Chief of Staff of the Second Army, later appeared to advocate during the course of the campaign, suggesting to the King that he should simply march along the line of a ruler from Gitschin to Berlin.[22]

Given the King's views, Moltke had to consider how to deal with a situation in which the initiative was surrendered to the enemy. He proceeded on the assumption that the Austrians would do what was best, and would make the best use of the railways. This led him to expect to have to face two armies, one in Bohemia and one in Moravia. This meant that Prussia must in turn concentrate on a broad front, organised into several armies. His great and well justified fear was that although mobilisation could be left until Austria made clear its hostile intention, it could not then be delayed further for diplomatic purposes without seriously endangering the situation. Above all, once the armies were mobilised, they must be used at once to gain the advantage of the superior Prussian organisation. Accordingly he addressed repeated memoranda to the King to ensure that this point was well understood.[23]

In the close attention which he paid to the developing situation during the months leading up to the outbreak of war in 1866, Moltke carefully assessed the possibility that the Austrians might seek to disrupt the Prussian concentration. He produced scenarios to cover every eventuality; but he was satisfied that in spite of the wide front of the concentration he could, with the aid of the telegraph, be confident of dealing with such an attempt. Moving on from that, he next prepared his plans for the invasion of Bohemia, assuming that his three armies would advance on the twenty fifth day of mobilisation. Where a decisive battle would be fought must depend on what the enemy did. What struck Caemmerer in particular was that Moltke was prepared to leave the Second Army, advancing from Silesia, on the left bank of the Elbe, and to fight the decisive battle with his forces separated by that river and two fortresses. Although this would appear risky, judged on more traditional strategies, Moltke emphasised in the official history of the campaign that such was indeed his intention.[24]

As it happened, this was a risk that did not have to be taken; but the tardy advance of the First Army, its failure to keep its left close to the mountains, and its diversion from the direct march on Gitschin created sufficient anxiety for Blumenthal and others to call for an early concentration of all the armies. This Moltke resisted, with the result that the decisive battle at Königgrätz was fought with a Prussian advance from two directions, with the junction of the armies taking place on the battlefield.

The failure of his subordinate army headquarters to grasp Moltke's intentions continued after the battle had been fought and won, as Schlieffen observed:

> Both army headquarters did not think of pursuing the enemy, still less of surrounding or annihilating him. All that had transpired so far was considered by them as an introduction to the war. The battles waged so far were not to be ascribed to one side or the other as considerable gain or loss. Strength had been tested and weighed on both sides. The troops would now have to be assembled into one mass and a decisive battle fought. But the 'decisive battle' had already been fought on the 27th, 28th and 29th … An attempt should have been made by immediate pursuit to recover what had been lost. Though Moltke's plan had been badly disfigured, the armies were placed not unfavourably for such a pursuit.[25]

Moltke's own comments on the missed opportunity of annihilation focused on the failure of the Army of the Elbe to get far enough forward, after its occupation of Problus meant that the double envelopment of the enemy had succeeded:

> The concern then was to annihilate him. The 16th Division could have been utilised for that purpose; it could have been sent ahead against the route of the enemy's retreat. Unfortunately, it was not at hand, for it was still crossing the Bistritz at Nechanitz. Had it utilised the bridge at Kuntschitz, it would have been on the battlefield six hours earlier.[26]

During the Franco-Prussian War, Moltke's strategy enabled his armies to win many victories, but none was so spectacularly decisive as the battle of Sedan, of which Schlieffen wrote:[27] 'A battle of Cannae had at last been fought, a complete surrounding of the enemy achieved.'[27] As several other writers have pointed out, however, the tasks facing Moltke in 1870-1871 were, in terms of their strategic difficulty, not as demanding as those in 1866. Fritz Hönig, one of the most penetrating military writers of the nineteenth century, argued that Moltke's achievement at Sedan was not to be compared with that at Gravelotte-St Privat:

> The great Moltke had up to August 18 to deal with quite other and far greater difficulties than those which he conquered between August 23 and September 2. For those who can judge, the two are, in my opinion, sufficiently distinct. In spite of 'friction and obstacles,' and of a constant struggle against the want of intelligence in those under him and against respect for those over him, Moltke really worked out the same task at Gravelotte as he did later at Sedan; the latter is only the fully developed idea of Gravelotte-St Privat ... Everything was more favourable for the operations at Sedan, and, above all, Moltke had then two generals under him, who understood him and anticipated his wishes; whereas, up to August 18, one of them had to be constantly held back, while the other had equally to be somewhat pushed on.[28]

As has been noted Moltke predictably believed that the sovereign was always the proper commander in chief. Nominally at any rate that was always his own personal experience, and it was a view that informed all his opinions on the subject of command. In practice, there were few occasions in which he had any difficulty in bringing William to his point of view, even when that anxious monarch started out with a different opinion. The General Staff collected together some of Moltke's concepts on the subject of command from essays written in 1859-1870 under the rather clunky title *Zusammensetzung der Hauptquartiere – Wahl des Feldherrn – Freiheit des Handelns*. which Professor Hughes renders more conveniently as *Thoughts on Command*.

Moltke distinguished between supreme commanders in no need of advice, where staffs merely execute their instructions, such as Fredrick the Great, and those 'who will not wish to do without advice.' That seems innocuous enough; but for Moltke such advice carried with it extreme risk:

> This advice may well be the result of the collective deliberations of a smaller or larger number of men, whose education and experience make them competent to judge correctly. But of that number, never more than one opinion must gain prevalence. The military's hierarchical organisation must assist both subordination and thought. Only one authorised person may submit to the commanding general this one opinion. The supreme commander chooses that person not according to rank, but according to confidence placed in him.[29]

It is not difficult to see in this Moltke's own view as to his relationship with the King. He was frequently obliged to give orders to generals much senior to him, and if sometimes he had to wrap those orders in monarchical clothing, he had no problem; his concern was to see his projects duly carried out. He mused on the situation where this precept was not applied:

If one surrounds the supreme commander with a number of independent men, the situation will worsen both as their numbers increase and the more distinguished and intelligent they are. The commander will hear the counsel of the one, then of the other. He will carry out one proper measure up to a certain point, then a better one in another direction. Then he will recognise the entirely justified objection of a third and the proposals of a fourth adviser. We will wager a hundred to one that with the very best intentioned measures he will probably lose his campaign.[30]

Moltke was also clear about the malign influence of advisers 'who know how to demonstrate with great perception all the difficulties attending every proposed enterprise.' Wherever anything goes wrong, they would be always right; because they never put forward anything positive, even success cannot refute them. However, the most unfortunate of all senior commanders were, thought Moltke, those under close supervision; which might be exercised 'through a delegate of the highest authority at his headquarters, or a telegraph wire attached to his back.' For such commanders, independence of thought or rapid decision became impossible.[31]

Historical examples of the mischief that could be caused by the lack of an unambiguous chain of command were much in Moltke's mind when he made these observations. The problems facing the military leadership in Denmark in 1864 and in France in 1870 were fresh in the memory, and so was the situation with the Austrian high command in 1859; a clear cut expression of responsibilities was essential. This was threatened as much by divided voices within the military as political interference. It was for this reason that he was always at pains to insist that no council of war ever took place during the wars of 1866 and 1870-1871. It was a suggestion that he particularly resented, and he included as an appendix to his history of the latter war an indignant refutation of the suggestion, headed 'Memorandum of the Pretended Council of War in the Wars of King William I' which opened fiercely:

> In the accounts of historical events, as they are handed down to posterity, mistakes assume the form of legends which it is not always easy subsequently to disprove. Among others is the fable which ascribes, with particular zest and as a matter of regular custom, the great decisions taken in the course of our latest campaigns, to the deliberations of a council of war previously convened.[32]

He went on to knock on the head the various stories that had circulated, beginning with the non existent council of war before Königgrätz, when only he and the King had been present together to agree the course to be taken.

Much the most important statement which Moltke produced which contained the core of his military philosophy was the document entitled *Verordnungen fur die hoheren Truppenführer*, translated in Hughes as *Instructions for Large Unit Commanders*: but perhaps more neatly expressed as *Instructions for Senior Commanders*. It was dated June 24 1869, and was based on a study, prepared by the General Staff's historical section on Moltke's orders, of the strengths and weaknesses of the Prussian army as revealed by the war of 1866. As Professor Hughes noted: 'This document became one of the most influential and enduring operational instructions ever written. Its principles endured for more than seventy years.'[33] Large parts of the document were written by Moltke personally, and he supervised the whole of its preparation. Other contributors were Julius von Verdy du Vernois, Hermann von Wartensleben, Karl von Brandenstein and Prince Krafft zu Hohenlohe-Ingelfingen, who represented the cream of the General Staff intellect.

The document began with an observation as to the difficulty of goal-oriented training in peacetime, and the consequent risk of the sudden transition to war. It continues:

> In peace, the moral element seldom comes to be of value; in war it forms the precondition of every victory, the true value of a unit. In war, the qualities of character weigh more heavily than those of reason. Many step forth brilliantly on the battlefield who would be would be overlooked in garrison life. In the conduct of war what one does often matters less than how one does it. A firm decision and persistent execution of a simple concept leads most certainly to the goal.[34]

As has been seen, Moltke was cautious about defining strategical concepts too closely. In peacetime it was impossible to learn the management of large units; only could one study factors such as the terrain and the experiences of previous campaigns. But here, too the rapid advance of technology, especially in terms of weapons and communications, had so changed circumstances that even the precepts of the greatest commanders of history were no longer applicable. General Caemmerer found in the instructions passages that contained the core of Moltke's strategic thinking, and which he distinguished from the basic principles on which Napoleon had proceeded. Moltke wrote of the powerful effect of flank attacks and the desirability of the forces being concentrated from different directions and not, as Napoleon would have it, coming together before the day of battle:

> If the army approaches the enemy while concentrated before the battle, then any new division of forces for a flanking attack as a turning movement against the enemy requires a flanking march within his tactical sphere of action. If one does not wish to engage in such a dubious enterprise, there remains only a strengthening of that flank from which the opposite standing enemy flank should be overpowered. But this is of use only in a frontal attack. This can nevertheless succeed if one is able to spare parts of the reserves in the centre and on the opposite flank.[35]

The strategic doctrines here set out were, General Caemmerer concluded, in sharp contrast to Napoleon's words and actual deeds; Napoleon considered 'the movement of masses on one line of operation and the pressure of masses on one point of the enemy's lines as the climax of all strategic wisdom.' On occasion, of course, Napoleon was obliged to enter the battlefield from two different directions in order to envelop his enemy. These were, however, with him only exceptions. As to this Caemmerer concluded his comparison with Napoleon: 'And what with him was an exception has become with Moltke the rule; what with him was the rule is with Moltke the exception.'[36]

One of the most striking features of Moltke's management of the enormous forces at his disposal was his of general directives rather than specific orders. Moltke himself never defined the term 'directive;' but in the Official History of the Franco-Prussian War, the General Staff definition was that 'directives are communications from a higher authority to a lower one, which convey guidelines rather than definite orders for immediate action. These guidelines should serve as a precept for subsequent decisions that must be taken independently.'[37] His successful employment of such modes of instruction led some observers to conclude that he had a dogmatic approach to leading by directives whereas, as Professor Hughes pointed out, his 'theory and practice recognised that either form could be appropriate, depending on local circumstances and personalities.'[38] He expressly stated that the basis of the orderly direction for an army was continuous communication between headquarters and units, maintained by orders from above no less than by reports and messages from below. During the wars of 1866 and 1870-1871 he frequently had to complain that information was not being supplied to him from the front. In 1870-1871 the distance of headquarters from the front line units was such that general directives had to be sent to the German commanders on the Loire, in the North, and in the East, and written exchanges of opinions with the chiefs of staff, or sometimes the army commanders, had to take the place of the oral discussions which would otherwise have occurred.

In his teachings as to the role of the supreme commander, Moltke was careful to emphasise that he must preserve his objectivity. Once battle was joined, the place of all higher commanders was in more rearward positions that allowed a sufficient overview, while remaining visible to their units:

> In large battles it will usually be irrelevant whether the supreme commander views any single part of the battlefield or not. He must act on the basis of reports, and will often have a clearer conception of the situation if he receives his information from all parts of the battlefield in the same manner. He can then calmly reach his decisions far from the confusing effects of the fighting. The decision of a battle begins when one side gives up the battle as lost. Many times battles have been won because the enemy believed himself beaten before the victor did, even though he was no less shaken. In case of doubt, one must therefore persist.[39]

Moltke was in no doubt that there was a risk that higher commanders might be tempted into 'useless interference with the independence of subordinate commanders in the forward line,' when their proper role was the correct employment of reserves.

He was however realistic that victory was not always wholly to be ascribed to the commander, writing:

> Success principally decides the reputation of a general. How much of it is his actual due is very difficult to determine. Even the best of men fail against the irresistible force of circumstances, and the same force will carry along the mediocre man. A capable supreme commander can easily be defeated by a less capable one; but only the capable will have luck in the long run. Where armies have commanders as in 1870, and where one has to reckon only with victories, strategy has everything it needs. We have had only victories. Gneisenau, however, led a beaten army to victory. We have not yet stood this highest test.[40]

Towards the end of his life Moltke began to realise, well before almost anyone else, that the growing power of the defensive meant that Germany should aspire only to limited victories and a strategic stalemate. However, the increasing military power of the French and Russian armies, and the likelihood of a two front war, made it necessary to seek to achieve a knockout blow against one adversary before turning on the other. It was a concept with which his successors constantly wrestled; but for Moltke it simply was not achievable. In 1890, in his last significant speech to the Reichstag he warned, presciently, that future wars could last for 'seven and perhaps thirty years,' with huge consequences for the social order.[41]

Looking at Moltke as a German legend, Arden Bucholz has observed that 'virtually on a par with Luther and Bismarck, Moltke comes with almost no negative baggage.' At the same time, he considered that making sense of him in the present day is difficult, not least because of the course of German history in the twentieth century. And because of the lack of negative baggage, the popular image of Moltke almost reaches hagiography. The image, however, is justified; Bucholz quotes Theodor Fontane, who wrote that Moltke 'embodied the Prussian ideal; he looked sound and true, with a Greek soul, the spirit of Frederick the Great and a unique character: judicious, selfless, disciplined, proficient and full of common sense.'[42]

3

Organisation and Management

To give effect to the strategic principles that he had evolved, Moltke had the benefit of an advanced and very sophisticated management system that was not matched in any of the armies against which he was required to fight. The Great General Staff was an organisation of which the origins went back a long way, the first traces of which having appeared in the time of the Great Elector. In 1655 two officers were appointed with the title of Quartermaster-General, whose functions included engineering, entrenching and construction of camps and, in peacetime, taking charge of castles and fortresses. Thereafter a close connection existed between the Corps of Engineers and the Quartermaster-General's staff. Gradually other, junior, quartermaster-generals were appointed; but although these and others were listed as belonging to the General Staff, in Frederick the Great's time he personally undertook not only the functions of the Chief of the General Staff, but many of the duties of other staff officers. He wrote or dictated, for instance, all the plans, orders and instructions himself.[1]

It became evident during the Seven Years' War that the functions of the Quartermaster-General's staff required additional officers, and their numbers were increased by 1767 to seventeen. Frederick himself, in his history of the war, explained their duties:

> The army has stood the test of many campaigns, but the want of a good Quartermaster-General's staff was often felt at headquarters. The King, being anxious to create a body of officers of this description, selected twelve officers who showed special aptitudes for these duties. They were instructed in surveying, laying out camps, placing villages in a state of defence and field bridging. They learned also how to guide columns marching, and especially how to reconnoitre marshes and rivers, so that they might not, by mistake or negligence, place an army with its flank on a shallow river or a passable tract of marshy country. Mistakes of this nature have led to the most serious results. They cost the French the defeat of Malplaquet, and the Austrians that of Leuthen.[2]

This body of officers continued to be known as the Quartermaster-General's staff; it was not until the time of King Frederick William II that the term 'General Staff' was formally applied, when it was given a distinctive uniform. By 1791 there were nineteen officers on the Quartermaster-General's staff, rising to twenty four two years later, but falling to fifteen in 1796; these numbers were exclusive of the engineer officers. In 1800 General von Lecoq issued a set of instructions detailing the duties of the Quartermaster-General's Staff, which included for the first time the giving of advice to commanding generals, if required to do so. Perhaps the most important function at this time, however, was the requirement that the Quartermaster-General's officers should supervise the preparation of reliable military maps of the country, a task principally carried out by a team of engineer surveyors.

In the early years of the nineteenth century the Quartermaster-General, based at Potsdam, was Lieutenant General von Geusau, who held a large number of other appointments. As a result of this, his two Lieutenant-Quartermaster-Generals, Colonels von Phull and von Massenbach, effectively managed the staff.

Christian von Massenbach, although he failed to distinguish himself when put to the test of actual war in 1806, nonetheless has some claim to being the real founder of the Prussian General Staff in the form in which Moltke was to inherit it. In 1802 he wrote the first of a series of memoranda for the King, dealing with a wide range of issues. These included a collection of impracticable plans of operations, which Bronsart von Schellendorff described in his comprehensive work on the duties of the General Staff:

> These plans were not merely prepared as an exercise, but Colonel von Massenbach seemed to expect that the examples they contained were to be of great value for all time, and were consequently fitted to solve the difficulties of less gifted individuals in the future. He attempted, moreover, by establishing what he was pleased to call 'Fundamental Treatises,' in which the changes that constantly occur in practically carrying out the act of war, had, naturally to be left out of consideration, to lay down rigidly fixed and indisputable maxims which, once in possession of the Prussian Quartermaster-General's Staff as its precious property, were invariably to prevent it making mistakes.[3]

Although parts of his memorandum were seriously criticised by some of the senior officers to which it was referred, the King ordered the production of a set of instructions for the Quartermaster-General's staff, which Massenbach drafted in 1803. That staff was now to consist of 34 officers, with support staff in addition. The duties of the staff were divided into permanent and current work; the latter was now expressly to include the development of the principles on which military operations were to be carried out.

During this period there developed a rivalry between the departments of the Adjutant-General and the Quartermaster-General. The former was responsible for officers' records, garrison and armaments, and the production of regulations. Gradually the Adjutant-General gained the ascendancy, with the result noted by Walter Görlitz;

> Thus the way was opened for the development ... whereby the Adjutant-General's department was ultimately to blossom into the all powerful military cabinet of the Prussian kings, a consummation that had its disquieting side, for the military cabinet's irresponsible *imperium in imperio*, and its ability to influence the sovereign by secret advice, was to provide at least one of the reasons for Stein's dramatic appeal for a reform of head and members.[4]

By 1806 the expanded staff was complete, and it is from then that the term General Staff appears to have been synonymous with that of Quartermaster-General's Staff. The gradual expansion of its functions, continuously adding more and more staff duties, meant that the term 'quartermaster' more or less ceased to have its original meaning of responsibility for the quartering and supply of troops.[5] 1806 was, however, to see the new organisation subjected to the actual test of war; and it failed to prevent the Prussian army going down to disastrous defeat at the hands of Napoleon.

Colonel Hittle, in his work on the development of the military staff system, has observed that the catastrophe of Jena gave a considerable impetus to considerations in Prussia of reform, not least in the General Staff:

> The collective German military mind has almost invariably demonstrated a willingness to indulge in self analysis, even when that investigation was likely to result in unflattering findings. The defeat at Jena provided the more progressive of the military leaders with an almost inexhaustible field for analysis, for it conclusively indicated that there was room for reform, not only in tactical thought, but in command organisation as well.[6]

The man on whom fell the task of reform was Gerhard Johann von Scharnhorst. He had joined the Prussian army from the Hanoverian army in 1801; when applying to do so he attached three conditions. The first was that he be given the rank of Lieutenant Colonel, the second that he be raised to the nobility and the third that he be allowed to carry out a reform of the Prussian army. Considering his humble origins (his father, who had been a sergeant major in the Hanoverian army, was a tenant farmer) and that his present rank was that of major, it is remarkable that the Prussian army was prepared to grant his requests. Scharnhorst was only 36 years of age; but he had already earned a considerable reputation during the wars against Revolutionary France before becoming Chief of Staff to the Commander in Chief of the Hanoverian Army.[7]

He was at once posted to the Quartermaster-General's staff, where he was responsible for military education. Soon after arriving in Berlin he founded the *Militärische Gesellschaft*, the object of which was army reform. The society attracted a number of promising young officers as members, including Hermann von Boyen, Carl von Grolmann, Carl von Clausewitz and Rühle von Lilienstern; its president was Lieutenant General von Rüchel, Inspector of the Guards and Governor of Potsdam. Walter Görlitz has pointed out that although Scharnhorst was no revolutionary, wishing to see reform develop organically, he was realistic about the political implications of some of his proposals:

> Scharnhorst was also perfectly clear in his mind that the creation of a militia, the introduction of universal service, necessitated the granting of political rights to the serfs on the great estates. This freeing of the peasants and the recognition of a universal duty of bearing arms were two things that went hand in hand. Hegel, who was to become the philosopher of the almighty state, had already indulged in reflection on an ideal constitution. In these the correlation between universal service and popular representation, both of which the author demanded, had been clearly apparent.[8]

Scharnhorst was a forerunner of Moltke in very many ways, flexible in his approach to military problems. In particular he foresaw that the increasing size of armies required that forces should be divided in their approach to the battlefield; he applied the principle 'never stand in concentration, always do battle in concentration,' which directly anticipated Moltke's own approach to strategy. Such a policy, he saw, called for increased responsibilities to be assumed by the staff in operational planning.

In the chaos that followed the disastrous battle of Jena, in which the Prussian army fell back in disorder, Scharnhorst, who had been serving as Chief of Staff to the Duke of Brunswick, became separated from the Royal headquarters, but fell in with General Gebhard von Blücher. He quickly became Blücher's trusted adviser, and accompanied him until they were obliged to surrender with the forces they had collected at Rakau near Lübeck. Following a prisoner of war exchange Scharnhorst was sent as an *Assistant* to General von Lestocq, commanding a Prussian corps serving with the Russians in East Prussia. It was Prussia's darkest hour; the French occupied most of the country, and Napoleon dictated humiliating terms aimed at reducing Prussia to a second class power.

Out of this catastrophe, however, emerged the conditions in which a comprehensive reform of the army, and in particular the General Staff, might be achieved, and Scharnhorst in the ensuing years was at the centre of this. In his first scheme, produced in early 1808, Scharnhorst proposed the organisation of the army into three army corps, and fixed the number of General Staff officers at twenty six, headed by a Quartermaster-General with the rank of Major General. Their duties were to be regulated by special instructions, which were not to be confined to the General Staff, but were to be published to all the generals of the army. The purpose of this was explained in the document. It was so that the General Staff officers should know what was expected of them, while on the other hand, the commanding officers 'should be cognizant of the duties of a General Staff Officer, so that misunderstandings, overlapping, wrong expectations, of accusations might be avoided.'[9]

Scharnhorst was determined that the efficiency of the General Staff should be subject to constant improvement:

> The practical training of General Staff officers was to be kept up in peacetime by ensuring an accurate knowledge of the condition and the tactical manoeures of troops, a general knowledge of the country, by exercises in the movements of troops in the field, and finally, by being employed in surveying. The summer tours were to be reduced to three months (partly for the sake of economy), and were not to be restricted to Prussia alone, but were to comprise foreign countries as well, 'in so far as they might possibly form a theatre of operations for a Prussian army at any future time.'[10]

Knowledge of the country was to be linked with a study of military history, so that the officers could consider the effect of the ground on the conduct of operations.

In the ensuing wars which led ultimately to the final defeat of Napoleon the General Staff played a crucial role. When peace came the organisation was further refined. One part was based permanently in Berlin, under its own Chief, and was known as the 'Great General Staff;' the rest of the officers were distributed among army corps and were known as the 'Army General Staff.' Both parts were at that time subject to the Second Department of the War Ministry. However, in 1821, upon the appointment of Lieutenant General Philipp Freiherr von Müffling as sole Chief of the General Staff, it was released from the direction of the War Ministry. This gave the Chief of the General Staff direct access to the King, which was of crucial importance to Moltke during the wars of German unification.[11]

Bronsart was clear that the independence of the General Staff which was thus conferred on it was of the greatest importance, and was 'one of the most important causes of the splendid achievements of the General Staff in recent campaigns.' It was essential, he argued, for the Chief of the General Staff, both in peace and war, to be one and the same man. In countries where the Chief of the General Staff was subject to the War Minister, it might be taken for granted that the latter might assume control at the most critical moment. This would be 'a terrible mistake':

> In the first place, it would be next to impossible that a man would be found who possessed at the same time the necessary qualifications of a War Minster and of a Chief of the General Staff, that is to say, was equally master of the art of military administration and of handling armies. Besides, the choice of a War Minister in many countries is often restricted by political considerations, such as his parliamentary connections.[12]

It should be noted that Bronsart, one of the key General Staff officers upon whom Moltke depended with such confidence, was himself subsequently to serve as War Minister.

Peacetime economic conditions soon resulted in the reduction of the General Staff. Officers were no longer attached to divisions. In 1824 the total number of officers in all was cut to forty six, against a theoretical war establishment of 101 officers, including forty five officers attached to infantry and cavalry divisions and twenty seven attached to the Army Corps. In 1828 instructions were issued for the structure of the General Staff attached to the army corps, which was divided into four sections – the General Staff, routine staff, legal staff and intendance sections. It has been pointed out that this arrangement 'with few minor changes was basically the same as the staff organisation utilised in the field commands of the German army in World War II.'[13] Thus it can be seen that the outline of the management system that was to be so important to Moltke was largely in place thirty years before he became Chief of the Great General Staff.

Crucial to the role of the General Staff was the right of a chief of staff as the commander's adviser to take part in command and control until a decision was taken. In the early years of the nineteenth century this was not something which more traditionally minded Prussian generals found easy to accept; General Yorck von Wartenburg, for instance, objected to General Neidhardt von Gneisenau exercising this right in relation to Field Marshal von Blücher. However, the harmonious relationship between Blücher and Scharnhorst when they came together in the grim days of 1806 had set the tone for the future, and the joint responsibility for their actions became, it has been said, the institutionalised right of General Staff officers.

Gneisenau, in his tenure of office as Chief of the General Staff, introduced the concept of mission oriented command and control, or *Auftragstaktik*, which became and has remained central to German leadership philosophy. A modern commentator has written of Gneisenau:

> He was the first to develop command and control by directives, thus giving latitude to the subordinate commanders for the execution of operations. Subordinate commanders were for the first time issued directives expressing the intent of the Royal headquarters in terms of clear objectives, but giving only general indications of the methods of their achievement. This enabled commanders and their General Staff officers to use initiative in taking advantage of unforeseen opportunities, provided that their actions were consistent with the main objective.[14]

Moltke, when he came to assume the duties of Chief of the Great General Staff, adopted Gneisenau's principles of command and control without hesitation; the directives which he issued were remarkable both for their clarity and the flexibility which he gave to his commanders in the field.

One reason why it was so important that the authority of the Chiefs of Staff of the major operational units should be enhanced and maintained was the practice in the Prussian army of appointing to the command of such units leaders who were chosen for their status and reputation rather than for their innate ability. Royal princes, such as the Crown Prince, Frederick Charles and the Saxon Crown Prince all performed well most of the time; but it was to their Chiefs of Staff that Moltke looked for the consistent application of his principles and the execution of his directives. When a

Chief of Staff was unable to control his commanding general, trouble almost invariably ensued. The aged Wrangel in Denmark; Vogel von Falckenstein in Western Germany; Steinmetz in Lorraine and the Grand Duke of Mecklenburg-Schwerin on the Loire all went off the rails at one time or another and caused Moltke substantial problems until steps could be taken to put matters right.

Bronsart noted that the 1824 peace establishment of the General Staff was less than half of that required for war, a situation which he regarded as extremely dangerous:

> This was the more so, as at that time General Staff officers were not often changed, and consequently there was no sufficient reserve of regimental officers who had served on the General Staff and could be reckoned on in case of emergency. The events of the years 1848 to 1850 disclosed many imperfections, chiefly caused by certain economies which had been carried to excess in preceding years. This led to a fresh work of reorganisation.[15]

The General Staff was, therefore, in April 1853, given a new establishment, as part of which General Staff officers were again attached to divisions in peacetime. The divisional and corps structure was changed, a corps now consisting of two divisions of twelve battalions each, rather than four divisions of six battalions. The total of the peacetime establishment was sixty four offices, of whom twenty eight served on the Great General Staff and the remainder with corps and divisions. In wartime, the establishment would rise to eighty three officers. There would again be a periodical rotation of General Staff officers to regimental duty; when the army was mobilised in 1859, this had ensured an ample reserve to provide the wartime establishment.[16] The regular alternation of officers between the Great General Staff and troop units also tended to diminish the lingering suspicion of these intellectuals on the part of field officers.

Between Müffling, who retired in 1829, and the provisional appointment of Moltke in 1857, there had been only two Chiefs of the Great General Staff. The first of these was General Wilhelm von Krauseneck. The son of a bourgeois judicial official in Bayreuth, he had joined the Prussian army in the ranks; after becoming an officer, he worked with Scharnhorst, and rose ultimately to the command of a corps. In his time first Moltke, in 1833, and then Roon, in 1836, joined the General Staff, followed by others who would in due course become household names. It was Krauseneck who established links with the Turkish army, as a result of which Moltke and others went to Constantinople as advisers:

> These were the first chords of the great symphony that was to come – and yet the era of Krauseneck was still subject to the paralysing influence of reaction. Even the recall of Boyen by Frederick William IV changed very little. Krauseneck, being of bourgeois origin, might still have some liberal and progressive views, but even if he had not been hostile to the thought of his time he was helpless in trying to influence it. In 1848 he heard the news of the revolution in France

with pleasure, but when the revolution spread to Berlin, he grew frightened and prayed for a return of the old order.[17]

Krauseneck was succeeded in May 1848 by Lieutenant General Karl von Reyher. He came from an even more humble background than his predecessor, being the son of a cantor and organist in a small Brandenburg village, where as a boy he worked as a shepherd. After joining the Prussian army as a clerk, he worked his way up to become an officer in a Uhlan regiment. In 1815 he joined the General Staff; later, as Chief of Staff of the Guard Corps he established a good relationship with Prince William. During the troubled March Days he served for a while as War Minister. He had been raised to the nobility, and adopted the conservative principles of a typical Prussian officer. Despite his origins, he was entirely opposed to the revolution, believing in the maintenance of order at all costs.

In his capacity as War Minister he had been concerned to limit the growing power of the Military Cabinet, a cause which one War Minister after another took up in the period after the March Days. Frederick William IV did all he could to make the Military Cabinet into a Royal Chancellery for all army affairs and to assert his military prerogatives. In the period between 1848 and 1851 the post of War Minister changed hands very frequently due to this ongoing struggle; six post holders left abruptly during this time as a result.[18]

With his transfer to the post of Chief of the Great General Staff Reyher found himself still in the forefront of the struggle with the Military Cabinet. When Manteuffel became its head the position became even more serious, a proposal being seriously considered that the Military Cabinet should absorb the General Staff. It was not the least of Reyher's achievements that he was able to resist the suggestion. He brought to the post of Chief of the General Staff a considerable intelligence and administrative ability, and total loyalty to the King. He was a careful student of military history, and applied himself to the task of improving the ability of the Prussian army to meet whatever challenges faced it. He had every confidence that its superior efficiency made it more than a match for the Austrian Army, and joined with Prince William in assuring the King of this. Frederick William, however, was not prepared to take the gamble; the result was the humiliating Convention of Olmütz.[19]

Reyher died suddenly on October 7 1857. Soon after this the King suffered a severe stroke, disabling him completely. This brought Prince William to the centre of the stage, first to act as the King's Deputy and then formally as Regent. The urgent need to fill Reyher's post was obvious; reluctant to make permanent appointments while merely the King's Deputy, he appointed Moltke as acting Chief of the Great General Staff on October 29. It was a decision he took with the encouragement of Edwin von Manteuffel.

Thus it was that Moltke inherited an organisation that would prove central to his successful management of the Prussian army during the wars of unification. During his time as Chief of the Great General Staff he was able to refine the structure, but he made no significant changes in principle. The officers of the General Staff contributed to his victories on the battlefield, which resulted in the huge respect in which he was held; in its turn this cemented the role of General Staff officers who brought to their duties both the confidence of success and the mounting respect for their achievement.

In the years after his appointment to lead the General Staff, Moltke's principal achievement was his selection of the key officers upon whom he particularly came to depend. Almost without exception they were men of remarkable ability. They repaid his trust in them with total loyalty, and he enjoyed a close personal relationship with them. One of their principal functions outside their work was to play whist with him, a game which he much enjoyed but which he played rather badly. Even privately with them, however, he was reluctant to unburden himself. As an example of his taciturnity, for instance, Verdy described a journey he made with Moltke on August 19, to Pont á Mousson, the day after the battle of Gravelotte:

> Moltke took Winterfeld and myself with him in his carriage, and we drove on in silence; nor did the chief break his train of thought except for three short remarks. The first time was when we crossed, on the way from Rezonville to Gorze, a part of the battlefield of August 16 and came across heaps of still unburied French Voltigeurs of the Guard, in whose foremost ranks lay a young non commissioned officer of our 11th Regiment still grasping in his hands his rifle with fixed-bayonet. Seeing him, the General said, 'This was the bravest of the brave.' Later on he remarked, 'I have learned once more that one cannot be too strong on the field of battle' ... The last remark of the General was made as we approached Pont á Mousson ... Then he exclaimed, 'What would be our feelings now, if we had been beaten?'[20]

Soon after his appointment Moltke had revised the organisation of the General Staff, restoring Grolmann's system of sections organised on a geographical basis, which had been abandoned by Krauseneck. There were now to be four departments responsible for planning and strategic analysis. The Eastern Department covered Russia, Austria-Hungary, Sweden and Turkey; the German Department covered Germany, Denmark, Switzerland and Italy; and the Western Department dealt with France, Spain, Great Britain, the Low Countries and the USA. The fourth department was responsible for railway organisation; it was central to the mobilisation process.

The first significant test of the General Staff under Moltke's leadership came with the mobilisation of 1859. This was based on the 1853 establishment of the General Staff and there was no difficulty in increasing the number of General Staff officers to the wartime complement. However, the problems which arose during the campaign of 1864 showed that there was now a clear need to raise the peacetime establishment, as Bronsart explained:

> No systematic mobilisation of whole Army Corps took place in this campaign, but only that of certain separate Divisions. Whereas, however, the General Staffs of Army Corps remained behind at their posts occupied with their peace

duties, the Divisions were reformed into Army Corps at the seat of war. The extra number of General Staff Officers required in consequence of this was met by detaching officers from the Great General Staff. But the latter was then barely able to carry on its own duties. An increase of the General Staff was therefore determined on, together with the strict separation of a special establishment of the General Staff for purely scientific purposes, to ensure the continuity of which certain specially fitted officers were to be retained and exempted from the usual spells of regimental duty.[21]

Reforms of this kind were always subject to budgetary considerations. Moltke had as early as May 1859 put forward a proposal for there to be scientifically trained officers who were to remain on the General Staff for extended terms without being obliged to return to front line duties; his concern was that the scientific work of the General Staff, particularly in geographical and historical studies, would be impaired. In addition to this, in the same month he applied for an increase in the overall establishment. These claims appear to have fallen on stony ground, only to be renewed in 1865.[22]

The General Staff budget was naturally always a matter of great concern to Moltke. A few months after his first appointment he had written to his brother Adolf to tell him something of his new circumstances:

As this position is properly that of a General of Division, and I hold only the rank of Major General, this appointment can be only temporary. I still wear the scarlet collar of the Infantry uniform; my salary too is 800 thalers less than that due to the position in the Staff. Otherwise I have all the functions and attributes of the Chief; an official residence, general orders, and so forth. My force consists of sixty four men, among the fifty of the so called 'Great,' but in reality very small, General Staff, and the staff of the nine army corps and eighteen divisions. The funds appropriated to the department amount to 26,000 thalers for general purposes, over which I have full control, out of which I have to pay for the trigonometrical and topographical survey of the country. In this I have at my command a corps of thirty officers, drawn from the army; I have also 10,000 thalers for travelling expenses.[23]

In fact, the plans for expansion were not carried into effect even in 1865, due to lack of funds and the continuing dispute between the Government and the Landtag. It was not until the Royal Order of January 31 1867 that a considerable enlargement of the General Staff took place, taking into account the experiences of the Austro-Prussian War and the substantial increase in the size of the army after the formation of the North German Confederation.

The new establishment in peacetime of the Great General Staff was to be 109 officers, divided between the main establishment *(Haupt-Etat)* of 88 officers, and the separate establishment for scientific purposes *(Neben-Etat)* of 21 officers. In addition the Kingdom of Saxony and the Grand Duchy of Hesse contributed an additional eight and two officers respectively. The proportion of officers attached to the Great General Staff had now risen to 42.2%. Even so, the basic headquarters staff with which Moltke took the field in 1870 consisted of only thirteen officers in addition to himself, made up as to the Quartermaster-General, 3 Chiefs of Sections, 3 Field Officers and 6 Captains. To these should be added the Intendant General and the Chief of Military Telegraphs, who accompanied the Royal Headquarters. It was a very modest number with which to manage not only the field armies, but all the other command structures with which Moltke had to deal.[24]

These, in addition to the three armies with which Prussia and her German allies began the war, included the lines of communication staff, military governments, army corps commands and divisional commands. The grand total of Prussian General Staff officers in the field amounted to 138, plus 23 extra officers attached to the General Staff; since the peacetime strength was only 109, another 52 General Staff officers had to be appointed, in addition to all those attached to the other German units. These now included those from Bavaria, Württemberg and Baden, and added a further 50 further officers, making a total of 211. During the course of the war the formation of other army commands, army corps, reserve divisions and the military governments of occupied France led to a requirement for additional General Staff officers. By the end of the war there were 155 Prussian officers alone holding General Staff posts with units in the field, a further increase of 17 officers.

The role of the Chief of Staff of an operational unit steadily evolved during Moltke's tenure of office, as Colonel Hittle has described:

> During the time he was serving as Chief of Staff the peculiar status of that official in relation to the commanding general was more firmly established. The General Staff officers serving in armies, corps and divisions tended more and more to represent the General Staff. The relationship of Moltke to the crown was similar to the relationship of the lower chiefs of staff to their respective commanders.[25]

Moltke, in the appendix to his history of the war of 1870-71 previously referred to, spelt out in detail the way in which, as Chief of the General Staff, he reported to the King:

> Excepting on the march and on days of battle, an audience was regularly held by his Majesty at ten o'clock, at which I, accompanied by the Quartermaster-General, laid the latest reports and information before him, and made our suggestions on that basis. The Chief of the Military Cabinet and the Minister of War were also present, and while the headquarters of the Third Army were at Versailles, the Crown Prince also; but all merely as listeners. The King occasionally required them to give him information on one point or another; but I do not remember that he ever asked for advice concerning the operations in the field or the suggestions I made. These, which I always discussed beforehand with my staff officers, were, on the contrary, generally maturely weighed by his Majesty

himself. He always pointed out with a military eye and an invariably correct estimate of the situation, all the objections that might be raised to their execution; but as in war every step is beset with danger, the plans laid before him were invariably adopted.[26]

Of course, since the functioning of the General Staff depended on the individuals concerned, it could never be said that it was free of any problems and worked as a perfectly functioning organisation. From time to time difficulties arose, and Moltke was obliged to intervene. One of the most well known instances of this was his replacement of Colonel von Krenski as Chief of Staff of the Detachment of the Grand Duke of Mecklenburg-Schwerin by Albrecht von Stosch, the Intendant General. But it was certainly true, as Colonel Hittle pointed out in the passage quoted above, that the General Staff officers in the field tended increasingly to represent Moltke, and it was in this way that Moltke could count on a remarkably consistent execution of his intentions. Stosch's temporary assignment to the Loire campaign was an especially dramatic example of the way in which Moltke intended to get a grip on not only the Grand Duke, but also Prince Frederick Charles. Colonel Lonsdale Hale put it thus:

> Stosch was an excellent soldier, a large minded man, but in view of the situation he was a good deal more. Owing to his high position on the supreme staff of the German forces, and his close professional connection with Moltke, the chief staff officer of those forces, he was, on the Loire, little less than Moltke present by proxy. The Grand Duke must now be aware that if he rebelled against his new chief staff officer, he would be rebelling against Moltke, whilst the Prince knew similarly, that although he might be determined to act in future in disregard of Moltke's expressed views and wishes there was present only a few miles away from him in the theatre of war, Moltke's personal representative, endeavouring to hold him in check.[27]

It was the ability to depend on the General Staff officers in the field which enabled Moltke to apply the principles of central command, which by then was an established doctrine. No longer was a commander a participant in the battle; instead, at a command post sometimes well behind the front line, and hence not distracted by being present at minor phases of the battle, he could calmly and quickly identify the key issues, and draft his instructions accordingly. In 1866 and again in 1871 Moltke was able to take his decisions from a long way back in the early stages of each conflict.

It was also thanks to the efficiency of his General Staff that mobilisation of the Prussian army could proceed so smoothly. Gustav von Stiehle, soon to be in the field as Chief of Staff of the Second Army, found Moltke during the crisis in July 1870 sitting peaceably on the sofa with one of Sir Walter Scott's novels in his hand. Upon Stiehle expressing surprise that he could be reading such a book at such a time, Moltke replied: 'Why not? Everything's ready. We've only got to press the button.'[28]

The point at which Moltke's authority became totally assured, and with it the power and influence of the General Staff as a whole, came on June 2 1866. Prior to this Moltke's authority had been boosted in 1857 when the War Minister, von Bonin, gave him the right to report direct to him rather than through the *Allegemeine Kriegsdepartement*. Now, on the eve of the Austro Prussian War, a Royal cabinet order was issued to the effect that the orders of the General Staff would be sent directly to units in the field rather than through the medium of the War Ministry. Professor Craig has explored the extent to which this explained the subsequent tensions that arose between Bismarck and Moltke, as suggested by the official historians of the General Staff, who wrote:

> When Moltke on June 2 finally stepped into Roon's place as the first military adviser of the King, he must have appeared to Bismarck to a certain extent as an intruder. It is from this standpoint that the later friction between Bismarck and the General Staff is to be understood.[29]

As Professor Craig pointed out, there exists no evidence to show that Bismarck raised any objection to the Royal order, making this not a very satisfactory theory. In any case the practical effect on Roon's political position was not great; it was the assertion of Moltke's military primacy that was so important.

By 1866, during the years of Moltke's leadership, the position of the Great General Staff had advanced a long way. In 1857 its status was such that it could fairly be described as a 'small relatively obscure bureaucracy'; at that time it was wholly subordinate to the War Ministry, exerting little or no influence on the corps commanders in whose hands real power lay.[30]

During the years that followed, Moltke's advice was more and more frequently sought on operational questions. Personally close to the King, he enjoyed in practice direct access to him, even though officially his communications went through the War Ministry. The limited influence of the Great General Staff was demonstrated, however, by its lack of involvement in the process of army reorganisation that began in 1860, which remained entirely in Roon's hands as War Minister. And even as late as 1864 there seems to have been an assumption that the initiative for the planning process for the conflict with Denmark lay with the War Ministry.[31]

The Royal order of June 2 1866 was not altogether well received by a few of the noble or long serving army commanders; but Moltke was perfectly able to deal with this jealous reaction to the assertion of the General Staff's authority. His practice was to write directly to the relevant Chiefs of Staff. He could, in any case, rely on the trust placed in him by the King; this, most of the time, was quite sufficient to keep fractious subordinate troop commanders in line.

Herbert Rosinski summarised Moltke's relationship with the Great General Staff in his work on the German Army in these terms:

His appointment as head of the General Staff, without effecting any fundamental changes in the constitution or methods of that body, marked an epoch in its development owing to the immediate intensification of all its activities. The career of its members was regularised, a more intimate contact with the general life of the army assured by the regular interchange of staff and regimental duty; its theoretical work – particularly the study of military history, the compilation and interpretation of statistical and other information, and the cartographical service – was revived and greatly expanded; the tactical and strategical training of the General Staff was much improved by better adaptation of tactical exercises and 'staff journeys' to wartime conditions and by their extension to cover strategical issues proper.[32]

4

Moltke and the King

Moltke's relationship with the King was, in the context of nineteenth century Prussia, an extremely important one. William was brought up as a soldier, and he remained a soldier all his life, Born in 1797, he was present at the battle of Bar sur Aube in 1814, where his father awarded him the Iron Cross for bravery, and the Tsar bestowed on him the Cross of St George. As the younger son of King Frederick William III he was not, of course expected at first to mount the throne; but as his elder brother remained childless it became increasingly clear that he might do so. As Prince of Prussia he led a quiet and orthodox military life, becoming a lieutenant general at the age of thirty two, when he was put in command of an army corps. Before this he had fallen in love with Princess Elisa Radziwill; but his hope of marrying her was dashed by his father's refusal to permit the match, as she was not of royal blood. Instead, William married the good, amiable, and beautiful Princess Augusta of Weimar in June 1829.[1] As the years went by, the Prince of Prussia became more and more clearly identified with the views of the reactionaries, and made no secret of his fierce opposition to liberal reformers.

When, therefore, the March Days burst on to the streets of Berlin, it was no surprise that he was a particular object of hatred to the mob which besieged the royal palace:

> A known and protected supporter of absolutism, all sorts of charges were hurled against him ... The windows of his residence had been broken, and repeated attempts had been made to storm it. The clamour against him surged so high that the King succumbed before it; perhaps hoping as well to make a little capital out of his compliance.[2]

William's first reaction to the upsurge of hatred against him had been one of defiance; his place was in Berlin, he declared, and he would die there. His brother was adamant, however; William was to leave the country at once, and go to England, on a face saving mission to Queen Victoria. After an adventurous journey, William arrived in London, where he watched with resignation events in Prussia. He did not, however, mean to walk away from his country, writing to Edwin von Manteuffel: 'Time will show that I shall devote all my energies to my country, even under these new conditions, if indeed I am to be allowed to return at all.'³

In June William returned, and took his seat in the National Assembly, wearing the uniform of a general. He was cheered by those on the Right, and hissed by those on the Left, but he was evidently no longer in physical danger. He loyally supported his brother in the complex political manoeuvring that followed the convening of the Frankfurt Parliament and the latter's refusal of the Imperial crown that was offered him. In June 1849 William was appointed to the command of the troops operating against the rebels in Baden and the Palatinate. After a short and successful campaign, in which Albrecht von Roon served on his staff, William's troops defeated the rebels before the end of July.

Back in Berlin, as tension grew in 1850, William was in favour of standing firm against Austria. Firmness, however, was not Frederick William IV's strong suit, and he wavered between an obstinate hatred of the Federal Parliament in Frankfurt and a reluctance to impose his will on the ministry, which wished to make concessions. Appalled by the humiliation of the Convention of Olmütz William wrote to Otto von Manteuffel, the incoming Minister-President:

> I have shown all through life that I am no popularity hunter, but there is a public opinion to which I take off my hat, the one that was shown when the army was mobilised. That must not be given a slap in the face.'⁴

The ultimate outcome of the Olmütz deal and the Dresden conferences that followed it was the restoration of the German Confederation, which William watched miserably but ineffectually; he was careful not to express himself publicly as critical of his brother but was privately outraged by what had happened. Looking ahead, however, in a memorandum which he wrote in February 1851, he showed himself to have a clearer view of the future than those immediately around him:

> The wounds may perhaps be cemented for a time, but not healed, and whether Germany is to live or die will depend upon a fresh crisis. Under Prussia's leadership she will live; under Austria's she will die; under the leadership of both she will continue to languish as hitherto, and that will be thanks to Dresden.⁵

In the years that followed William largely avoided controversy. By now he was evidently going to succeed to the throne, if he survived his brother, but he was still able to lead a more or less military existence, apart from a few state visits abroad. Most of the time he spent in Coblenz, where he was Governor General of the Rhineland. In 1854 he was raised to the rank of Field Marshal. In the following year he performed one of the most important functions of his military career, when he presided over the commission that finally settled the adoption of the needle gun for the Prussian infantry. In 1857, however, this period of William's life came to an end, with the serious illness of Frederick William that led to the establishment of the regency.

King William I.

Initially for three months only, it was renewed from time to time, until William was permanently appointed as Regent in October 1858.

As has been seen, the provisional appointment of Moltke as Chief of the Great General Staff was one of William's first acts. In making this decision, he was appointing a man who was well known to him. Indeed, it was early in Moltke's career on the General Staff that he first came to William's attention, when he saw 'a plan worked out by a young Moltke,' which impressed him so much that he remarked: 'I wish an eye to be kept on this officer, who is as thin as a lead pencil; he may certainly rise to be something.'[6] Thereafter he will never have lost sight of Moltke; the General Staff was generally close to the Royal family, and there were frequent occasions when William met Moltke in a social environment. Moltke's appointment as aide de camp to Prince Henry in Rome will have further enhanced his relationship with the Royal family; and there were frequent encounters between the two men in the military sphere as well, especially when they attended annual manoeuvres. Moltke's letters to his wife contain frequent references to the Prince of Prussia which show that, always allowing for their relative positions in the hierarchy of Prussian society, they were on easy and familiar but no doubt very correct terms. In February 1851 William paid a visit to Prince Charles, who was Moltke's commanding general at the time in Magdeburg, as Moltke wrote to his wife:

I received him at the station at 8.15 in the evening and conducted him to his quarters. The board of officers were assembled in the hall, and the prince was genuinely pleased to see his Badeners again. The bands of both regiments played a grand tattoo. The prince visited the general as he lay in bed, then we had supper, in which the prince joined – twelve covers, oysters, salmon, caper sauce, ices, champagne. Next day at 10.45 the Staff assembled at the railway station, and then the prince left for Brunswick, evidently pleased with his reception. To me he was very friendly.[7]

When in 1855 Frederick William wished to appoint Moltke as adjutant to his nephew, his brother was at first opposed, not to Moltke but to any such appointment being made at all. However, he quickly became reconciled to the plan, and thereafter the contact between Moltke and William became extremely close. During the next two years the Prince of Prussia had the opportunity to get to know Moltke and his qualities to such an extent that Manteuffel's suggestion that Moltke be appointed Chief of the Great General Staff met with ready approval.

From then on Moltke's influence over the King began steadily to increase. At first he was able to involve himself only to a limited extent in William's decision making. During the struggle over army reform, for instance, Moltke played little part. And until Edwin von Manteuffel was finally moved by Bismarck out of harm's way in 1865, there is little doubt that the Chief of the Military Cabinet exerted more influence over William's thinking than the Chief of the Great General Staff. During the first part of the Danish war Moltke had been effectively sidelined until it became clear that he should be sent to take over from Vogel von Falckenstein as Chief of Staff of the Prussian forces. There, he performed with marked distinction, as William recognised in a letter he wrote to Moltke on August 14 1864:

When I despatched you to the seat of war, I could not foresee with any degree of certainty that your position there would be of any long duration, or that you would find much opportunity of proving your military talents in any very brilliant manner. From the moment, however, that your present position became an established fact you have rewarded my confidence and my expectations in a way that demands my heartiest thanks and full recognition. Both these accordingly I now most joyfully beg to offer you.[8]

He also conferred on Moltke the Order of the Crown First Class with Swords. On the same day Franz Joseph sent the Grand Cross of the Order of Leopold. As Moltke told Mary, however, it was William's letter that pleased him most. What did not please him, however, were rumours that he might be put in command of an army corps; he wrote that he had been too long out of the regular army, and had not 'sufficient talent for matters of detail to be able to take the chief command of a corps.' He thought that he would certainly do best to close his career with this campaign, adding that he 'should be very glad indeed to became Willisen's successor at Rome.'[9]

Moltke was always inclined, of course, to offer downbeat predictions about his own future, and there can be no doubt that the suggestion that he might retire as Chief of the Great General Staff existed nowhere outside his own reflections. In March 1865, as the possibility of a war with Austria became a serious eventuality, Manteuffel wrote to Roon that in the event of a war William intended to take command of the army in person, and was accustomed to the idea that Moltke would be his Chief of Staff.[10] In fact, the King regarded himself as the effective day to day commander of the army even in peacetime, as he crisply pointed out to the War Minister, when the latter complained of commanding generals going straight to the King and bypassing the ministry: 'The Commander in Chief commands the army not the War Minister,' he wrote in the margin of one of Bonin's reports.[11] Meanwhile, Moltke's attendance at the Royal Council meetings that preceded the war of 1866 demonstrated William's confidence in him; in May 1865, the King asked Moltke, hitherto a silent participant, what was the opinion of the army. In reply, Moltke gave his own opinion that annexation of the Duchies was the only desirable solution. The gain, he said, was so great that it was worth a war, and so far as he knew, the army also favoured annexation.

The King's order of June 2 1866 that the orders of the General Staff would go directly to the troops put into formal practice what had already become a reality; Moltke was now William's primary adviser. Thereafter, it would be, with few exceptions, Moltke's will that would prevail.

It was not always entirely plain sailing, since on occasion William had quite a lot to say, particularly when he became agitated about the progress of a battle. Professor Craig, in his history of the battle, described an incident referred to in Oscar von Lettow-Vorbeck's account of the campaign:

> At about noon, when the wounded Lieutenant Colonel Heinrich von Valentini came out of the Holawald, leading some shattered battalions of the 31st and 71st Regiments, which had led the way into the wood at 8.10 am and had stood under heavy fire ever since, the King spurred angrily toward them and, reproaching Valentini, said to the weary files: 'I'm going to send you forward again! Let's see you fight like brave Prussians.'[12]

Frederick Charles, who was present at this unfortunate incident, could not let it pass:

> The sovereign himself was being less than generous to troops who had fought well; and no man was more jealous of the reputation of his command than Frederick Charles. He remonstrated with the King, pointing out that the 31st and 71st had more than done their duty, and assuring him that he had reserves enough to hold the contested wood.[13]

As the battle wore on, without any sign of the arrival of the Second Army, and with little progress on the front of the Army of the Elbe, there were a number of exchanges between Moltke and the King on the Roskosberg to illustrate the confidence of the former and the anxiety of the latter. At one point the King, anxious about the situation in the Holawald, exclaimed: 'Moltke, Moltke, we are losing the battle.' Moltke's calm reply was: 'Your Majesty will today win not only the battle, but the campaign.'[14] Later, the King asked about preparations for a retreat, if this became necessary; Moltke's response was: 'Here there will be no retreat. Here we are fighting for the very existence of Prussia.' These anecdotes do show just how much Moltke had to calm the fears of those around him.

When, finally, Bismarck was the first of those on the Roskosberg to notice the signs of the Second Army's advance, Moltke took one look through the proffered telescope, and then rode over to the King, saying: 'The campaign is decided and in accordance with your Majesty's desires!' Perplexed, the King irritably said that he did not know what Moltke was talking about, and they should concentrate on what was happening today. Moltke was adamant: 'No, the success is complete. Vienna lies at Your Majesty's feet.'[15]

The reality of the King's authority was well illustrated towards the end of the battle, when Moltke was trying to organise the pursuit of the beaten Austrians. The King had left him, in order to congratulate his victorious troops, and could not be found to approve Moltke's plan of procedure. As a result, Moltke was unable to issue the necessary orders until 6.30 pm, and Benedek was able to extricate a substantial part of his army.

Similar incidents occurred during the Franco-Prussian War, when William's nerves, and those of others at the Royal Headquarters, were stretched extremely tight. One instance was recounted by Fritz Hönig, towards the close of the battle of Gravelotte, when Fransecky's II Corps was moving up to the front. The King ordered the corps to attack Point du Jour, a decision which Moltke disapproved. On this occasion at least the Chief of the General Staff's advice was not followed:

> When Moltke saw that no attention was paid to his advice, and when the King's idea had become an order, and the II Corps was marching towards the defile, he slowly turned away from the King, moved about one hundred paces to the right, and pretended to be busy about something. He intended to thus give it to be understood that he did not approve of what was coming, and those around who saw this action so understood it; indeed, the scene made a great impression on them. When, later on, the point of the II Corps was approaching the wood, Moltke followed it for a few paces along the main road, and a number of staff officers came up to him, while the King, with Bismarck, Roon and Podbielski, remained near Malmaison.[16]

Another reported incident relates to this period of the battle, and was described by Alfred von Waldersee, serving as aide de camp to the King. It was an echo of the similar occasion during the battle Königgrätz:

> Steinmetz came up and reported that the troops were not advancing further, 'Why are they not advancing further?' asked the King in excited tones. 'They

have no longer any leaders, Your Majesty: the officers are dead or wounded.' After some time the King was again indignant and expressed himself to Moltke complaining of the troops and of their not gaining ground. Moltke replied with equal heat: 'They are fighting for Your Majesty like heroes!' 'I am the best judge of that,' the King retorted. Whereupon Moltke gave spur to his horse and dashed forward down the incline towards Gravelotte where the head of the 3rd Division was now to arrive.[17]

American General Philip Sheridan accompanied the Royal Headquarters and recorded his impressions of Gravelotte-St Privat in his memoirs, although not always the most accurate of observers. He described the manner in which reports of the progress of the battle were made:

> These reports were always made to the King first, and whenever anybody arrived with tidings of the fight we clustered around to hear the news, General von Moltke unfolding a map meanwhile and explaining the situation. This done, the Chief of the Staff, while awaiting the next report, would either return to a seat that had been made for him with some knapsacks, or would occupy the time walking about, kicking clods of dirt or small stones here and there, his hands clasped behind his back, his face pale and thoughtful. He was then nearly seventy years old, but because of his emaciated figure, the deep wrinkles in his face, and the crows feet about his eyes, he looked even older, his appearance being suggestive of the practice of church asceticism rather than of his well-known ardent devotion to the military profession.[18]

The state of mind of those at the Royal Headquarters towards the end of the battle was the subject of a characteristically highly coloured report by the journalist Archibald Forbes. Whether his account is at all reliable is decidedly open to question. He described how, when the attack of the II Corps went in, the King sat on a makeshift bench in the village of Rezonville anxiously awaiting news, and forcing himself to keep still; Bismarck, equally tense, pretended to be reading letters:

> The night came down like a pall, but the blaze of an adjacent conflagration lit up the anxious group here by the churchyard wall. From out the medley of broken troops littering the plain in front, came suddenly a great shout that grew in volume as it rolled nearer. The hoofs of a galloping horse rattled on the causeway. A moment later, Moltke, his face for once quivering with excitement, sprang from the saddle, and running towards the King, cried out: 'It is good for us; we have won the plateau, and the victory is with your Majesty!' The king sprang to his feet with a 'God be thanked!' Bismarck, with a great sigh of relief, crushed his letters in the hollow of his hand.[19]

Inevitably, there were many moments when even Moltke's marble calm was tested to the limit; and many more when the King gave way to extreme anxiety. Throughout it all, however, Moltke 'entirely preserved his quiet manner with his subordinates, and his peculiarly careful modesty towards the King.'[20]

Moltke was given an opportunity to summarise his relationship with the King in the course of an interview with Count Bethusy-Huc, who put to him a suggestion that was apparently widely discussed. The count recorded Moltke's response:

> At that time (about 1885) a legend was in circulation, not only in society talk, but in the press, which, though apparently to the Field-Marshal's credit, was really distasteful to him. The story was that on the evening of the battle of Gravelottte King William asked his Chief of the Staff what was to be done if the enemy still held his position next morning. Moltke was said to have answered, 'Attack him again, your Majesty,' and when the King replied that after the heavy losses he could not bring himself to agree to that, Moltke was said to have added, 'In that case I should beg leave to resign.' I was rightly in doubt, says Count Bethusy-Huc, about the genuineness of this legend and when in confidence I asked the Field-Marshal about it he declared it from beginning to end an invention, without the slightest justification in anything that took place on that evening. He added: 'I should never have left my King in the lurch like that, least of all during war, in face of the enemy. It would be contrary both to discipline and to military honour. But such legends might have arisen, by misunderstanding, from something that did happen more than once in both wars. The King who, as you know, thoroughly studied all my plans before they were carried out, had a very sharp eye, far keener than either the public or the army knew, for any weak points in them, and sometimes insisted very strongly that they should be modified to meet his objections, which in themselves were justified. That was not always possible, at least, not for me. There are in war many situations in which it is quite impossible to make a plan without a weak point, and in which you must necessarily rely to some extent upon good luck and the bravery of your troops. On such occasions, when the King could not be induced to let fall his theoretical objections, I more than once had to say, 'then your Majesty must be so gracious as to give your own orders. My wisdom is at an end; I can suggest no other course.' This declaration invariably led to the approval of my plan.'[21]

Once the Army of Châlons had been disposed of at Sedan, and the Army of the Rhine safely shut up in Metz, and the Royal Headquarters had settled down in Versailles, there were less sudden crises to test the King's frayed nerves. Away from the immediate battle front, Moltke's magisterial command of the situation from day to day was generally enough to soothe his jittery Royal master. However, from time to time the King's pessimism got the better of him, although usually not to the point of affecting the conduct of operations. One instance of it doing so, however, occurred during Ducrot's offensive from Paris at Champigny, which began on November 30. On the night of

December 3 the Crown Prince of Saxony sent a decidedly pessimistic report to Moltke, to the effect that the troops of his Army of the Meuse, manning the threatened sector, were exhausted. After a conference with the King, Moltke ordered the Third Army to reinforce Fransecky, upon whose front a further assault was expected. The situation appeared critical and the King was profoundly anxious, writing an angry note on the Saxon Crown Prince's report which, he thought 'gives no confidence in the issue of a battle tomorrow, if the enemy debouches from five bridges and turns Brie.'[22]

Moltke was not convinced that the situation was critical, as indeed it was not. But that night he sat down to write a reassuring note to the King, pointing out that there were 58 battalions and more than 200 guns in the sector, and that both the Third Army and the Army of the Meuse had orders to have other reinforcements ready if necessary. The King's anxiety was not wholly assuaged by this; he made a marginal note that the 58 battalions were only the equivalent of 30.[23]

Pondering the situation overnight, Moltke decided that he must be seen to have covered every eventuality if William's nerves were to be calmed, and so he wrote a memorandum setting out the steps that would be taken in the event of a French breakthrough.

He suggested that it might temporarily be necessary to raise the investment on the north of Paris until the First Army could be pulled back from Rouen to reinforce the position. The Guard Corps and the IV Corps could be pulled out of their lines and moved to the threatened sector to deal with the breakout, while the XII Corps and the Württemberg Division hung on to the enemy's flanks. If the French marched east, they would have to be prevented from damaging the vital rail links. It would have represented a huge rearrangement of the troops investing Paris, but it was written to demonstrate that even a successful breakout could be coped with.[24]

The Crown Prince's diary of the war records a number of occasions when his father's gloom got the better of him. On December 15 he noted: 'His Majesty is in great excitement and ill humour not less over the military situation than over the course of politics.' Moltke tried to cheer up the King by observing that although the commandant of the besieged fortress of Longwy had declared that rather than surrender he would be buried beneath the last stone, such protestations were usually followed immediately by the capitulation of the fortress. The Crown Prince noted that 'Count Moltke's bearing and way of speaking at such moments are quite inimitable.'[25]

Three weeks later, at a time when a lot was going on, the Royal pessimism again asserted itself:

> We are once again politically and strategically in an extremely critical situation, calling for attention to every quarter of the heavens at one and the same time, inasmuch as the efforts to relieve Paris are being directed from all sides and with great masses of men. The King's mind is naturally greatly exercised by all this, and for the last few days his outlook on the immediate future has been of the blackest; we have accordingly had to do what we could to encourage him and raise his spirits, whereas General Count Moltke never loses his quiet composure.[26]

One of the threats which caused the King particular agitation was the movement of Bourbaki's Army of the East, which threatened the forces besieging Belfort. Werder, commanding there, had suggested in a report that it might be better to abandon Belfort, and concentrate on defending Alsace. The Crown Prince recorded Moltke's reaction to this proposition:

> One must have seen General Count Moltke's face and known him too as well as I do to form a conception of the look with which he communicated this telegram to me in the King's antechamber, then read it out at the report, and with what an air of imperturbable icy calm he added: 'Your Majesty will, I trust, approve of this answer to General von Werder, that he has simply to stand firm and beat the enemy wherever he finds him.' I cannot say how admirable beyond all praise I thought General Moltke at this moment; any other man would have launched out with reflections and exclamations – he in one second relieved the whole strain of the situation and, thank heaven, restored General von Werder's steadiness.[27]

However, by far the most important issue involving Moltke and the King in a direct confrontation was the dispute over the bombardment of Paris, which broadened into the fundamental question of the relative roles of the Chancellor and the Chief of the Great General Staff. Moltke, and most of his colleagues, (although not Roon) considered that the proposed bombardment of the city was a futile distraction from the essential military operations, and did their level best to put paid to the idea. Bismarck, on the other hand, saw it as a means of accelerating the end of the war; the longer it was prolonged the greater was the risk of foreign interference. He was able to rely on the constant support of Roon, whose strong feelings on the issue led him to write a remarkably angry letter to Moltke on December 11:

> The declarations made by Your Excellency at today's report suggested to me reflections which I did not wish to express at the time, in order to avoid all controversy in His Majesty's presence, but which I am not however able to leave unspoken. Several months ago, Your Excellency issued His Majesty's order as to the bombardment of several forts: the Third Army was charged with its execution for this limited objective. At that time Your Excellency did not appear to doubt the possibility of carrying this out. However subsequently the strangely long delay required by the technical services for commencing the attack has became longer and longer.[28]

He was surprised, he went on, to hear Moltke 'declare that the projected attack was absolutely impracticable and pointless.'

Moltke's resistance to the idea could not prevent a meeting to discuss the matter being held on December 17, in the presence of the King, who had, in the meantime, been subjected to ceaseless pressure from Bismarck. It was not a placid meeting; Blumenthal, who was disgusted to see that some of his colleagues appeared to have changed their views in deference to what appeared William's opinion, observed that 'the War Minster glared at us most angrily and resentfully.'[28] The upshot was an agreement to stockpile munitions for a bombardment of the southern forts and to shell Mont Avron as a trial run. Bismarck, of course, was delighted with this, although still profoundly concerned that the military were interfering in political questions.

The bombardment of Mont Avron on December 27 and 28 proved surprisingly successful, the French abandoning the position during the night of December 28/29 and meant that the bombardment of the city would now go forward. After a delay due to bad weather, it began on January 5. The prevailing conditions continued to hamper the effectiveness of the bombardment, but the effect on some of the forts was very apparent. This was less so in the case of the city itself; after the first few days the shelling of the city was confined to the hours of darkness. In fact, civilian casualties were surprisingly low; although 1,400 buildings were damaged there were only 97 killed and 278 wounded in the three weeks of the bombardment. Nonetheless, the fact that the operation was carried out at all in the face of Moltke's objections was entirely due to the fact that the King was persuaded that it was necessary.

It was one of the crucial factors that led to the climax of the dispute between Moltke and Bismarck. So serious had the conflict became that the Crown Prince attempted to mediate, arranging a meeting between the two men in his presence. This occurred on January 13; much to the Crown Prince's disappointment it failed to resolve their differences. Sharp things were said by both of them:

> Under such circumstances agreement was clearly out of the question, and I could not even gain this much, that at any rate at coming reports at His Majesty's mention might be avoided of the differences of opinion actually existing. It will rather come to this, that each separately for himself will lay his views before the King, and His Majesty must decide between them.[30]

The Crown Prince was obviously right that it would therefore be for the King to take a view; his father would, however, be faced with an extremely difficult decision, given his instinctive inclination always to put the army first. Professor Craig described his response:

> What went on inside the King's mind as relations between Bismarck and Moltke reached their final crisis is not known. In the long series of disputes since the beginning of the war, the sovereign had seemed, on the whole, to be more sympathetic to the soldiers than to his Chancellor. Now, however, he reversed his position completely. On January 20, when the French expressed a desire to discuss terms, he authorised Bismarck to begin armistice talks – an action which foreshadowed the end of Moltke's ideas of an extension of the war. And five days later he at last took action to end the bitter struggle over spheres of competence and to satisfy Bismarck's frequent complaints concerning the boycott imposed on him by the General Staff.[31]

The action which he took came in the form of two orders, the first forbidding Moltke to communicate with the French without first asking the King if Bismarck should be consulted, and the second that Bismarck was to be kept fully informed about future operations.

Moltke was appalled. His first thought was to resign, and on the evening of January 25 he produced a fierce memorandum, drafted originally by Bronsart von Schellendorff, which concluded with the sarcastic suggestion that in future it should be for Bismarck to advise the King in military matters and accept responsibility for future operations. Having slept on it, Moltke drew back from the inevitable consequences of such a confrontation and wrote a second memorandum, defending his conduct. He concluded this with a statement of his own position as he saw it:

> I believe that it would be a good thing to settle my relationship with the Federal Chancellor definitively. Up till now I have considered that the Chief of the General Staff (especially in war) and the Federal Chancellor are two equally warranted and mutually independent agencies under the direct command of Your Royal Majesty, which have the duty of keeping each other reciprocally informed.[32]

Although a reply was prepared to this, it seems that William decided not to send it, and preferred to leave matters as they now stood.

In coming down on Bismarck's side in this controversy, the King displayed, having regard to the pressures of the soldiers around him, considerable moral courage, as well as political wisdom. The subsequent armistice negotiations were conducted by the Chancellor in accordance with his own ideas, to the bitter frustration of the senior military commanders. A major point of principle had been established; it was, however, one that might not stand if in the future a Chancellor with less natural authority than Bismarck was obliged to face a united military opinion. All the same, in reviewing the King's relationship with Moltke, it is not unfair to give him great credit for being able to see the wood for the trees.

5

Blumenthal

Arguably Moltke's most important collaborator, and certainly preeminent among those who served in senior staff posts, was Albrecht Karl Leonhard von Blumenthal. Much the best sources for an understanding of his contribution during the wars of German unification are his own candid and revealing diaries of the campaigns of 1866 and 1870-71. Although these display his vain and querulous personality with awful clarity, these characteristics should not obscure his very real ability or the crucial role that Blumenthal played as Chief of Staff to the Prussian Crown Prince in these campaigns.

Born in 1810, Blumenthal was the son of a Prussian cavalry officer who was killed at the battle of Dennewitz in 1813, and he was brought up by his grandfather. Enrolment at the cadet school at Kulm was a natural step in his education. From there he progressed at the age of fourteen to the Berlin *Kadetteninstitute,* where he seems to have enjoyed a valuable education in mathematics and history, but not in languages. Blumenthal himself described the rest of the curriculum: 'To the matter of bodily exercises, however, much greater care was given, and I fancy that I particularly distinguished myself in drill, swordsmanship, dancing, riding etc, and so increased my physical strength that I managed to undergo all the hardships of my first manoeuvres without any undue strain.'[1]

Thereafter, at the age of seventeen, Blumenthal was commissioned as a Second Lieutenant in the Guard Reserve Regiment at Potsdam. It is some indication of the pace of advancement in the Prussian peacetime army of that time that it was not until 1844 that Blumenthal received his first promotion, to the rank of First Lieutenant. In the meantime, after attending a course at the Garrison War School between 1830 and 1833, which inspired him with the determination to pursue a successful military career, he had been posted to Coblenz as Adjutant and Paymaster to a Guard Landwehr battalion. While serving there he took up in particular the study of military history. He also studied the Italian and English languages. 'I soon dropped the former as useless for the practical purposes of life, but in the latter I was fortunate in finding a very pleasant opportunity of studying it intimately. In the summer of 1839 I married a young English lady whose mother came to live a short time in Coblenz. I was in this way thrown among a great many Englishmen, and saw much of their ways and heard much of their language.'[2] By an odd coincidence, the two men with whom Blumenthal was to work most closely, Moltke and the Prussian Crown Prince, also married English women.

An important step towards a successful General Staff career was appointment to the Topographical Section; unluckily, when offered the chance of this in 1841, ill health prevented Blumenthal taking it up, and it was not until 1846 that he obtained such an appointment. By 1848, still only a First Lieutenant at the age of thirty eight, Blumenthal was becoming discouraged. 'Despairing of anything like early promotion, I find consolation in the thought that I have done my duty to the best of my ability. I have always endeavoured, both in private life and in my military career, to get as much change as possible of scene and work, so as to keep my body healthy and my spirits young.'[3]

But the course of European history was about to change, and with it the progress of Blumenthal's military career. He wrote the brief autobiographical note pondering his lack of advancement in January 1848. Within two months Europe was shaken by the upheavals of that year. The war planning of the Great Powers was thrown into chaos as the political situation changed at bewildering speed. During this time the Prussian army was involved in the Schleswig-Holstein war of 1848-50, and also in the suppression of insurgency in Baden in 1849. But with the reaction came a return to Great Power confrontation; in 1850 the Prussian army was mobilised in preparation for a war against Austria. That possibility disappeared with the conclusion of the Convention of Olmütz, which left many of those in the Prussian army feeling humiliated and profoundly depressed at the lost opportunity. Among the latter was Moltke, at that time serving as Chief of Staff of the IV Corps based in Magdeberg. He wrote mournfully to his wife in January 1851 as the subsequent demobilisation process drew to its close:

> That our whole policy has been so presented that we must now accept many humiliations, that we must give up everything we have claimed and attempted during the last three years, I quite understand. But that we should muster five hundred thousand men to yield at all points, and help the Austrians over the Elbe on Frederick the Great's birthday, that is difficult to understand. What disasters a single day has brought upon us![4]

Next month he was still fuming, writing to his brother Adolf that 'a more disgraceful peace was never signed;' but his spirits were somewhat reviving, and he remarked that 'Prussia will stand yet at the head of Germany.' All the same, Moltke did not begin to foresee that it would be he who led Prussia to that position within fifteen years or that by 1857 he would be acting as the Chief of the Prussian General Staff.

During this period Blumenthal's career was also transformed. By the outbreak of the Schleswig-Holstein War of 1864 he had risen to the rank of Colonel, and was appointed to be Chief of Staff of the Prussian I Corps, assigned to the combined

Blumenthal.

Austro-Prussian army which was to carry out the military operations against Denmark. The commander of the I Corps was Prince Frederick Charles, a Royal prince who was nonetheless a career soldier who was highly regarded. Blumenthal's appointment, and his progress up the General Staff ladder owed much to the trust and confidence which Moltke reposed in him and it was through Blumenthal that Moltke, with no direct responsibility for the conduct of the war, and who was not otherwise always fully informed of the progress of the operations against the Danes, was able to keep himself in the picture. Their private correspondence enabled Moltke from Berlin to offer a stream of thoughtful advice to Blumenthal, and to be sufficiently on top of the situation to offer advice to the King. This was just as well, since the overall command of the Allied army was in the hands of the aged and eccentric von Wrangel, and his wilful and incompetent chief of staff Vogel von Falckenstein.

Blumenthal thus found himself at the epicentre of Prussia's first important military operations since the Wars of Liberation against Napoleon in which his father had died. Regrettably, he did not keep a diary of this campaign; his private comments on it might have been very instructive. As it was, though, his regular private correspondence with Moltke was invaluable to the chief of the General Staff, and gives some insight into the strategic thinking of both men. The allied operations began on February 1, when the army crossed the River Eider at various points. In the plans he had prepared for the campaign, Moltke had aimed to trap the Danish army in the Dannewerk, the lines of fortification that for nine hundred years had covered Schleswig, but Lieutenant General Christian de Meza, the able Danish Commander in Chief, was too quick for the Allies, and abandoned the position and fell back northwards. Danish public opinion was outraged by the giving up of a line of defence that had been expected to impose a substantial check on the Allied advance, and it cost de Meza his job, although he had in this way saved the Danish army from encirclement.

Back in Berlin after paying a visit to the theatre of operations, Moltke sat down to write to Blumenthal on February 21 to deal with a number of the most pressing questions. Moltke's return to Berlin had followed an explicit order to Wrangel that his forces should halt, following the unauthorised crossing of the border of Jutland and the occupation of Kolding. This the Commander in Chief had received with unbridled fury, despatching a violent letter of protest to the King. Awaiting with what he described as 'reverent expectation' revised orders which would enable the advance to continue northwards, Wrangel observed: 'To recall the Prussians from their career of victory is quite impossible for me, for the curse of the fatherland would strike even my grandchildren. The diplomats may counsel such a thing but they may be sure that their name will be affixed to the gallows.'[5] It was around army commanders such as this that seasoned staff officers sometimes had to work.

In his letter to Blumenthal, Moltke reviewed the course of the operations thus far, and added his private comments on the current views which appeared to prevail at Wrangel's headquarters:

> As for what is happening now, the idea dominating the headquarters staff, absolutely correctly from the military point of view, is to occupy Jutland while observing Fredericia and Düppel. This conquest could be completed before the end of the month, if it were not for obstacles. The halt previously ordered decided me to return home, my special mission having ended. But, in the meantime the frontier has been crossed, and the measures taken here have only been such as most carefully to meet our confederate's scruples …. If insurmountable political difficulties prevent an invasion of Jutland, it will then only remain, certainly, for us to concern ourselves seriously with Düppel.[6]

Moltke was, as he had told Blumenthal, strongly of the view that militarily the correct course to pursue was to occupy Jutland, and he strongly urged that this be done. It would be necessary first, however, for the political objections of the Austrians as well as those of the lesser German states, to be overcome. The task of doing this fell to Edwin von Manteuffel, who was sent to visit Vienna and the other capitals for the purpose. In the meanwhile Moltke set out the military arguments in a memorandum to the King of February 22, pointing out that Jutland could be speedily overrun, while a successful siege of Düppel would require a siege of several weeks.[7] Manteuffel's journey was not entirely fruitful, and the Austrian views against an advance into Jutland were embodied in a paper presented by General Huyn. Moltke regarded

Huyn's arguments as rubbish, and demolished them in a report to Roon of February 28 and a private letter to Blumenthal on the same day.

> It is a pure masterpiece of staff pedantry. The temporary occupation of Schleswig is presented as the object of the war, whereas it is only a means to force Denmark to accept certain conditions relating to the Duchies, a means that has obviously proved insufficient. On this false base has been erected an enormous strategic dissertation throwing light on what has never been in dispute, that the Danes as masters of the sea can concentrate their forces at Düppel or Fredericia in order to take the offensive against us.'[8]

Outlining the course he thought should be followed if the Prussians were compelled to assault Düppel, Moltke favoured an attack on the south end of the line of forts that made up the Danish position there. An attack at the other end of the line could, he believed, be at risk of being taken in flank. Moltke concluded his letter to Blumenthal with the fervent hope that their discussion of a direct assault on Düppel would prove academic: 'Please God, however, that we can exchange Alsen for Jutland. Meanwhile, I will be very happy if you would continue to keep me informed confidentially.'[9] Blumenthal and Moltke were united in a powerful distaste for embarking an formal siege operations at Düppel, just as they would be in 1870 when the issue arose again during the investment of Paris. Ultimately, however, again as in 1870, views based on issues wider than the purely military were to prevail, although in the meantime Blumenthal was looking hard at ways to avoid the necessity for a direct assault on the Düppel lines. In the meantime, however, the Austrians began to give way over a move northward and by March 4 Moltke was able to tell Blumenthal that he hoped that a positive order to invade Jutland would be sent that day. This would not, however, enable Blumenthal and Frederick Charles to escape from their sojourn in front of Düppel; Moltke asked Blumenthal to tell the Prince how much he regretted 'not to see him at the head of an expedition into Jutland instead of being charged with such a difficult and thankless task as an artillery assault on Düppel. But this attack is considered in high places as an inevitable necessity.[10]

Blumenthal had not found it difficult to persuade both Prince Frederick Charles and Wrangel that the projected assault was an unnecessary and potentially very expensive operation. As early as February 23 Wrangel had opposed it on the basis that it would take a long time to bring up the necessary siege artillery, because of the lack of the necessary rail links, and because the roads to Düppel were in a very poor state due to the weather. It would thus take a month to get the artillery into position. Pointing all this out in a despatch to the King, Wrangel went on: 'Therefore it is better to give up that plan altogether, especially since the conquest of that little corner of earth would be of no real gain. It would not even lead to the possession of Alsen, since the passage thither could not be effected without the help of a fleet.'[11] Meanwhile Frederick Charles complained to the King that the projected assault would cost a lot of men and money. He could not see, he told him, any military necessity for it.[12]

Blumenthal, however, had now come up with a better idea of his own, about which he wrote to Moltke on March 4. His plan was to mount a seaborne assault on the island of Alsen from Ballegaard. If successful, it would effectively outflank the lines of Düppel, and would also offer what ought to be an effective political substitute for the projected Düppel assault. Moltke responded promptly and with cautious enthusiasm in his letter to Blumenthal of March 8. 'The thought of avoiding, thanks to a landing on Alsen, the difficult operation of a siege of the Düppel position deserves mature consideration.' There were, he thought, a number of conditions precedent that must be fulfilled before such an operation could be launched. A lot of preparation would be required; if the operation were to be carried out in the near future the attackers must be prepared to do without the missing siege artillery; and the cooperation of the fleet would be required. The Danish ironclad *Rolf Krake* was a serious threat and could on her own, unless some means was found of preventing it, disrupt the landing before half the troops had crossed. The availability of sufficient artillery seemed to Moltke to be the key point whether the assault was aimed at Düppel or Alsen; regretting a press leak about the Prussian observation post on the Broager Pensinula, separated from the Düppel position by the Wemmingbund, Moltke hoped that the batteries there would 'not only interdict the Wemmingbund to enemy ships but that they will also inflict heavy losses on the large bodies of troops that must, immediately after an attack, be established behind the entrenchments.'[13] When Blumenthal put forward his scheme to Frederick Charles, the latter was at first very dubious; it seemed a very high risk operation. Gradually, however, Blumenthal overcame his doubts, and Frederick Charles submitted the plan for approval to Army Headquarters on March 10.

In the desire to find out some way to avoid a costly assault on Düppel, the local commanders were strongly supported by Moltke; but the political imperative for the attack was very strong, and was being strongly urged from Berlin. In different ways, and to some extent for different reasons, Bismarck, Roon, Manteuffel and the King all applied extreme pressure. Manteuffel, in a letter to Frederick Charles on March 10, spelled out the position bluntly. If the assault was further postponed, he wrote, people would begin to doubt the Prince's determination. It was crucial to take Düppel before an armistice was concluded. He went on: 'This is a matter not of the importance of the position, not of the question whether it can be held without Alsen, whether Alsen should be captured, whether without Alsen's capture the taking of Düppel is not worthless – this is a matter of the renown of the Prussian army and the position of the King in the councils of Europe.'[14] Manteuffel, for his part, was not impressed by Blumenthal's Alsen scheme, fearing its vulnerability both to the weather and the Danish fleet. To follow up his written advice, Manteuffel was sent off to headquarters to make sure that the need for an assault was accepted there.

Having himself reluctantly accepted the position, Moltke was at pains in his discussions with the King and Roon to emphasise that the local commanders should be left to plan and execute the assault on Düppel in their own way, free from interference from above. He was reluctantly coming to the conclusion that Blumenthal's plan for an attack at Alsen was too risky, since the Prussian navy was doubtful of its ability to operate effectively there; on March 17 he explained to Blumenthal the difficulties perceived by the navy in operating in waters in which it could encounter the main Danish fleet. Unfortunately efforts to strengthen the navy by the purchase of ships from abroad had not been well managed. He hoped, though, that the project would not be abandoned. However, just then two important events occurred: an operation in which a battalion of Prussian troops landed on the island of Fehmarn was brilliantly successful, and the next day the Prussian navy fought a most encouraging if ultimately indecisive battle off Rügen. In the face of this, Moltke began to think that the risks of a seaborne operation might have been overdone. By March 25 the objections to the Alsen landing had been overcome and final approval was given, enabling Blumenthal to get down to the work of the detailed planning of this operation, as well as the assault on Düppel. As to this, Moltke's insistence that Blumenthal and Frederick Charles should have freedom to plan the operation seems to have won the day; he was able to write reassuringly on the subject to Blumenthal, saying that 'any sensible soldier must see that one cannot hope for an immediate solution before Düppel and that it must take time; have no concern about this. I would also like to believe that the Prince will not be given too narrow instructions. One cannot respond positively to the boldest hopes, and a good rider does not attempt, even on his best horse, a jump which will break its back. Our troops will certainly show what they are capable of, but it is necessary that the assault is properly prepared.'[15] And he was able to confirm his belief that the need for this was appreciated in Berlin when he wrote to Blumenthal again on March 21.

Moltke, although glad that the projected landing on Alsen had been authorised, was nonetheless still very anxious about the risks involved, and wrote regularly to Blumenthal with his suggestions for the operation. On March 27, for instance, he wondered whether it might be possible to establish a battery east of Rackebull facing the narrowest part of the Alsen Sund, without alerting the enemy. But his main anxiety continued to be about the reality of naval cooperation, without which he was all too well aware of the devastation which the Danish fleet could cause. Blumenthal however, was pressing ahead with his plans, which were extremely bold, and which were designed to gain the maximum advantage of complete surprise. He proposed to cross the northern end of the Alsen Sund; although this meant crossing at a point twice as wide as would be found further south, the Danish troops on Alsen were concentrated in the south of the island, and Blumenthal reckoned he could get enough troops ashore in the first wave to secure the beachhead before the Danes were able to react. The jumping off point would therefore be at Ballegaard, from which he hoped to despatch 1,500 troops in each wave. The boats available restricted him to this number; the second and subsequent waves would follow at intervals of ninety minutes. On the mainland, Blumenthal began covertly to transfer the newly arrived heavy artillery into a position from which it could cover the crossing and in particular to deal with the *Rolf Krake* if and when it put in an appearance.

His preparations completed, Blumenthal fixed the night of April 2/3 for the crossing. As the hours ticked by, all seemed to be going well. The weather was fair, and the waters of the Sund remained calm. Blumenthal had concentrated a force of twenty six battalions in and around Ballegaard in preparation for the assault, and these began to move up to the embarkation points, but suddenly there was a sharp change in the weather, and as it continued to deteriorate it became clear that the assault could not proceed. Blumenthal, naturally, was deeply disappointed and frustrated at what, as later became apparent, was the loss of an outstanding opportunity of achieving a complete surprise. This would have enabled Blumenthal to get sufficient troops across to withstand any counter attack and then proceed to overrun the whole of Alsen. Significantly, too, there had been no sign of the *Rolf Krake*.

Moltke, in sympathising with Blumenthal, was clear that the intrinsic merits of his plan should not be forgotten:

> I see from your letter of yesterday that God did not wish the operation so long prepared by you to be carried out, I believe, however, that even now there is no case for it to be definitively abandoned, for only in this way could the war be brought to an end, since this would have led to the destruction of the enemy army. Even a successful assault on Düppel may not achieve this; it will result in the retreat of the Danish troops to Fünen where they will confront us anew in that island position.[16]

For the moment, however, the element of surprise having been lost, Frederick Charles and Blumenthal had to resign themselves to carrying out the assault on Düppel, for which they were to have the assistance of the redoubtable Lieutenant General Eduard von Hindersin, who on April 7 was despatched to oversee the artillery assault. Writing to tell Blumenthal of this, Moltke was quick to reassume him that he was not about to lose control of the operation: 'If I see Hindersin again before his departure, I will call his attention above all to the necessity of an absolute agreement with you if it is to succeed.'[17]

As Blumenthal turned his attention once more to the preparations for an assault on the Düppel position, he and Moltke continued to exchange frequent letters on the situation. On April 12, in contemplating the proposed attack on the Danish position, Moltke sent Blumenthal his hopes that it would fall without too dear a sacrifice, since 'we will hardly gain much material advantage there, above all if, as I believe, the Danes get out in time.' He had not, however, forgotten the Alsen operation, and devoted the rest of his letter to a consideration of its revival.[18] Three days later he sent Blumenthal a plan of Sonderburg and of the heights of Düppel, the latter annotated with a report prepared in 1849. It still seemed to Moltke that the Danes were waiting only for an 'honest opportunity' to pull out of the Düppel position, something that Gerlach could not do until he faced a serious attack. He was in no doubt that the assault would be successful; when it was, he hoped 'that full justice will be given to your personal disinterestedness and your indefatigable activity.'[19]

Moltke did not have long to wait. By April 18 the heavy artillery available to Hindersin had reached a total of one hundred and eighteen guns. The long period of preparation had not only enabled the Prussian artillery to cause extensive damage to the forts; it had also led to a progressive deterioration of the Danish morale. Blumenthal and Frederick Charles had at first intended to launch the infantry assault at dawn, but the experience gained from the dawn raids which had been undertaken had shown that the Danes were ready at that time to repel attacks with grape shot. It was instead decided only to send the infantry forward after a further heavy bombardment. When therefore Lieutenant General von Manstein, in command of the assault force, which comprised a total of 8,000 men, moved forward at 10.00 am, his leading troops soon overran the six southernmost forts, all of which had fallen by 10.22 am. Manstein then turned north; the garrisons of the remaining four forts put up a fierce resistance, but by 1.00 pm the Danish position was no longer feasible, and the survivors streamed back cross the bridge to Sonderburg.

The news of the long awaited victory was received in Berlin, and throughout Germany, with the greatest enthusiasm. Moltke hastened to write to Blumenthal, to whom he believed that much of the credit should go. 'I send you my sincere congratulations for the brilliant victory achieved on April 18 by our brave troops, and to which your tenacity, your intelligence and your forbearance has so effectively contributed. The significant losses which this great feat of arms has cost show clearly that the greatest sacrifices still will not guarantee success if the gun and the pickaxe have not prepared it.' Turning to the next steps in the campaign, he speculated upon the possibility that the Danes would transfer their army to Fünen, abandoning Alsen. If they remained in Alsen, they risked losing everything if, with artillery superiority, Blumenthal succeeded in forcing the passage of the Sund. Moltke had always favoured the idea of a descent upon Fünen; the moment for this would come, he thought, when the Danes showed any sign of pulling troops out of Alsen. In the meantime, there would very likely be an armistice when the London Conference convened on April 25.[20]

During the days after the victory at Düppel, Moltke was much exercised by Wrangel's wrong headed conviction that the next step should be an assault on the Danish position at Fredericia, a project which he regarded as absurd. It took all his influence (which was by now somewhat increasing) to put paid to this idea. In the end he was successful in this; but the promotion of the idea from Wrangel's headquarters was a further indication that Vogel von Falckenstein was quite unsuited to his position as Chief of Staff. Moltke would have liked to visit the theatre of operations but had no wish to do so as a mere spectator. Meanwhile in Berlin, where he was heavily dependent on Blumenthal for information, he was frustrated by not knowing exactly what was happening. On April 28, congratulating Blumenthal on the award of the Pour le Mérite, he wrote:

> Since April 17 I have not received any letter from you, and for me this is a real hardship. If this is because, since the assault, nothing important has occurred in your front, it is nonetheless vitally important for me to be kept informed of

intentions and plans. I am often asked, at what notice, for my opinion on important questions, but at other times it is not thought necessary to tell me what is proposed or what has occurred. It is thus necessary for me to seek, at least in a private correspondence, sufficient information to keep me up to date with what has transpired.[21]

During the armistice Blumenthal paid a visit to Berlin, and a fascinating glimpse of him at this time is provided by Prince Krafft zu Hohenlohe in his memoirs:

> On my return from the theatre of war, I was again a frequent visitor to the 'Democratic Club.' It was only natural that everything that had taken place in the [theatre of] war was discussed most eagerly on those occasions. One day I was on my way there when I happened to meet Colonel von Blumenthal. He had taken advantage of the armistice to visit his family in Berlin for a few days on leave. I had to half drag him to the club, to which he had to devote at least an hour of his precious leave, drinking coffee. You can imagine the cheering that greeted him and the questions with which he was bombarded. Every one of them asked him why this and that had happened or had not happened. As these questions all came at once, of course he could not answer any of them, but sipped his coffee quite unhurriedly, sitting next to Werder, who was later to become the hero of Belfort. When everyone finally expected him to speak and fell silent, he said: 'Honoured friends, instead of answering everything I should like to give you only my main impression of the campaign as a whole.' Everyone listened attentively. 'Namely,' he continued, 'that we don't have a single general in the whole Prussian army who is capable of leading his six battalions in a strategic campaign that is changing daily and – you must not take this amiss – I'll make no exceptions, not even for you, dear Werder.' Everyone looked at him in amazement, but soon a mood of general merriment provided the right response to this marked paradox. For Blumenthal loved working in paradoxes.[22]

For Moltke, whose intense professionalism demanded total commitment to the task in hand, these days when he was kept out of the loop were profoundly frustrating. They were, fortunately, not to be prolonged. Manteuffel in particular had been increasingly disturbed by the evident lack of organisation at headquarters, from which had been put forward a series of irrational proposals. He was in no doubt that, instead of keeping Wrangel under reasonable restraint, Vogel von Falckenstein was encouraging the commander in chief in his wilder flights of fancy. Manteuffel had little difficulty in persuading both the King and Roon that Moltke should take Falckenstein's place as Chief of Staff of the Allied forces. Falckenstein himself was given command of an enlarged III Corps, operating in the north of Jutland. Moltke, delighted to be given the chance to exert a direct influence on operations, set off at once, arriving at headquarters on May 2.

It did not take him long to settle in, and on May 6 he wrote a long letter to Blumenthal to review the situation in the light of the ongoing discussions about a possible armistice. He thought that, while negotiations continued, the Danes would not embark on any significant operations. By now, unexpectedly, the Danes had abandoned their strong position at Fredericia, and it seemed to Moltke that they had in any case abandoned any attempt to hold on to the mainland:

> On the contrary, they wish to occupy the islands under the protection of the sea and of their fleet, and to pursue a naval war while waiting for foreign cabinets or some European imbroglio to restore their lost territories. I do not believe, therefore, that they will give up any of their islands of their own accord or without another defeat. Will the Danes conclude a reasonable armistice, or continue their resistance? That question will no doubt be answered when the conference resumes in London on May 9. After this date it does not seem to me that we can avoid undertaking something, even at the risk of heavy losses.

All this, he thought, pointed to the need to launch an assault on Alsen; a demonstration should be made opposite Sonderburg, where the Danes had been preparing a defensive position, 'but it is still at Ballegaard that the crossing will be most easily effected.'[23]

Blumenthal began to put in hand the plans for the revived project of the Alsen crossing, although the immediate occasion for it disappeared when an armistice, effective from May 12, was negotiated. But there was no great expectation that matters would be resolved swiftly on the political front, and preparations continued apace. In the meantime there was a further significant change in the command structure, when Wrangel was relieved of his command and replaced by Frederick Charles, with whom Moltke enjoyed an excellent relationship. The command of the I Corps, in succession to Frederick Charles, was given to Lieutenant General Herwarth von Bittenfeld; but Blumenthal remained as Chief of Staff, and it was with him that Moltke continued to work closely in the planning of the Alsen operation. The extension of the armistice until June 26 meant that they had plenty of time to prepare.

Thus it was that when the end of the armistice neared, Moltke was able to issue instructions to the I Corps requiring an immediate descent on Alsen as soon as hostilities recommenced. Herwarth had some 25,000 men available; the defenders, now commanded by Steinmann, numbered about half that. On the night of June 28/29 the attacking force closed up to the embarkation points, and the crossing began at 1.30 pm, the first wave landing at about 2.00 am. Once again, the Danes were taken by surprise, and the beachhead was rapidly reinforced before Manstein, leading the attack, deployed for an immediate advance. The Danes were soon rapidly in retreat, and before long it was clear that their position was impossible. Steinmann fell back to Hörup Haff and the Kekenis peninsula; it was a position judged too strong to attack, and he was not molested as he embarked his troops, the last of which left Alsen on July 1. It was a brilliant victory, and the Prussian losses were, to Moltke's great relief, very low.

With this victory, in which Blumenthal had again played a prominent part, there was little prospect of the Danes being able to put up any prolonged resistance; and the next armistice, which came into effect on July 20, marked the end of active operations. Blumenthal returned to peacetime duties with his reputation greatly enhanced, especially and most importantly in the eyes of Moltke, who had come to regard him as one of his most able and trustworthy subordinates.

6

The Campaign in Bohemia

It was therefore somewhat unexpected that, when hostilities against Austria loomed in the spring of 1866, Blumenthal was not at once earmarked for a staff appointment. Instead, he was given a field command, much to his own surprise, as he recorded in his diary on May 13.

> Today I received an order which gave me the greatest joy. I am to go to Wetzlar on the 17th to take up the command of a brigade, or, rather, mixed force, consisting of the 28th and the 65th Infantry Regiments, the 8th Battalion of Rifles (Jägers), the 7th Hussars and two batteries of Artillery. It seems to me that the appointment has been made in Berlin, so that I am not to be employed on the General Staff, but as commander of an independent mixed force, and this suits me exactly.[1]

However, this posting was not destined to stand for long; on May 18 Blumenthal was ordered to stand by for another appointment, which he guessed was probably not to be Chief of Staff to Frederick Charles, 'for a man of his impatient temperament would have telegraphed for me long ago.' Next day he learned that he was to be Chief of Staff of the Second Army, commanded by the Crown Prince. Blumenthal was delighted. 'The position is exactly the one I should have most desired. The youthful buoyancy of the Crown Prince's nature suits me much more than the severe earnestness of Prince Frederick Charles. Light heartedness is the spirit in which to go to battle.'[2]

On May 20 Blumenthal reported for duty at Berlin, where he had a lengthy discussion with Moltke before meeting his new army commander. 'The Crown Prince was most gracious, and told me quite plainly that he wanted General von Goeben himself, but now was very glad that it was I ... He made a most charming impression upon me, and appears to be entering upon the war in the most cheerful spirit, although he, too, would willingly see it avoided if possible.'[3] The partnership between the two men which now began was to prove extremely successful; the Crown Prince displayed a remarkably mature understanding of the quirks of his occasionally hot headed Chief of Staff, and thereby succeeded in getting the best out of him. Moltke, highly appreciative of Blumenthal's performance during the Danish war, had the greatest confidence in him and kept him fully and continuously informed as to his intentions.

Moltke appointed to the key post of Quartermaster General of the Second Army Major General Albrecht von Stosch, another of the senior staff officers in whom he and the Crown Prince had particular confidence. Moltke was under no illusions about Blumenthal's headstrong nature and the need to keep it under control. For Stosch, though, the assignment was by no means an easy one.

It was much about this time that Blumenthal joined Hohenlohe and his cousin, the Duke of Ujest, for lunch at a restaurant on the Unter den Linden. Hohenlohe recorded the meeting in his memoirs:

> The landowners of Upper Silesia, of whom the Duke was one, were all very worried. Had the King himself not said that if Austria began to invade soon, he would not be able to protect the unfortunate Upper Silesia for the time being? The Duke of Ujest's concerns contrasted very oddly with Blumenthal's confidence in victory. 'How can that be so', he said, 'the Austrians have so many good riflemen and other light infantry they will be far superior to us in wooded terrain.' 'In wooded terrain,' retorted Blumenthal, 'we are superior to them, for our officers are better trained than the Austrians.' 'But on the plain?' asked the Duke anxiously. 'I feel quite sorry for them there,' said Blumenthal as he sipped a glass of red wine, 'for there we will shoot the poor fellows dead.' His prediction proved to be accurate.[4]

During this period of intense anticipation, Blumenthal was engaged in assembling his staff. One of his earliest duties was to attend the key meeting on May 25, when Moltke set out for the benefit of the King his appreciation of the current position. During the course of the discussion, at which Blumenthal was uncharacteristically silent, there was a vigorous debate about Moltke's plans for the deployment of the Prussian armies. Among those particularly critical of Moltke's proposals was von Voigts-Rhetz, serving as Chief of Staff of the First Army. Blumenthal noted that the King feared an Austrian advance directed on Berlin, and there was a widely held view that Moltke had stretched the Prussian armies over too wide a front:

> Voigts-Rhetz blamed the disposition of the forces, as being too greatly extended for the first forward movement, stretching as they do from Zeitz to Upper Silesia – a matter of sixty miles. General von Moltke justified it by reason of the improved means of transport, namely, the railroads, which alone made such an extension possible. In the successive marches onwards, the columns can always be brought into close touch.[5]

At this meeting William rejected the more bellicose advice of the military, led by Roon, and was not prepared to go as far as Bismarck wanted in giving an ultimatum to Saxony; this last proposal was fully supported by Moltke, who worked to get his forces into Saxony as soon as he could.

If Blumenthal had at the meeting been quietly supportive of Moltke's strategy, his mood did not last. By June 1 he was recording his severe disapproval:

> This afternoon I was with General von Moltke, who communicated to me the information that the whole army would very likely be moved further eastwards, from which I gather that it is proposed to remain on the defensive rather than assume the offensive. This continued changing of plans is dreadful, and will jeopardise everything. It does not signify whether a thing can be better done, provided only that the plan adopted be adhered to. I am afraid that General von Moltke is very much under the influence of others, and can come to no decided conclusion. ...For all I have heard, it is Voigts-Rhetz who counsels the more towards Silesia. That is all right for the defensive, but I cannot admire a man who tries to force his convictions upon others at the risk of jeopardising everything.[6]

On June 4 Blumenthal left Berlin to establish the headquarters of the Second Army at Freiberg. By now it was beginning to look likely that at least one further corps would be attached to the Second Army, with possibly another; Blumenthal noted that handling some 120,000 to 130,000 men would be 'no easy job;' adding flippantly: 'personally I have never considered myself much of a General, and I am well assured that others think with me in this respect at least.'[7]

Having settled in, and having toured the positions occupied by his troops, Blumenthal sat down to give Moltke the benefit of his views on the situation. Writing on June 8, he told Moltke that 'our conjecture has almost attained certainty that, if war breaks out, the Austrians intend to advance through Upper Silesia past the fortresses upon Breslau.' To meet this advance, Blumenthal proposed to take up a position behind the Neisse between Grothkau and Patschkau; his intention was to concentrate on the Neisse by June 16. What he did want, however, was reinforcement by another corps, which he thought should go to Brieg. As it happened, his letter crossed with a telegram from Moltke: 'Think this over: if another Army Corps were sent to you by railway, where would you wish it to go? Greiffenberg, Liegnitz, Breslau or where? Reply tomorrow morning.'[8] Blumenthal at once confirmed his view that it should be to Brieg that the reinforcements should go.

However, Moltke was disturbed by Blumenthal's insouciant announcement that he was going to take up a new position, and on June 9 sent him a peremptory telegram: 'As His Majesty reserves for himself the direction of operations, important changes in the position of the army must not be made without His Majesty's approval. Agree substantially with your views.'[9] To this, Blumenthal responded at once, confirming that the move to the Neisse was suspended, although commenting crossly in his diary on Moltke's telegram: 'I dare say he may be right; but one thing I see, and that is, that we are not to be given a very free hand!'[10] Meanwhile, however Moltke wrote

him a rather more emollient letter explaining calmly but firmly his own command
intentions:

> Do not infer from my telegram of today that it is the intention, once the opera-
> tions of the army have begun in the face of the enemy, to restrict them by instruc-
> tions from above. My whole endeavour would be directed to preventing this. But
> the general instructions whether an army is to proceed offensively or defensively,
> whether it is to advance or retire, can be issued only by His Majesty, for the
> movements of the one army must necessarily be connected with those of the
> other.

His point made, Moltke approved of the move to the Neisse, and confirmed that the
Second Army was to have the Guard Corps, which would as requested go to Brieg.[11]
   The timing of these exchanges is not without significance. It was only on June 2 that
the King had issued his famous Cabinet Order to the War Minister conferring on the
Chief of the General Staff the sole responsibility for the issue of operational orders
to the army commanders. It is hardly surprising, therefore that, encountering only a
week later a display of independence on Blumenthal's part Moltke should have acted
to reinforce the message that the maintenance of a centralised command structure was
essential to effective coordination. His calm assumption of what was effectively the
supreme command was, after Königgrätz, never to be challenged again. The apocry-
phal story of the divisional commander (von Manstein) who, receiving written orders,
remarked that they seemed all to be in order but asked 'who is General von Moltke?'
has occasionally been quoted as an indication of how little known he was to the army
as a whole. This, of course, is absurd; the senior members of the officer corps were few
enough in number for the Chief of the General Staff to be sufficiently well known. In
the improbable event of some such remark being made, it may have reflected an ironic
recognition that Moltke was now really in charge.
   Both Blumenthal's conviction that the Austrians were planning an advance
through Silesia, and Moltke's eastward shift of his forces, were based on very specula-
tive assessments of Austrian intentions. Certainly Benedek's forces were assembling
in Moravia, but this was as much to keep them well back and hence leave options open
as it was to aim at an invasion of Silesia. The only Austrian forces taking up a forward
position were the 1st Corps (Clam Gallas) at Prague, together with Edelsheim's 1st
Light Cavalry Division, which were to move up to the Iser and to establish links with
the Saxon army. Moltke was still concerned that Benedek would make Silesia his
objective when he wrote to Blumenthal on June 11. Noting that the advance of the
First Army into Bohemia would only be effective in giving the Second Army indirect
support if there were substantial Austrian forces already there, Moltke observed:

> A vigorous leader like Benedek is not sure to be thereby induced to give up his
> operations in Silesia. There he has Hungary and the Galician Railway behind
> him and will lead all his forces against whatever he has in front of him. The

Austrians, taught by the ill success of their turning movements and positions in reserve, have probably fallen into the opposite extreme of 'going for the enemy.'[12]

On June 13 Blumenthal wrote back to Moltke to review the situation as he now saw it. He remained certain that Benedek would take the offensive into Silesia, either by taking the bull by the horns and advancing between Patschkau and Ottmachau, or by falling on the Second Army's left flank and then heading directly for Breslau. He thought the second option the more probable. But the long delay in commencing operations, which had caused Moltke such profound concern, was also getting on Blumenthal's nerves, and he ended his letter with a gloomy warning that waiting for the enemy to strike would demolish all their plans.[13]

However, the mercurial Blumenthal soon changed his mind about this. On June 15, after a visit to the Second Army's position behind the Neisse, he was recording in his diary: 'I have given up all hopes of Austria attacking us here. It is a great pity, for in three days we shall stand 130,000 strong (according to field- states), and in a most favourable position.'[14]

But events at last were gathering pace. The final breakdown of the diplomatic processes meant that the restraints that had shackled Moltke for so long were about to be removed. On Saturday June 16 Prussian troops invaded Hanover, Saxony and Hesse; next day Austria and Prussia were at war and, at last, on June 18, the Austrian Army moved out of its positions around Olmütz, moving to Josephstadt in Bohemia rather than directly on Silesia.

By June 19 it was becoming clear to Moltke that he would be fighting an offensive campaign, and the immediate need was to coordinate the movements of his armies to ensure that, from their widely scattered start lines, they would be able to support each other. On the previous day he had written to Major General von Stülpnagel, another of the senior staff officers whom he particularly trusted, to set out his view of the position. Stülpnagel was serving as Quarter Master General of the First Army, and Moltke undoubtedly found him a more reliable contact there than the obstreperous Voigts-Rhetz. Reporting on events in North Germany, Moltke thought it still possible that it would come to a fight in Saxony:

But if not, North Germany has been conquered without a shot having been fired. But this success is real only if we know how to maintain it and the decision lies in Bohemia. It is very hard at present to decide whether the First Army should reinforce the Second or the Second the First. It depends on whether the Austrians turn their main forces against Silesia or against Lusatia … we must needs wait for more light … It seems to me not improbable that Benedek will take the decisive direction of Berlin in order to unite again with his 1st and 2nd Corps.

Confronted by the thought that each of the armies was 130,000 to 150,000 strong, and would take some beating, Moltke concluded his letter on a confident note. 'As

Stülpnagel.

soon as ever General Herwarth becomes available, that moment I think we will, in God's name, march into Bohemia.'[15]

Next day Moltke sketched out his planned advance by the whole army into Bohemia:

> News received indicates that the principal Austrian forces are concentrating towards northern Bohemia. The First Army will take the offensive in that direction. The Second Army must move towards the First in order to unite with it by advancing into Bohemia. One of General von der Mulbe's divisions will remain in Saxony; by June 25 150,000 men will have united at Gitschin. The Second Army by its offensive will immobilise at least two Austrian Corps at Neisse and Grulich and will debouch with two Corps.[16]

That evening telegrams went out to the armies with orders based on Moltke's succinct note of his intentions. Blumenthal, when he received his telegram, found himself 'quite in accord with this plan. I do not, however, consider it necessary that we should unite with Prince Frederick Charles on the battlefield, as he is strong enough to do without us … If the Austrians retreat, we shall have time to unite with him from Braunau etc. and if they accept battle, then, coming in as we shall from the direction of Glatz County, we shall strike him in flank and rear. Rapidity is now the essential factor.'[17]

Blumenthal and Moltke were in no doubt that the march through the mountains which the Second Army must now undertake was a decidedly risky business. Blumenthal noted that 'our march over the mountains is a most critical operation and open to failure,' while Moltke, in issuing his detailed orders on June 22, added in those to the First Army a firm reminder of the need for cooperation 'as the weaker Second Army has the more difficult task of issuing from the mountains, it is the more incumbent on the First Army, as soon as ever its junction with the force of General von Herwarth has been effected, to hasten especially in advance in order to shorten the length of this critical operation.'[18] This would not be the last of the hurry up messages that Moltke sent during the campaign to the First Army headquarters, and he supported it with a careful analysis of the available options in a private letter to Stülpnagel on the same day.

Notwithstanding his acceptance of the need for haste, Blumenthal asked Moltke for a rest day on June 23 and for permission to move the VI Corps into the county of Glatz, to both of which requests Moltke unhesitatingly agreed. He sat down on June 24 to write a private letter to Blumenthal. In this he frankly recognised the difficult tasks which confronted the Second Army, especially at Nachod: 'The V Corps has there a difficult task. It must cover the flank of the whole army. It may well be that General Steinmetz will be obliged to retreat northwards on Braunau. It would be necessary for the Guard Corps to cover it and protect its retreat. See to it that the operations are judiciously and properly conducted.' Moltke went on to complain about the quality of the available intelligence, but hoped that the union of the army would be assured if only there was a rapid advance from both sides:

> We are on the eve of decisive events. God will not desert us. I am hardly able to get to bed at all. Since yesterday evening we have been negotiating for the surrender of the Hanoverian Army ... Falckenstein has assembled 40,000 men behind them, and I have done all I can to collect some troops in front of them; I am having great difficulties, but I hope tomorrow to have enough strength for us to impose our conditions. The King will then have conquered all North Germany in eight days. We could well lose Saxony in the next few days, but no matter, it is in Bohemia that the decision will come. A Saxon-Bavarian invasion of Saxony does not bother me. Once we have finished with Hanover, the Bavarians will have enough to do at home. God be with you.[19]

For Blumenthal the first crisis of the campaign was at hand. On June 24 he was dismayed to find that as a result of his dispositions the headquarters of the Second Army was undefended:

> I discovered ... after dinner, that when Steinmetz moves forward we shall be so exposed that we shall have no escort. If the Austrians know it, all they will have to do is to reach out and grab us! It is through my carelessness that my Prince has thus been brought into danger. This shall never happen again. I am awaiting daybreak in the greatest anxiety.[20]

On June 27 the Second Army fought its first battles in the mountains. To the north, von Bonin's I Corps suffered a largely avoidable reverse at Trautenau, and retreated to its start line. Steinmetz, however, met with more success at Nachod. Moving forward from the town early in the morning, the V Corps at first encountered little resistance, and got through the narrow defile and on to the plateau above Wysokow before any significant Austrian forces came up. These were units of Ramming's 6th Corps, which launched a series of fierce attacks on Steinmetz's position, suffering heavy casualties in the process. Although forcing the Prussians back to the edge of the plateau, Ramming failed to press the infantry attack here, turning instead to his cavalry, a stroke which Steinmetz countered with his own horsemen. While this struggle was going on, Steinmetz was able to reinforce his position; a fresh series of Austrian infantry attacks, uncoordinated, broke down with heavy losses, and by 1.00 Ramming was in full retreat. Blumenthal and the Crown Prince, accompanied among others by Stosch and Colonel Walker, the British military attaché, spent fourteen hours in the saddle, before returning tired but exhilarated from Nachod to their headquarters at Camenz.

There, the news came of Bonin's defeat by Gablenz at Trautenau; the advance of the Guard Corps next day, however, made good this setback by forcing their way through the Eypel Pass and defeated Gablenz at Soor. And on the same day Steinmetz followed up his victory at Nachod by defeating the Archduke Leopold's 8th Corps at Skalitz. It was a decisive day for the campaign of the Second Army; at the headquarters as the day wore on there was a lack of reliable information about the success or failure of each of the three corps engaged, and this led to serious anxiety among the staff. Blumenthal and the Crown Prince were unconcerned, the former remarking with characteristic aplomb: 'What a shame we can't be with Steinmetz! I'd just like to watch how the old fellow finishes them off.' The Crown Prince was more philosophical: 'Well then, we've done our duty and taken care of everything that good will and our limited understanding make possible. Now it's up to God.'[21]

These victories meant that the Second Army was safely through the mountains and it had, in the process, inflicted considerable damage on the confidence of the Austrian commanders and the morale of their troops. Blumenthal, never patient at the best of times was, however, discontented with the performance of some of his subordinates, writing on July 1:

> Our Generals are, for the most part, lacking in war experience, and the way in which they cling to peace traditions greatly increases difficulties. When several Army Corps have to move over hill and down dale, through narrow defiles, woods, and gorges, it should be well understood what care is necessary to prevent the march being hampered with baggage and supply wagons. These should all be left to follow well in rear, and the troops be made to subsist on provisions which each man can carry on his person, say for three days at least.'[22]

Moltke's continuing anxiety was the slow progress which the First Army was making. On June 29, he sent a pointed telegram to Frederick Charles: 'His Majesty expects that the First Army, hastening its advance as much as possible, will disengage the Second Army which, in spite of a series of successful combats, is still for the moment in a difficult situation.'[23] And he telegraphed Blumenthal at the end of the day to say that the First Army had twice been ordered to push forward. By then, in fact, Frederick Charles had fought and won a battle at Gitschin, and on the following day Moltke, by now en route to the front with the rest of the Royal Headquarters, issued firm instructions to the two army commanders intended to keep alive his hopes of fighting a successful battle of encirclement:

> The Second Army will maintain itself on the left bank of the Upper Elbe, and will hold itself ready to join its right wing, through Koniginhof, to the left wing of the advancing First Army. The First Army is to advance without stopping in the direction of Königgrätz. General Herwarth's mission is to attack any substantial enemy forces threatening the right flank of his movement, and to cut off the bulk of the enemy.[24]

The instruction that the Second Army should remain on the left bank seemed clear enough. Moltke was understandably surprised, therefore, to receive from the Crown Prince on July 1 a telegram announcing that Bonin's I Army Corps was to cross the Elbe and advance to Miletin, with the rest of the army following next day. Moltke received this at Reichenberg, which the Royal Headquarters reached in the morning, and his response at 1.45 pm was swift: 'According to yesterday's cypher telegram Second Army was to maintain itself on the left bank of the Upper Elbe. Had that telegram not yet been received or what reasons led to the decision to go with the whole army on to the right bank?'[25] Thinking further about it, Moltke sent another telegram to Blumenthal later that day, announcing his intention to go that evening to Gitschin, and suggesting that a talk with one of Blumenthal's officers would be desirable.

As recently as June 20 Blumenthal had appeared to have taken on board the advantages of keeping the Prussian armies widely separated. His proposal to cross to the right bank of the Elbe suggested that (as was also the case with Frederick Charles and Voigts-Rhetz) he now wanted the armies to draw together. Moltke's rebuke, albeit very tactfully expressed, can have done nothing to improve Blumenthal's temper, which was inclined to fray under pressure, although he failed on this occasion to record it in his diary. Rather than send one of his staff to see Moltke, he decided to go himself, making the lengthy journey from Königinhof by carriage. However, his subsequent recollection of the circumstances of this trip, as he recorded it, was not entirely accurate; he describes the receipt of orders indicating that the two armies were to reconnoitre in force on both banks of the Elbe. This, he thought, was 'a little too strong:

> I felt sure that they did not quite know what they were doing at headquarters, and were trying to gain time to think by ordering a reconnaissance in force. With a matter of 250,000 men in hand, reconnaissances of this sort are sure to lead

to our being beaten in detail. At ten o'clock I jumped into my carriage, and in company with Verdy drove the twenty-eight miles through Miletin to Gitschin, to have a talk with the King and Moltke about it. I think I persuaded the latter both of the futility of reconnaissances in force and of the expediency of marching straight on Vienna after the first battle won, without looking to the right or to the left. I said straightforwardly to the King: 'Your Majesty should just lay your ruler on the map in a line between Gitschin and Vienna, draw your pencil along the ruler, and march straight along that line.' He laughed in his kindly way, and doubtless thought that I was not in earnest.[26]

In fact, the meeting included not only Moltke, the King and his Adjutant General Lieutenant General Gustav von Alvensleben, but also Voigts-Rhetz, who had come to Gitschin from the First Army headquarters at Kamenetz. Alvensleben, Blumenthal and Voigts-Rhetz now all argued for an immediate union of the armies, a cautious view no doubt stimulated by the fact that all touch with Benedek's army had now been lost. Moltke was far from pleased that this should have been allowed to occur, but remained convinced that the Austrians were still close at hand. In the end he prevailed, and it was agreed that the First and Second Armies should remain separated until Benedek was located. At that stage the intention was that July 3 should be a rest day for both armies, save that the I Corps should move via Miletin towards Bürglitz and Cerekwitz. It was to reconnoitre towards Josephstadt, and be in a position to link with the First Army's left as and when required. Herwarth, meanwhile, was to move on Chlumetz, to observe towards Prague and to secure the crossings of the Elbe as far as Pardubitz.

The conference concluded, Blumenthal and Verdy set off back to the Second Army headquarters, arriving there at 2 am. By then, however, the situation had profoundly changed. Soon after Voigts-Rhetz had returned to his headquarters at Kamenetz there arrived the comprehensive and reliable report of Major von Unger that a large part at least of Benedek's army was in strength behind the Bistritz. This was before 7 pm; it is instructive to see what Frederick Charles and Voigts-Rhetz did with this priceless intelligence. Instead of at once passing it to Moltke at the Royal Headquarters, only six or seven miles away by a good road, they sat down to work out their own scheme for a frontal attack on what at this stage they seemed to assume was only part of the Austrian army. By 9.00 pm the orders for an advance by the First Army astride the Horitz-Königgrätz road, and by Herwarth towards Nechanitz, were ready for despatch to the divisional commanders. At 9.30, belatedly recognising the desirability of some cooperation from the Second Army, Frederick Charles despatched a message to the Crown Prince to notify him of his intended attack on Benedek and requesting support. Blumenthal, still chafing at Moltke's rejection of his own proposals, recorded this in his diary as a message from Frederick Charles 'that in carrying out his reconnaissance in force he had fallen into imminent danger, and prayed me to come to his aid.'[27] Blumenthal sent back to say that Frederick Charles could only look for the support of the cavalry and the I Corps, as the rest of the army was needed to support its own reconnaissance.

This was at about 3 am. However, in the meantime, Voigts-Rhetz had finally made his way to Royal Headquarters at Gitschin to report what had happened, arriving at about 10.00 pm where the King was awoken by an aide de camp to hear the news. It was passed on at once to Moltke, who sprang out of bed saying 'Gott Sei dank!' He would have been entitled, however, to be extremely angry with Voigts-Rhetz; the intelligence had reached the latter over three hours earlier and orders had been issued which it was effectively impossible to recall without causing great confusion. Moltke at once grasped that the whole of Benedek's army was present and that the ineffectual steps taken by the First Army to obtain help from the Second Army would produce by no means enough support if this was the case. Left as things were not only might the First Army's frontal assault end in wholly unnecessary defeat, but the opportunity of a crushing victory would have been thrown away.

Moltke's response was immediate, despatching at 11 pm an order to the Second Army which replaced his previous instructions. After briefly outlining the changed situation, he ordered the Second Army 'to make the necessary arrangements to be able to advance with all our forces in support of the First Army against the right flank of the enemy's probable advance, and in so doing to come into action as soon as possible.'[28] The vital importance of this order was such that it was entrusted to the King's ADC, Lieutenant Colonel Finck von Finckenstein, who rode off at once to the headquarters of the Second Army at Königinhof; a second copy went back to the First Army headquarters for onward despatch by another route. Finckenstein reached Miletin at 4.00 am on July 3, and Blumenthal at once woke up the Crown Prince before issuing the necessary orders for the advance of the whole army.[29] Blumenthal was as always greatly invigorated by the prospect of action: 'At seven o'clock the whole of the troops were in motion. We rode after them at 7.30. It was very cold but bracing. I had no feeling now of weariness, although the previous day I had only a short hour's sleep from 5.30 to 6.30.'[30] Blumenthal and the Crown Prince rode forward to the head of their marching columns, and by 11.00 had reached Chotoborek, from where they could see the general outlines of the battle. The progress of the Second Army had been slower than was hoped; Verdy, in his memoirs, recalled how difficult it was for the troops to make progress over the rain sodden countryside:

> The infantry, closed up in sections as long as we could use the broad highway, had to shift to files when it became necessary to leave the high road for the byways; and it wasn't long before the difficulties caused by the unfavourable weather and the condition of the soil made themselves felt. The cold rain, which had streamed down almost without interruption during the night, held on through the whole course of the forenoon.[31]

Until they reached Chotoborek, it had been by no means clear to Blumenthal and the Crown Prince that the crisis of the campaign had arrived; but the extent of the battle and the forces engaged which they could now see left no room for doubt. 'This is the decisive battle,' he told the Crown Prince, and as the situation developed this became still more apparent. Hohenlohe, who had been fretting that his artillery was to follow both divisions of infantry, had been relieved to get orders to move off after the 1st Guard division, and he too reached Chotoborek at this time.

Pointing out a prominent tree (it was in fact two lime trees either side of a crucifix), on the Horenowes ridge, the Crown Prince told Hohenlohe that there was the Austrian right flank, and in opening fire he should keep it on his right. Blumenthal, meanwhile, was disconcerted by the failure of von Hartmann's Cavalry Division to put in an appearance: 'It might almost have disappeared into the earth; and when severe strictures began to be passed on the leaders, I comforted myself with the reflection that it would turn up somewhere unexpectedly. However, nothing was ever seen of it, nor did it appear on the battlefield until about four o'clock in the evening.'[32] As the Second Army pushed forward, the retreating Austrian troops fell back from the Horenowes ridge. A series of bitter combats took place along the front of the Second Army in the villages of Maslowed, Chlum and Rossnitz, but in spite of the desperate courage of their opponents, the Prussian troops pushed remorselessly on. Blumenthal could soon see that the Prussians were victorious: 'From the heights of Horenowes, at between two and three o'clock, we saw that the battle was won; but it was after five o'clock before the enemy ceased to hold isolated posts. Then they retreated in headlong flight towards Pardubitz.'[33]

Moltke had watched the battle develop from Royal Headquarters, displaying an icy composure which was not shared by the King or indeed anyone else, as described in Chapter Four. Throughout the battle Moltke issued only one written order, jotting down in pencil on a small card a hurry up order to Herwarth at 1.45 pm.

Moltke's style was not to interfere; although the outcome of the battle turned entirely on the ability of the Second Army to arrive in time, he felt no need to send off anxious enquiries to Blumenthal about his progress. He was entirely confident that the Second Army would appear and ensure victory. If Frederick Charles, Voigts-Rhetz and Herwarth had better grasped the extent of the opportunity, that victory would have been even more crushing than it was, since the First Army need not have committed all its reserves, and Herwarth could have encircled the Austrian left. As it was, though, Moltke had succeeded in uniting his armies on the battlefield so that further intervention by him was unnecessary, and had won a quite stunning victory.

For Blumenthal the day ended with the pleasure of witnessing the historic meeting when the Crown Prince met the King near Rossnitz. 'It was a touching and soul stirring meeting between the father and his victorious son. The King embraced him affectionately, and afterwards shook me very warmly by the hand. The Prince said, "I know to whom I owe the conduct of my army." His words went straight to my heart, and the feeling of chill which the events of the day had caused quite disappeared.'[34]

For the victorious Prussians, however, there was no time to rest on their laurels. The retreating Austrian army must be followed up, a task in which Moltke and his field commanders were hampered by the lack of any really effective cavalry pursuit. The following days saw a considerable strain being placed on the warm relations between

Moltke and Blumenthal, as the former continually pressed for the greatest urgency on the part of the Second Army in its southward march. Blumenthal was always hyper-sensitive to any criticism, and invariably suspected Royal Headquarters of lacking a proper appreciation of his army's achievements – as for instance on July 9, when he and the Crown Prince drove over to Pardubitz, the Austrian von Gablenz having turned up to seek an armistice.

As it happened, Blumenthal need have had no anxieties; Moltke sent Gablenz away without giving him the opportunity to see the King.

> We found at Headquarters that the importance of our successes was not appreci-ated, but there was no intention of granting the armistice. The requests, or, rather the demands, of the Austrians were so impudent and so insulting that Gablenz was not received by the King at all, and, to our inexpressible joy, had to retire without his interview.[35]

Blumenthal was ill later that day, and it was some while before he was well again. He had however recovered enough by the following day to enter into a dispute with Moltke as to the direction to be taken by Second Army, which Blumenthal believed should take up a position to the south west of Olmütz to be closer to the First Army. He wanted to move to Prossnitz, where, he argued, the Second Army would at least be capable of detecting the withdrawal of the enemy, and of supporting the First Army in good time if necessary:

> At nine o'clock in the evening General von Moltke came in unexpectedly. I submitted this idea to him, but he turned a deaf ear. Instead of discussing the point with me, he began to find fault saying that we "had marched too slowly." I said nothing further on the subject, but left it to his good sense to reconsider the matter on his way home.'[36]

Next day Moltke, as Blumenthal complacently recorded, issued an order allowing the Second Army to broaden the front of its advance and to break the railway line between Olmütz and Vienna. The move to Prossснitz was to lead shortly to a brisk engagement at Tobitschau, but in the meantime Blumenthal had become further enraged by what he saw as Moltke's critical attitude. On July 15, Captain Mischke, of the Second Army staff, returned from Royal Headquarters after an interview with Moltke: 'During the morning Major Count Graben came in also from there. The dispositions which Moltke communicated to Mischke were absolutely incomprehen-sible in several points, and when I heard from Mischke that Moltke had several times broken out into reproaches about our slow rate of marching, I could contain myself no longer.' Blumenthal complained to the Crown Prince, who was, he recorded, 'so vexed and annoyed at these reflections, so unjust and uncalled for that he spoke of handing in his resignation of the command.' Instead, however, Stosch was called upon to go to Royal Headquarters 'to point out to Moltke his mistake, and if this did not satisfy him, to go to the King and show how General von Moltke was to blame for having changed the direction of the march after having first directed us upon Hohenstadt.'[37]

Moltke, after receiving the report of the customarily tactful Stosch, was unruffled, issuing fresh orders to the Second Army on the morning of July 16:

> From the report of the Second Army of the 15th instant, and from the oral expla-
> nations of General von Stosch, it seems in all probability that the entire Austrian
> Army has left Olmütz. It will therefore be sufficient for us to observe this place
> with a much weaker detachment than previously intended. His Majesty, there-
> fore, approves of the proposal that this task should now be carried out by the I
> Corps alone, especially since it will shortly, be reinforced by the reserve Corps of
> General von der Mulbe.[38]

Any reassurance which Blumenthal might have drawn from Moltke's readiness to reconsider his plans was however swiftly dispersed when on July 19 he received a further report of the discontent at Royal Headquarters:

> Rittmeister von Plotz came in from Headquarters at about eleven o'clock pm,
> and we heard more about the charges Moltke was making against the Second
> Army of having marched too slowly. I was exceedingly vexed, and felt that I
> must have a court of inquiry to put an end, once for all, to this unjust accusation.
> We cannot race up and down these hills. Our men are so worn that they have
> implored me to give them a day's rest.[39]

Moltke, however, was adamant that the greatest possible effort must be made for the Second Army to push on to the south as quickly as it could. His concern was the prospect of an imminent encounter with the reassembled Austrian army which was taking up a position along the river; for Moltke, it was 'in all circumstances desirable to appear on the Danube with the greatest possible total strength,' as he emphasised in his orders to all three armies issued on July 19.[40]

A further confrontation with Blumenthal was avoided, however, when the nego-tiations which had been going on for several days led to an armistice for five days being agreed, commencing on July 22. Moltke however was still anxious to deploy his maximum strength on the Danube, writing that day a personal letter to Blumenthal to outline the steps to be taken to prepare for further operations, should these become necessary after the expiry of the armistice period. He was emphatic in his demand for the fullest report about various aspects of the Second Army's readiness, pointedly concluding his letter: 'Please let me know as soon as possible, and in the light of the information you have received on the points set out … so that I may here be in a posi-tion to understand exactly what forces are available for our next operations.'[41]

There were, however to be no further operations; preliminaries of peace were signed on July 26, although not before Bismarck had had to overcome the extrava-gant demands of the military for even more in the way of annexations than he had achieved. There was, however, to be another incident to put the relationship of Moltke and Blumenthal under further strain, as the latter ruefully recorded in his diary:

> A letter of mine which I had written to my wife from Trübau had fallen into the hands of the Austrians, and had been reproduced in many of the south German newspapers. Certainly the letter was mine in substance, but it had been mistranslated from the English in which language I had written, and moreover, the sense had been intentionally perverted. I should not have been much disturbed about it, only, unfortunately, Moltke had been somewhat roughly handled by me in it, and he is the last of men I should wish to pain, for I honour him exceedingly. It was very mortifying to me to have made myself a laughing-stock through this letter, and be represented to the world as a conceited ass. I can put up with this, however, as I do not care one jot what people think of me.

Next day Blumenthal got a copy of his letter as published, and gave it to the Crown Prince to put before the King and Moltke. 'The King was highly amused and laughed heartily, but Moltke did not wish to read it. He said that it was addressed to my wife, and had not been intended for him. I should not have expected any other treatment from him, for I know full well what a perfect gentleman Moltke is.'[42] Blumenthal should have been somewhat chastened by the experience, but on the evidence of his later diaries this hardly seems to have been the case.

7

Sedan

When in July 1870 war broke out with France, the Crown Prince, who was to command the Third Army, perhaps surprisingly made Stosch rather than Blumenthal his first choice as Chief of the Staff. This request was refused; Moltke, who shared the Crown Prince's high opinion of Stosch, had earmarked him as Intendant General. Disappointed in this, the Crown Prince naturally turned to his 'old and trusty friend' as his Chief of Staff. Blumenthal was at that time commanding the 14th Division, in the Rhineland; ordered back to Berlin, he proceeded on July 20 to Potsdam, where he went at once to call on the Crown Prince:

> He received me with that kindliness which is his characteristic, and asked my advice whether, as future commander of the Army of the South, he ought not to proceed at once to Munich, Stuttgart, and Karlsruhe, as Count Bismarck wished him to do on political grounds. He desired to take me with him. I was, however, opposed to the notion, as the whole situation was too uncertain, and we should not have a reply ready, if questions were asked. The journey was therefore postponed;[1]

Blumenthal was pushing at an open door; Moltke had already advised earlier that day that the Crown Prince should not yet go to South Germany. However, since the south German troops were to form part of the Third Army, and for political reasons Bismarck was keen that it should take place as soon as possible, on July 26 Blumenthal accompanied the Crown Prince as he set out to visit Prussia's South German allies. In Saxony, they found that 'the enthusiasm is wonderful, and it is universal' and when they got to Munich, they found the same thing. Blumenthal recorded 'an unaccountable throng of people from the station to the Residency. Everywhere shouting and hurrahing. Most exciting!'[2] And the Crown Prince was similarly touched by the fervour of his greeting:

> The assembled multitude welcomed me almost as if I was in a Prussian town; and so it went on everywhere … At the railway station at Munich there awaited all

the Royal Princes, the Staff and Guard of Honour of the Infantry and Cavalry, as well as an extraordinarily large number of the public, whose cheers gave me a tumultuous and enthusiastic welcome.'[3]

Blumenthal and the Crown Prince journeyed on to Stuttgart before arriving at Karlsruhe on July 28 where the welcome was just as warm. Even more importantly, some intelligence about French movements was beginning to arrive; Blumenthal noted that the Emperor was said to have attended a meeting in Nancy with his generals on the previous day. Speculating on what might be the enemy's intention if he crossed the Rhine, Blumenthal found it difficult to fathom:

It is not at all improbable that he will cross near Strasbourg, and will operate in the direction of South Germany, counting upon the vacillation of the South German states, and possibly in the expectation that the Italians will enter into alliance with him and invade us through Tyrol. This plan, however, appears to me so extravagant that I cannot believe in it. It is to be hoped that we will not allow ourselves to be harassed, but quietly await the turn of events, and then, when all is ready, take the offensive and march on Nancy.[4]

This last suggestion was certainly Blumenthal's own idea; Moltke's objective was the French army and he would have regarded it as entirely premature to think yet of an advance towards Nancy unless French movements made this desirable; there was no sign that this would be the case.

By now the pace of events was quickening. Blumenthal began to establish his head-quarters at Speyer, where he was soon recording that he 'had a frightful lot of work to do, assisted by Gottberg, to bring everything into order.' He went on to note that Moltke had ordered the Third Army to advance on Strasbourg if it possibly could, but that this could not be complied with, as the Bavarian Corps would be only half complete by August 2. In fact, Moltke had not directed an advance on Strasbourg, nor had he issued an order about it. Hearing from Gottberg of a French movement from Bitsche through Weissenburg, he thought that it would be 'desirable to bring the Württembergers and Badeners over to the left back while the bridge at Maxau can still be used.' There would be no danger, he pointed out, from the right bank as soon as the Third Army took the offensive towards Hagenau-Bischweiler. He asked Blumenthal to submit this to the Crown Prince for consideration while he sought authorisation from the King.[5] Blumenthal's answer was to tell Moltke that the French were collecting bridging material to the south of Lauterburg, to which Moltke responded that as soon as the Baden and Württemberg troops had joined, the Third Army should advance on the left back of the Rhine to seek and attack the enemy.

Blumenthal was by now getting a bit rattled by the pace of events and the pressure upon him. His door, he noted fretfully in his diary, did not remain closed for two minutes consecutively; he replied on July 31, in a message over the signature of the Crown Prince, that the Third Army, was not yet ready to march. This, predictably, brought a sharp and immediate response from Moltke enquiring when it would be ready for operations; Blumenthal replied at once that this would be on August 3. This reached Moltke just before his train bearing the bulk of the Royal Headquarters was due to leave Berlin for Mainz on the afternoon of July 31, and Moltke was profoundly dissatisfied. Blumenthal's telegram had been far from reassuring as to the projected advance of the Third Army; as Verdy recorded, 'it seemed as if they meant not to begin the march until the very last detachments and columns had arrived, while we wished for as speedy an advance as possible, in view of the general situation, and especially of the intended cooperation of the Third Army with the two others.'[6]

Moltke's reaction was to draft a very firm order indeed that the Third Army should advance at once. By now, the Royal train had set off on its slow journey; it was not until the following morning that Podbielski, when the train stopped briefly, left his carriage and brought the draft telegram to Verdy. The latter was horrified; by virtue of his service on Blumenthal's staff during the 1866 campaign, he was very well aware that he burned on a very short fuse indeed, and that such an order would cause a major row. Verdy's advice to Podbielski was emphatic: 'If you wish to create strained relations with them, during the whole of this campaign, send it; but I am perfectly sure that they will feel offended, and, I think, not without some cause. For, a good reason of some kind there must surely be, for their not yet fixing the date of starting.' Just then, Moltke joined them; when Podbielski explained Verdy's concerns, he asked: 'Well, but how are we to manage it then?' After a brief reflection, Verdy offered to go in person to see Blumenthal, and Moltke, invariably fair minded, readily agreed. Just as soon as Royal Headquarters got to Mainz, Verdy was sent off on a circuitous and difficult journey to Speyer.[7]

He finally reached the headquarters of the Third Army at 6.00 pm August 1, where he met first with the Crown Prince. He found the latter in high spirits as a result of the warmth of the reception accorded to him and to his officers since they had arrived in South Germany. He was however chafing to be involved in the fighting at the decisive point, fearing that only the weaker part of the French Army stood before him. Verdy reassured him that Moltke 'would no doubt do everything he could not to let the Crown Prince of Prussia play a secondary part in this war,' although he added that this could only be attained if the Third Army assumed the offensive immediately.

When Blumenthal joined them, Verdy carefully explained just how important it was that the advance to crush the forces opposed to it should begin as soon as possible. In response, Blumenthal was able to satisfy Verdy that it was indeed his intention to advance as soon as he could; and the text of a telegram was agreed on, confirming to Moltke that the Third Army would cross the frontier on August 4.[8] Blumenthal was under no illusion as to the reason for Verdy's visit, noting that he had come 'very likely to see how everything was progressing with us.' Predictably, he did not allow Verdy to depart without ventilating his usual grievances about the orders he received:

> I could not ... conceal from him my opinion that the instructions given from Headquarters as regards the general idea are very defective, for as far as the Third Army is concerned, nothing whatever has been said of the role it is to play.[9]

And he told Verdy that he would write to Moltke to set out his views.

This he did, getting in response a characteristically soothing but also very comprehensive letter from Moltke on August 4. 'The intentions explained in your letter of yesterday quite correspond to the views and intentions of these headquarters. The Third Army is left quite free in the execution of its mission. Direct cooperation with the Second Army is at present impossible owing to the Hardt mountains.' Moltke was careful to emphasise, however, that notwithstanding its freedom to achieve its objectives, the Third Army was still subject to the strategic control of Royal Headquarters, observing that 'only from here can the accord of the operations of both armies, with due regard to the enemy's measures, be secured.'[10] Once Moltke had got the Third Army in motion, he was prepared to go along with the detailed proposals which Blumenthal put forward, even though the delay in commencing operations had put paid to his initial hopes of encircling the French army. He was entitled to believe that Blumenthal, despite his querulous complaints, fully understood his overall intention, and that, albeit belatedly, his dispositions were consistent with it, so he had no hesitation in sending his short tempered subordinate a suitably placatory response. Moltke's reaction to Blumenthal's display of independence was in sharp contrast to the way he was at this time dealing with the eccentric and self willed antics of Steinmetz on his other flank. Blumenthal was one of those that Moltke knew he could generally trust to conduct operations competently.

Even now, however, Moltke could feel discontented with minor details. On August 4 the Third Army fought and won the battle of Weissenburg on the River Lauter, defeating the isolated division of General Abel Douay, from MacMahon's corps. As late as the morning of August 6 Moltke was still waiting for a full report, and hardly surprisingly sent an irritable telegram: 'Till now not the smallest detail of the action at Weissenburg has reached the King, nor any approximate statement of our losses, while French newspaper accounts are already known here. Omission to be repaired at once.'[11]

Blumenthal was by now preoccupied with his plans to attack MacMahon's corps in position between Reichshoffen and Wörth, an operation he intended to carry out on August 7. In fact, however, the battle came about almost by accident on August 6 and the Crown Prince and Blumenthal, unaware of how extensively their troops were committed, at one stage ordered von Kirchbach, the commander of the V Corps, to discontinue the action and avoid anything which might induce a fresh one. After a fierce encounter, however, the French were driven in headlong retreat from their positions, and by 4.30 the Crown Prince was able to telegraph his father with news of the victory.

Next day the Crown Prince and Blumenthal were able to give a first hand account of the battle to a distinguished visitor. William Howard Russell, the special correspondent of the Times, finally caught up with the Third Army headquarters to which he was to be attached. His conversation with the Crown Prince was interrupted by Blumenthal's arrival, as he recorded: 'At that moment there entered an officer, middle aged, with grey hair and moustache, of distinguished appearance, rather under the middle size, and of slight, well knit figure. His eyes, blue and clear, rested on us.'

Blumenthal took Russell into his map room to explain the current situation. Blumenthal impressed his visitor by a characteristic display of self-confidence, telling him:

> The French are now quite broken in upon. We have thrust them back and got through their first line, broken up their combinations, beaten their best general, and I believe their best army. They fought magnificently, I must say that! Never was there in the world fiercer fighting than at Reichshoffen you see there, and Froeschwiller over there. But you see they have no chance. They are quite outnumbered … If the Bavarians had come up a little sooner, or if they had marched faster, I don't see how MacMahon could have escaped. Poor fellow! He is a good soldier and made a fine fight. His change of front was very clever. Now, I don't know what he will do … I wish you had seen that battle, because I should have liked you to have seen the stubborn way in which our Germans attacked again and again, and fought through most difficult ground, some of them very young troops, who had never seen a shot fired.[12]

Moltke was understandably extremely pleased to receive the news of Wörth writing to Blumenthal on the morning of August 7 with 'Hearty congratulations on your brilliant success,' and going on to tell him of the simultaneous victory at Spicheren. Speculating as to what the French might do next, Moltke thought that perhaps their 'most correct measure' would be to strike at the Second Army, which was still somewhat strung out as a result of the speed of its advance; but based on the performance of the French so far he certainly did not expect them to show such a 'vigorous resolve,' and was more inclined to think that they would fall back towards Metz, and hence away from MacMahon. What was important was to know the latter's line of retreat – to the west where he might seek to regain touch with the French main body, or southwestwards away from it.[13]

Moltke sent Major von Holleben of his staff to take this to the headquarters of the Third Army where he arrived on August 8, waking Blumenthal at 6.00 am. The latter recorded the conversation in his diary in a distinctly sour frame of mind:

> The same old story! Congratulations upon the victory; satisfied with everything; also much good advice to carry out plans which have been carried out long ago. Still, a sort of impatient feeling is apparent, as though we ought to be getting along more quickly, whereas we have pressed our men to the utmost in fact, too much.[14]

Blumenthal was as always quick to resent any advice which appeared to carry any hint of criticism; his sensitivity on the subject of the speed of his progress was perhaps due to a private recognition that it certainly left a lot to be desired.

During this crucial period of the frontier battles, Moltke was encountering not inconsiderable difficulty in getting his subordinates to implement his intentions.

Steinmetz was of course the worst, being openly insubordinate. This was testing Moltke's patience to the limit. But in minor ways he also encountered practical problems in the failure of the army staffs to send in prompt reports. Blumenthal himself had been reproached for this, although the record of the First Army in this respect was especially bad. It seems to have derived from a belief on the part of army commanders and their chiefs of staff that they possessed an autonomy that was in fact quite inappropriate to their situation. It may be that Moltke's normal willingness to trust the man on the spot had fed this dangerous misapprehension. At all events Blumenthal's diary was full of complaints that he had been obliged to draft revised orders for his army when Moltke issued fresh instructions.

Perhaps as a reminder of his ultimate authority, and particularly for the benefit of the still intractable Steinmetz, Moltke found it necessary to telegraph each of the army commanders on August 8: 'His Majesty has ordered that all military messages, reports and questions from the army commands must be addressed to me.'[15] With the campaign entering its most critical phase, Moltke could not afford maverick behaviour on the part of his subordinates, but his assertion of his authority nonetheless caused resentment. Blumenthal was in a particularly tetchy frame of mind on August 11. The forward movement of the armies was leading to overcrowding on the limited number of roads available, and Blumenthal blamed Moltke for it. As usual, he was in no doubt that he knew better:

> The Second Army has pushed its left wing in front of us. We are closely packed in each other's way, and I cannot conceal from myself the notion that General von Moltke has manoeuvred us into a pretty mess, and I think he has incorrect notions of what troops are capable of, and of what they can be called to do and still retain their organisation. According to my notions the French have retreated behind the Moselle. Everything points to that conclusion ... I should advance to the Moselle on a broader front, and not keep the columns so crowded together, send strong advanced guards a day's march ahead, and then concentrate upon the spot where reconnaissances have shown the enemy to be in position. This crowded order of march fatigues the troops most unnecessarily.[16]

Blumenthal was nonetheless always avid for recognition, and was always careful to record it, noting on August 13: 'I received a very charming letter from General von Moltke, from which I gather that the King is very much pleased with us.'[17] Moltke's letter is not included in his *Military Correspondence*; but he was well aware of the beneficial effect of approbation on Blumenthal's temperament, and was sincere in his appreciation of the Third Army's successes.

The Third Army continued to push westward in pursuit of MacMahon, with whom touch had not yet been regained, while the First and Second Armies closed in on Bazaine, On August 16 leading units of the Second Army encountered the Army of the Rhine as it made its way out of Metz towards Verdun, and inflicted a sharp defeat on it at Vionville-Mars La Tour. Bazaine, as a result, fell back to a defensive position outside Metz. Meanwhile the Crown Prince and Blumenthal had intended to go to Pont à Mousson to meet the King; but just as they were about to set off on August 17, news arrived of Mars la Tour, with the suggestion that a decisive battle would be fought next day. The Crown Prince was all for going to witness it, but had to be firmly restrained by Blumenthal; as he put it, 'it became my duty to support him in his resolution to deny himself. It is his duty to remain with his army, for everything may not go according to our expectations, and some important decision may have to be taken, in which case his absence would, to say the least, be unfortunate.'[18] On the same subject, the Crown Prince was less explicit in his diary, remarking of the expected battle: 'Of course I could not go there now, but at the very least I might stop where I was, well out of the range of my army, as a mere onlooker, and I believe I have done my duty in exercising this self-denial.'[19] After an anxious two days of waiting, news came of the victory at Gravelotte-St Privat, and on August 20 the Crown Prince and Blumenthal set off to meet the King and the Royal Headquarters at Pont à Mousson:

> They found the King in an agitated state. He was intensely strained by the fatigues of the campaign, and had become quite nervous. What affected him most were the terrible losses among the officers in the battle of the 18th ... The King appeared concerned about the operation leading up to the battle, but kept returning to and harping upon the losses of his brave officers, and among them his dearest.

Blumenthal noted the contrasting demeanour of the Chief of the General Staff: 'Moltke was cold and calm, as always, and was not troubled with cares, a state of mind I cannot share with him.'[20]

The Sedan campaign was now entering its most crucial phase, and Moltke was beginning to feel the lack of firm intelligence about French intentions. By August 23 the indications increasingly pointed to the likelihood that MacMahon was on the move from Châlons. That day Moltke wrote to Blumenthal to tell him, stressing thte importance of maintaining a strong cavalry screen in the front of the advancing Third Army: 'According to the reports received here it is not improbable that the enemy's army assembled at Châlons is marching away from there. In that case it is desirable to ascertain by cavalry, pushed on beyond and to the north of Châlons, the precise direction of the enemy's march.'[21] Next day, on his way to his new headquarters at Bar le Duc, Moltke stopped at the Third Army for a conference with Blumenthal. Confirmation had been received from cavalry patrols that MacMahon had pulled out of Châlons and was making for Reims. That left unanswered the question of what the French were doing. Blumenthal saw it as a move designed to frustrate a direct advance on Paris: 'It seems as though they mean to take up a position to a flank which we cannot pass, and one from which they will be able, if necessary, to relieve Metz. The idea is not a bad one, but if they are attacked and beaten it is all up with them.'[22]

Of all the German leaders Moltke was the most dubious about the notion that MacMahon would set off on an extremely hazardous flank march in an effort to relieve Bazaine. As usual regarding the most probable enemy move as being that which seemed the most advantageous, he found it difficult to accept that the French would embark on so rash an adventure. But as time went by, it became clear that this was just what was happening, and during August 25 Moltke sat down to draft march tables that would be appropriate if, by that evening, there came news that the Army of the Châlons had reached Vouziers. And, that night, reports indeed arrived indicating this, including a telegram from London with a report taken from *Le Temps*. Next day, probing along a wide front, German cavalry patrols located the French army as it pushed through Vouziers. Blumenthal and the Crown Prince were in no doubt that their army should wheel to the right and that the prospect of a crushing victory was within their grasp. With characteristic panache Blumenthal outlined the situation on the map to William Howard Russell. 'These French are lost, you see. We know they are there, and there – MacMahon's whole army. Where can they go to? Poor foolish fellows. They must go to Belgium, or fight there and be lost, 'pointing to the area between Mézières and Carignan.[23]

Moltke had, on the evening of August 26, following a further discussion with Blumenthal, given orders for the wheel to the north. It was a decision not without risk. The intelligence available to him did point firmly to MacMahon being committed to an operation to relieve Bazaine, but it took the German armies away from their supply columns and into the hilly and densely wooded region of the Argonne. Blumenthal had some concerns about what the enemy might do:

> The most unfavourable turn affairs could take would be that MacMahon should throw himself now with his whole strength upon us. We should only be able to oppose some 80,000 men to him, as we have no supports in hand within twelve or sixteen miles. He, however, must be ignorant of our march, and believes us to be on the way to Paris.[24]

On the following day, however, came news that the French had left Vouziers and Grandpré, and Blumenthal began to wonder what McMahon could be up to, since he was now within two marches of the Belgian frontier. Moltke was also uncertain but, determined to press on, issued orders that the Army of the Meuse, commanded by the Crown Prince of Saxony should advance to Nouart, Stenay and Rémonville. To both the Third Army and the Army of the Meuse he wrote at 11.00 pm on August 28 to suggest that the appearance of large French forces near Buzancy indicated that MacMahon was indeed heading for Metz. By now Moltke was issuing orders direct to corps headquarters, in his determination to close in on MacMahon's army, a practice which was beginning to irritate Blumenthal: 'According to my way of thinking, it is an immense error to keep continually making changes with every new report which comes in. The information is for the most part unreliable, or exaggerated and misinterpreted, and continuous alterations create a sort of nervous uncertainty which soon communicates itself to the troops.'[25] When he encountered Moltke on

Crown Prince Albert of Saxony.

the morning of August 29, Blumenthal could not resist a feeling of self satisfaction: 'On our arrival Moltke met us with the news that the French had got away, but soon word was brought in from our Cavalry Division which threw doubt on this report.. The worst of it was that Moltke had kept back the Bavarian and the VI Corps, which he now much regretted.'[26]

Moltke took the Crown Prince and Blumenthal to the Royal Headquarters at Grandpré; by the time they arrived there, his cause for concern that MacMahon might have eluded them began to fade. The capture of a high ranking French staff officer, taken with all the other reports coming in, made it clear that MacMahon was by now scarcely able to escape, and Moltke gave orders for a general attack on the Army of Châlons, secure in the knowledge that practically all his troops were in position to take part. The Third Army was to take a largely supporting role; it was ordered 'to start early and more with its right wing by Buzancy on Beaumont, and must be ready to support the attack of HRH the Crown Prince of Saxony with two army corps while the other corps are at first to keep rather to the direction towards Le Chesne.'[27] Blumenthal rather sourly commented: 'The pity is that we are still twelve miles from him, and therefore owing to want of time the fruits of victory may not be fully reaped.'[28]

Next day, however, Blumenthal's pessimism proved unwarranted, as his army caught up with the retreating French. The battle of Beaumont was decisive in its consequences, driving MacMahon back to the Meuse with little option but to retire into Sedan, into which most of his battered units retreated on the night of August 30. Late that night, Moltke wasted no time in issuing orders that the French were next day to be closely followed up: 'The forward movement is therefore to be configured tomorrow as early as possible, and the enemy to be vigorously attacked wherever he stands this side of the Meuse and to be squeezed into the narrowest possible space between that river and the Belgian frontier.'[29] His satisfaction with the day's proceedings did not prevent him, however, from making a sharp comment to Blumenthal about one of the Third Army's units:

> His Majesty observed with displeasure that the II Bavarian Corps, which according to army orders was to follow the I Bavarian Corps directly as reserve, was not deployed one mile behind it at Sommauthe, but was found in column of march after 9.00 pm with its rear at Buzancy. The corps would therefore have been in no position to give support if support had been required.'[30]

Not much more needed to be done; the marches of the Third Army and the Army of the Meuse on August 31 ensured that on the following day they would be in position for a decisive attack on MacMahon. During the afternoon Moltke and Podbielski went over to the Third Army headquarters for a final briefing meeting with Blumenthal, who memorably noted it in his diary: 'In the afternoon General von Moltke was with me. He came in rubbing his hands, with a sardonic smile on his face, and said, "Now we have them in a mousetrap.'[31] Even now, however, Moltke was taking no chances; a report by one of his most trusted staff officers indicated the possibility that MacMahon might be taking the last available option to extricate himself, and at 7.45 pm he sent an urgent note to Blumenthal:

> Lt Col von Brandenstein, just returned from Remilly, confirms that the French have marched off westwards leaving all baggage behind, and will perhaps continue this march through the night. By that means the attainment of a great result might be frustrated. Your Excellency will consider whether it might not be practicable to cross the Meuse in the night with the XI Corps and the Württemberg Division, so that the attack may be made in the morning at dawn on a deployed front in the direction of the road Sedan- Mézières.[32]

Blumenthal, on receipt of this, issued the necessary orders, and wrote to the Crown Prince of Saxony to suggest that he should not push forward too rapidly, so that the Third Army should have the time to seal off MacMahon's escape route to the west.

Thus it was that Moltke had set the stage for what would be one of the most decisive battles of military history, in the most theatrical setting imaginable. He was in no doubt about the result, and neither was Blumenthal, who wrote in his diary:

> From the very outset it was unmistakably evident that we were bound to win:
> still, at every repulse of our people which was quite easy to follow, owing to the
> clearly marked lines of smoke, there rose in the hearts of the exalted personages
> and their entourage cares and anxieties which were almost laughable to those
> having a clearer insight into the situation.'[33]

The Crown Prince and his headquarters staff arrived on a height above Donchéry at
about 6.00 am; the Royal Headquarters was posted about a mile away, on a hill above
Frénois. From each location there was a spectacular view of practically the whole
battlefield, and the steady advance of the German troops could be closely followed.

There was little left for Moltke to do. His commanders well understood their objectives, and from the moment that the door was shut on the escape route to Mézières
there was nothing that the French could do to avert the inevitable outcome. When
MacMahon was wounded, and the command passed briefly to Ducrot, the latter
grasped the reality of the position, and prepared to make an attempt to break out
to the northwest. But it was too late. Wimpffen's assumption of command, which
led to a reversal of Ducrot's plan in a doomed attempt to smash through the encircling German forces from Balan in an easterly direction, made no difference to the
outcome. The advance of the Army of the Meuse towards and then over the Givonne
forced the French troops inexorably back. At Bazeilles, in spite of bitter resistance,
von der Tann's Bavarians pressed remorselessly on, while the rest of the Third Army,
across the Meuse at Donchéry, drove forward on the west of the French positions.
Compressed into a rapidly shrinking triangle, the French units began to disintegrate
under a pitiless artillery bombardment.

Throughout the day, Moltke found it unnecessary to send out any written orders.
From Frénois he could see with his own eyes that the mousetrap had closed on its
hapless prey, and that it was only a matter of time before the French capitulated.
When the end came, and Napoleon had sent General Reille up to the height above
Frénois, Moltke issued at 7.15 pm a characteristically laconic order to his commanders:

> Negotiations have been opened; accordingly attacks may not be made by our side
> during the night. But any attempt of the enemy to break through our line must
> be repelled by force, if the negotiations do not lead to a conclusion, hostilities
> will begin again, but only after communication from here. As such the opening
> of artillery fire from the height east of Frénois may be taken.[34]

That night Moltke conducted the negotiations with Wimpffen; try as he might,
Wimpffen was unable to persuade his adversary to relax his implacable insistence on
the surrender of the whole French army. Blumenthal, who attended the negotiations,
could justly record in his diary: 'To such an event as this history can hardly find a
parallel. Our trophies are enormous, and at present cannot properly be estimated.'[35]

8

Versailles

The victory might have been immense, but it was not long before Blumenthal was grumbling again, writing querulously in his diary on September 3:

> After everything had been carried out with such precision up to date, suddenly there set in the wildest confusion in the communication of orders, which nearly drove me mad with annoyance. It was indeed too distressing. The written orders of Moltke and Podbielski did not tally with the orders communicated verbally: in short, it looked as though they had intended to bring chaos and confusion into our counsels, then to withdraw and let the thing work out its own salvation.'[1]

Moltke had long since got used to the outbursts of his talented subordinate, and even if Blumenthal expressed himself as forcibly in the letter he wrote to the Chief of the General Staff to complain, the latter would have been unmoved by it. It was almost invariably Blumenthal's habit, when under stress, to blame other people for his difficulties, and as the war continued there would be plenty of occasions when the pressure got to him.

For the moment, however, the issues confronting Moltke and Blumenthal concerned the logistics of the advance on Paris. On September 9 Moltke met Blumenthal; both were in a cautious frame of mind, as the latter noted:

> Moltke said to me that we ought too proceed by easy marches, so as not to leave the Crown Prince too far in rear. He had, however, no objection to our advancing as far as Meaux, and there halting; for then we should be in a position to march into Paris immediately, should circumstances demand it; and, furthermore, we would have a start, if required, on the other side of the Seine.[2]

Three days later the always touchy Blumenthal received a great blow to his pride, when he read the letter from the King to the Queen about the battle of Sedan:

The battle is very shortly described therein, and nothing whatever is said of the Crown Prince's army; in fact, one would suppose that it was not there at all, when the truth is that it was the Third Army which struck the decisive blow. I have now been through three campaigns, and have grown quite accustomed to having the operations, in which I have had the luck to be successful, depreciated; but it pains me to see the doings of the Crown Prince intentionally minimised.'[3]

Blumenthal was, however, very much more gratified by a meeting on September 14 with Russell, just returned from London, where he had been able repeatedly to tell people of his conversation with Blumenthal three days before Sedan, when the latter showed him on the map how the French would be surrounded at Sedan.[4]

Moltke continued to plan for the investment of Paris, meeting Blumenthal on September 15 to finalise the arrangements, whereby the Third Army would cover the south of the city while the Army of the Meuse took the north. The investment was to be completed by September 19, and for once Blumenthal was 'quite in accord with Moltke'; adding that he was pleased 'that it is to take place as I had previously planned, and as I had laid down to my Staff officers as the plan I should adopt.'[5]

Blumenthal reported to Moltke the completion of the investment on September 19, and on the actions at Petit Bicêtre, Chatillon, Choisy le Roi and Chevilly. In reply, Moltke stressed the importance of tightening the screw on the beleaguered city, recommending that all possible steps should be taken, such as the flooding of Auteuil, where the principal bakeries were located, as well as the destruction of the Arceuil aqueduct.[6] He agreed on September 27 with Blumenthal that there was no point in engaging in any costly operation at the present time: 'Before any real action is taken, we must await the arrival of the siege artillery, of which the first part left Nancy today and will arrive tomorrow at Nanteuil sur Marne.' Colonel Rieff, the siege artillery expert was travelling with the guns and would, after reporting to the Royal Headquarters, come on to Blumenthal to discuss the necessary arrangements. But Moltke's letter brought news which Blumenthal found much less agreeable; it had been decided that the Royal Headquarters would be based at Versailles.[7] Blumenthal had on September 20 established his headquarters at the prefecture there, and greeted the news with dismay:

We shall, I suppose, have to move out of our beautiful palace and seek some humbler abode. I do not mind that so much, but the close propinquity of the King's Headquarters has its drawbacks, especially for me, as I have not always sufficient command over myself to return the diplomatic or evasive answer to all the unnecessary questions and unsolicited conundrums set to solve. I am afraid I shall become again somewhat caustic or brusque, without wishing to be so and shall get myself disliked.[8]

In addition to keeping Trochu and the Army of Paris tightly bottled up, Moltke had also to be concerned with the steps being taken in the provinces to mount an operation for the relief of the city. The most pressing threat clearly came from the direction of the Loire, and on October 6 a lot of attention was directed to this. Quite whose idea it was to mount an operation to deal with this threat is far from clear. It was probably on that day that Moltke made some pencilled notes as to the units to take part in a thrust south towards the French Army of the Loire. It would involve a division of the XI Corps, the I Bavarian Corps and two cavalry divisions. The intention would be to move through Étampes, which would be close to that town by October 7. These operations were, Moltke intended, to be under the control of the Third Army.[9]

Characteristically claiming the credit for this, Blumenthal wrote in his diary on October 6:

> I came to the conclusion that a determined assault was in course of preparation on the part of the regular troops, in order to break our line and form a junction with the Army of the Loire. With this prospect in view, I approached General von Moltke when he appeared at half past five, and proposed that a force consisting of the I Bavarian Corps, supported by the 22nd Division (von Wittich), together with the three cavalry divisions, the whole under General von der Tann, should move against the Army of the South and give it a sound drubbing.[10]

Meantime the Crown Prince was noting in his diary on the same day that 'not without difficulty have I succeeded in obtaining permission from the King himself to instruct Lieutenant General von der Tann to leave Longjumeau forthwith.'[11] Whoever was the progenitor of this operation, it marked the beginning of a lengthy campaign, or series of campaigns, that was to subject the German army to its most searching test of the war against the Government of National Defence. For the moment, however, all seemed to be going well, and von der Tann was soon able to report that he had advanced to Orleans.

Meanwhile the seeds had been sown of the controversy that was to poison relationships between the military and civil powers of Germany. On October 7 Blumenthal met with Rieff and General Schulz to plan for siege operations against Paris if they should become necessary, having been told by Podbielski that the matter would be placed in the hands of the Third Army. To Blumenthal's great annoyance, he then learned that this was not to be the case:

> Why, I should like to know? I fancy that there are several who want to have their say in the matter, and this they would not have were it put into my hands. It is really most extraordinary that, in spite of the fact that Moltke and I continually come to an agreement on certain points, there invariably steps between us some third person, so that matters are eventually arranged quite otherwise than I expected. It may be that he is prevented from acting exactly as he wishes.[12]

One of Moltke's most persistent concerns at this stage of the war was the important manufacturing centre and military base at Bourges. He repeatedly urged an advance towards this as being the most effective blow that could be struck against the nascent military power of his enemy. On October 12 he explained to Blumenthal why he regarded this as so important:

> The greatest difficulty encountered by the enemy in forming new army corps is the lack of artillery and trains. The centre of the organisation of the artillery of the Army of the Loire is at Bourges. It is there that are located several artillery depots and workshop. One also finds the principal cannon foundry, pyrotechnic workshop, cartridge factory and major powder stores. At Châteauroux is to be found the only supply train still available … there would be nothing more decisive in preventing the formation of an army behind the Loire than a surprise attack by our forces on Bourges and Châteauroux, an attack that would have as its result *la destruction au fond* of the establishments and stores found in these towns.

He firmly urged Blumenthal to ensure that von der Tann had this in mind in the conduct of his operations.[13] Blumenthal took this on board, but his solution, as he noted on October 14 after hearing to his disappointment that von der Tann was not moving south from Orleans as suggested, was that Werder might be asked to move on Bourges from the east.

Blumenthal was by now getting thoroughly fed up with the proximity of the Royal Headquarters, which required 'reports about everything,' as a result of which his temper was getting shorter, as he had predicted. 'Curiosity and impatience are the chief demons with which I have to deal, and these annoy me so intensely that I am often prompted to return a sarcastic answer, or make some bitter retort, for, after all, I have a good deal of the Below blood in me.'[14] His spirits were lifted, though, on October 18, which was the Crown Prince's birthday:

> At 8.00 am three massed bands appeared, and commenced with the hymn "Nun danket alle Gott." My feelings were quite overcome by the music, and when the Crown Prince entered my room suddenly, and, with the kindest and most gracious expressions of gratitude, handed to me the Iron Cross of the First Class, I quite broke down, and could not utter a word.[15]

To an increasing extent the issue of how to bring the investment of Paris to a successful conclusion was coming to dominate the regular discussions between Moltke and his senior colleagues. He and Blumenthal spoke for practically all of them in disfavouring a bombardment on the commencement of siege operations. Blumenthal noted on October 20:

> This should be our keynote, namely, to lay stress upon starvation, rather than bombardment, as the actual means to be adopted for reducing the garrison. It is quite possible for us to starve them out, and within a few months. Their sorties

Roon.

cannot be really dangerous to us now, as their army is still feeling the influence of its recent defeats.[16]

He was very pleased to be confirmed in this view on the following day, when in conversation with Moltke, who considered that it never would come to be a question of bombardment, as the French would be starved out long before that could arise.'[17] Bismarck, of course, was of a different view, and went out of his way to be charming to Blumenthal, who was fascinated by the Chancellor, and flattered to be the recipient of his attention during lengthy discussions after dinner. He did not get on so well with Roon, reporting on October 31: 'I got into a lively altercation with the War Minister, who is just as bloodthirsty as he was in 1864, and always wants to hear the first cannon shot fired. It was a very pleasant and most interesting evening, and it was almost 11.00 pm before I got to bed. Bismarck talked a good deal as usual.'[18]

Blumenthal's outspokenness led him into another confrontation on October 30, as the Crown Prince noted; never one to take insults lying down, he was extremely angry at comments made by Prince Charles, the King's brother, about a march past of the Landwehr Guards Division. The prince 'spoke so roughly about it to General von Blumenthal that the latter there and then gave him back as good as he got, not to be forced into the necessity of officially reporting the King's brother; amongst other things the prince said that such like confusions could only happen in such an army as the Third was.'[19]

Meanwhile things were not going as well as had been hoped on the Loire, and Blumenthal chafed at interference with his conduct of operations. He decided to mount an operation against Blois and Tours:

> The Crown Prince has consented to my plan, and now I have sent Bronsart to Moltke to communicate it to him. I am sure that he will have no objection, but it is to me like a millstone round my neck that I am not allowed to do anything independently, but always have to sound others, and make all sorts of inquiries, lest objections should be raised in the circles of the highest and most unjust. In a word, our wings are cut and we are pinioned.[20]

Blumenthal was soon, however, engaged in another dispute with Moltke over the operations of von der Tann and Wittich, objecting to orders that they move forward.

> I cannot say that I at all approve this idea, for it throws to the winds my plan, which has hitherto been followed, of remaining quiet until all should be ready for a big stroke. It may easily lay us open to defeats in detail. I drove over to Moltke at once, and we came to terms as soon as he had heard what I had to say. He now desires nothing more than that they should make reconnaissances in force, which they are both doing. Wittich is making one today, but I greatly fear that he will come upon very superior forces in doing so.[21]

His annoyance deepened on the following day, when he confided to his diary that he considered that operations were being conducted in an 'inexpressibly distressing manner.' What upset him was what he considered the very exposed position of Wittich's division:

> As the Crown Prince was going to an audience with the King, I begged him to explain the question emphatically to His Majesty and pray him to allow us to support Wittich with the 4th Division, which has just marched in, and then permit him, in conjunction with von der Tann, to carry out the movement which appears so desirable. It was all in vain, as the King fancies our own position in front of Paris to be extremely hazardous, and will not sanction army troops being sent away. We shall have to wait another day. I have not been so depressed for a long time, or so despondent as I am today.[22]

Next day he tried again, sending first Bronsart to Moltke, and then the Crown Prince to the King. Both were unsuccessful, leaving Blumenthal perhaps brooding on the comments of Prince Charles, to moan in his diary: 'There is a limit of work in every human body, and it is not at all to the point that I should be working myself to death, night and day, while a whole crowd of military loafers are kicking their heels about in dozens, doing nothing but passing worthless criticism on other people's work.'[23]

When on November 7 it was decided to strengthen operations against the Army of the Loire by forming a detachment under the Grand Duke of Mecklenburg-Schwerin he was momentarily gratified, 'as he was so smart and quick in apprehending his task that I have the greatest hopes of him.' The Grand Duke was to command a force comprising the I Bavarian Corps, with Wittich's 22nd Division and the 17th Division, together with two cavalry divisions. Von der Tann had sent word from Orleans that he was expecting to be attacked, a fear which Blumenthal dismissed out of hand, 'as the enemy cannot be ready for it yet.' Next day, as reconnaissance reports indicated that von der Tann was right, Blumenthal managed to conclude 'that a battle is nearer to hand than has been anticipated by those in the councils of the King. All my prayers and entreaties have been in vain, and now people will not be surprised that it should have made me ill. My conscience is, however, clear.'[24] When the news came of von der Tann's defeat at Coulmiers on November 9, Moltke came over to Blumenthal to discuss the situation; it was certainly a setback, but the two men were optimistic that the situation would very soon be reversed. Moltke, as usual, was able to impart some of his calm confidence to his mercurial subordinate.

As to the Detachment, whatever may have been the genesis of the decision to strengthen operations against the Army of the Loire, there was at least a general agreement as to its objectives. But it did not take long for the management of its operations to give rise to disputes. Moltke had a clear idea of the need to strike quickly at the Army of the Loire before it was able to develop further, and was soon taking a close personal interest in its operations. This annoyed Blumenthal, who was distinctly put out by Moltke's wish to exert his own control over the Grand Duke's movements, grumbling on November 13 about 'the very decided tendency here to dictate every move to the Grand Duke, and this ought to be resisted. If I were in his place, I should report nothing but just cut the telegraph wire.' A further instance of this arose on the next day, when the Grand Duke's latest report arrived and which caused 'great agitation,' and which led Blumenthal to observe: 'when I see agitation abound it always annoys me, but when there is absolutely no foundation for such weakness it makes me wild.' What was irritating Moltke was the move of the Detachment towards Chartres, and the fact that its forces were too much divided. Blumenthal thought that 'no doubt the Grand Duke had good reasons for his action,' but this did not by any means satisfy Moltke, who wanted Blumenthal to issue more prescriptive orders. This Blumenthal stoutly refused to do and, according to his diary, he persuaded Moltke for the moment to relent.[25]

Moltke's other immediate preoccupation was the movement of the Second Army from Metz towards the Loire to take a hand in the campaign there, and by November 15 the first units of Frederick Charles' army were beginning to arrive. Manstein, with the IX Corps, led the movement, reaching an area to the east of Étampes that day. For the present, though, it was the Detachment that was, or ought to have been, in contact with the enemy, and its movements still gave rise to profound discontent, as Blumenthal noted next day: 'Moltke came to me today, and complained that the Grand Duke reported so little, and said that I ought to order him to take the offensive. That is not at all necessary. The Duke will do that of his own accord, and up to now it seems to me that he has done perfectly right.'[26] Moltke was certainly not mollified by observations of this kind, and his impatience and frustration were to mount in the coming days.

At Versailles, Moltke was coming under increasing pressure on the subject of the bombardment of Paris. This was being applied in particular by Bismarck, who lost no opportunity of propounding his views. One occasion for this came after dinner with the King on November 21, when he seized the opportunity to try to brainwash Blumenthal, explaining that the bombardment was a political necessity. Blumenthal would have none of it., and robustly set out the military arguments against it, which he recorded in trenchant terms:

> I could only reply that I considered it would be a great military fault, and that I would rather retire than permit it. His politics should have nothing to do with this question; it is purely a military one, and the honour of the army is at stake. I can perfectly well see that the Crown Prince has been worked on, and would very much like to see a bombardment take place such as a subaltern would indulge in. I cannot consent to such inanity, and would rather give up my command than yield to such infantile counsels. When once firing commences, there ought to be no cessation whatever. Once the task is undertaken, we must go through with it, or else accept the blame of the whole world. If I could only see some purpose in a bombardment I would not object, but if people think that the bursting of a few shells in the suburbs of Paris will bring about a capitulation, they labour under a childish illusion and greatly misjudge the French. In the open field I will gladly go at them, but behind walls and ramparts they will become real heroes, and we shall forego all our advantage.'[27]

Returning to his headquarters, Blumenthal sat down to write a strident note of his views on the subject, which he sent to Moltke. In it, he recounted his conversation with Bismarck, and set out in colourful language and considerable detail the objections which he had noted in his diary. He closed with his own recollections of the bombardment of Fredericia in 1849 and in particular Düppel in 1864 where 'I thoroughly bombarded the redoubts … for four weeks with excellent artillery without seeing the least benefit in attaining our objective, until the time we embarked on a formal siege.' In the present campaign, he pointed out that Toul and Phalsbourg had 'been shelled rigorously without any conclusive result.' Moltke was pleased with this memorandum, noting in the margin: 'Spoken with vigour with a point of view that I share.'[28]

A few days later Bismarck tried to persuade the Crown Prince of the need for a bombardment. Notwithstanding Blumenthal's suspicions that the Crown Prince had been 'worked on,' he stuck to the party line, repeating the arguments put forward in Blumenthal's memorandum. As a result of this, the Crown Prince felt two days later on November 28 the call for a bombardment was

> becoming a perfect mania in Berlin … and I even hear that Countess Bismarck-Schönhausen points me out to all and sundry as more particularly the guilty cause of its postponement. And she is quite right, for above all things I do not wish fire to be opened till in the opinion of professional gunners and experts the necessary ammunition each single siege gun requires for an effective, uninterrupted bombardment is there on the spot.'[29]

In the west, the Detachment was still operating very ineffectively, and on November 22 Moltke ordered that it should move immediately towards the Loire, in order to cooperate with the Second Army. Indicating that the Detachment would have to operate on the left bank of the river, Moltke added that it was desirable that, by a rapid march, it should seize a bridge over the Loire. If that was not possible, the Second Army would provide pontoon equipment. Next day, Moltke wrote to Blumenthal to confirm that the rest day applied for by the Detachment could not be granted; by November 26 the force must be on the line Vendôme-Châteaudun. Blumenthal was in full agreement, describing the Detachment's planned wheel to the left as 'a most excellent move,' adding that the rest day 'cannot be dreamt of.' But once again the Detachment failed to make the progress hoped for, reporting an encounter with strong French forces near Brou. Blumenthal, observing that he 'would have gone forward at all hazards and routed the lot,' noted that Moltke had by now had enough, and had decided to do something about it. 'General von Moltke was very much vexed with this tardiness, and proposed to the King that General von Stosch should be sent to the Grand Duke as Chief of the Staff to hurry him up.'[30]

Moltke had, since the formation of the Detachment, effectively taken the management of the campaign on the Loire into his own hands, and with the decision to send Stosch there, and the arrival of the Second Army, Blumenthal's responsibility for it more or less came to an end. Thereafter, sharing the general view at Versailles of Frederick Charles's excessive caution, he confined himself to acerbic comments about the lack of progress in dealing with the Army of the Loire. He had plenty to occupy himself, in any case, with the continued operations of the Third Army before Paris, where the issue of the bombardment of the city came more and more to dominate German military planning.

The repulse of the French sortie launched on November 29 after four days of bitter fighting marked the effective end of Trochu's efforts to break out of Paris. It was also the occasion for a serious row between the Crown Prince and his Chief of Staff, who had failed to consult his army commander over the arrival of orders for Fransecky, whose corps was heavily engaged in resisting the French assault.

Blumenthal described the incident in his diary:

> In the morning the Crown Prince was very much put out that I had not had him
> called, as he said he ought to be informed of all orders as soon as they arrive. I
> said to him I could not think of waking him for such details; moreover, that it
> came into my province, and not into his, to issue the subsequent orders. I told
> him that I was not in the position of an adjutant who merely had to carry out
> orders; that I was only too willing to leave him all the honour of the command
> and do all the work, but that my position could not be reduced to that of an
> adjutancy ... It is not possible for him to feel offended, as he is always governed
> by the best intentions, but he does not grasp the exact relationship in which I
> stand to him.[31]

The Crown Prince, for his part, did not refer to the incident in his own diary.
Blumenthal, always in need of being publicly appreciated, was cheered two days later
to learn from a Russian visitor, Prince Georgi, that he had a remarkable number of
admirers in Russia.

Dining with the King on December 8, Blumenthal had a long talk with Moltke
about the demand for a bombardment. They agreed that it was likely that hunger
would bring about a capitulation within a few weeks, and that in any case it would be
wrong to commence a bombardment until the stocks of ammunition were sufficient.
Moltke, was, however, contemplating going some way to meet Bismarck on the issue:

> He is going to put the case to some of the artillerists as to whether a partial
> cannonading of Paris might not be possible without opening regular parallels. I
> imagine he overestimates the range of our weapons, and the normal effect that
> such a cannonading would have.'[32]

Tempers were becoming frayed over the issue: on December 11 Bismarck uncharacteristically overreached himself by suggesting that the delay in bombarding Paris
might cause civil unrest in Berlin, which prompted the King to issue instructions to
the Governor there to face steps to suppress it. Bismarck, greatly embarrassed, had
to explain that he meant only that people were getting impatient, adding that 'military men were calling out for bombardment.' At this Moltke, the Crown Prince told
Blumenthal, was 'in a high state of indignation. Blumenthal himself was enraged to
learn that it was being suggested that his own objection to the bombardment was as a
result of 'female influence,' a reference to the Crown Princess and the Queen.[33]

The 'military men' to whom Bismarck had referred were led by Roon, who had been
recruited by Bismarck in his campaign to persuade the King that the bombardment
must commence without delay. Roon had greatly encouraged Bismarck by assuring
him that the necessary siege artillery and ammunition were available, and he did
not hesitate to take on Moltke directly, writing a strongly worded letter to him on
December 11, following a meeting with the King. Moltke's statements to the King

about the difficulties of carrying out the bombardment had seriously annoyed Roon, who wrote:

> 'The declarations made by Your Excellency at today's report suggested to me reflections which I did not wish to express at the time, in order to avoid all controversy in His Majesty's presence, but which I am not however able to leave unspoken. Several months ago, Your Excellency issued His Majesty's order as to the bombardment of several forts; the Third Army was charged with its execution and the War Ministry was to take measures to bring up artillery and ammunition sufficient for this limited objective. At that time Your Excellency did not appear to doubt the possibility of carrying this out. However subsequently the strangely long delay required by the technical services for commencing the attack has become longer and longer.'[34]

Moltke next day delivered a dignified response, denying that he had said that the proposal was impossible or pointless; but that in the face of all the difficulties he was 'resolutely opposed to the idea, which I consider inopportune, that it should be commenced now.'

On December 17 the King held a conference to discuss the question. It was an entirely military conference, and included Hindersin and Kleist, respectively the Inspectors General of Artillery and Engineering, and also Schulz and Rieff who had been working on the plans for the bombardment. It also included Roon who, as Blumenthal described, found himself in a minority of one:

> The professional soldiers all deprecated the useless and childish idea of a bombardment. The War Minister alone was in favour of it, and he glared at us most angrily and resentfully. I really hope that this futile idea, with all the sacrifices it must cost us, will be rendered unnecessary by a speedy capitulation.[35]

Bismarck had another tête-á-tête with Blumenthal on December 19, when he made a further determined effort to win him round, employing all the considerable charm of which he was capable. Blumenthal recorded the discussion:

> He combated all my arguments so cleverly and with such flattering unction that I nearly laughed aloud. He said to me that it was never his wish to bombard; he was perfectly aware that the town could not be touched by our fire; but the political necessities of the case rendered it most important that we should show we are in earnest. We are compelled to bombard, even if it be only fifty shots fired at the forts; otherwise it would be impossible to prevent foreign Powers – Russia and England he meant – from intervening. All thought that our resources were at an end ... He had no compunction in laying on flattery thickly, but to such influences, thank God, I am as impervious as armour plate.'

Bismarck went on to complain bitterly 'of the treatment he was receiving at the hands of the King and of Moltke, who had left him for some time now without any information regarding the course of events; in fact, they had both been quite discourteous to him.' Warming to his theme, Bismarck went on to tell Blumenthal that 'he would not remain Minister one hour after the war was over.' He seemed to Blumenthal to 'be quite beside himself, going on to complain of the discourteous letters which he said he had received from Moltke and Podbielski.'[36]

Things were going from bad to worse for Blumenthal. The news that the overall conduct of the bombardment was now to be in the hands of Kameke and Hohenlohe in succession to Schulz and Rieff did not particularly disturb him, but his incipient paranoia led him to speculate on the wider implications. 'So we are again to have new brooms and new oars. Who knows that I shall not now be turned out? In spite of all intrigues, they will not find it easy to do so.'[37]

Kameke was, he found, of much his own view as to the inadequacy of the supplies of ammunition for the siege artillery, and this confirmed Blumenthal in his opinion that in any case the bombardment would be of little effect on the morale of the Parisians. He was momentarily cheered by the remarks of the King on New Year's Day: 'He thanked me for all that I have done in previous years in such kind tones that I could find no words to reply. He wishes, evidently, to speak kindly to me before others to compensate me for the many vexations and slights that I have had to put up with of late.'[38]

Two days later, however, he was enraged by a suggestion that the secret of the bombardment, due to start on January 4, had not been kept and that he or his staff were to blame, and he at once went off to see Moltke and Podbielski about it. Next day he was again seriously upset by the suggestion that his opposition to the bombardment was due to the influence of the Crown Princess, which he denounced as an 'infamous untruth.' Moltke, anxious to retain control of events, meanwhile called for reports twice daily as to the effect of the bombardment.[39]

There was not a great deal to report, though, and Blumenthal would have liked to wash his hands of the whole thing, observing on January 8 that he had 'no wish to look on the bombardment. It does not meet my approval on principle, and at the same time I cannot alter matters.'[40] Events elsewhere in France were more encouraging, however, and even at Paris the feeling was growing that the end was near. This did nothing to help Blumenthal's mood, though, and another issue arose on January 21 with the Crown Prince, this time over his agreeing to a cessation of hostilities along the front of the V Corps, a step he had agreed with Moltke: 'The Crown Prince's displeasure I cannot account for (he did not make it apparent to me personally), but I assume that he cannot bear my arranging anything on my own responsibility.'[41] Blumenthal's ill temper continued on the following day. He recorded in his diary: 'I am possessed by a feeling that everyone is hostile and unjust towards me, and yet I have done nothing to anyone. I am, I know, very intolerant and curt. Perhaps it is an inward result of this senseless and purposeless bombardment, which is costing us so many lives.'[42] By January 24 he had cheered up considerably, believing that the 'superheated advocates of bombardment' now saw that he was right. He added, unctuously, that 'it is not however an unusual thing to find in the world that those who have tendered sound and wholesome advice, which has not been followed, are hated and loathed because they stand as a reproach to the people.'[43]

The war, indeed, was drawing at last to an end. Blumenthal professed himself as 'well contented with the wise moderation' that Bismarck and Moltke had shown in the negotiations for an armistice. Although he was to be subjected to many further irritations, which he querulously recorded in his diary, the pressure was off. He worked himself into a fury when he mistakenly supposed that Metz was after all to be restored to France, bewailing the loss of the good military frontier; but this misapprehension lasted only twenty four hours, and he was able to record his 'astonishment and joy' that Metz was to be retained, a development which he put down to an intervention by Moltke. It was soon time for the Royal Headquarters to return to Berlin, and Blumenthal followed, travelling slowly across France, and reaching Berlin on March 21. Next day he went to the Emperor's reception where he was able to reassure himself that his achievements were recognised: 'There met many retired generals who had formerly been my commanding officers – a strange feeling. Kindness and hearty sincerity surrounded me on all sides – perhaps, too, a little envy and malice.'[44]

It had been an enormously demanding war for Blumenthal, and he was entitled to feel that his own contribution to the German success had been very considerable. He was the most gifted of all Moltke's subordinates and, in spite of the quirks of his mercurial temperament, the most reliable. Most of the time he had an intuitive grasp of Moltke's intentions, and acted promptly to realise them, in spite of the vanity and flashes of temper which led to so many complaints in his diary. For Moltke, working with Blumenthal was never dull, and there were many times when his excitable subordinate tried his patience. But the two men formed a really effective partnership that was one of the key elements of Moltke's success in conducting the wars of German unification.

9

Stosch

Albrecht von Stosch was a very different personality from Blumenthal. Although he too could be outspoken he was altogether more considered in his views and more tactful in expressing them. It was these qualities that led Moltke, whose appraisal of the two men was characteristically accurate, to appoint Stosch to serve as Blumenthal's No 2 in the Austro-Prussian War. As he explained to Stosch when the latter reported for duty in Berlin, his duties as Quartermaster-General of the Second Army would be to ensure that Blumenthal's inspired ideas were carried into effect and Stosch appears from the outset to have accepted this as his responsibility, as well as understanding the problems it would cause hm.

Stosch was born on April 2 1818 in Coblenz, to a family that had, with the ennoblement of his father, risen above its middle-class origins. His father enjoyed a successful career in the Prussian army, rising to the rank of General in 1840. After his death in 1857 one of his senior colleagues commented on his thoroughness and prudence, 'the clarity of his reasoning powers, and his nice sense of tact in society,' all of which were qualities which would in turn stand his son in good stead over a long career in the army, the navy and politics.[1]

The young Stosch grew up, therefore, in a very orthodox military family, absorbing the basic values of a conservative society which remained with him all his life. After his education in the State Schools and the Coblenz gymnasium he went, predictably, to the Prussian cadet school at Potsdam and thence, in 1832, to the Chief Cadet School in Berlin. Leaving in 1835, he was commissioned as a second lieutenant in the 29th Infantry Regiment based at Coblenz, enjoying the benefit of the social connections in the city with which he had grown up. Since the demands made on his time by his military responsibilities were not great, he was able to broaden his education by the study of law, economics, and literature.[2] In 1839 he passed the entrance examination for the General Military School in Berlin which was, or ought to have been, the gateway to more rapid advancement.

Stosch greatly enjoyed his time in Berlin, making many lifelong friends. Each summer he returned to regimental duties, the first year in Silesia and the second in Danzig. During the winter he moved in the highest social circles, and got to know

Stosch.

many of the great and the good. Prussian court society was a very enclosed world in those days. During his third year he met and secretly became engaged to Rosaline Ulrich, his future wife; his chances of marrying her were not improved by the fact that his prospective father-in-law was an extreme democrat, for whom a lieutenant in the Prussian army held few attractions. Stosch however persevered and in 1843 Dr Ulrich gave his consent to the engagement. That year Stosch was posted to the Guard artillery in Berlin for a nine month term, which was something of a plum job; and following this he did a tour of duty with the Topographical Bureau of the General Staff. Ten young officers a year were selected for this assignment which lasted three years, at the end of which two were chosen to join the General Staff. It was a career advancement that Stosch greatly desired, and he worked extremely hard for it. His battalion commanders gave him excellent reports; but the endorsement of his record with the words 'inclined to indiscipline' arising from an incident with his superior at the Topographical Bureau proved fatal to his chances of selection. Stosch was mortified, as he recorded in his memoirs:

> This blow struck me in my innermost soul. I know I had learned and accomplished something. I had considered myself more intelligent and more clever than all my comrades. Now I was shown the opposite. Entrance into the General

Staff would have made me a captain within two years and would have aided me financially. I had been a second lieutenant for twelve years already and now had the prospect of remaining one for at least twelve years more. It was a hard lesson in humility but it has been advantageous all my life.'[3]

At this point in his life Stosch's military career seemed to be going nowhere, but the events of 1848 were to prove a turning point. During the troubled period that followed the 'March Days' in Berlin, many army units were affected by unrest. This included the 29th Regiment at Coblenz, and General von Thile, the commander of the VIII Corps, determined that it should be posted to the French frontier in the hope that the move away from its base would restore its discipline. The citizens of Coblenz protested vigorously at this, to the point that the Chief Magistrate of the city repre-sented to Thile that unless he withdrew the movement order there would be a revolt. Thile gave in, to Stosch's fury; when he told the other lieutenants what had occurred they united behind a demand that the move be carried out.

Thile not surprisingly refused, but the affair so upset him that he wrote out his resignation. Stosch was ordered by the Chief of Staff to take it to Berlin, with the injunction that he should use his influence to ensure that the resignation would be refused. When in the presence of the King the acting War Minister, General von Reyher, asked for his opinion, Stosch dutifully reported that the Chief of Staff believed that Thile 'was the only man for the job.' Pressed to give his own opinion, Stosch felt obliged to say that Thile should not continue in post, and he shortly found himself taking back to Coblenz the formal acceptance of his commanding officer's resignation.[3] The whole experience brought out the all Stosch's conservative instincts and fired his own ambitions, and he wrote later:

> I had looked deep into the world and was inclined to take a part in events. The direction was preordained both by family tradition and my professional feelings; I would have gone vigorously into the field against all revolutionaries without any pangs of conscience.[5]

One other event occurred during his visit to Berlin which at the time he would have had no reason for regarding as especially important. While there, he apparently first made the acquaintance of Moltke. The latter, then a colonel, had been serving on the staff of the VIII Corps in Coblenz, until being posted to Magdeburg as Chief of Staff of the IV Corps. There is, however, no record that anything of significance passed between them.[6]

Returning to the Rhine, Stosch resumed his duties as a second lieutenant. At the age of thirty, he had not made a great deal of progress in his military career. He was of course by no means alone in serving such a long apprenticeship in a junior rank; his experience was typical of a number of very successful Prussian soldiers who had to wait a long time before the system combined with some fortunate circumstance to provide an opportunity to progress. In September 1848 Stosch had an interesting assignment observing the situation in France as it appeared from conditions in the frontier districts. This was followed by a short period of service with the units engaged in restoring order in Baden and Hesse. His next posting was as adjutant to a Landwehr brigade based in Trier. He served three years there in what he evidently regarded as a dead end job in a provincial backwater, and he turned to politics for intellectual stimulus, writing articles on the subject of the army for local newspapers. He still hoped for a transfer to the General Staff, but this did not materialise, although he was promoted to first lieutenant in June 1849. As adjutant to the brigade he was heavily involved in the 1850 mobilisation of the Prussian army that was followed by the Convention of Olmütz and, like many others, was shocked by the deficiencies of the process.

His lack of success in getting a transfer to the General Staff was due to the perception that he was politically unreliable. Thus, although promoted to the rank of Captain in 1852, and appointed as first adjutant to the division, he was the only one holding such a post to be returned to regimental duties when General Staff officers were appointed to the position. He served as a company commander for a year, becoming increasingly discouraged by his lack of progress; but then, at last, achieved his ambition by being appointed to the General Staff and taking up a post on the staff of the VIII Corps at Coblenz. There he made the acquaintance of the Prince of Prussia, who was serving as military governor of the Rhineland and Westphalia at the time, and who was impressed by a lecture Stosch gave on the subject of the needle gun. In later years he would remind Stosch of how he had been the first to demonstrate to him the potential importance of the weapon.[7]

Stosch's career was now gathering momentum. In April 1856 he reached the rank of Major, and was posted to Posen on the staff of the 10th Division, where he formed a lasting friendship with General Heinrich von Brandt. From the latter, who was a well known writer on military affairs, Stosch learned a great deal, and he looked back on his time in Posen in the course of which he was promoted to lieutenant colonel, as giving him profound professional satisfaction. On the other hand, he did not think much of Posen society, which he found extremely boring.

He was therefore very pleased when in 1861 he was appointed as Chief of Staff of the IV Corps, based in Magdeburg. In this position he was getting very close to the most senior echelons of power in the General Staff, including for instance Moltke, who had by now been Chief of the General Staff for four years. In this position he had begun to inculcate the consistent ethos among his officers that was to be at the heart of his military success. Moltke was extremely impressed with Stosch's performance on the staff ride of 1861, remarking that the latter's insistence that his officers write a daily report was making too much work for him.[8] He acknowledged that Stosch was doing well in his present post, and noted that he might be appointed as a brigade commander. Stosch also enjoyed another good relationship with his corps commander, von Schack who held the highest opinion of him.

All seemed set fair for Stosch's career; but in November 1863 he was seriously injured in a riding accident, so much so that his condition gave rise to some anxiety for his life. As a result, although the crisis was soon overcome, he was sidelined for some eighteen months, and was in particular prevented from taking any part in the Austro-Prussian campaign against Denmark. Although, slowly, he recovered from the injury, he walked with a limp for the rest of his life. He passed the time in writing articles for *Die Grenzboten*, a Saxon magazine edited by his friend Gustav Freytag, covering not only the Danish War but also the American Civil War. By now Stosch was making influential friends such as the Chief Minister of Baden, von Roggenbach. He also developed an especially close friendship with Karl von Normann, who in 1864 became secretary to the Crown Princess; through him, Stosch first made the acquaintance of the Crown Prince and he formed a close and enduring friendship with the Royal couple. Stosch was also close to a number of rising General Staff officers, such as Julius von Verdy du Vernois. Although his injury kept him off duty for such a long time, he was not forgotten; Moltke thought him 'a promising personality,' and that he would 'accomplish even more as a troop commander than in the General Staff.'[9] His close relationship with the Crown Prince, however, did him no good professionally; the Military Cabinet was deeply suspicious of anyone high in the Crown Prince's favour. As a result Stosch was passed over first as Chief of Staff of the II Corps, commanded by the Crown Prince; when the latter sought to have him appointed as his adjutant, this too was refused, to his great annoyance. Stosch's connection with the Royal couple was enough for him to be categorised as a liberal, and although he seems always to have held entirely orthodox political and social views, it was a reputation that never left him.

By the spring of 1866 relations between Austria and Prussia had deteriorated to the point at which war had become a distinct possibility, and this entailed the making of appointments to key positions, as the Prussian army prepared for the conflict. Passed fit for duty, Stosch received on May 8 news of his appointment as Quartermaster General of the Second Army, to be commanded by the Crown Prince, in which capacity he would be serving as No 2 to the mercurial Blumenthal. Stosch made his way at once to Berlin, but missed the Crown Prince, who had gone to Potsdam, so he visited Moltke. He found the Chief of the General Staff feeling decidedly frustrated by the continuing uncertainties of the political situation, which among other problems was causing protracted delays in the formation of the army staffs. That being so, Stosch asked why he had been ordered to Berlin in such a hurry.

Moltke explained, patiently if somewhat wearily, the difficulties he was encountering, but went on to explain that as far as Stosch was concerned, his principal responsibility would be to give practical effect to Blumenthal's inspirations.[10] Working with Blumenthal was always going to be difficult: Stosch was fortunate to have the very able, and very tactful, Verdy as one of his assistants.

While waiting to go to Breslau, the intended headquarters of the Second Army, Stosch had the opportunity of attending a three hour meeting of the Royal Council on May 25. Stosch was particularly impressed with Bismarck's efforts to bring the vacillating King William to the point of decision, writing to his wife that the Minister President 'was decidedly the clearest and keenest. I had the conviction that he directed

the whole state proceedings with the sole purpose of influencing the King for war.'
Stosch also observed at first hand the negative feelings towards Moltke displayed by
von Voigts-Rhetz; the latter, who was to serve in the key post of Chief of Staff of
Frederick Charles' First Army, contradicted Moltke at great length without offering
any suggestions of his own. For his part, Moltke, as was to be expected repeatedly
asserted the importance of embarking on hostilities without delay; only in this way,
he said, could they be sure of victory.[11]

Leaving the meeting, the Crown Prince expressed his frustration to Stosch: 'We
know just as much as we did before – the King does not want to [go to war] but
Bismarck does.'[12] It seemed to Stosch that it was entirely likely that the King's views
would prevail, but at all events he and the rest of the Crown Prince's senior staff were
able to leave early in June for Silesia to supervise the preparations for a war that might
never come.

Verdy, looking back on the war of 1866, described Stosch:

> He had a tall, imposing figure, and always carried himself rigidly erect, even
> though he limped slightly …He was also the picture of virile strength, which
> was expressed in indefatigable activity. His powerful frame was surmounted by
> an expressive head, out of which two shrewd eyes looked sharply into the world,
> and his candid features gave the impression that he grew more joyful the more
> difficult a situation became.'

He evidently enjoyed the complete confidence of the Crown Prince, whom Verdy
recorded as saying: 'As soon as I see Stosch, if only from afar, I get an extraordinary
feeling of well being; it is always a pleasure to me when I see his splendid counte-
nance.'[13] Stosch soon came to appreciate the problem of working with Blumenthal;
and found it best to transmit his suggestions to the arrogant and impatient Chief
of Staff by transmitting them through Verdy. Stosch noted approvingly of the latter
that he was 'developing the unusual talents of asking the right questions, giving
the right instructions, forming correct opinions of people and synthesising reports
correctly.'[14]

Once hostilities commenced, the Second Army moved forward to undertake its
potentially hazardous advance through widely separated mountain passes, which
exposed it to the risk of being defeated in detail as it emerged. On June 27 Stosch
at last had his first experience of combat when, riding with the Crown Prince and
Blumenthal towards the town of Nachod, which had been occupied by Steinmetz's
V Corps, they came under brisk rifle fire. The Crown Prince's adjutant, fearful of the
danger, asked Stosch to persuade him to withdraw. Stosch replied that he was under
fire for the first time in his life, and suggested that the adjutant should ask Blumenthal
to get his army commander out of harm's way. Stosch rode on, meeting Verdy; when
he saw a Prussian battery retreating, he ordered it back into action,, and then gave
instructions that the road should be cleared so that promised reinforcements could
come up, a move which probably saved Steinmetz from defeat.

After their success in the early battles of the campaign the Prussian armies moved forward to the decisive encounter with Benedck's concentrated army. Some questions have been raised as to the events of the night of July 2, when orders were issued which brought the Second Army down on Benedek's flank. No mention is made in the accounts of the Crown Prince, Blumenthal or Verdy of any decisive intervention by Stosch; but Professor Hollyday, Stosch's biographer, has noted that in Stosch's own account it was he who persuaded the Crown Prince to issue orders which caused the Second Army to appear on the scene earlier than expected on the following day, and concluded that neither Blumenthal nor Verdy was present at the material time. The order in question to which Stosch refers must have been issued before Finckenstein arrived at the headquarters of the Second Army at 4.00 am, with Moltke's orders for the army to advance. Since Blumenthal made the long journey back from Gitschin to Königinhof during the night of July 2/3, returning only at 2.00 am, he was certainly not there when the first news of the proposed reconnaissance in force by Frederick Charles arrived during the evening of July 2. Since no doubt some orders were issued during the evening in response to this information, Hollyday is almost certainly right that they would have been initiated by Stosch, in the absence of Blumenthal. These orders related, in all probability, to the advance of the I Corps and the cavalry, which was all the support Blumenthal was able to promise the First Army in his reply of 3 am to Frederick Charles's second message. Such earlier orders of course, were overtaken by the later orders issued to the units of the Second Army after Finckenstein's arrival; but it is probably not unfair for Stosch to claim that, at the least, his orders got the Second Army moving forward sooner than would otherwise have been the case.[15]

During the battle on July 3 Stosch, no doubt to his discontent, played a passive role, but with the rest of the staff was in no doubt of the completeness of the victory and the decisive nature of the Second Army's part in it. He described it as 'the best and greatest day in Prussia's history.'[16] On the following day Stosch went with the Crown Prince to Royal Headquarters to discuss the terms of any possible armistice; Blumenthal did not accompany them, but since he felt strongly that the Austrians must not be let off the hook, no doubt sent them off with firm instructions to demand the strongest conditions. After some vigorous debate with Moltke and Bismarck the Crown Prince's arguments were largely accepted.

Relations between the Second Army and Royal Headquarters did not remain peaceful for long, since Blumenthal was greatly provoked by what he felt were Moltke's unfair comments on the progress of his army; it must be recorded, however that in these disputes Stosch supported his chief, and after the particularly violent upset of July 15 it was Stosch who was sent off to Royal Headquarters in Brünn to put the Second Army's case. As has been seen above, Stosch was able to pour oil on troubled waters, which temporarily resolved matters.

While at Royal Headquarters Stosch had the opportunity of a long discussion with Bismarck. He observed in his diary that the 'gentlemen of the Foreign Office speak of their chief with as holy a respect as believers of the Prophet.' He noted Bismarck's view that Austria must be excluded from Germany, but that no territorial gains should be made at Austria's expense, as her support might later be needed. Bismarck remarked that 'dazzling military success' was the best prop of the arts of diplomacy.[7] Bismarck, treating Stosch as a personal confidant of the Crown Prince, was in an expansive mood; he needed the support of the Crown Prince and rightly saw Stosch as a powerful influence on him.

The extent of that influence was widely remarked; Stosch himself wrote on July 27: 'The world begins to believe in my power, entirely forgetting that the young Prince himself has none yet.' And he ascribed part of this to the influence of the Crown Princess, which he regarded as very great: 'She determines the course of his ideas, even when far from him, and it is touching to see how he depends on her.'[18]

The relationship with the Crown Prince, which exercised both a positive and a negative effect on Stosch's career, remained of enormous significance to him. Stosch stayed in Bohemia with the Second Army for six weeks after the armistice, returning to Berlin to be placed temporarily on the retired list before, on September 27, he was appointed as Director of the Military Economic Department of the War Office. The appointment brought with it a brief to reorganise the department, the performance of which had, during the course of the war, been regarded as thoroughly unsatisfactory. Nominally, Stosch reported to Roon, but in practice, as Professor Hollyday points out, he was left very much to himself; he appears to have had only two business meetings with Roon during his four years in the War Ministry.[19]

Stosch's association with the Crown Prince inevitably had the effect of drawing him towards the world of politics, due to his patron's liberal views. Soon after his appointment was confirmed in December 1866 he found himself at the centre of a major controversy on his own account. Following the end of the war, negotiations had been on foot between Moltke's Quartermaster General Theophil von Podbielski and the Saxon War Minister General Georg von Fabrice. The convention arrived at between them in September 1866, which met most of the terms demanded by Fabrice, profoundly upset William when it was leaked in the press, and he absolutely refused to accept it. By January 1867 Bismarck was obliged himself to take a close interest in the negotiations, since he was anxious that a deal be struck as soon as possible in order to smooth the way towards the establishment of the North German Confederation. The brief given to Stosch, who was asked to take over the negotiations, was to ensure that Saxony should not be able to take up a privileged position. On the other hand, he was to allow Saxony to maintain an independent military administration, provided they bore the cost of it.[20] A number of other concessions were offered, which were thought to be generous enough to get a deal.

Bismarck was enraged to discover that this was not the case, Fabrice continuing to raise objections, and he hardened his heart. He did not, however, give Stosch fresh instructions, who proceeded to negotiate a settlement of the dispute which he believed was within the sprit, if not the letter of his instructions. When summoned by Bismarck to explain himself, Stosch was given a vey hard time; he recorded that Bismarck:

went over my work with me like a schoolmaster does with the opus of a stupid and refractory pupil. There was not one good thing in it. From the inaccessible heights of his superiority, he overwhelmed me with the full abundance of his anger and the pointed arrows of his scorn. He demonstrated that I had seriously wronged King and Fatherland, Emperor and future Empire. Every objection was cut off short. I could do nothing but remain silent and leave.[21]

Bismarck now took over the negotiations himself, and succeeded in achieving a result with which he was satisfied, before leaving it to Stosch to conclude the final settlement. Even then, the Saxon Army Corps entered the army of the North German Confederation without being bound by the military terms of the constitution, which applied to all the other member states.

For Stosch, the matter did not end there, since as Director of the Military Economic Department of the War Ministry it was his responsibility to produce the Confederation's military budget. In doing so he sought to limit the independence of the Saxon War Ministry to budget separately, which produced a furious dispute. In this, Stosch had the support of Roon and Podbielski, the acting War Minister in Roon's absence on leave. But the constant need to balance the interests of all parties in his progress towards unifying the members of the Confederation meant that Bismarck would do all he could to avoid a confrontation, as the Saxons well knew, and in further lengthy discussions tried to take advantage of this. Stosch was now perceived as being extremely anti-Saxon and was especially unfavourably perceived by the Saxon Military Plenipotentiary in Berlin, Colonel von Brandenstein, who thought him 'completely incalculable in his perfidious insolence.'[22] In the end the Saxons did go over Stosch's head to appeal directly to Bismarck; and after further protracted discussions largely got their way.

Stosch had conducted the negotiations with great force and skill, and demonstrated his considerable abilities, even though he took such an inflexible line in trying to break down Saxon military independence that in the end Bismarck was obliged, with his view of the bigger picture, to overrule him. In spite of the end result, he appears greatly to have enjoyed an experience which he felt broadened the scope of his ambition.[23] He was already beginning to consider what his position might be if war broke out with France. He did not want to go back to the situation of being No.2 to Blumenthal, and hankered after the appointment of Chief of Staff for himself. The alternative, which he wished to avoid, was the post of Intendant-General; when the suggestion was made he originally recoiled in horror, because he wished to serve in the field. Stosch remained deeply interested in politics, although in order not to prejudice his military career he avoided any public involvement. He shared the widely held view that a French war was more or less inevitable, writing to his friend Freytag in November 1867: 'Napoleon has become the slave of his bigoted wife and speeds toward the abyss. Since the beginning I have expected a great crisis, and cannot believe that I delude myself. For this reason I work like a horse in order to prepare the Army, improving it by all the experiences of the last war.'[24] In spite of his personal brushes with Bismarck, he retained a considerable admiration for him, It was not, however, uncritical; Stosch looked at him with detachment, noting in August 1867:

> The more Bismarck increases [in power], the more uncomfortable persons who think as individuals and act independently become to him; the more nervous he becomes, the more he fears sharp personal conflicts. I know from my own experience that there are days of spiritual overexertion when I can indeed give orders, but when business with able, independent officials is more burdensome.[25]

Later, he described Bismarck as

> vigorous and bold in thought and clear in what he wants; he will never set a goal beyond his reach. He will ruthlessly destroy men and situations that stand in his way ... Bismarck only uses liberalism and the Constitution in order to lead and sway the King and the Conservatives, but never as an assured element of power. Bismarck wants a united monarchical Germany.[26]

Stosch remained in close touch with the Crown Prince, accompanying him during a state visit to Italy in May 1868 and to the opening of the Suez Canal in the following year. In Italy he encountered Theodor von Bernhardi, the Prussian military attaché who very much disapproved of what he supposed to be his politics. Bernhardi wrote in his diary when he learned of his coming: 'General von Stosch! The future war minister of a Progressive Party ministry. That does not please me at all.'[27] For his part, Stosch took a poor view not only of Bernhardi, but also von Usedom, the Prussian Minister, who was hostile to General La Marmora; and he prevailed on the Crown Prince to write a report to the King which proposed the recall of the whole of the legation. As a result Bismarck sacked Usedom, which no doubt pleased Stosch, but which the Crown Prince later regretted. Bernhardi himself was a man of unlimited self-esteem and remarkably poor judgment. Stosch, when in later life commenting on a book which Bernhardi had published, wrote to Freytag:

> Bernhardi's new volume has stimulated and entertained me in many ways. The book has the advantage that one can read it for five minutes and can put it aside again. One meets with a throng of people who are more or less slandered. Wise alone ... is Bernhardi. People who have done nothing in life like Etzel, Gewin etc are praised; a man like Moltke is represented as limited.[28]

Stosch was by now able to exercise a good deal of influence over the Crown Prince, and recorded in his diary that the Crown Prince kept telling him that he was the only person who really instructed him. Stosch was, for instance, active in trying to persuade the Crown Prince to support Bismarck, writing to him in February 1869 about a dispute in the Prussian State Ministry:

Since it is of the greatest importance for our progress that Count Bismarck remains the victor in this battle, I would like to ask Your Royal Highness to support him vigorously, and by no means to take steps against him because of his 'tactlessness' in Your Royal Highness's house, about which Your Royal Highness writes so ill-humouredly. Count Bismarck is the only one who helps us forward.[29]

In such matters Stosch had, of course, to contend with the Crown Princess, who was almost invariably very much opposed to Bismarck, and advised her husband accordingly. For Stosch, the main thing was Bismarck's progress towards German unity, which he believed would ultimately require liberal support; but he was optimistic about the outcome, writing to Freytag in April 1870: 'When I compare our situation with that in Austria or France, I cannot stop thinking that we are called to be a Great Power! The House of Hohenzollern is the representative of godly order in Europe, and we must hope that our young Prince has the pride and the will for such a position.'[30] Stosch's political activity, albeit indirect and at one remove, shows him to be an unswerving supporter of the movement to national unity, and certainly was excellent preparation for a future political career. For the present, though, it was his military responsibility that was uppermost in his mind; it was almost time for his military skills to be tested to the limit.

10

The Loire

During his time at the War Ministry in the inter war years Stosch was of course not reporting directly to Moltke. Although the question of high level military appointments in the event of war was one for the Military Cabinet, the proposed appointment of Stosch as Intendant-General was so important that the Chief of the General Staff must necessarily be consulted, and there can be no doubt that Moltke, who had formed the highest regard for Stosch's abilities in 1866, wanted him in that post. Logistics would play a vital part in Moltke's strategy for the conquest of France, and it was essential that the responsibilities of the Intendant-General should be in hands that he could rely on. Moltke shared with the King and the Crown Prince a conviction that Stosch could be depended on to discharge these responsibilities with firmness and tact. Professor Hollyday is surely right to discount the suggestion that Stosch was a tactless individual. Indeed, the patient and thoughtful way in which he had carried out Moltke's original injunction 'to realise Blumenthal's gifted ideas' in 1866 is sufficient evidence in itself to demonstrate that when required Stosch was able to act in the most diplomatic way. Patience and determination were certainly to be required of him in the Franco Prussian war.

As was the case with practically all the senior players in Berlin, the crisis in July 1870 came as a complete surprise to Stosch. On July 15 he was recalled from leave, to learn what was to be his assignment in the war that was about to break out. Although the Crown Prince had strenuously argued for Stosch as his Chief of Staff, Moltke would have none of it, telling the Crown Prince that Stosch was regarded as 'absolutely indispensable' in the post of Intendant-General.[1] Roon was of the same opinion, observing that Stosch 'was the only General who could direct the provisioning of the Army in war.'[2] For Stosch, in spite of the compliment paid him, it was a huge disappointment, since he had aspired above all to be a commander in the field. He was obliged to find comfort in the sheer scale of the task set him. He later wrote: 'My consolation lay in the great labour and immense responsibility of my task.'[3] As the Official History of the war observed:

The successful feeding of such considerable bodies of troops as were collected on the French frontier at the end of July was beset with great difficulties owing to the short time permitted for preparation. Yet the German War Minister and the Intendant-General of the army, Lieutenant General von Stosch, overcame them successfully.[4]

The mobilisation of the forces of the North German Confederation began on July 16, followed over the next three days by Bavaria, Württemberg and Baden. The plans for the mobilisation and deployment of the German armies had been perfected long in advance. Moltke, in his own history of the war, summarised the position:

The orders for marching, and travelling by rail or boat, were worked out for each division of the army, together with the most minute directions as to their different starting points, the day and hour of departure, the duration of the journey, the refreshment stations and place of destination. At the meeting-point cantonments were assigned to each corps and division, stores and magazines were established; and thus, when war was declared, it needed only the royal signature to set the entire apparatus in motion with undisturbed precision.[5]

That the plans would work smoothly, Moltke had no doubt, and there is no reason to doubt the story that, once the mobilisation was well under way, he was found unconcernedly sitting on a sofa reading a novel.

No such leisure was available to Stosch, for whom the enormous tasks of his department began at once. The mobilisation of the German armies, which brought about half a million men into the field by the beginning of August, naturally demanded the maximum exploitation of the railway lines running to the French frontier; during that first fortnight, therefore, the *Intendantur* could not use any of the railways for bringing up supplies, while as the troops moved up to the frontier the roads were crowded with the marching columns. Some lessons were there to be learned from the war of 1866; only a week after Königgrätz Moltke was writing to his army commanders to draw their attention to the reasons why the supply of the troops had on occasion gone so badly wrong. It was due, he said, to a number of irregularities, including confusion of convoys and the resulting obstruction of roads, the failure of the military police to maintain order, the use of unsuitable vehicles, a lack of leadership causing congestion especially in defiles, and a general irresponsibility towards the blocking of roads.[6] These difficulties had led to very severe problems in feeding the troops, problems which were compounded by the fact that the Prussians were unable to make any effective use of the Austrian railways as they advanced deeper into the country.[7]

It has been generally accepted that the supplying of the German armies in 1870-1871 was very successful. Certainly Moltke thought so, contending that they were the best provisioned in the history of great wars and that 'provisioning difficulties were overcome without endangering the health of man or beast.' Anton von Werner, the historical painter who accompanied the German armies, observed that the French frequently remarked of German soldiers: 'Ils sont tous d'une santé insultante,' which he attributed principally to Stosch. Stosch began the war by putting in place a plan of centralised procurement, taking provisioning from corps commissaries and putting it in the hands of those on the lines of supply, the *etappenintendanten*. His biographer recorded Stosch's brisk and direct approach:

> Stosch cut through much red tape by avoiding the clogged channels of regular military communication. Instead of sending orders to the commissaries of each corps and army, he found that he got speedier results by communicating directly with the army corps commanders, who trusted him. He was able to overcome the difficulties of royal interference, blocked railways, opposition of subordinates, rapidly changing lines of supply, the provisioning not only of mass armies, but of prisoners of war and the French civilian population as well, and the cattle plague. [8]

Stosch also enjoyed the confidence of his colleagues on the General Staff, and especially that of the King, who after the war told an old friend that 'the provisioning of the army exceeded anything previously heard of.' This view has however been challenged by Martin van Creveld:

> While the Prussian army did, in 1870, have a supply service theoretically capable of catering to its needs, this service proved an utter failure in practice. Though marching performances were not terribly high – the pace of the advance seldom averaged more than ten miles a day for a fortnight at a time – the method of deployment had thrown the train apparatus out of gear even before the campaign started.[9]

Van Creveld goes on to observe that but for the fact that the Prussians were operating in a country rich in agricultural produce, and except for the units investing Paris were widely scattered, the resulting need to live off the country might have led to disaster. On the other hand, it must be said that the marching performances referred to were in fact quite high; the difficulty of the supply columns, following the long lines of combat troops, in keeping up was not at all surprising. Certainly it was the ability to live off the country that permitted the armies to keep moving. And van Creveld's comments that the railway system could not cope with a rapidly changing system is equally a statement of the blindingly obvious. The problems were, he noted, due to the railway traffic, the difficulty of keeping up the railheads with the speed of the advance, and the difficulties of bringing supplies from the railhead to the front. His final conclusion was unsurprising if something of an overstatement:

> It is the fact that Moltke's forces could only live as long as they kept moving, and experienced the greatest difficulty in staying in one place for more than a few

days at a time, that the supreme proof lies that the military instrument in his hands did not, after all, belong to the modern age.[10]

Actually, there is not a lot of evidence that the German forces were obliged to move solely to gather supplies. However, there is some truth in van Creveld's conclusion. Moltke and Stosch were operating in what was essentially a period of transition between the wars of Napoleon and the twentieth century, and their success in supplying their armies is not really appropriately judged against modern standards. They had to deal with operations on a gigantic sale, and the demands on the supply services were correspondingly huge. It was perfectly normal to utilise the resources of the country where possible, as an English nineteenth century historian noted:

> There is no question that all administrators recognise the necessity for appropriating everything that may be of use to an army in the theatre of war; this forms the foundation of the supply system of all continental armies. With all their very complete arrangements for reserve rations, provision columns and magazines, the Germans, in their regulations, rigidly enjoin their generals not to bring up any provisions from the rear as long as it is practicable to obtain them either by purchase or by forced requisitions. The Austrian regulations, likewise, only admit of a call being made on the reserves stored in the rear, when the local sources fail to furnish sufficient means.[11]

One aspect of the supply system in 1870-1871 that did not generally create any problem was the replenishment of ammunition. Van Creveld notes that the average expenditure of infantry ammunition over the five months' campaigning was fifty six cartridges for each infantryman, rather less than he carried on his back and only about a third of the stocks available. Similarly, the expenditure of artillery ammunition was surprisingly low, amounting to 199 rounds per gun for the whole of the war, a figure only about 30% greater than each corps carried in its munition columns.[12]

As the war against the Government of National Defence developed, Stosch was closely involved in the decision making processes at Versailles. One of the issues most causing concern there was the performance of the Detachment commanded by the Grand Duke of Mecklenburg-Schwerin. There was particular dissatisfaction with his Chief of Staff, Colonel von Krenski, who was blamed for not keeping his noble master in order. As early as November 14, Verdy was noting the anxiety in his diary:

> We can make nothing of the operations of the Grand Duke of Mecklenburg, it being not easy at this distance to judge of what is going on on the spot. One of us will probably have to go there. It is Bronsart's turn, and as he has now recovered from a slight indisposition, it is likely to be he.[13]

However, as days went by, the discussion of possible candidates focused on Podbielski and Stosch. After a meeting on November 25 when the issue was discussed

Stosch spoke to Verdy about it : 'I would be ready to assume this difficult post, and, if the conversation returns to it, you can mention me as a candidate.' Stosch, it is not difficult to assume, would have been more than ready at last to take his chance in the field. Next day Verdy told Moltke of Stosch's remark, and the Chief of the General Staff had no difficulty in agreeing that Stosch could go, albeit temporarily, to the Loire to sort things out.[14] First Roon, and then William were consulted, and readily gave their approval, and Stosch set off to the Loire that same day. Fritz Hönig, in his history of the Loire campaign, reviewed the decision:

> The naming of General von Stosch as Chief of Staff of the Detachment was a real event, for, without a doubt, the General was one of the most outstanding men of that great time and had the reputation of a distinguished officer of the General Staff. Assured in his bearing, he combined a high degree of commonsense with good judgement and a wide and inclusive point of view. The General, as a result of his high rank, could expect that more attention would be paid to his advice than that of Colonel von Krenski, and, moreover, he was in such close contact with Count von Moltke that professional relations between them were expected to be advantageous. He was completely informed of Moltke's ideas through his participation in the conversations which preceded the Chief of the General Staff's daily reports.[15]

Colonel Lonsdale Hale, in his account of the Loire campaign , said much the same:

> Von Stosch was an excellent soldier, a large-minded man, but in view of the situation he was a good deal more. Owing to his high position on the supreme staff of the German forces, and his close professional connection with von Moltke, the chief staff officer of those forces, he was, on the Loire, little less than von Moltke present by proxy.[16]

Stosch. heading for the Detachment's headquarters at Châteaudun, encountered the 4th Cavalry Division and the 22nd Division at Bonneval, and found at once that the morale of the Detachment was extremely low, due not only to the physical discomforts that the men had endured, but also to the fact that for days 'there had been only a perpetual irritating skirmishing with guerrilla bands,' rather than one big battle. He went on to Châteaudun to meet his new commander:

> The Duke received Stosch with a somewhat distant manner; the change of a Chief Staff officer without consultation with him was a departure from rule, and he might fairly suspect that Stosch had been sent to keep a watch on him. But soon Stosch discovered that the discontent of the Grand Duke arose from the same cause as did the general depression, hard work with no result.[17]

Stosch was, of course, also very much concerned with the problem of getting the Second Army to move more aggressively. Frederick Charles appeared to recognise that more might have been done in a conversation he had with Alfred von Waldersee on November 30, when he observed that 'the favourable moment for the offensive is gone,' adding that he was now reduced to a waiting attitude. It was this negative frame of mind that Stosch sought to change, when he had a meeting with Stiehle, the Chief of Staff of the Second Army, on November 30 at Bazoches les Gallerandes. It had been at Stiehle's request that they met:

> The purpose of Stiehle in meeting Stosch was twofold: first to learn from Stosch the views held by Moltke as to the course of the campaign on the Loire, past, present and future: secondly, to justify the action of the Prince in the past and present, and his proposed action in the future.[18]

When they parted, however, the two men were no nearer agreement, since Stiehle was sticking to the view of the situation held by Frederick Charles. When he reported the outcome of the meeting to his commander, the latter wrote to the Grand Duke, who had been placed under his orders on November 25, setting out his view of the situation and reiterating his intention to stand on the defensive, adding a paragraph intended to keep Stosch in his place: 'Until the situation on the enemy's side is clearer, I must reserve to myself the communication to your Royal Highness of my further plans for driving the enemy out of Orleans.'[19]

Frederick Charles had entirely miscalculated the strength of the enemy forces facing the Detachment, suggesting that only the 17th Corps and a part of the 16th Corps was in its front, and in consequence assigning the 22nd Division to relieve a brigade of the X Corps at Pithiviers. Actually, however, the Detachment was to be confronted by the 16th Corps, two divisions of the 15th Corps, and two and-a-half divisions of the 17th Corps. On December 1 the advanced guard of von der Tann's 1 Bavarian Corps was driven out of Villepion, falling back on Orgéres, as the Army of the Loire embarked on a further advance intended to lead to the relief of Paris. This was the force that Stosch, though greatly outnumbered, resolved to attack on December 2. To do so, he first had to persuade the Grand Duke to agree and then to obtain approval of his intention from Frederick Charles. This arrived at midnight on December 1/2; by then Stosch knew the full situation following the Bavarian retreat from Villepion, and he took the bold step of defying the instruction to give up the 22nd Division, resolving to employ it for his battle on the following day.

In spite of the great disparity of force, Stosch conducted the battle on December 2 with great aplomb. There were in effect two separate battles, around Loigny and around Poupry to the east. When the French began their advance, Stosch had only von der Tann's 1 Bavarian Corps in line, which he positioned to the north east of Loigny. He knew that it would not be before 11.00 am that the 17th (Tresckow) and 22nd (Wittich) Divisions would be able to come up in support. Strong French columns moved forward on the Bavarian position, of which the key point was Château Goury. It was upon this walled farm that the French concentrated their assault at about 1.00 pm. For a while it was touch and go; but soon the leading troops of Tesckow's division came up to relieve the pressure on Château Goury before swinging to the right to capture Loigny. Gradually the German line advanced; an abortive attempt by de Sonis's 17th Corps failed to relieve Chanzy, and the French were driven back to Villepion, a position which they abandoned during the night.[20]

Although he had thus disposed of two of Chanzy's corps, Stosch still had serious problems to face, as two divisions of the 15th Corps began a threatening advance in the direction of Poupry. The responsibility for resisting this fell upon Wittich's 22nd Division, which Stosch was in the process of ordering to take part in the attack on Loigny. Recognising the danger, Wittich swung his division to its left, facing eastwards; it was obliged to fight with its back, effectively, to the remainder of the 2nd Army of the Loire. And it, too, was heavily outnumbered. Nonetheless, after a fierce struggle in the woods east of Poupry, the French advance was first held, and then thrown back, as darkness fell. There had been heavy casualties on both sides, the German losing a total of 4,144 men; the French losses exceeded 6,500. Nonetheless, it had been a remarkable victory.

At Versailles Moltke was having a difficult time soothing the King, who was extremely jumpy as a result of a report that there were 20,000 French troops in Montargis; it was necessary to send Verdy to him to calm him down. The King was agitated about the order Moltke intended to send, and did send at 1.10 pm, to Frederick Charles to the effect that it was 'absolutely necessary that the Second Army moves without delay directly on Orleans for a decisive attack.'[21] Moltke had evidently abandoned all hope of seeing Frederick Charles pursue the correct strategic objective, which was the destruction of Chanzy's army and not the capture of Orleans. This was a pity, because the Detachment's success on December 2 gave Stosch the opportunity to strike first southwest, and then south. This was his intention, and in reporting to Frederick Charles that the enemy had been driven back on Terminiers and Artenay, he added that 'if the enemy is to be pursued tomorrow, it is absolutely necessary that the Second Army should attack Artenay and cover the Orleans-Paris road.'[22]

This suggestion made no impression on Frederick Charles; complying strictly with Moltke's order of 1.10 pm he and Stiehle issued orders for an advance next day for a concentric advance next day on Orleans, ignoring the fact that the success of the Detachment, of which Moltke of course was unaware, had entirely changed the situation. This was in spite of Waldersee's confirmation to him that it had been 'a brilliant victory.' Stiehle wrote to Moltke that night to update him as to the Second Army's intention to endeavour to reach Orleans by the direct road. This, Colonel Hale regards as a 'great blunder' that might needlessly prolong the war.[23]

Frederick Charles and Stiehle had little reliable intelligence as to the dispositions of the French, except the information given by Stosch, which was more or less accurate. For December 3 the key role was to be played by Alvensleben's III Corps, which was to plunge into the Forest of Orleans, while Manstein's IX Corps moved directly down the Orleans-Paris high road. Behind these came the X Corps of Voigts-Rhetz, designated as the reserve. All made progress, although Frederick Charles, determined to press on as fast as possible, issued orders at 2.45 pm calling for a night attack if necessary. This was to apply also to the Detachment; the 17th and 22nd Divisions, leading its advance, were to take Château Chevilly before pausing. Behind them, von der Tann had the task of following the 17th Division with his 2nd Division, while the rest of his corps moved on Sougy, which he took without difficulty. The 17th Division reached Chameul with little resistance, at which point Tresckow heard of the order for a night attack, Wittich, also aware of this order, had the 22nd Division either side of the Chevilly road.

Stosch was appalled by the order for a night attack on a fortified position, which he thought much too risky, and set off to see Frederick Charles about it. He caught up with him at about 5 pm at Creuzy, three miles from Chevilly, and reported to him that the Detachment faced strong hostile forces. Frederick Charles was unimpressed, saying to Stosch:

> Many prisoners of many regiments of the 3rd Divisions of the 15th Corps have been captured at Artenay; the Grand Duke has made a mistake, this division cannot be opposite him; he has nothing much opposed to him, and he has been allowed himself to be drawn away from the real point for attack.[24]

As for the 'strong hostile forces,' Frederick Charles dismissed them as merely franc-tireurs and Gardes Mobiles; it was in fact Barry's division of the 16th Corps. However, on Stosch's urging, the commander of the Second Army was at least prepared to listen to advice, and countermanded the order for a night attack, telling Stosch that the Detachment should remain for the night in its present position. Hale described the conclusion of the meeting:

> Stosch was already riding away when the Prince repeated the words 'But tomorrow we must be in Orleans'; Stosch replied, 'It will not be our fault if we are not.'[25]

Wittich and Tresckow were not at all impressed with the suggestion that their divisions spend the night where they were; Wittich observed:

> There was nothing for my men but the bare plain covered with wet snow, a bivouac without straw, wood, water or food. My troops had been fighting during the whole of December 2; the leading troops had arrived at 10 pm that night, the last at one in the morning, in the icy bivouac at Anneau, where they had little to eat.[26]

Finding that the village and Château of Chevilly had been abandoned by the French, the two infantry divisions spent the night under shelter there.

For the following day the Detachment was ordered to cooperate with the IX Corps in attacking the French position at Gidy. The X Corps remained in reserve, while the III Corps pushed on through the forest. At 9.00 am Frederick Charles paid a 'short, stiff and frigid' call upon the Grand Duke, discounting the latter's suggestion that the French were retreating over the Loire, but repeating that Orleans must be occupied that day. Accordingly, the Detachment pushed on down the road on the right of the IX Corps; as it advanced, it found the enemy resistance crumbling. A squadron of the 4th Hussars from Stolberg's 2nd Cavalry Division captured an entire battery of 9 guns, with wagons, men and horses; then three more squadrons charged three French squadrons on the Châteaudun road, routing them completely.[27]

The position at Gidy, abandoned by the French, was occupied by 11.00 am. The advance guard of the 17th Division under Colonel von Manteuffel reached the entrance gate to Orleans at 6.00 pm. Its defenders refused to open the gate, so Manteuffel reported back to Tresckow and then had a meeting with the Grand Duke. After prolonged negotiations conducted by Tresckow with a French staff officer, it was agreed that the French would give up the city; and at 1.00 am the Grand Duke, leading the 17th Division and a Bavarian brigade, their bands playing, marched into the city. When the news reached Frederick Charles at 3.00 am, he was far from pleased that his intention to make personally a triumphant entry to the city had been thwarted.

As usual, Moltke responded to the news of the victory with a telegram calling for the beaten enemy to be vigorously pursued. Frederick Charles assigned this task to the Detachment; when Stosch pointed out how exhausted were his troops, all he could obtain was a rest day on December 5. That day the cavalry riding on ahead encountered the advanced posts of the newly created Second Army of the Loire, commanded by the energetic Chanzy. On December 7 the Detachment advanced westward, with the 17th Division on the river road to Meung and the 1st Bavarian Division towards La Bourie. Further north, the 22nd Division reached Ouzouer. As night fell, the Detachment occupied a front of 14 miles, all along which there had been contacts with the enemy; Stosch, next day, would have to fight a major battle with only 27,000 infantry against heavy numerical odds. That night Stosch sent a full report of the fighting on December 8 to Moltke, both by letter and telegram, and the latter responded at once, sending a telegram which reached the Second Army headquarters at 10.00 am on December 9, requiring that the Detachment should be supported by at least one division on the right bank of the Loire, together with further activity on the left bank.[28]

His first step was to shorten his line, bringing the 22nd Division south; this left his front as no more than seven miles. During December 8, in spite of a briefly successful advance early in the day, the French were beaten all along the line. Chanzy, however, was made of sterner stuff than some of his colleagues, and prepared to stand and fight on December 9. This he did to no little effect, launching a series of heavy attacks that were only beaten off with great difficulty. He was still fighting on December 10, enjoying an early success with the recapture of Origny. Bringing back the 1st Bavarian Corps into line, which had been promised a rest day, and using his artillery to break up the French attacks, Stosch succeeded in holding his position. By night fall the Second Army of the Loire had shot its bolt, and Chanzy had no choice but to retreat to Vendôme.

The Bavarian official historian gave high praise to the efforts of the French, and in particular of Chanzy:

> Although the French had the advantage of superior numbers and a better firearm, it cannot be denied that at some points they fought with remarkable bravery and great devotion. It must at any rate be allowed that the tenacity and endurance with which the enemy's troops made their stand for four days, is a proof of the conspicuous energy and inspiriting activity of their leader, General Chanzy.[29]

Stosch, who had won a remarkable victory at odds of four to one, was recognised at Versailles as having done a brilliant job. On December 12 William sent him the Iron Cross First Class. He returned to the Royal Headquarters on December 19, where Moltke told him: 'We have felt your energetic hand.'[30] The undemonstrative Chief of the General Staff was profoundly impressed by Stosch's report of the battle of Beaugency: 'Victory after victory: our brave troops have only to be led to the right spot and then you can sleep in peace. You can't help taking off your hat even to the very drivers of the transport.'[31] The King told Stosch that he had fulfilled all his expectations and had done exactly what he wished.

In discharging his functions as the Grand Duke's Chief of Staff he was obliged to handle his Royal master with considerable tact, as not all his military colleagues had a high regard for the Grand Duke's ability. On one notable occasion Prince Albrecht senior, the commander of a cavalry division who as the brother of the King, did not regard himself as bound by questions of military rank, came into the room where the Grand Duke and Stosch were discussing the day's operations. He breezily asked: 'Well then, Stosch, what shall I do today?' This did not go down well with the Grand Duke, who snapped: 'I command here.' This cut no ice with the Prince: 'We all know what the score is, so need not inconvenience ourselves; so, Stosch, what shall I do?'[32]

The striking success of Stosch's brief assignment on the Loire, which was so readily appreciated by his immediate colleagues, was not widely appreciated by popular opinion. Nonetheless, informed commentators, such as Fritz Hönig, realised the extent of his achievement at Beaugency. He regarded this as due to Stosch's 'strong will and iron firmness. Up to this point he had only proved himself to be an excellent chief of staff; from then on he showed himself a hero in his bearing, thoughts and actions.' When he came to write Stosch's obituary, Hönig described his performance at Beaugency as 'perhaps the greatest performance with insufficient resources in the entire history of modern warfare.'[33]

Back at Versailles, Stosch was inevitably drawn into the disputes over the bombardment of Paris. He took a middle position between those who supported Bismarck's call for an immediate bombardment and those who, like Moltke, were complete opposed. He certainly favoured a direct attack on the city, but did not favour a bombardment. He went about his duties as Intendant-General, on the whole keeping out of the controversy; personally, he hoped to be sent to the field again.[34]

It was he who persuaded the Crown Prince to attempt mediation between Bismarck and Moltke, writing to him on January 14 1871 to set out the present position of the dispute which during a meeting between the two men had 'ended with an explosion of suppressed rancour on both sides.'[35] It was a demonstration of Stosch's willingness to get involved in what were essentially questions of personality and politics; he had a huge respect for both of the antagonists, remarking: 'For me, Moltke and Bismarck alone remain above reproach in their specific greatness.'

During the peace negotiations with the French, Stosch served as a general adviser on military issues to Bismarck, and later conducted a series of direct negotiations himself on detailed logistical questions. On one occasion, disregarding Bismarck's instructions, he concluded a convention with Jules Favre as to the rations to be provided by the French for the Army of Occupation. Since William signed the ensuing decree, there was not much Bismarck could do about it, but the incident appears thereafter to have rankled.

After accompanying the Emperor home to Berlin, Stosch was appointed temporary Chief of Staff to Manteuffel, the commander of the Army of Occupation. In this capacity he was an interested observer of the feud between Manteuffel and Bismarck, which threatened to escalate. Those close to Stosch feared that his public reputation would be tarnished by his association with the unpopular Manteuffel, but he was sure that he had managed to keep clear of the dispute. When Manteuffel returned to Germany, he continued in France as acting Commander in Chief; when Manteuffel came back, Stosch returned to Berlin.

During this period there had been extensive negotiations between the Crown Prince and Bismarck as to the possibility of appointing Stosch to the position of Chief of the Imperial Admiralty. He had always been interested in the navy, and was keenly interested in the appointment, which was intended to carry 'as much independence as the Constitution allowed and Bismarck would permit.' On January 1 1872 he took over the duties of Chief of the Admiralty from Roon who had previously discharged them as part of his junctions as War Minister. One of his earliest decisions was to obtain the Emperor's approval to the redesignation of the Royal Prussian Navy as the Imperial German Navy. His biographer reviewed his outstanding qualifications for his new post:

> He had varied experience as a military administrator and demonstrated great resourcefulness and a considerable talent for improvisation. He showed himself eager to assume responsibilities and was frank in making his opinions known. With these characteristics, he combined an abundant reserve of energy and a great capacity for work.[37]

He quickly mastered the problems of his new office and proved an extremely successful naval minister, managing technical and political issues with equal dexterity. His term of office was however marred by an intensifying feud with Bismarck. This was not only due to sharp disagreements on policy issues, but also because Stosch was seen, particularly by the Chancellor, as a potential successor with dangerous liberal views and a close association with the Crown Prince. Stosch finally resigned on March 20 1883, in part as a result of another crisis prompted by Bismarck's constant determination to retain all his powers and to reduce those of anyone else who might oppose him. This particular crisis concerned the scope of the War Minister's authority; but it was not the only reason for Stosch's resignation, since after more than eleven years of constant struggle he felt he had had enough.

In retirement, he remained a close confidant of the Crown Prince, which was of course enough to ensure that Bismarck's resentment towards him would continue. And he was also seen by others as still a possible candidate as Bismarck's successor. He wrote on July 7 1884 to the Crown Prince commenting ironically on the effect of this belief:

> To be sure, I am a dangerous man, the candidate of the Left Liberals for the Chancellorship, as the Chancellor, according to the best informed sources, recently maintained, but I believe that Your Imperial Highness has known me to be a faithful man and knows that I am free from egotistical goals and party motives.[38]

In fact, Stosch was strongly opposed to the influence of the Left Liberals on the Crown Princess, and approved of Bismarck's attacks on them. His own influence over the Crown Prince continued to the latter's accession as Emperor Frederick III, and during his tragically brief reign. Had the Crown Prince come to the throne a decade earlier, Stosch would no doubt have had an important part to play in the government; as it was, Bismarck remained in power, and Stosch, although taking a keen and continuing interest in both politics and the Navy, remained an observer rather than a participant in the affairs of state. He was highly regarded in the Navy, and the Emperor William II warmly recognised his achievements. He died suddenly on February 29 1896, having, as his memoirs showed, found great happiness and contentment. He could look back on his military career with great satisfaction as one of Moltke's closest and ablest colleagues.

11

The Red Prince

Prince Frederick Charles Nicholas was born on March 20 1828 at Berlin, the only son of Prince Charles, a younger brother of King Frederick William IV and King William 1. From the outset he was destined for a military career; when, at the age of eighteen, he went to Bonn University, there was appointed as his military tutor Major Albrecht von Roon. He was an apt pupil, entering the army in 1848, and was made captain of cavalry. Known as 'the Red Prince' from the colour of the Guard Hussar uniform which he preferred, he served on Wrangel's staff in Schleswig that year, and in the following year served on William's staff in the Baden campaign. He was seriously wounded at the battle of Wiesenthal. During his convalescence he began a thorough study of military history, and as he progressed through the army to the rank of Lieutenant General, he continued his researches. Though a Royal prince, and though he soon developed a somewhat overbearing personality and a touchy sense of his own importance, he was no fool, and took his profession extremely seriously.

He wrote a number of influential essays on the art of war, one of which was to lead him into some difficulty. Privately printed for colleagues and friends, these essays included one entitled 'A Military Memorial,' which addressed the differences between the French and the Prussian armies, and the ways in which the latter might be victorious if it came to war:

> What will be our fate in a war with France? We can conquer her, I shall answer; and we shall conquer her with a single blow, if we know how to detach ourselves, in time of war, from the routine of the drill ground, the demands of regulations, and from our system of skirmishers. Here is the difficulty, this is my only anxiety. The motive power which these forms give is insufficient to maintain discipline, to bring the soldiers up to the enemy, and to make them sustain their fire. Thank God, we have others, and we shall know how to bring them to our aid. Already several times we have succeeded in overturning the legions of the Emperor of the Gauls, and what we have done, with the help of God, we can do again.[1]

This essay was published, entirely without his authority, in Frankfurt in 1860, and caused a considerable stir in France. Frederick Charles was seriously annoyed by this unauthorised publication, not least by the addition of a preface which was entirely at odds with his opinions; and he was rash enough to bring an action against the publisher which, to his intense chagrin, was unsuccessful.

As the extract from the essay quoted above suggests, Frederick Charles was not altogether convinced that the greatly increased firepower provided by the needle gun would be as decisive as had been claimed. In this he revealed the decidedly conservative aspect of his thinking. It was a characteristic which he displayed throughout his military career, in which his innate caution frequently got the better of his offensive instincts.

Another essay by Frederick Charles, in which he revealed a good deal of himself, written in January 1860, was entitled 'The Origins and Development of the spirit of the Prussian Officer its Manifestations and its effect.' In this essay he reached the conclusion 'that in the Prussian Corps of officers nowadays there is a stronger desire for independence from above and for taking responsibility upon one's self than in any other army,' and that 'this habit of thought has undeniably had an influence on our battle tactics.' He quoted as an example: 'One day when a staff officer was duly carrying out an order he had received, a high ranking general rebuked him, saying 'Sir, the King made you a staff officer so that you should learn when <u>not</u> to obey.' Ironically, one historian of the German Army has put the general's words into Frederick Charles' own mouth, suggesting that Moltke quoted them with approval.[2]

The essay is especially notable, however, for the very personal account which its author gives of the expectation that an officer slighted by the Commander in Chief (i.e. the King) should resign rather than have the finger of scorn pointed at him. Although his reference is to the King, it is immediately plain that it is the Military Cabinet that was in Frederick Charles's mind:

> I have been in that position myself, and I did what the Army expected of me. At first it was badly received and permission refused. I then had to find out for myself that an injury can grow and grow, so that everything seems to inflame it even further. I no longer felt I was standing on the same solid ground as the rest of the officers. In the end I got my way, and went on twelve months' leave. Everyone else, quite understandably, took this to mean the end of my service and so did I. Things are not the same for a Royal Prince as they are for other people; and that is just as true of my retirement, my atonement, as of my reinstatement. Over this affair I was deeply hurt by Major General von Manteuffel, just as all other officers in the Army have been. But I do not intend to go into that matter here, and although it really is the right place for describing the harm he has done to the army, I shall choose some other occasion.

In fact later in this essay, Frederick Charles went on to take a further swipe at Manteuffel, complaining that 'boot licking is not punished, but rewarded by success,

Prince Frederick Charles.

telling tales commands a hearing like the secret police;' both these he described as 'particularly acceptable' to the Chief of the Military Cabinet. Outspoken comments of this kind are not often found from the pen of a cautious member of the Royal family; rather more to be expected was the list of qualities which Frederick Charles looked for in the Prussian officer:

> Affection, aptitude and zeal for the chosen profession, a sense of the importance and status of an officer, a mind receptive to the spirit that has always marked the Prussian Corps of Officers and which should continue to do so in the future.[3]

Moltke's close contacts with the Prussian Royal family meant that he was well acquainted with Frederick Charles socially as well as professionally. During the staff ride of 1854 Moltke served as chief of the staff under Reyher, the Chief of the General Staff, and worked closely with the two royal princes who took part:

> Princes Frederick William and Frederick Charles accompany it this year. I have seen some excellent work with the latter, who has a real passion for the business, and told Reyher that, although he is a general, he will be glad to place himself

under my command. I am to lead the expedition. Reyher will criticise the affair as a whole.[4]

Moltke, who greatly enjoyed working on the staff ride, found it illuminating as to his colleagues' ability, particularly in respect of Frederick Charles:

> [He] has an absolute passion for the business, which is very creditable to his powers of insight. He does his work very well. I believe he is the man who will some day restore the ancient glory of the Prussian arms. He is a very good comrade to the officers of the General Staff, though in general not liked by other officers, whom he repels by his strict morality and somewhat rough manner. Prince Frederick William is a truly lovable man.[5]

Frederick Charles reciprocated Moltke's good opinion of him, and always enjoyed a good personal relationship with him. In 1860, by which time Moltke was Chief of the General Staff, he met the prince on the road, as he reported to Mary: 'He jumped immediately from his carriage, and we chatted there on the road for more than a quarter of an hour together. He would much have preferred coming on directly with us.'[6] Politically, Frederick Charles was among the more hawkish of the Prussian military. During the struggle with the Landtag, he was in favour of purging the ministry of its less reliable members and putting a soldier, preferably Roon, at its head.[7]

As relations with Denmark began seriously to deteriorate, Moltke sent a copy of his projected plan of operations in December 1862 to Frederick Charles for comment. The prince's reaction on February 5 1863 was favourable; Moltke's ideas were, he wrote, in accordance with his own thoughts and what he knew of the situation; the only proper objective if war broke out must be the Danish army. He went on, however, in his lengthy memorandum, to review in detail the way in which the invading army must deal with the Dannewerk. If he was to command the expedition, he added in a postscript, he would want to be sure of keeping the III Corps under his hand.[8]

As 1863 drew towards its close, the plans for an Austro Prussian advance into Jutland were firmed up. Overall command was to go not to Frederick Charles, but to the aged Wrangel, in spite of the fact that the Austrians had indicated a willingness to put its army corps under the command of Frederick Charles.[9] The latter would command the I Prussian Corps. The selection of Wrangel was made with his experience in the Schleswig Campaign of 1848 in mind. The Field Marshal was, however, already eighty years old, of uncertain temper and judgment, and these shortcomings were compounded by the appointment of the wilful and unreliable General Ernst Vogel von Falckenstein as his Chief of Staff. Frederick Charles, on the other hand, would have the benefit of Blumenthal as his Chief of Staff, an arrangement which provided Moltke with what was, for a long time, his only reliable source of information as to events in Jutland.

Moltke's plan for the campaign was based on his proposals of December 1862. However, when it was considered at a meeting called by the King on January 20, it ran into immediate opposition from Bismarck, who was appalled at the suggestion that the whole of Jutland should be occupied; only after Bismarck threatened to resign was this omitted from the instructions to Wrangel. These, unfortunately, gave the latter too much freedom of interpretation; although Moltke was clear that the Dannewerk should be turned from its left, when Wrangel met with his senior commanders he insisted on a frontal assault by the I Corps on the Missunde position. Frederick Charles and Blumenthal tried their best to talk him out of this, but Wrangel would brook no argument, and the attack went ahead, with the predicted lack of success. It was, however, enough to alert de Meza, the Danish Commander in Chief, to the danger of being trapped in the Dannewerk, and he ordered an immediate retreat. Blumenthal wrote indignantly to Moltke to protest about the way in which the Danes were allowed to make their escape:

> There are but few men, indeed, who can execute a simple plan in a simple way. The Danish Army does us the kindness of so placing itself that by making a detour we can bring it into the greatest possible embarrassment; instead of this, we run so violently at their strongest position and produce such terror there, that an early opportunity is taken by them to sound a retreat. The Danes on February 4 were wiser than we; we made our detour two days too late.[10]

Neither Moltke nor Wrangel had given up the idea that Jutland would have to be overrun, but the suggestion was still extremely sensitive in political terms. On February 11 the King ordered Moltke to visit the front to form a view as to the future course of the campaign. While there, he visited Frederick Charles at his headquarters at Gravenstein six miles behind the Düppel lines; he noted that an assault there would not be possible for several weeks. Moltke's dislike of this operation meant that he enthusiastically received Blumenthal's plan for a landing on Alsen, both when the latter first mooted it, and later when Frederick Charles formally proposed the scheme. Unluckily the weather intervened; planned for the night of April 2/3, the crossing had to be abandoned.

Frederick Charles had been fiercely opposed to the proposed assault on Düppel, and did all he could to promote alternatives to what he regarded as an expensive and unnecessary operation. To the King he wrote: 'Is it supposed to be a military necessity to take the bulwarks? It will cost a lot of men and money. I don't see the necessity.'[11] The ferocity of his objections attracted the attention of Manteuffel, who wrote to him on March 10, with undisguised relish, in an attempt to bring Frederick Charles to heel:

> If your Royal Highness goes on demanding more weapons, if you go on postponing the attack, then doubts will arise in people's minds concerning your Royal Highness's determination; and I should not desire, for the sake of the army and of the person of our royal highness and of the hope which I place in it, that an armistice should be concluded while our troops were still standing in front of

Düppel. This is a matter not of the importance of the position, whether it can be held without Alsen, whether Alsen should be captured, whether without Alsen's capture the taking of Düppel is not worthless – this is a matter of the renown of the Prussian army and the position of the King in the councils of Europe. The prize is worth streams of blood, and for its sake that blood will be spilled with joy by everyone from the highest officer down to the drummer boy.[12]

When the assault on Alsen had to be aborted, Frederick Charles reluctantly gave in, but emphasised that he was doing so only for political reasons.

The successful attack on the Düppel position brought forth a surge of patriotic opinion in Prussia, and immensely strengthened Bismarck's hand in his political management of the situation. Euphoric, the King telegraphed to Frederick Charles: 'Next to the Lord of Hosts, I thank my noble army and your leadership for this day's glorious victory. Express my highest acknowledgements to the troops and my thanks for their exertions.'[13] He followed this up with a personal visit to the troops; Moltke was decidedly put out that he was not asked to accompany William on this occasion.

His frustration at being so out of touch was now, however, to come to an end. Manteuffel, who had been dismayed at the disorganisation of Wrangel's headquarters, knew what to do about it. Falckenstein was removed as Chief of Staff, and assigned to command the III Corps operating in northern Jutland, and Moltke took his place, arriving on May 2. A further change in the command structure was made on May 18, when Frederick Charles was appointed Commander in Chief of the Allied forces in succession to Wrangel, Lieutenant General Herwarth von Bittenfeld taking over the I Corps.

Moltke and Frederick Charles worked closely with Blumenthal in the planning of the descent on Alsen, which was to take place after the armistice came to an end. The assault took place on the night of June 28/29; characteristically relaxed, Moltke played whist until 10.00 pm before proceeding to join Frederick Charles and key members of his staff to witness the successful crossing to Alsen. The island was soon overrun; it had in fact been a much more brilliant success than the storming of Düppel, and it shortly brought the Danish campaign to an end. Moltke later accompanied Frederick Charles when the latter went to Vienna formally to report the disbandment of the Allied army; he enjoyed the trip, and wrote to Mary a lively account of the extravagant celebrations which he attended there.[14]

12

Königgrätz

When the army commands were assigned at the start of the Austro Prussian War in 1866 there was no doubt that Frederick Charles would play a prominent role. His was to be the First Army, to consist of the four divisions of the III and IV Corps, intended to operate without their intervening corps headquarters, together with the Cavalry Corps of Prince Albrecht senior. In addition, provisionally, there would be the II Corps, commanded by Lieutenant General Stefan von Schmidt. For his Chief of Staff Frederick Charles would have the very able Lieutenant General Konstantin von Voigts-Rhetz; the Quarter Master General would be Major General Wolf von Stülpnagel. These two principal staff officers were in marked contrast to each other. Voigts-Rhetz had enjoyed a successful career, and had been head of the General War Department in the War Ministry in 1859. In that capacity he had become a great admirer of the new guns produced by Alfred Krupp, with whom he had a close friendship. He did not, however, get on well with Moltke, of whom he was professionally jealous. Stülpnagel, on the other hand, was one of Moltke's closest associates, and it was to him that he looked for reliable information. Stülpnagel had been Chief of Staff of the III Corps; since the divisions of this corps were to operate independently, he was assigned to the headquarters of the First Army.

It was to Stülpnagel that Moltke wrote on June 14 to respond to the letter Frederick Charles had sent to the King three days earlier, following the decision to attach the Guard Corps to the Second Army rather than the First Army. This followed the transfer of the I Corps, and led Frederick Charles to conclude that the centre of gravity of the operations would now be in Silesia. In the light of this, he suggested, should not the rest of the First Army be moved to link directly with the Second Army? He added, probably between clenched teeth, that it would be an honour to serve under the Crown Prince, even though the latter was younger. In fact, an order to the First Army to concentrate between Niesky and Hirschberg had already been issued. To Stülpnagel, Moltke wrote to comment on the sound sense of Frederick Charles's letter, but also to note that the apparent movement of a second Austrian corps into Bohemia would relieve the situation in front of the Crown Prince.[1]

On June 18 Moltke wrote again to Stülpnagel who had been asking for instructions as to the next move of the First Army. He was still somewhat in doubt about the intentions of the Austrians, which must determine the question:

> It is difficult at the moment to decide whether the First Army should support the Second Army directly, or the Second the First. That depends on whether the Austrians turn their main force toward Silesia or Lusatia … It is very easy to give orders for something that doesn't turn out right later on, and consequently we must wait for more light.[2]

The next day, however, Moltke was relieved to get intelligence reports that Benedek was moving into Northern Bohemia.

Once Saxony had been dealt with, the invasion of Bohemia could begin. Frederick Charles rode to the border with his leading troops, which were directed towards the Bohemian town of Reichenberg. With bands playing, the 7th and 8th Divisions crossed the border on the roads from Zittau, Seidenburg and Marklissa. Theodor Fontane recorded a description of the scene by an observer:

> A toll house with a black and yellow crossing barrier marked the border between Saxony and Bohemia. Here the Prince stopped. Uhlans, who formed the advance guard, crossed the border first; then came the infantry. Whenever the forward ranks of a battalion reached the barrier and saw the Austrian colours, they raised a joyful shout, which was taken up by the rear ranks and repeated over and over, until the troops reached the toll house and saw their 'soldier prince' standing by the border marker. At the sight of him the hurrahs turned to a jubilant roar, which stopped only when replaced by the sound of a war song which was taken up and repeated by every battalion as it crossed to Bohemian soil. The commander stood quietly on the highway, watching the passing regiments with silent pride. And well might he have felt this way, for never had an army crossed a foreign border that was better armed, better supplied, and inspired with a higher feeling than the one that crossed from Saxony to Bohemia.[3]

As Professor Craig noted, the comment on the army's supplies was wide of the mark; inadequate preparations had been made, and the further the army advanced the worse the situation became.

These supply difficulties soon began to slow up the advance of the First Army. This was not, however, the only reason why its progress was not as fast as Moltke would have liked. Frederick Charles was an intelligent, capable commander, but he was also extremely cautious. He was on record as saying, basing his words on Clausewitz: 'The best strategy is always to be really strong, first in general, and then at the decisive point. There is no loftier or simpler law in strategy than to hold one's strength together.'[4] Anxious not to walk into an Austrian trap, he did hold his troops together, with the result that the First Army reached Reichenberg on a very narrow front. Since

Frederick Charles had in addition Herwarth's Army of the Elbe under his command, he was also anxious not to push too far forward until he was in contact with it. The fact that the First Army's cavalry had been kept in the rear, apparently because the staff thought it could not be used effectively in the mountains, meant that it was not available to Frederick Charles for reconnaissance. As a result, he was in ignorance of the position of the Austrians, and he resolved to wait until he knew of the progress of the Army of the Elbe.

Frederick Charles sent a telegram on June 23 to Moltke expressing the fear that without the I Corps his army would not be strong enough, especially since the Army of the Elbe was not sufficiently advanced, to tackle the Austrian forces being concentrated in Bohemia. Moltke responded that same day to Stülpnagel, although his letter was delayed three days in transit to the First Army headquarters. First, he confirmed that the I Corps had been assigned to the Second Army. He went on to stress that the possibility of strengthening the left wing of the First Army had been a possibility considered in case the Austrians were already concentrated behind Reichenberg. This could now, however, be ruled out. The bulk of the Austrians were in the Second Army's front: 'only a vigorous advance by the First Army can disengage the Second.'

When this message reached Frederick Charles on June 26, he ordered a movement by Lieutenant General Friedrich von Horn's 8th Division towards Turnau on the Iser. This advance ran into the Austrian cavalry division of Baron von Edelsheim at Sichrow and encountered vigorous resistance; only when Lieutenant General Eduard von Fransecky's 7th Division came up did the Austrian cavalry fall back. Frederick Charles now ordered both divisions to push forward to the bridgeheads on the Iser. Fransecky's advance guard found Turnau abandoned, though the bridge over the Iser had been destroyed; his engineers at once set about building a pontoon bridge, and Fransecky consolidated his position. Horn, meanwhile, was advancing towards Podol. Later that day, in response to an order from Benedek, Prince Albert of Saxony, commanding the Saxon Corps and that of Clam Gallas, ordered that Turnau be retaken, and at 8.30 pm there was a fierce encounter at Podol which ended in the defeat of the Austrians.

Determined to follow up this victory, Frederick Charles was convinced that the Austrians would make a stand at Münchengrätz, in a position that would threaten his advance towards Gitschin. With characteristic thoroughness he spent the whole of June 27 preparing an elaborate attack on what he supposed to be the enemy's positions at Münchengrätz. Herwarth was to attack across the Iser, while the First Army would come down on the enemy flank and rear. Albert, however, had seen the impossibility of his position; long before Herwarth advanced at 9.00 am on June 28, his troops were well on their way to Gitschin. Rearguard actions held up the Prussian advance for a while, but by 1.00 pm the Iser had been crossed at all points. These engagements had cost the Prussians a total of 341 casualties; the Austrians and Saxons lost over 2,000. The success, such as it was, brought a further set of problems for Frederick Charles; he had 100,000 men concentrated in a very restricted area, and feeding the troops proved extremely difficult.

Moltke's anxiety about the First Army's slow progress was sharpened by his concerns about the exposure of the Second Army. At 6.35 am on June 29 he sent an emphatic telegram to Stülpnagel, pointing out that the Crown Prince, with three corps, had his back to the exits from the mountains, facing four enemy corps in his front and one on his flank:

> I believe it absolutely necessary that the First Army should disengage him: it has five corps available and has before it only the 1st and 3rd Austrian Corps with the Saxon Corps. The opportunity of making use of so great a superiority will perhaps not recur.[5]

Moltke added that he was not being kept sufficiently in the picture, and called for a response. An hour or so later a separate telegram, with a similar injunction, went direct to Frederick Charles.

Moltke, with the King and the Royal Headquarters, set off next day in six trains for the front. Just before leaving Berlin, news came in that the Second Army had now occupied the line of the Elbe, and en route to Reichenberg Moltke issued the following order:

> The Second Army will remain on the left bank of the upper Elbe, and will hold itself ready to unite its right wing, via Königinhof, with the left wing of the First Army as it advances. The First Army will advance without delay in the direction of Königgrätz. General Herwarth's mission is to attack the important enemy forces which would threaten the right flank of this movement and to cut off the bulk of the enemy.[6]

The target for the First Army was of course Gitschin, and it was towards this town that two of its divisions were moving on June 29. From the direction of Turnau Lieutenant General Ludwig von Tümpling's 5th Division advanced on the position taken up by Clam Gallas along the heights north of the town. From the west, Lieutenant General August von Werder's 3rd Division was advancing along the road from Münchengratz, where the army headquarters remained for the day. Frederick Charles accordingly played no part in a hard fought battle that did not begin until late on June 29, and ended in darkness when Werder captured Gitschin at 10.30 pm. Total Prussian casualties amounted to 1,552; Austrian losses were 4,898 and the Saxons suffered 613. Among the Prussian casualties was Tümpling, wounded in the arm during his division's attack on the key position of Diletz. His reward for this was a telegram from Frederick Charles: 'It is fine when a Prussian general bleeds. It brings the army luck.'[7]

Frederick Charles and Voigts-Rhetz arrived in Gitschin on June 30. The Chief of Staff described the scenes they found:

> The battlefields were dreadful to look at, and the worst thing is that there was no means of carrying the wounded to lazarets as quickly as one would have desired.

Often one finds these hapless persons days later lying half dead in the fields. The inhabitants have all fled, and there are seldom people in the villages and, when there are, they themselves have nothing to live on, so how can anything be done for the sick and the wounded?[8]

For the moment still free from the actual presence of the Royal Headquarters, Frederick Charles and Voigts-Rhetz directed the First Army towards Miletin and Horitz, intending to pull the Army of the Elbe along with them. While Moltke was still thinking in terms of encirclement, none of his army commanders could see beyond the need for a junction of the armies. By now all touch with the enemy had been lost. Moltke and the Royal Headquarters arrived at Gitschin on July 1 and next day he convened a staff conference, attended by the King, his Adjutant General Gustav von Alvensleben, Voigts-Rhetz and Blumenthal. All three generals contended for a junction of the armies, fearing that Benedek might interpose between them and defeat their divided forces; what nobody knew, of course, was exactly where the Austrians might be. Moltke's best guess was that they would be taking up a position along the Elbe, with their flanks resting on the fortresses of Josephstadt and Königgrätz. A junction of the armies on the right bank of the river would, in Moltke's view, deprive him of the chance of winning a battle of encirclement, and he was adamant that his forces should remain separated. His views prevailed (to the particular annoyance of Blumenthal) and the armies enjoyed the benefit of a rest day while cavalry patrols sought the whereabouts of the Austrian army. Shortly before 7.00 pm the crucial information as to this reached Frederick Charles's headquarters at Kamenetz, when Major von Unger brought news of his discovery that a large part at any rate of the Austrian Army was in the valley of the Bistritz and on the heights behind it. Frederick Charles reacted with an impressive speed, which commentators have contrasted with his previously cautious and slow moving responses to rapidly changing situations. His momentous decision to attack the Austrians with his entire army was described by his biographer as the greatest and most far reaching of his career as a military commander.[9] With Voigts-Rhetz he at once began to work out his plan of attack. The army would advance down the Horitz-Königgrätz road, led by the II Corps and the 7th and 8th Divisions at 2.00 am, followed at 3.00 am by the 5th and 6th Divisions. Herwarth, meanwhile, was to move in the direction of Nechanitz. Frederick Charles had got the idea that Austrian forces had crossed the Elbe near Josephstadt; he wrote to the Crown Prince that he looked on it as their intention to operate against his left flank, which would compel him to divide his forces. For the support of his left flank therefore he asked the Crown Prince to move the Guard Corps across the Elbe towards Josephstadt.[10]

This frontal assault demonstrated all too clearly how far Frederick Charles and Voigts-Rhetz had failed to grasp Moltke's intention, and the orders which they issued to some extent limited the latter's options. As it was, it was not until after 10.00 pm that Voigts-Rhetz took the road to Gitschin, and insisted on awakening the King with the news. William, naturally, sent him at once to Moltke, who had also retired. The

Chief of Staff rose, saying 'Thank God,' and hurried to the King to explain the situation. He was with him for only ten minutes before obtaining the Royal approval of his intention to attack next day with all three armies in cooperation. Not much could be done to alter the plans of the First Army; it was essential, however, that the Second Army should advance as quickly as possible with all its forces, rather than lending distant support to the left flank of the First Army. This would involve the whole of the Second Army advancing on the right bank of the Elbe in the narrow space between that river and the Bistritz. Accordingly, he issued an order to the Second Army 'to advance with all your forces to the support of the First Army against the right flank of the presumed enemy advance, coming into action as soon as possible.'[11] This order went off at once in the hands of the King's ADC, Count Finck von Finckenstein, while Voigts-Rhetz took another copy to send by an alternative route. This done, Moltke returned to bed.

Next morning the Prussians were up betimes. At 1.30 am Frederick Charles and his staff rode out of Schloss Kamenetz in a windy night; as dawn broke, a drizzling rain came on. At 4.00 am Moltke, with Podbielski and Wartensleben, drove in his carriage to Horitz, to pick up their horses and ride to Milowitz By 5.45 all the units of the First Army had taken up their jumping off positions, while Herwarth reported to Frederick Charles that he would reach Nechanitz between 7.00 and 9.00 am. This being the case, the army could advance, and at 6.00 am Frederick Charles issued the order to move forward. Between his view of this movement and that of Moltke there existed a wide gulf; for Moltke, the attack of the First Army was to take hold of the Austrian Army while the Second Army arrived on its flank. Frederick Charles, on the other hand, was driven by a personal desire for victory, and saw his attack as being decisive in achieving this. What he was immediately worried about, as he rode forward towards Dub was that the Austrians might not still be there, murmuring to Major von Unger, 'I hope they haven't withdrawn.' As they rode up the hill of Dub, they could see that the Austrians were still in position, and he warmly shook his staff officer's hand. Mindful of the fact that his troops had had no more than a cup of coffee, Frederick Charles decided to defer his attack, long enough to give them a short break and a good meal.

This, however, was not to be. Soon after 8.00 am Moltke ordered Frederick Charles to begin his attack along his whole line, This decision came as a profound disappointment; Moltke's concept of the battle now became clear to him. The First Army would not have the glory of smashing through the enemy centre, but must pin it down for the decisive action on the flanks. Moltke was grimly aware that this would mean that the First Army would have to endure heavy casualties, but he explained to Bismarck that 'the important thing was to hold the enemy for a battle of the whole.'[12] Professor Craig has written that 'this diminution of role was disappointing to Prince Frederick Charles, and it was to leave him with a lasting feeling of resentment which he sought, not entirely successfully, to control.' Duke Ernst of Saxe-Coburg-Gotha put it rather more pungently: 'Prince Frederick Charles always regarded the famous and extraordinary course of the tactical developments on July 3 as a blow from a malevolent fate against his own fame and self esteem.'[13]

However disappointed he may have been with Moltke's plan to limit the First Army's part in the opening stages of the battle to a holding operation, Frederick Charles loyally executed his instructions. The role of his army had been expected by Moltke to lead to heavy casualties, and the effectiveness of the Austrian artillery ensured that this was the case. Reference has already been made to the Prince's stern response to William, when he the King angrily reproached Valentini's battalions retreating from the Holawald. This was not all that Frederick Charles had to put up with; Herwarth's slow progress on the right wing, which he explained was due to his lack of cavalry, led to the transfer of Alvensleben's cavalry division from the First Army's reserve, without reference to the army commander.

As the morning wore on, the First Army's casualties mounted, particularly in the Swiepwald, where Fransecky was fighting desperately to hold the position. Late in the morning Moltke decided to take a closer look at the fighting in the First Army's front, as he recorded in an account written many years later:

> Close in front of us lay the wood of Sadowa [the Holawald] in which Horn's brigade was being held under fire by the enemy's artillery. I remember noticing a deer jump out in high gambols right through the middle of the battalion of troops posted in the wood. With Wartensleben I rode over a piece of the road leading to Lipa, where we met an ownerless bull, which was strolling quite quietly through among the shells which were falling to right and left of it.[14]

On his return to the headquarters staff accompanying the King, he found that in his absence Frederick Charles had ordered up Lieutenant General Gustav von Manstein's 6th Division which was paraded before the King before crossing the Bistritz. There, it was obliged to endure the Austrian artillery fire; the movement had been ordered so that the division would be ready to advance as soon as the advance of the Second Army made itself felt. It was a pointless and impatient move, and directly contrary to Moltke's intentions as to the conduct of the battle. In fact, the Second Army was now closing on the Austrian right; but it was still Moltke's determination to hold back Manstein until the right moment. Frederick Charles, on his own initiative ordered Manstein to commence his advance, an order which Moltke was obliged to countermand. It was all too evident that even now Frederick Charles had not grasped the supreme importance of holding Benedek's army where it was, while the movements of the Prussian flanking units advanced around it. The Second Army's position was, evidently, entirely satisfactory for the purpose; this, however, could not be said of the Army of the Elbe, to which at 1.45 pm Moltke sent an urgent message:

> Crown Prince at Zizelowes. Retreat of Austrians to Josephstadt cut off. It is of the greatest importance that corps of General von Herwarth advance against the wing opposed to it while the Austrians are still making a stand in the centre.[15]

It was not until about 4.15 that Moltke finally released the brakes on the advance of Frederick Charles' troops. By now, the progress on both flanks of the Prussian army was such as to provide the possibility of achieving Moltke's *Kesselschlacht,* and Frederick Charles rode forward to meet his cousin Frederick William amid the ruins of Chlum. Even now, however, the resistance of the Austrian artillery, which remained in action until nightfall, prevented the victors from realising the full extent of their victory; by the time the two wings of the Prussian army met, Benedek had most of his army over the Elbe.

Next day, when Gablenz arrived from the Austrian high command to seek an armistice, it was the headquarters of Frederick Charles that he reached first. 'Does your army <u>need</u> an armistice?' asked Frederick Charles. 'My Emperor no longer has an army. It is as good as destroyed,' was Gablenz's reply.[16]

The contribution made by Frederick Charles to the Prussian victory at Königgrätz was, therefore, limited by Moltke's assumption of effective control of the First Army. Some sense of this, and perhaps of jealousy of the acclaim which Moltke received, inspired Frederick Charles later that year to write:

> It was our entire Army and not the genius or talent of any single leader that brought us victory … There were no geniuses … Therefore it is my opinion that our battles and campaigns were won by our work in peacetime.[17]

In the course of his book 'The Moltke Myth,' a modern American writer, Terence Zuber, was obliged to elevate Frederick Charles to the status of the real hero of the Wars of German unification. As the title of the book suggest, it is an attention-seeking attempt to rewrite history by an exercise in contrived iconoclasm. The title itself is presumably designed to pique the interest of all these readers curious to know how it could be that for a century and-a-half everyone could get it so wrong, and that it was not until Mr Zuber arrived on the scene that all became clear. Mr Zuber himself evidently suffers to some extent from a persecution complex, explaining in a shrill preface how he, and he alone, is possessed of the necessary clear-sightedness to write history:

> 'The Moltke Myth' challenges the orthodox opinion that Moltke was a military genius. For that reason, some professors, often the same ones who tried to suppress my 'Schlieffen Plan' argument, have once again gone to no little amount of trouble in an attempt to keep 'The Moltke Myth' from being published. These professors' comments to editors concerning 'The Moltke Myth' were usually uninformed, often unprofessional, sometimes not even polite, finally descending to being vicious. These professors are concerned that 'The Moltke Myth' will overturn their previous apple carts, and they are not scrupulous in the methods they use to protect their interests.[18]

Well, he got his book published, and in order to support his thesis that Moltke was 'on par with "Fighting Joe" Hooker and Burnside,' he proceeds at length to excuse, or deny, the failings of Frederick Charles throughout the wars of unification. As part of this exercise he triumphantly proclaims Frederick Charles as 'the most brilliant trainer and tactical thinker in a Prussian army that excelled in both.'[19] He brushes aside the conclusions of two of the leading modern historians of the Austro Prussian War in Gordon Craig and Geoffrey Wawro by the clumsy reiteration of statements of his own opinion, and then proceeds to denounce Arden Bucholz for a neglect of Moltke's actual plans and orders and a reliance on secondary sources. Along the way one by one all the eminent historians who preceded them are similarly consigned to the rubbish tip. Zuber sounds one note throughout; to explain the Prussian victories he must find some one other than Moltke to be responsible, and Frederick Charles is the man. There is not much, therefore, to be found in Zuber to assist in a balanced appraisal of the contribution of Frederick Charles to Prussian success, either in 1866 or later in 1870-1871; and it would be a tedious and unrewarding exercise to seek further enlightenment there.

At the end of a review which is more balanced and thorough than Zuber's book deserves, Wilson Blythe, writing in the *Michigan War Studies Review,* commented that Zuber 'fails to diminish or "demythologize" Moltke's established reputations ... He misguidedly calculates that glory is a zero sum commodity, in which laurels must be snatched from Moltke in order for Frederick Charles to enjoy them.'[20]

13

Metz

_____

There never was a perfect sympathy between Frederick Charles and his cousin the Crown Prince, partly due to the fact that they were very different personalities and partly due to a sense of rivalry between them. For this reason some of Frederick William's comments about his cousin must occasionally be viewed with a degree of caution. Nonetheless, his diary entries relative to Frederick Charles immediately prior to the declaration of war in 1870 do make interesting reading. On July 16 the King had, somewhat testily, refused to decide on the appointments to the highest commands, and the allocation of senior General Staff officers. Next day, after attending a Sunday morning service at the Potsdam Garrison Church, the Crown Prince found his father more prepared to consider this crucially important question:

> Afterwards in Berlin I attended a council of war at the Palace, at which His Majesty showed himself more compliant than yesterday. It was noteworthy how no one would speak right out when the question came up as to Prince Frederick Charles and his appointment to a high command, until His Majesty in some excitement insisted on an expression of opinion, and then how all were unanimous that the Prince should lead that Army (the Second Army as it is entitled) which the King would accompany and so be on the spot to exercise special control.[1]

Quite what the reservations at which the Crown Prince hinted were not expressed; and it does seem surprising, to say the least, that there could have been much doubt about the suitability of the appointment, and most historians have accepted that it was inevitable. On the other hand, could it be that Moltke, remembering some of the problems he had faced in his dealings with Frederick Charles in 1866, had dropped a few hints here and there?

At all events, it was to the Second Army that Frederick Charles was appointed, and Major General Gustav von Stiehle became his Chief of Staff. Of the latter, Waldersee wrote that a great deal was thought of him: 'I do not know much of him, but in any case he brings freshness and youth to his work.'[2] Much of the input from Moltke into the operations of the Second Army came in the form of the many letters which he sent Stiehle in the course of their regular correspondence. Born in 1823, he reached the rank of Major in 1859. He was responsible for organising the new military schools established at Potsdam and Neisse and from 1860 became head of the military history section of the General Staff. In 1864 he served on Wrangel's headquarters staff and in 1866 he was an aide de camp to the King, in which capacity he conducted the military side of the peace negotiations at Prague.

The advance of the Second Army required it to march through the hills and forests of the Pfalzwald, but it was not until it reached the frontier that it began to encounter delays in its progress. These had nothing to do with any excess of caution on the part of Frederick Charles; they were caused by the irresponsible and wrong headed actions of Steinmetz and the First Army, which occupied roads intended to be used by the Second Army. Sorting all this out caused Moltke quite unnecessary difficulties, and it took a good deal of time and effort on his part to resolve the problems. In addition to this, Steinmetz was failing to keep Moltke informed, as he told Stiehle on August 11:

> Thank you for all your reports, the more so as we have none from the First Army. I am not even able to tell you the direction in which I, VIII and VII Corps are marching today. Sufficient steps have been taken to remedy this state of things. The position behind the Nied is perhaps in spite of all only a position of observation, with the principal forces remaining behind the Moselle. I suggest for your consideration whether it would be best to halt the III Corps to let the others come up.[3]

The situation and intention of the enemy was only now becoming evident. Moltke's plan to deal with them was manifestly not understood by Steinmetz; Frederick Charles, on the other hand, was clear about what Moltke was trying to do, as he showed by the letter which he wrote to him from Püttlingen on the morning of August 11;

> Just arrived here, I hasten to let you know my views. It appears that this union of masses of the enemy will lead to a battle. It does not seem likely that the enemy will leave his good position and attack us, although this would be more in character than their strict defensive up to now. This defensive has been unsuccessful and one can conceive of his taking the offensive. Although this is to me improbable, I shall hold myself ready for it so that he cannot fall on any isolated corps before the Second Army has been united … I would not dispose more troops in the enemy's front than are necessary to hold him there, as was the case with my army at Königgrätz, and to prevent him breaking through our centre. I will direct the principal effort against the enemy's right flank; I will attack there in force keeping at least one corps echeloned in reserve.[4]

Moltke was pleased to see that he and Frederick Charles were in tune; replying, he speculated that the French units behind the Nied might fall back and that the main body of the enemy be found south of Metz behind the Seille or the Moselle. By the time his reply reached the Second Army, however, it had been reported that large masses of the French had again been seen marching towards the Nied.

With the handling of the Second Army by Frederick Charles during the ensuing days Moltke was perfectly in accord. After the battle of Borny-Colombey, and the retreat of the Army of the Rhine into Metz, the important thing was to get sufficient troops forward to prevent Bazaine making a dash for Verdun. On the evening of August 15 Moltke issued instructions to all three armies outlining the situation but, as he made clear, the next important move would be made by Frederick Charles:

> The fruits of the victory can be reaped only by a vigorous offensive by the Second Army towards the roads from Metz to Verdun by Fresnes and Etain. It is left to the commander in chief of that army to carry that out on his own judgment, with all the available means. If as a result the Second Army finds itself in advance of the First Army, care must be taken for the dispositions to be made with a view to continuing the advance to be foreseen, and to ensure that the troops have as much rest as possible.[5]

Next day was fought the encounter battle of Vionville-Mars la Tour. As yet unaware of the seriousness of the battle Stiehle left for Moltke at Pont-à-Mousson a brief report as he was setting off to the battlefield at 2.00 pm. That evening Moltke replied: 'In my opinion, driving back northwards the principal forces of the enemy which have left Metz is the decisive thing for the outcome of the campaign … Not till this purpose has been fulfilled will the First and Second Armies be able to separate to continue the march westward.'[6]

Headed off by the battle of August 16, Bazaine fell back towards Metz. It was not immediately clear what position he was taking up, but it was now evident that there was a real prospect of swinging around to the right with a view either to shutting the French up in Metz or driving them back towards the Belgian frontier, and it was as early as 1.45 pm on August 17, on the height south of Flavigny, that Moltke issued the necessary orders for the right wheel, requiring the Second Army to 'advance en echelon between the Yron and the Gorze stream (on the general line from Ville-sur-Yron to Rezonville).' The VIII Corps was to follow this movement on the right wing of the Second Army. Considering the scale of the forces involved, and the critical nature of the battle to be fought, this order is astonishingly brief, and demonstrates the confidence which Moltke was prepared to place in his subordinates. The imprecision was, in Hönig's view, deliberate; it ensured that the Second Army, continued to move forward, its right flank covered by the First Army. It was, thought Hönig, 'a work of genius.'[7]

Frederick Charles rode out from Mars-la-Tour at 5.30 am on August 18. During the rest of that day he received only three messages from Moltke, all of them brief and only one of them an order. Sent at 10.30 am, it reported the latest position of the French Army, and went on:

His Majesty is of opinion that it will be advisable to move the XII and the Guard Corps in the direction of Batilly, in order, if the enemy is retiring upon Briey, to come up with him at Ste Marie aux Chênes, or, if he remains in position on the heights, to attack him from Amanvillers inwards. The attack must take place simultaneously, by the First Army from the Bois de Vaux and Gravelotte, by the IX Corps against the Bois des Génivaux and Verneville, and by the left wing of the Second Army from the north.[8]

This order reached Frederick Charles at about 11.00 am but at almost the same time a crucially important report arrived which completely altered the situation. Lieutenant Scholl had been reconnoitring the French position to the north from Batilly and had discovered that there was a French camp at St Privat. Frederick Charles had, an hour earlier, ordered the IX Corps to advance towards Verneville and La Folie; he now saw the risk of an isolated attack, and attempted, too late, to rescind the order.

Hönig severely criticised both the Royal Headquarters and both army commanders for the failure adequately to reconnoitre the French position. It was a failure which effectively ruled out the possibility of coordinating the attack of the two armies, each of which when the battle started brought their units into action in succession. Moltke clung to the idea of a simultaneous assault long after the battle commenced, by which time there was little more he could do about it. Hönig gives credit where it was due for the ultimate victory:

> The true mark of a general is the manner in which he makes good a situation which at the beginning has gone wrong. If Prince Frederick Charles must be blamed for too much caution and delay before the battle, justice compels us to emphasise the fact that the prince, from the moment of the receipt of the report of Lieutenant Scholl, showed himself throughout to be equal to the general situation in its widest strategical sense, and that his direction of the battle from that moment need shun no criticism, being fully equal to that of Napoleon; this careful general did not quit the point where the decision took place until the blazing flames of St Privat had been extinguished. Indeed, if any individual persons can be described as the victors of St Privat, they are Prince Frederick Charles and the Crown Prince Albert of Saxony.[9]

Hönig's review of the events of August 18 is primarily concerned with the battle of Gravelotte rather than the whole of the battle; nonetheless, as the quotation above shows, he was prepared to acknowledge that it was, in the end, Frederick Charles and the Second Army that ensured the overall victory which, in its strategic consequences was the most important battle of the whole war. But it was, nonetheless, Moltke's victory:

> In spite of 'friction and obstacles,' and of a constant struggle against the want of intelligence in those under him and against respect for those over him, Moltke

really worked out the same task at Gravelotte as he did later at Sedan; the latter is only the fully developed idea of Gravelotte-St Privat. As at Sedan, so on August 18 two armies had to quit their lines of communication, and to change front, in the one case to the north, and in the other to the east; and this in a narrow space, after weighing various contingencies. Everything was more favourable for the operations at Sedan, and, above all, Moltke had the two generals under him, who understood him and anticipated his wishes; whereas, up to August 18, one of them had to be constantly held back, while the other had equally to be somewhat pushed on. The latter certainly cancelled the proportion of blame which was his due, while the former was by his actions at Gravelotte finally and for ever struck out of the list of leaders in war; but Gravelotte-St Privat is, and will continue to be, Moltke's grandest feat.[10]

With Bazaine securely penned into Metz, Moltke wasted no time in reorganising his armies. For the investment of the fortress he selected the II, III, IX and X Corps together with the whole of the First Army and the 3rd Reserve Division. This force was placed under the command of Frederick Charles. Moltke was reasonably confident that it was quite sufficient to deal with the Army of the Rhine; but he wrote to Stiehle on August 21 to emphasise that a breakout in a north easterly direction was much less dangerous than an advance towards the south, which would interrupt the line Frouard-Strasbourg, so important to the advance towards Châlons.[11]

Frederick Charles was evidently discontented by the provision of General Staff officers, and perhaps also by the realisation that his immediate task did not offer much prospect of military excitement, since Moltke was obliged on August 22 to explain to him that it would not be possible substantially to reduce the strength of the General Staff with the Royal Headquarters or back at home; he did, however agree to the request that Major von Holleben should be attached to the Staff of Crown Prince Albert. Mindful of the ambitions of Frederick Charles, Moltke went on:

> The difficulties and the disagreeable features of the very important task which has fallen to Your Royal Highness are clearly understood, but may perhaps be of short duration. If the enemy succeeds in breaking out, it will probably be attempted in the direction of Nancy, when the investment will at once became a campaign in the open field. Since, in this case, we can count on an effective and vigorous pursuit, the other two armies would, in my opinion, continue their march. If the French Army in Metz is unable to break out, it cannot without relief exist long there. Your Royal Highness will achieve, in its capitulation, one of the greatest successes recorded in military history.[12]

Moltke had learned long since the right way to appeal to the Red Prince.

Frederick Charles proceeded to conduct the investment of Metz with characteristic efficiency. It did, however, bring him into conflict with Bismarck, who had persuaded the King to authorise a safe conduct for General Bourbaki to leave Metz in order to travel to England to meet the Empress Eugénie before returning to the fortress. Frederick Charles had been extremely suspicious of the contacts which Bismarck had made with Bazaine and his agents; his concern seems to have been that these negotiations would deny him the honour of receiving the capitulation of the fortress. It was a view with which Moltke had a good deal of sympathy. When Bourbaki got back from England, Frederick Charles withheld permission for him to return to the fortress for so long that Bourbaki went off to Tours to serve the army of the Government of National Defence.

The Crown Prince recorded in his diary the views held by the military at Versailles of this incident:

> Prince Frederick Charles is against receiving the French intermediary, for he is rightly enough afraid that in the end the capitulation will come to be signed at Versailles instead of before Metz, and he, after being detained there for months, will only be a looker-on; however, he is now pacified on this point, having been assured that he is to sign the stipulations whatever they are.[13]

Bismarck was, however furious, and wrote a long letter to Stiehle to protest:

> I appeal to your Excellency's clear judgment and to your own perception, so that you will understand how discouraging it must be for me when, through this kind of failure to execute explicit Royal orders, the danger arises that in the whole constellation of political calculations one single cog, which is necessary in its place, will refuse to do its work. How can I have the courage to proceed with my work if I cannot count on Royal orders being faithfully executed? ... Your Excellency knows that my whole energy has been devoted, and with success, to providing for the victorious progress of our arms a free field, undisturbed by foreign influence. I must then demand that the army show the same confidence in me that His Majesty the King has shown in the approval of my plans.[14]

Bismarck can have felt no surprise that it was Frederick Charles who was behaving in this way; the prince had always been one of the most hawkish among the military, as well as the one above all most sensitive to issues of prestige.

Moltke was in no doubt that the siege of Metz, while it lasted, was much the most important military operation, and one in which he took a close interest. On September 5, for instance, fresh from the victory at Sedan, and with all the consequent moves to oversee, he wrote to Stiehle to set out his views on how to destroy the morale of the garrison:

> Now that every prospect of relief has been taken away from the army in Metz, the important thing is to make its stay there still more disagreeable, and for that purpose one means is to disturb it every night. I think this can be done as well with field guns as with 12-pounders and is possible at very great ranges if

only you can see the enemy's camps or find their distance exactly. Even against the town – a target you cannot miss – the 6-pounder with the same charge and loading as the 12-pounder will do. Perhaps also with pick and spade you can increase the difficulty for the enemy of breaking through in face of the advantage of the defensive on which you lay stress. But you should allow an officer from the fortress to look round at Sedan in order to convince himself of the helplessness of the position.[15]

14

Le Mans

After the fall of Metz, the Second Army became the largest field force available to Moltke, and he was determined to make the best use of it. The strategic situation with which he had to deal was far more complex in the second phase of the war than it had been before the battle of Sedan. It was the operations on the Loire, to which the bulk of the Second Army now proceeded, that would be decisive, as Colonel Hale noted:

> The ultimate issue of the whole campaign depended on the successful course of the campaign on the Loire, and upon maintaining the investment of Paris unbroken; failure in one meant, perhaps, failure in the other. Real anxiety hardly existed during the first war, it was absent hardly a day during the second.[1]

Moltke and his staff entered the war against the Government of National Defence confident that it would not be prolonged; that Paris would soon surrender, and that when it did France would also capitulate. Famously, as late as September 21, he wrote to his brother Adolf that he hoped by the end of October he would be shooting hares in Creisau. This confidence was not shared by most of the other Prussian leaders; Bismarck, Roon and the King very much doubted that the war would end so quickly, and Frederick Charles was very much of their view.

One of the factors which Moltke underestimated was the effect of the establishment of the franc- tireurs. Their performance was extremely variable; but some franc-tireur groups were excellent irregular troops, and did real damage to the German war effort, not least by the difficulty they caused in the requisitioning of supplies. Moltke wrote sternly on October 27:

> The audacity of the franc-tireurs must be punished by severe reprisals, as the war is assuming a horrible aspect. It is bad enough when armies have to tear each other to pieces, but to set nations against each other is not an advance but a lapse into barbarism.[2]

Frederick Charles was very much affected by the success of the franc-tireurs, commenting later on their effect:

> The franc-tireurs, aided by the country, have done the French good service. Now I am reduced to a waiting attitude … There is for a leader nothing more oppressive than a situation that is not clear, nothing more trying than bands of irregular troops aided by the population and the nature of the country, and relying for support on a strong army in the neighbourhood.[3]

His personal experience of the way in which the population responded to the government's urging in the second phase of the war was vividly summarised by Colonel Hale, describing the prince's ride towards Pithiviers on November 20. In the course of this he was able to make his own assessment of both the nature of the country in which his army would have to fight, and of the attitude of the population:

> He recognised at once, fully, that the whole character of the war had altered; that it was not merely the hostile army that was his enemy, but the whole of the population also and that from the physical nature of the country both these enemies would derive great assistance. During the ride, the farms and villages were found deserted; in the fields bodies of armed men were visible; bullets fell all round irregularly; prisoners, some of them priests with gloomy faces, bearing expressions of deepest hatred, came before the prince; the roads were in many places cut through and destroyed, the sign-posts carried away; and the bells of the churches signalled from church tower to church tower the march of the invaders. By this gloomy November picture the prince was so deeply impressed that he repeatedly made remarks to those around him about the rising of the Spanish nation against Napoleon 1.[4]

One outcome of the fall of Metz that was of especial significance for Frederick Charles was the King's announcement on October 29 that both he and the Crown Prince had been promoted to the rank of Field Marshal. The latter was uncomfortable about it, since such a promotion had never before been granted to a Royal Prince, and in any case he felt that Moltke, who was made a count, should have come first. A few days later, he reflected on the matter in his diary:

> When Prince Frederick Charles heard of his appointment as Field Marshal, all he exclaimed was: 'At last.' This one word says everything. Subsequently he expressed the opinion that the fact that he as senior General of the army did not receive this rank has prevented others from obtaining it … It is plain that, as I said just now, how he looks upon this honour as a right hitherto unwarrantably withheld. For how long will the possession of this rank he has laid claim to satisfy his boundless ambition and overweening vanity? Not a doubt he will soon be dreaming of fresh distinctions and privileges of exceptional sort and

Stiehle.

will never show himself contented, making a point of it at every opportunity to gratify his own will and pleasure.[5]

The Crown Prince really did not like his cousin very much at all, and was especially scornful when he began styling himself as Prince Field Marshal in correspondence.

In anticipation of the imminent fall of Metz, Moltke had, on October 23, determined how to employ the forces thereby released. Manteuffel, with the First Army, was to advance into northern France; Frederick Charles, with the Second Army, consisting of the II, III, IX and X Corps and the 1st Cavalry Division was to have Bourges as its target. By the time the fortress capitulated on October 29, though, Moltke had somewhat varied his plans; Fransecky's II Corps was to be diverted to strengthen the army of investment around Paris, while Frederick Charles marched off as quickly as possible with the rest of his army in the general direction of Troyes towards the Seine and the Middle Loire. Moltke set out in a letter to Stiehle dated November 1 his assessment of the objectives which the army might have when it reached its new theatre of war:

> Only the course of events will determine the tasks that will have to be undertaken by the Second Army during its advance. I hardly think it will be necessary

to give support to General von Werder, who is provisionally in a defensive position on the line Vesoul-Gray-Dijon. The south of France will hardly make great
efforts on behalf of Paris. On the other hand, there are three points on the left
flank where the most severe losses to military France can be inflicted, Châlons
sur Saone, Nevers and above all, Bourges, where there are the great arsenals and
the Chassepôt cartridge manufactories ... The main object remains as before, the
destruction of the enemy's forces in the field, and the speedy reinforcing of the
forces at Paris, so as to render possible the sending out of detachments.[6]

Moltke thought that it would not be necessary for the Second Army to operate as a
single body; one corps would be enough for each of the named objectives. The letter
did not show Moltke at his most prescient; within a month Frederick Charles was
fighting a major campaign against a very substantial French army. Within a fortnight Moltke was obliged to eat his words, after von der Tann had been defeated
at Coulmiers. He wrote to Stiehle on November 14 to observe that 'it shows the
resources of France and the patriotism of the people, that after the whole army had
been captured, yet in a comparatively short time a new army, which is not to be
despised, has been put into the field.'[7] He acknowledged that it was not at present
feasible to destroy the arsenals at Bourges or to drive the Delegation out of Tours;
the Second Army must continue its advance westwards to deal with the situation.
He was very grateful for the rapid approach of Prince Frederick Charles; 'it has
pulled us through a sort of crisis.'

In the days following, however, there was increasing dissatisfaction at Versailles
with the situation of the Second Army and of the Detachment of the Grand Duke of
Mecklenburg-Schwerin. The performance of the Detachment was in particular giving
rise to concern. Much of the difficulty derived from the fact that neither the Grand
Duke or Frederick Charles was keeping Moltke fully informed. Moltke and Frederick
Charles had different ideas as to the employment of the Detachment; Moltke wanted
to use it for a blow at the left flank of the Army of the Loire, while Frederick Charles
preferred that it go off in a south-westerly direction threatening Tours.

It was at this point that the King intervened, sending Waldersee to Frederick
Charles's headquarters with instructions to send him daily reports. The King told
Waldersee that it was a critical moment; the Army of the Loire had been greatly
strengthened. 'I saw that coming,' he said, 'but these gentlemen always know everything better than I and have been declaring that the war is at an end.' Waldersee
noted in his diary that this was principally a reference to Podbielski, who annoyed the
King by his habitual over confidence. Since the King tended to pessimism, Waldersee
thought it a good thing that someone take the opposite point of view.[8]

Waldersee took with him a letter to the prince; he arrived at the headquarters on
November 26:

At about 1.00 pm I arrived in Pithiviers and made my way at once to the prince.
He read the King's letter through very slowly, then heard what I had to say, and

declared that he entirely shared the King's opinion but that he had the best hope that all would be well. He wished, however, the Grand Duke of Mecklenburg would make a move but it was always a business to get the Grand Duke to come along – he would never carry out punctually what he was told to do.[9]

Waldersee was extremely uneasy about the way in which his visit would be regarded by Frederick Charles; the Prince, he thought, must by reason of his 'jealous disposition' regard him as an undesirable kind of monitor. He decided to do something to pre-empt this:

> After lunch, I availed myself of a suitable opportunity to pay the Prince some compliments on his gifts as an army leader- I knew one could safely go to great lengths in this kind of thing – and I expressed the hope that he would regard me merely as being there to further his wishes with the King, and I intimated that I intended, above all, to write nothing but what he wished me to write. I must admit that it was not quite straightforward to talk like this, but it was good policy, for it evidently pleased him.[10]

On November 25 at 1.00 pm Moltke sent a telegram placing the Detachment, hitherto reporting to the Third Army, under the orders of Prince Frederick Charles. Colonel Hale observes that, having regard to the prince's different view of the employment of the Detachment, Moltke's decision seems at first sight incredible. He explains it, however, by reference to Moltke's workload, of which the task of conducting the Loire campaign was a substantial part. It was, he thought, 'mentally and physically, beyond the power of any human being in the position of Moltke – a position in which the strain, already enormous, was increasing hourly.' It was no wonder that Moltke temporarily relieved himself of hands on responsibility for the Loire.[11]

He was not, however, comfortable with leaving it at that; it was on the following day that he announced to the Grand Duke that he was sending Stosch to serve as Chief of Staff of the Detachment. It was by this means above all that Moltke intended to put matters on the Loire in order and, as has been noted above, it was a move that proved entirely successful. It was a step taken not merely to improve the staff work of the Detachment, but to ensure that on the Loire there was a man capable of promoting Moltke's strategic intentions in a practical fashion.

As his correspondence with Stiehle demonstrated, Moltke certainly needed all the help he could get if he was to make any headway in prevailing on the Second Army to do what he wanted. Frederick Charles was candid in his refusal to execute Moltke's strategy in a letter which he wrote to the King on November 26, in reply to the letter which Waldersee had brought to him. In this letter the prince emphasised that he must not run any risk at the present time. On the other hand, although he faced a far more numerous enemy, over a front of twenty eight miles, he was no danger to himself, only some inconvenience. He would welcome, he said, a French offensive, particularly if it took the direction of Fontainebleau. On the other hand, he regarded it as far more difficult to drive the French out of the Forest of Orleans, because of his lack of reliable information about the location of their main body.[12]

What Frederick Charles did expect was that 'the fight against Orleans will probably last many days and be very bloody.' But he would undertake it unless ordered otherwise. He went on:

> One must do in war what is most inconvenient to the enemy, not that which he likes. To me it seems clear that the enemy wishes me to attack, and wherever I may make the attack I shall come on a series of small strong localities prepared for defence. Since I must always so arrange as to be able to get in front of an enemy who, when I am engaged with him, may march past my flank on Paris, I am unfortunately more restricted in the choice of the direction of my attack than I should be after the fall of Paris.[13]

He remarked that under the existing circumstances he must employ the Detachment tactically, not strategically, against the Army of the Loire, a conclusion directly contrary to Moltke's wishes. The latter was quite unaware of this correspondence.

On November 28 the French advance led to the outbreak of the battle of Beaune la Rolande. Frederick Charles was at his headquarters in Pithiviers when news came not only of fighting at Maizières, but also of what appeared to be French movements in the Loing valley, which the Prince now erroneously concluded was the real direction of the French offensive. After a brisk exchange of telegrams with Voigts-Rhetz, upon whose X Corps the attack had principally fallen, Frederick Charles set off from Pithiviers to see for himself what was happening. It seems to be common ground that he was an indifferent horseman; Hönig noted that he never moved faster than at a trot, while Waldersee wrote that he was 'only a mediocre and somewhat nervous horseman.'[14]

As a result he only got to Barville between 1.00 – 2.00 pm, and once there concerned himself solely with the measures being taken to resist the advance of the French 20th Corps; with the events at Long Cour, where Voigts-Rhetz was fighting a fierce battle, he did not concern himself. At 5.30 pm, as he was about to return to Pithiviers, Waldersee reported to him. The latter had been present throughout, and had been in close touch with both Voigts-Rhetz and Alvensleben. Mindful of the prince's cautious disposition, Waldersee said: 'A complete victory has been won, it will be a Rossbach for the French if there is a vigorous pursuit.' Frederick Charles was unimpressed, convinced that the strength of the enemy was exaggerated. He gave brief instructions to Stiehle before riding back to Pithiviers, accompanied at his request by Waldersee, who continued to explain to him the extent of the combat:

> Waldersee, from his personal observation, was convinced that the fight had been far more than a demonstration or a mask for strategical movements, and he endeavoured to induce the prince to accept as correct his opinion that two hostile army corps had taken part in the battle, and that its issue had been so

decisive, that any belief in the advance down the Loing valley could no longer be entertained. But the prince firmly held to the opinion that the strength of the enemy had been overestimated; he still believed that the fight was but the introduction to a powerful offensive movement, and he considered it necessary to put in the Loing valley stronger forces than had been there up to the present time.[15]

In this belief, Frederick Charles sent off a telegram to the King which minimised the extent of the battle and its outcome, information which was incorrect due to his failure to get more involved.

Moltke himself had written on November 27 a letter of great clarity setting out for Stiehle the situation as he saw it in terms that made clear that he expected the Second Army to take the offensive; Stiehle only received this on November 29, after the battle of Beaune la Rolande, but it made little impact on him or his Royal master, In his letter, Moltke summarised the position of the various forces operating against the French, as well as the anticipated sortie from Paris. He emphasised the special significance of the campaign on the Loire:

> It is the struggle which you are going to engage in against the only real army that France can put into the field that has a truly decisive importance. If (and I sincerely hope this does not happen) you lose the battle, my plan will be to lift the blockade of Paris without regard to the loss of our siege equipment. The Crown Prince of Saxony would operate with General Manteuffel against the concentration in the north, and the Crown Prince of Prussia with you against the Army of the Loire. In this way our decisive superiority will bring us victory, and we shall return to Paris which because of the broken rail lines will not have been able to be revictualled, and after the surrender of which we will recover our guns.[16]

Had he listened to Waldersee, on the evening of November 28, Frederick Charles might well have been able to inflict a terminal defeat on the forces in front of him; as it was, two days later, he was grumbling about the missed opportunity. He was still bemused by his lack of information about the French forces in the Forest of Orleans, and cited the activity of the franc-tireurs as substantially responsible for this. By now, however, he was convinced that he did have the bulk of the Army of the Loire in front of him; sending to the Grand Duke an outline of the situation as he saw it, he said that it was probable that on the following day the Detachment would only have to face the 17th Corps and a part of the 16th Corps. For his part, he intended to stand on the defensive. As a result of his misconception of the true situation, Stosch and the Grand Duke were obliged to fight the battle of Loigny-Poupry on December 2 against an enemy that was numerically by far superior.

Hale is especially critical of Frederick Charles for his reference to his 'further plans for driving the enemy out of Orleans:'

Specially noteworthy is it that here for the first time in the Loire campaign the mere regaining possession of Orleans appears as the objective of the operations. Moltke, up to this time, certainly cannot be credited, or rather discredited, with concurrence in this novel idea.[17]

However, the position completely changed two days later; at noon on December 2 Moltke despatched a telegram to Frederick Charles, after having heard from Stosch of the situation of the Detachment. Moltke's telegram, which reached Frederick Charles at 1.30 pm, read:

> According to a report, the bulk of the Army of the Loire is now in position south of Artenay. The Grand Duke , on his own, is not in a state to resist an offensive from this point on Toury. His Majesty reckons that it is absolutely necessary for the Second Army to move directly on Orleans without delay for a decisive attack. This morning we have recovered from the enemy, in front of Paris, several points of the line of advanced posts which had been lost yesterday.[18]

Frederick Charles could say, therefore, that by December 2 his intention to drive the enemy out of Orleans was not inconsistent with the instructions which he was receiving from Versailles.

Moltke's telegram was illustrative of the extreme frustration being felt at the Royal Headquarters at the situation on the Loire. Hale says of the telegram 'that it may be doubted whether in the records of this campaign there exists one more extraordinary in its character.' Certainly it marked a change of policy; up to this point, Moltke had aimed at the destruction of the Army of the Loire by a blow at its left flank, and thereby protect the Paris road; now, he directed the Second Army to bludgeon its way forward to capture an open city. It is also surprising that, at the time the telegram was sent, Moltke was still unaware of the battle raging at Loigny-Poupry; no report had reached him since the battle began; the first he knew of it was from a telegram sent by Waldersee to the King between 5.00 and 6.00 pm to the effect that a complete victory had been won.[19] It appears that there may have been a strong feeling at Versailles that the recapture of Orleans would be the stroke that brought the war to an end; that, at any rate, is what Hönig suggests. If so, it is a rare example of Moltke giving way to impatience, abandoning what he knew to be the correct course in favour of the only means of getting Frederick Charles to move forward. That was clearly how Blumenthal interpreted it, writing in his diary on that day:

> The Crown Prince told me that the King has now positively ordered the prince to attack the Army of the Loire. Surely it is impossible for him to ignore such an order, and he must now go forward (Fabius Cunctator). A Prussian Field Marshal is bound to go forward.[20]

At all events, when he got the order Frederick Charles determined to carry it out literally; possibly he was annoyed by the way it was worded and the criticism it implied. The instructions for the advance were issued at 10.00 pm on December 2; in these he made it clear that what he was ordering was in compliance with orders he had himself received. Hale is sharply critical:

> In this plan and scheme there is no strategy, notwithstanding the fact that on this long front of forty miles there is plenty of scope for its employment. It is all tactics, tactics of a kind almost barbaric: those of weight and brute force. The influence of ground on tactics, and the selection of the ground most suitable for a force weak in infantry but strong in the other arms are alike ignored.[21]

Nor, strangely, did the orders for December 3 take any account of the outcome of the battle of Loigny-Poupry, described by Waldersee as 'a brilliant victory,' and of which Frederick Charles had a full report before the orders went out.

In the event, the two day second battle of Orleans resulted in an outstanding victory, even though the manner of it was highly displeasing to Frederick Charles. When the news arrived that the Grand Duke had ridden into the city he was outraged; Waldersee, who enjoyed recording scenes like this, wrote:

> It was a thunderbolt. The Prince was beside himself. He had intended to make a formal entry into Orleans; his joy had vanished, and all owing to the Grand Duke, of whom he had an enduring dislike.[22]

Summing up the performance of Frederick Charles during this battle, Colonel Hale showed why he deserved only limited credit for his victory:

> It sometimes happens when the line of action taken in war by a leader appears to have been dangerous and even foolhardy, and yet has resulted in a brilliant success, that there is attributed to him a species of marvellous insight into the state of affairs on the side of the enemy and his moral condition. But though the Prince achieved his aim on December 3 and 4, the success of the dangerous and hazardous operation adopted was in no way due to his possessing any insight of this kind. Rarely has any leader entered so completely blindfolded into a battle as did Prince Frederick Charles into the second battle of Orleans. Of even the general disposition of the enemy he knew very little … As regards the morale of the enemy he was equally in the dark.[23]

With Orleans taken, the next task was to deal with Chanzy's army; Stosch, in the three day battle of Beaugency, achieved a brilliant success without a great deal of help from the Second Army. Following this up with characteristic caution, Frederick Charles missed an opportunity to smash Chanzy completely, although in his defence it must be said that the weather made rapid movement extremely difficult. Moltke prescribed limits to the advance of the Second Army; with its main body at Orleans, it should not probe forward beyond the line Tours-Bourges-Nevers. He was concerned that his army commanders might fail to see the wood for the trees, and on December 17 he sent a letter to Frederick Charles and Manteuffel to spell out the strategy that must now be pursued:

> The general situation requires that after a victory the enemy is pursued only as far as it is necessary to disperse the bulk of his forces and thus render it impossible for them to concentrate again for a considerable time. We cannot follow the French all the way to their last strongholds such as Lille, Le Havre and Bourges; we do not wish to occupy permanently distant provinces such as Normandy, Brittany and the Vendée; we must resolve to abandon certain points which we have taken, such as Dieppe and eventually Tours, in order to concentrate our principal forces at a small number of important points.[24]

Moltke's prescription for the Second Army was that it should now be concentrated around Orleans and this, with the exception of the X Corps at Vendôme, was its situation for most of the rest of December. Towards the end of the month, however, there were indications that Chanzy's army was gathering strength. This was confirmed by an advance of two divisions under Jouffroy towards Vendôme, and Moltke concluded that the time had come to make an end of Chanzy. The forces constituting the Detachment were once again put under the command of Frederick Charles; with the return of Stosch to Versailles, it had a new chief of staff in Waldersee. Moltke's conclusion was entirely correct; Chanzy was preparing to advance in support of the planned offensive by Bourbaki with the Army of the East.

On January 1 Moltke sent a telegram to Frederick Charles:

> His Majesty orders the Second Army to take the offensive against the enemy advancing from the west towards the line Vendôme-Illiers. The Grand Duke of Mecklenburg takes the command of the XIII (17th and 22nd Divisions) which, with the 2nd and 4th Cavalry Divisions, is added to the Second Army. Maintain the occupation of Orleans and reconnoitre the country on the right bank of the Loire. The II Corps marches on Montargis; General Zastrow is recalled westwards. A feldjäger is on the way.[25]

He wrote the same day to Stiehle to set out in more detail his intentions; the reaction of the latter, uneasy at the very substantial numerical superiority of Chanzy's army, was to ask how soon Fransecky would get to Montargis. Moltke's answer was that his leading troops would be there by January 5. For the next few days Moltke's attention was concentrated on the operations in the east, and the dispositions that must be made to counter Bourbaki's offensive, and he was content to leave Frederick Charles to get on with the task of smashing Chanzy's army.

His confidence that he might safely do this was entirely justified. With a clear objective, and no requirement that he take account of any other movements, Frederick Charles could be seen at his best. Notwithstanding the odds against him of two to one, the Prince resolved to attack all along his front. For this, he planned to stick to the main roads, since the dreadful weather conditions would make the side roads almost impassable.

The advance began on January 6. Frederick Charles conducted the campaign with brutal efficiency, pressing forward in the face of sustained resistance; he had occasion to be severely critical of Duke William of Mecklenburg-Schwerin who had, he considered, performed less than adequately with his 6th Cavalry Division in the fighting around St Amand; when Duke William reported to Frederick Charles on the evening of January 6 he was told peremptorily that he must restore the situation on the following day by retaking the village. On his left, Voigts-Rhetz made slow progress; all the advancing units were materially delayed by changes in the weather. A thaw on January 7 had been followed by a hard frost that night, and the resulting black ice made movement next day appallingly difficult. Nonetheless, and notwithstanding the courageous fight which the French put up, the advance of the Second Army was inexorable.

On January 9 a heavy snowstorm made conditions even worse, but Alvensleben's III Corps pressed on towards the line of the Huisne, on which Chanzy's defensive position was based. By nightfall on January 10 Changé, the key to the French position, was taken. Next day further strong resistance was encountered, but by now Manstein's IX Corps was at hand in support, enabling Alvensleben to get around the left of Chanzy's position. While on the right of the Second Army's advance the XIII Corps had been making progress, on the extreme left Voigts-Rhetz broke the defence of Jauréguiberry at La Tuilerie; on January 12 he was able to march into Le Mans as Chanzy mournfully pulled his troops out of the city.

It had been a comprehensive victory; Frederick Charles had executed in full his mission of smashing the 2nd Army of the Loire. Significantly, apart from a couple of communications about the destruction of railroads, Moltke had not felt it necessary to offer any advice or instruction as the battle proceeded. Frederick Charles, at the admittedly considerable cost of 3,400 casualties, had wrecked any prospect that Chanzy might have had of lifting the investment of Paris.

Thus, on a triumphant note, ended the career of Frederick Charles in the field. He had been, overall, a very successful army commander; not, perhaps, as great as he may have believed, but a good deal better than his cousin, among others, would have conceded. He was not always responsive to Moltke's instructions, and frequently appeared not to understand the strategy which he was required to follow; and he was, often, guilty of extreme over caution. This caused Moltke extreme frustration, as his correspondence with Stülpnagel in 1866 and Stiehle in 1870 demonstrated. Waldersee, never reluctant to express his opinion, and by no means always a reliable commentator, called Frederick Charles 'a fortunate, rather than a great, military leader.' He wrote, long after the events of 1870-1871, a not very flattering character study of the Prince:

Prince Frederick Charles was a man of only mediocre intellect – a man of slow understanding as they say; he read with deliberation, and did not like to have matters reported to him hurriedly, as he found it difficult to follow. By dint of iron diligence he sought to make good this shortcoming, and he held fast by what he had once mastered; moreover, he had a good memory. His whole heart was devoted to the military calling from the close of his university career. He gave himself up to soldiering and hunting exclusively. He was one of those few Princes who regarded a soldier's carer as their life's vocation and who never tried to go in for anything else; and thus he developed into a real General *de Métier*. Military histories were his favourite study, and in this field he had acquired considerable knowledge which he liked airing in conversation and in other ways. He culti-vated the society of well read officers and was appreciative of their stimulating talk. In later years – that is, after the war of 1870-71 – he welcomed scholars to his soirées and music was a source of pleasure to him … The Prince (though I do not think he realised this) was a much better teacher for infantry than for cavalry. Himself only a mediocre and somewhat nervous horseman, he would never have been qualified to lead cavalry, as he lacked promptness of decision and of apprehension; besides, he had never applied himself to mastering the details of cavalry service. On the other hand, alike by his whole character and by inclina-tion, he was an excellent infantry man and, as has been said, he improved this aim greatly … As a military leader, Prince Frederick Charles was notable by his great prudence; a sort of Fabius Cunctator – if a little exaggeration be allowed – he held it as a maxim that one could not be too strong when going into battle; hence arose difficulties at times.[26]

Discounting the characteristically waspish style of its author, this analysis was not far wrong.

15

Crown Prince Frederick William

Having served as First Adjutant to the young Crown Prince during two crucially important years of the latter's life, Moltke always remained extremely fond of him. In later years, when the Crown Prince was serving as an army commander, their relationship remained tranquil, since Blumenthal, as his Chief of Staff, absorbed most of the stresses that inevitably occurred. For his part, Frederick William was devoted to Moltke, and in his diary of 1870-1871 there are constant references to his admiration for him. In particular, surrounded as he was by strong and voluble personalities, he noted Moltke's clarity of thought, writing for instance on November 23:

> We are at a crisis of the most exciting and interesting strategical combinations. Day by day Count Moltke expounds the situation of affairs with the utmost clearness, nay, to some extent with over-much sobriety: he has always thought out and calculated everything and invariably hits the nail on the head. War Minister von Roon, who has an asthmatic cough, spits copiously, and is fond of shrugging his shoulders if any piece of news sounds strange: this sort of pantomime, joined to the Olympian calm and confidence that Lieutenant General von Podbielski shows under all circumstances, often makes more impression on the King's now highly nervous temperament than Count Moltke's admirable clarity.[1]

A few days later, the Crown Prince was reflecting again on Moltke's mastery of the complex tasks confronting him:

> In these times our military experiences from day to day are for all the world as they are laid down in the books. Combinations have to be made for three armies, quite separate and distinct, but still working in cooperation; successes alternate with reverses and surprises – in a word, the higher strategy and tactics are the order of the day. General Count Moltke in all this remains always his own calm, clear-headed matter-of-fact-self - a veritable worker of miracles; for me it is a pleasure of the rarest sort to hear him make his daily report. If only the dark side

– our inevitable losses – were not inextricably bound up with these impressions and experiences![2]

In Blumenthal, the Crown Prince had an extremely able, but also extremely assertive, Chief of Staff, who assumed a good deal of independent authority. Colonel Hale devoted a chapter of his book on the Loire campaign to an analysis of the role of chief of staff in the Prussian army:

> In the German army this officer is intended to be the confidant, the adviser of his General, and his alter ego; but sometimes this position is not real but only nominal, owing to a fault in coupling together two incompatibles .... The chief staff officer should be the mental complement of the commander with whom he serves. With an over cautious commander, a bold chief staff officer full of daring and enterprise; with an impulsive commander a chief staff officer who is cool-headed; with a commander who before he acts is prone to weigh and consider long, a chief staff officer prompt in decision; with a commander difficult owing to temper a chief staff officer of perfect tact; with an ignorant commander, mistaking his ignorance for wisdom, a chief staff officer full of knowledge, artful in concealing his superiority in the possession of wisdom, but tactful enough to induce him to accept it as his own.[3]

As Hale goes on to point out, serving as a chief of staff to a Royal commander was especially difficult; he quotes an unnamed general in the German army as remarking: 'if you want to have your nerves tried, become chief staff officer to a Royal personage in war.' True authorship of orders issued and of decisions taken, necessarily depended on the personalities concerned. At the Royal Headquarters, this invariably meant Moltke, since as a rule the King abstained from interfering with Moltke's decision. With the Second Army, the issue of an order 'seems to have meant Prince Frederick Charles accentuated and emphasised always by Stiehle; or Stiehle accentuated and emphasised by him.'[4] The consequence of this was that here the staff took only one view of a matter.

The situation was different at the Crown Prince's headquarters:

> There is no doubt who was the predominant partner here. It was not the Prince; charming and fascinating as he was, he had not in him the power to hold under complete control such a strong nature as that of Blumenthal, for whom, however, he had a warm and sincere regard.[5]

Hale describes the incident previously mentioned and recorded by Blumenthal in his diary (but not by the Crown Prince in his) in which Blumenthal explained the view which he held of their relationship. His position could not, he said, be reduced to that of a mere adjutant. The Crown Prince's response was characteristic; he replied good humouredly that Blumenthal could do whatever he wished and he would not interfere,

Crown Prince Frederick William.

but that he must be kept informed of everything. Blumenthal thought he did not grasp their exact relationship.[6]

Reflecting on the Crown Prince's assignment to the Third Army in 1870, Waldersee noted:

> The distribution of the army is to my taste, it is very right that the southern Germans should be placed under the Crown Prince. We are all alike working for his future. For one thing, his personality must make an excellent impression, especially in comparison with the Kings of Bavaria and Württemberg. It strikes me as noteworthy that he has Blumenthal again under him after what passed between them in 1866, but it is a good move, and Blumenthal is an excellent Chief of the General Staff for a great army.[7]

Moltke was fifty five when appointed as adjutant to Prince Frederick William, who was then twenty years old. From the start they enjoyed a warm friendship, although the outgoing young prince was of a very different nature from his taciturn mentor. By the time came for Frederick William to marry Princess Victoria in January 1858 Moltke had already assumed the post of acting Chief of the General Staff, but he was naturally in attendance upon him at the ceremony. Moltke wrote to Mary with a detailed description of the wedding:

> The ceremony was proceeded with according to the not very lengthy English form. Both parties had to repeat the formula put to them by the archbishop. They vowed to remain faithful, the one to the other, for better for worse, for richer for poorer, until death do them part. Under this condition the prince took his future wife with a feelingly spoken but firm and audible 'I will.' I was truly quite pleased with his bearing during this ceremony. One could read on his somewhat pale face how much impressed he was with the seriousness of the ceremony, and yet he maintained that firm manly bearing which became him so well in the eyes of the public present. Everyone who could see him as I did must have felt obliged to love him.[8]

Frederick William grew up with a conviction that the democratic representation of the people was a fundamental right. He was sustained in his liberal views by his wife, and together they attracted a good deal of opprobrium, not least from Bismarck. After the latter's appointment as Minister President the Crown Prince, as he had become on his father's accession to the throne, felt increasingly isolated. In June 1863 he rashly stated in a speech at Danzig that he had known nothing of the decrees curtailing the freedom of the press, and had taken no part in the discussions which had led to them. His remarks caused a furore, and the King was extremely angry, telling him that he must take back his words, and not to repeat them again. The Crown Prince wrote a long and angry letter himself to Bismarck denouncing his advice to the King as dangerous for both the monarchy and for Prussia, and would lead to a breach of the people's rights. Bismarck endorsed the letter with the comment 'Youth is hasty with words;' and he never ceased to be mistrustful of both the Crown Prince and his wife.[9]

The Crown Prince, who had thought that he might perhaps have Goeben as his Chief of Staff of the Second Army when the Austro Prussian war began, told Blumenthal that he was glad that he had been appointed. The latter was well supported, with Stosch as his Quartermaster General and Verdy among other talented staff officers. Blumenthal was pleased with his first meeting with the Crown Prince:

> 'He made a most charming impression upon me, and appears to be entering upon the war in the most cheerful spirit, although he, too, would willingly see it avoided if possible.' Next day confirmed Blumenthal's initial impression: 'I cannot express the satisfaction which his joyous, frank bearing imparts.'

On June 27 the Crown Prince had his baptism of fire as he accompanied the V Corps under Steinmetz as it crossed the frontier at Nachod and ran slightly unexpectedly into determined opposition. As he made his way forward to see what he could of the battle, the Crown Prince was caught up in a chaotic situation, as he described in his diary:

I looked round for a better place, which would give a general view, and tried to get to another hill, but was suddenly caught in a detachment of the 4th Dragoons, who tore over a hill top in mad confusion, hurrying out of the battle, with loose horses and riders of different arms running off in all directions. To resist the torrent was impossible, especially as I found myself between this wild rout and a column of infantry, as well as the artillery and ammunition wagons; in fact, just in front of me, some guns had been dismounted. It was only the almost total block of the road that checked the dragoons whom I ordered peremptorily into arrest, while loose horses crushed me between the wheels of the wagons.[11]

It was a scary moment; but soon afterwards Stosch brought up columns of infantry to stabilise the situation and by nightfall the Crown Prince was able to celebrate his first victory.

Apart from the defeat of Bonin's I Corps at Trautenau, the campaign went well for the Crown Prince's Army. It culminated in the arrival of the Second Army in time to ensure victory at Königgrätz. That evening, as he grieved to learn of the death of Hiller von Gärtringen, the Crown Prince heard cheering:

We thought the King must be coming, but it was Fritz Karl. We waved our caps to each other from afar, and then, amid the hurrahs of the troops of my extreme right, and his extreme left wing, with whom I raised an enthusiastic cheer for our King, we fell into each other's arms. Such greetings, again, must be lived through; two years ago I embraced him before Düppel as a victor, today we were both conquerors, and when his troops were hard pressed, I had decided the day with the advent of my army.

The Crown Prince went on to look for his father:

Finally, after much seeking and asking, we found the King. I informed him of the presence of my army on the field, and kissed his hand; and then he embraced me. Neither of us could speak for some time; then he was the first to find words, and told me he rejoiced that I had so far achieved successful results, and had shown capacity for command.[13]

The King presented his son with the order Pour le Mérite, an honour he had already awarded him for the previous victories, although the Crown Prince had not yet heard of this. He was careful to give credit where credit was due; when the King shook hands with Blumenthal, he told his father: 'I know to whom I owe the conduct of my army,' praise which, Blumenthal wrote, sent straight to his heart.

As he rode among his victorious troops the Crown Prince was greatly moved by what he was seeing:

It is a gruesome thing to ride over a battlefield, and the ghastly mutilations that meet ones eye are indescribable. War is an appalling thing, and the man who brings it about with a stroke of his pen at the 'green table,' little recks what he is coujuring.[14]

It was, however, after the fighting was concluded, that the Crown Prince made his greatest contribution to the outcome of the war, when he intervened to persuade his father that he must take Bismarck's advice as to the peace terms to be imposed on the defeated Austrians. After a long and emotional discussion with the King, the Crown Prince was able to emerge to tell Bismarck that his father had given in. William did so with a bad grace, however, scrawling an angry note on Bismarck's final memorandum on the peace terms:

If what the army and the country are justified in expecting – that is, a heavy war indemnity from Austria or an acquisition of land sufficient to impress the eye – cannot be obtained from the vanquished without endangering our principal objective, then the victor at the gates of Vienna must bite into this sour apple and leave to posterity the judgment of his behaviour.[15]

In 1870 Frederick William and his wife shared his father's hope that war could be avoided over the issue of the Hohenzollern candidature for the throne of Spain, and after a meeting with Bismarck he believed that there would be no war. Bismarck, however, was less than candid with him in encouraging the Crown Prince to believe that he too did not want war. When, after the publication of the Ems telegram, the two men met again, the Chancellor was still shedding crocodile tears over the outbreak of a war that he had wished to avoid but which had become inevitable. The Crown Prince was impressed, noting in his diary that Bismarck explained his view of the situation 'in clear, earnest and dignified language, without any of those jests and gibes he is usually so fond of.' Moltke and Roon accompanied them to meet the King at Brandenburg to discuss the question of mobilisation. The King had made his way back from Ems to be greeted at every station by enthusiastic crowds. When they got to the Potsdam station at Berlin the news from Paris made it clear that war was declared. The King accepted the need for an immediate mobilisation of the VII and VIII Corps to cover Mainz; the Crown Prince, however, went further, urging a full mobilisation of all the armed forces; and with little further discussion this was decided upon. Father and son then drove off through crowds who stood 'shoulder to shoulder all the way from the station to the Royal Palace, uttering one unbroken storm of cheers.'[16]

Waldersee's prediction of the beneficial effect on the South Germans of the Crown Prince's appointment to the command of their troops as part of the Third Army was almost immediately proved correct. At Stuttgart on July 28 the Crown Prince and Blumenthal were met by cheering crowds; the experience was repeated as they journeyed on, as the Crown Prince recorded:

> At my departure the crowd was still greater than in the morning and the cheering
> never-ending; in truth these South Germans gave me just as warm a welcome as
> we are accustomed to receive in our old provinces. I felt almost embarrassed in
> presence of the King, who sat beside me in the carriage, for it was manifest these
> compliments were paid not to him, but to me as representative of the Power that
> had undertaken the solution of the German question.[17]

They went on to Baden, where they were received with similar enthusiasm, and the
Crown Prince spent time with his sister and her husband the Grand Duke. On July
30 the Crown Prince and Blumenthal arrived at Speyer, where they were to meet the
rest of their headquarters staff. The Crown Prince was conscious of the importance of
the moment: 'Thus then we stand at the beginning of a historical world crisis! I am not
despondent, but yet the gravity of the situation makes my heart tremble in view of the
battles we shall have to fight.'[18]

On August 4 the Third Army fought and won the battle of Weisssenburg; as he
rode among his troops that night he was especially moved by their courage and devo-
tion. He was also profoundly saddened by the casualties that had been sustained,
particularly among the officers. That night, in the house of the Catholic curé, he was
overwhelmed with grief at the thought of their losses of the day.

Two days later the Third Army defeated MacMahon's army at the battle of Wörth.
The Crown Prince was composing telegrams announcing the victory as the fighting
came to an end:

> At the same hour the firing entirely ceased, and in a moment a deep stillness
> reigned, as though nothing had happened, while the lovely summer's evening
> spread its mantle over hill and plain ... One must be familiar with the sight
> of battlefields and of the look of troops that have just been in action to form
> any conception of the appearance of the bloody field of Worth; to describe it is
> impossible.[19]

August 7 was decreed as a much needed rest day; the Crown Prince spent it in
continuing to visit the wounded and the large number of French prisoners. Among the
latter he was surprised to encounter bitter feelings about Marshal MacMahon, 'whom
they blamed for bad leadership, called him "un cochon," while they designated the
emperor as "une vieille femme."' He was not altogether pleased to be asked by some
French officers if he was Prince Charles; he replied that his uncle was with the King;
'they took me, of course, as everybody does, for my cousin.'[20] Next day the army moved
forward to the line of the Saar, where he expected that the French might make a stand.

On August 12 the Crown Prince received a bundle of five letters from his wife,
which brought the first news as to how the reports of the victories of the Third Army
had been received in Berlin. He was moved to tears to hear of 'the lively interest and
sympathy expressed by all classes in unpremeditated and quite unaffected language,'
particularly when he thought of the cost in human suffering of these battles.

It was not until August 20 that the Crown Prince again met his father, driving to the Royal Headquarters at Pont à Mousson. The King presented him with the Iron Cross of the 2nd class for Weissenburg and of the 1st for Wörth; he at once asked that the same awards be made to Blumenthal, because he could not 'wear this order before this man who had done such distinguished service had received it.' The King duly granted his request. After this there was a short Council of War attended by Roon and Moltke, following which the Crown Prince paid a visit to Bismarck, whose son Herbert had been wounded at Mars la Tour:

> All goes well today; General von Moltke remains always entirely unperturbed, confident, clearheaded and firmly resolved to move on to the main objective-Paris; in a word, he is the complete veteran in all points! Count Bismarck I found moderate minded and speaking, I should say, very reasonably, his views clear and decisive on all points, calmly and coldly watching events, and in no way unduly sanguine in consequence of our successes so far.[21]

As the Prussian armies marched on in pursuit of the Army of Châlons, the Crown Prince paid a visit to the Royal Headquarters at Bar le Duc. He found Moltke and the King excited at the prospect of cutting off MacMahon who appeared to be attempting to go to the relief of Metz. Moltke's hopes were high; he was aiming now at the possibility of surrounding the French army and capturing it in its entirety, an ambition which the Crown Prince found over optimistic. As the days passed, however, it became increasingly clear that this was a realistic possibility. The Crown Prince was struck by the gloom of the population, regarding MacMahon's position as hopeless, and 'complaining loudly of the plundering and thieving committed by their own soldiery, and by way of contrast holding up ours as a good example.'[22]

The Crown Prince was taken ill on August 27, and for the next couple of days was confined to bed; but as the endgame for the Army of Châlons developed he and Blumenthal rode forward each day to be near the head of the Third Army's advance. By August 31 it was clear that MacMahon could not easily escape the net that was being tightened around him. On September 1 both the Royal Headquarters and the headquarters of the Third Army were in a position to see almost the whole of the battlefield. Blumenthal described the Crown Prince's reaction:

> Both points of observation were beyond the range of shot, and it became very difficult for me to restrain the Prince from going in closer. As far as the selection of the place was concerned, there could be no two opinions, but the Prince could not brook seeing the fight going on and he not taking part in it. I cannot deny that was my own feeling, too; but I am now old enough to be able to restrain such youthful ardour, and am quite content to find myself looking on at this sort of thing, in calm serenity, from a safe distance.[23]

In his diary the Crown Prince described the famous scene at the end of the battle when General Reille came up to the King to present Napoleon's letter. The King and the Crown Prince stood in front of a dense half circle of royalty and nobility as well as Bismarck, Moltke and military leaders. The Crown Prince was amused to note that 'the Grand Duke of Saxe-Weimar endeavoured by shifting his position this way and that to get as near as possible to me.'[24] Later, when he returned to his headquarters, the band of the 58th Infantry Regiment played 'Heil dir im Siegerkranz' and the hymn 'Now thank we all our God,' which moved him to tears. Next day he reflected on the extent of the victory and its significance, observing that on the previous day everything had happened too quickly to take it all in. He remained, however, anxious as to what the immediate future held.

Once the investment of Paris had commenced, and the Royal Headquarters had to Blumenthal's annoyance arrived at Versailles, its proximity meant that the Crown Prince saw a lot of his father and of Moltke, and he began regularly to attend the daily reports which the latter made to the King. In the early days of the investment he observed that Moltke and Roon were frequently at loggerheads, 'the gist of their mutual reproaches being that the departments are kept separated by too hard and fast a line and not enough reciprocal interchange of information practised.'[25] At one such daily report the subject of the annexation of Alsace was discussed; Blumenthal noted that the Crown Prince 'spoke most earnestly and with so much emotion of the dangers that might arise out of Alsace' that he suspected that the Duke of Coburg and Professor Samwer had been getting at him.[26]

As the autumn wore on, the issue that occupied most discussion at Versailles was of course the bombardment of Paris. The Crown Prince loyally supported Moltke and Blumenthal in their opposition to the project; but their long struggle to resist it ended in failure, and it finally began with the shelling of Mont Avron on December 27, an operation which, to the amazement of the Crown Prince and Blumenthal, and no doubt of Moltke as well, proved extremely successful. The bitterness with which the issue had been debated had deepened the gulf between Bismarck and Moltke.

The Crown Prince took up the question of their relationship on January 8:

> I had today at my quarters a lengthy discussion with General Count Moltke, in which I talked over the present situation with him in detail, and convinced myself that he is deeply offended at Count Bismarck's arbitrary and despotic attitude. He has the feeling that, in military matters no less than in political, the Federal Chancellor is resolved to decide everything himself, without paying the smallest heed to what the responsible experts have to say; besides which, he is offended because Count Bismarck addresses inquiries and writes communications to the General Staff relating to circumstances so exclusively concerned with recent strategical questions that he (Count Moltke) has already more than once been compelled summarily to abandon matters of the sort.[27]

This led in due course to the Crown Prince's attempt to mediate between them described in Chapter 4. In the end of course, their conflicting positions were resolved comprehensively in Bismarck's favour.

The Crown Prince will have been equivocal in his response to this outcome. Looked at from the point of view of liberal politics, it was of course right that the government should prevail over the military; but when the government was led by Bismarck, the Crown Prince shuddered when he contemplated the future. He wrote in his diary on December 31 of the reputation which Germany had gained under Bismarck's leadership:

> What good to us is all power, all martial glory and renown, if hatred and mistrust meet us at every turn, if every step we advance in our development is a subject for suspicion and grudging? Bismarck has made us great and powerful, but he has robbed us of our friends, the sympathies of the world, and – our conscience. I still hold fast today to the conviction that Germany, without blood and iron, simply by the justice of her cause, could make 'moral conquests' and, united, become free and powerful A preponderance of quite another kind than that gained by mere force of arms was within our reach, for German culture, German science and German genius must have won us respect, love and – honour. The insolent, brutal 'Junker' willed it otherwise …
>
> The future holds for us the noble, but infinitely difficult task of freeing the beloved German Fatherland from the baseless suspicion with which the world today regards her. We must prove that the power acquired is not to beget dangers, but to bring with it a blessing, the blessing of peace and civilisation.[28]

These profoundly held convictions ensured that, in the years before the day when, as a sick man, he ascended the throne, the Crown Prince remained an object of Bismarck's profound mistrust. Although they had, on occasion, been able to work together for the benefit of their country, there could never have been a productive relationship between them as Emperor and Chancellor. Naturally, in view of the subsequent course of German history, it has been a source of endless speculation as to where that would have gone had Frederick III not died so tragically young.

The Crown Prince was a man of great charm and integrity, and of warm humanity, qualities which communicated themselves to his troops, who idolised him. He was touched by their celebration of his birthday on October 18:

> The lovely sunny day opened with a salute of music performed by the band of the 9th Division quartered here. Men of the Royal Grenadier Regiment in particular had hung up festoons of flowers, and without a sound decorated the outside of the house and my room with them. Bonbons and tokens of affection from far and near took me by surprise at breakfast.[29]

His popularity extended to the South Germans; a few weeks later, as the Crown Prince rode past a party of Bavarian troops working on the establishment of a battery at Plessis-Piquet, Major General von Schulz overheard one of the men say: 'If he had led us in 1866, we'd have beaten the lousy Prussians.'[30]

As a commander the Crown Prince was content to act in effect as a non executive chairman of the organisation, leaving Blumenthal wide latitude as a very able, and particularly assertive, managing director. Every partnership must evolve its own private rules, and in both Bohemia and France the two men worked, almost all the time, extremely well together.

The last word on the Emperor Frederick III may be left to the eighty seven year old Moltke. When, although gravely ill, the Emperor attended the wedding of his son Prince Henry to Princess Irene of Hesse on May 24 1888, Moltke spoke for many who were there when he said that he had seen many brave men, 'but none as brave as the Emperor has shown himself today.'[31]

16

Manteuffel

From the day on which he assumed responsibility for the post of Chief of the Great General Staff, Moltke naturally had to deal with a wide range of other post holders whose position and influence to a greater or lesser extent impacted on his work. As the years went by, his influence and that of the General Staff grew; but especially in the early years his relationships with other senior officers and advisers to the King were of great importance.

It was on the advice of Edwin von Manteuffel that Moltke was originally appointed as acting Chief of the General Staff in 1857. Earlier that year Manteuffel had become Chief of the Military Cabinet, a post in which he exerted a great deal of political as well as military influence. He always held a high opinion of Moltke; since the latter was careful to avoid getting involved in controversial political issues there was little danger of their being at odds. On military matters they were generally in agreement, and it was at Manteuffel's suggestion that Moltke went to Allied headquarters in Jutland in 1864 to clear up the shambles that had been presided over by the aged Field Marshal von Wrangel and his Chief of Staff Vogel von Falckenstein. Manteuffel held the post of Chief of the Military Cabinet until 1865, when he was shunted sideways by Bismarck to the position of Governor of Schleswig. By then the Minister President, and Albrecht von Roon the Minister of War, had had more than enough of Manteuffel's interference with their efforts to resolve the conflict with the Landtag over the issue of army reform.

Karl Rochus Edwin von Manteuffel was born at Magdeburg in 1809. He was a cousin of Otto von Manteuffel, Minister President of Prussia from 1850 until 1858. At the age of 17 he joined the Guards Dragoon Regiment, becoming a Lieutenant in 1828, a rank in which he remained until 1843, when he was promoted to Captain. In 1848 when he became a major and was serving as adjutant to Prince Albrecht, he found himself during the March Days in the royal palace in Berlin. He earned the disapproval of General von Thile, a close military adviser of King Frederick William IV, by pointing out on March 18 that the King was a descendant of Frederick the Great, who would never have considered the suggested retreat to Potsdam.[1] Next day he reversed this advice, but the King, characteristically, hesitated to take it until it

Manteuffel.

was too late. He had, however, been impressed by Manteuffel's firmness, and after the disturbances had subsided remembered him as a useful source of constitutional advice. From then, as Professor Craig observed, 'he was very seldom very far from the centre of power.'

Manteuffel, described by one historian as 'one of the high priests of military orthodoxy,' had a predictably old fashioned view about duelling, profoundly disapproving of the introduction of tribunals of honour designed to stamp out the practice. He wrote in 1871 to the historian Ranke:

> In the army I was brought up in, it simply was not done to ask a judge to get you satisfaction. You got it for yourself. You drew your pistol, and if the other man refused to fight you had him soundly beaten by your own fellows.[2]

He had suited his own conduct to these principles when in 1861 Carl Twesten, a Berlin city councillor, had suggested in a pamphlet that Manteuffel, in seeking the extension of the term of military service to three years, was aiming to divide the army from the Prussian people, and that this could 'produce an atmosphere of distrust between the military and civil society such as existed in its fullest flower before 1806.'[3] Manteuffel promptly demanded that Twesten either withdraw, or fight a duel; Twesten chose to fight, and Manteuffel shot him through the arm. Following this, he insisted that he should be punished according to law, and spent several weeks in undisguised satisfaction in confinement in a castle in Magdeburg.

Manteuffel was always perfectly indifferent to the effect of his actions on those who opposed him, and delighted in rubbing this in, going out of his way to be arrogant and unyielding as possible. An instance of this was when Rudolf von Auerswald went to see him on behalf of the moderates in the Landtag, in an effort to get him to persuade the King not to dedicate the standards of the new regiments formed in 1860, at the height of the *Konfliktzeit*. Manteuffel's response was contemptuous:

> I do not understand what Your Excellency desires. His Majesty has ordered me to arrange a military ceremony. Am I to renounce this because there are a number of people sitting in a house in the Dönhoffplatz, who call themselves a Landtag and who may be displeased with this ceremony? I fail to see how these people concern me. As a general I have never yet been ordered to take my instructions from these people.[4]

Manteuffel relentlessly kept up the pressure for an unyielding position on the conflict over army reform, writing to Roon on April 3 1862:

> How can the three-year service be given up during his reign without bringing shame upon the personal position of the All Highest?... The army will not understand it; its confidence in the King will be shaken, and the consequences for the internal condition of the army will be incalculable.[5]

The most extravagant manifestation of his political views was his belief that sooner or later revolution would come and that it would be necessary to suppress it by a military coup d'état. He carried with him a vivid recollection of the events of 1848, and he was determined that never again should an uprising have any chance of success. In the overheated political atmosphere of Berlin in 1861 Manteuffel had little difficulty in inducing the King to take steps to prepare for armed conflict if that became necessary. During that year Major General Hiller von Gärtringen, later to die a hero's death at Königgrätz, prepared a plan for military action. This was not the work of a lone extremist; the plan was discussed in the Military Cabinet and in the presence of the King.[6] In January 1862 the King approved a plan of action, which included the delivery of sealed orders to the units which were to take part, to be opened only upon receipt of telegraphic instructions. It was, in the context of the time, merely a precaution against the breakdown of civil authority; but it represented to Manteuffel the opportunity to smash the liberal movement completely, and he was eager for it. Fortunately for Prussia, it never came; but during the fevered days of 1862 there was even talk among the most reactionary of those around the King of making Manteuffel Minister President.[7]

In the letter to Roon quoted above Manteuffel spelled out his belief that somehow the struggle must go on until a Landtag sympathetic to the monarch was elected. If that did not happen, then 'we shall see bloody heads and then good election results will come.' For a man holding such views to take the first position of government would have meant catastrophe.

However, Manteuffel, for all his extreme monarchical convictions, had no time whatever for incompetents, however aristocratic their connections might be. When, with the rank of Major General, he became Chief of the Military Cabinet, he also became head of the Personnel Division of the War Ministry. It was an appointment of huge significance; he was reported as saying of his work there:

> That was my greatest achievement. If I had not cleaned things out we should not have won in 1864, 1866 and 1870. The officers were much worse in the early fifties than in 1806.[8]

He may well have been right. His ruthless efficiency in weeding out useless officers was of far reaching importance, and influenced the history of his country to an extent even greater than his political activity or his career in the field.

Since Manteuffel was so very close to the King, it was Moltke's practice during the Danish war to keep him fully informed of any matters relevant to the future conduct of operations, and of course any personnel questions. He sent him, for instance, a copy of his letter of April 12 to Blumenthal commenting on the plan to storm the Düppel position; and on April 21 he sent a copy of the confidential report he had received from Captain von der Burg of the General Staff. In respect of this he was careful to emphasise that the candid comments of a junior officer on the performance of his seniors should not be held against him.[9]

During the period in which Moltke was intensely frustrated by the lack of information reaching him, Manteuffel seems not to have responded to Moltke's concern that he should be kept in the picture. Commenting on the debates that followed the victory at Düppel, Moltke wrote to Manteuffel that he was 'completely ignorant of the outcome of the discussion', and he asked that since Manteuffel was more fully in touch with the situation he should give him the information necessary for his continued planning. He ended his letter with a plaintive reproach:

> For five days I have been without any news of the orders given, without any report form the theatre of operations, and under these conditions it is particularly difficult to form an opinion.[10]

For Moltke to have to write in these terms illustrates just how far he still had in 1864 to travel before he reached the position he would occupy in 1866 and beyond.

During the Danish war Manteuffel's influence was at its height. It is noteworthy that in spite of Bismarck's extreme reservations about the Chief of the Military Cabinet's political conduct and attitudes, it was to the latter that he turned to carry out an extremely delicate mission in February1864. The dispute between Prussia and Austria over the need to carry the war into Jutland threatened to destabilise the alliance, and Manteuffel was chosen to go to Vienna to negotiate an agreement with the Austrian leadership to permit an advance northwards. His selection was due to the fact that his strong pro-Austrian attitudes would make him *persona grata* with Franz Joseph and his advisers. It was, however, a risky decision, as Professor Craig pointed out. Manteuffel's sympathy for Austria involved a belief that Prussia should agree to help her recover Lombardy, in exchange for agreement over Jutland and a promise of the Duchies after the war.[11] Bismarck, of course, was having none of that, and insisted on a strictly limited definition of the scope of Manteuffel's brief in Vienna. The latter's views were certainly shared by a number of senior officers, who regarded France as the real enemy and Austria as Prussia's natural ally. It was a view to which Moltke was privately sympathetic.

In Vienna, Manteuffel entirely justified Bismarck's decision to entrust him with the mission, using his diplomatic skills and personal charm to persuade the Austrians to agree to the advance into Jutland. Rechberg, the Austrian minister, was warm in his praise: 'If ever again a disagreement should arise between Berlin and Vienna, may the King send back General Manteuffel at once.'[12]

After the war, Bismarck's desire to see Manteuffel safely out of the way as Governor of Schleswig was firmly supported by Roon, whose realistic grasp of political reality left him out of sympathy with Manteuffel's extreme views.[13] Furthermore, in addition to his disapproval of Manteuffel's political activity, the War Minister had fallen out with Manteuffel over the latter's refusal to acknowledge that he was in fact Roon's subordinate. During the Danish war they clashed severely over Roon's allegation that Manteuffel had withheld from him reports to the King from commanding generals. Manteuffel had always taken the view that the existence of a constitutional War Minister was a direct threat to the royal military prerogatives, and had strenuously sought to limit the minister's powers. General Eduard von Bonin, serving as War Minister for the second time, was an earlier victim of these views. In 1859 Manteuffel and Gustav von Alvensleben, the Adjutant-General, held that the question of raising additional regiments was exclusively one for the Crown to decide. In this view they were warmly supported by the King, to whom any compromise on the issue was anathema; when this was put squarely to Bonin, a firm supporter of the 'New Era 'government, he promptly resigned. Many years later, in his memoirs, Bismarck brushed under the carpet the critical constitutional question involved, suggesting that it was a question of competence, when he described Bonin as a man who could not even 'have kept a drawer in order, much less a ministry.'[14]

Manteuffel continued to use his dual position as Chief of the Military Cabinet and head of the Personnel Division of the War Ministry to withhold from the War Minister any information which might find its way to the Landtag. This included, for instance, communications from the King to commanding generals and any orders pertaining to questions of command. He also did all he could to exclude his personnel function from the War Minister's control. Although Tresckow, his immediate successor, did not pursue this policy so assertively, the next holder of the post from 1871, von Albedyll, had worked in the Personnel Division under Manteuffel, and applied the latter's principles so successfully that the position of the War Minister was greatly weakened.

Prior to his appointment as Governor of Schleswig, Manteuffel's most recent demonstration of his extremely reactionary views had been to scupper a plan put forward by the Landtag, and approved by Bismarck and his ministers, in an endeavour to bring about a reconciliation. On May 2 1865 Manteuffel wrote to the King:

> Who rules and decides in Prussia, the King or the ministers? ... Your Majesty's ministers are loyal and devoted, but they live now only in the atmosphere of the Chamber. If I may express my opinion, it is this: Your Majesty should hold no Council but should write to Minister Bismarck saying: 'Now that I have read the proposal, I have decided that the government will not agree to it.'[15]

William had no difficulty in accepting this advice. He usually fell in with Manteuffel's suggestions. When Bismarck proposed that the latter be posted to Schleswig as Governor, he took a good deal of persuading that he could do without the man who had sustained his monarchical convictions for so many years, but in the end Bismarck and Roon got their way. As Chief of the Military Cabinet Manteuffel was succeeded by Hermann von Tresckow, who proved to be a good deal less overbearing than his predecessor. Manteuffel's removal from the front of the political stage, however, by no means marked the end of his contribution to his country's history.

When Manteuffel went to Schleswig as Governor, he vigorously applied Bismarck's policies that were designed to provoke the Austrians, notwithstanding his own sympathies for them. He was firm on the principle of joint sovereignty of the Duchies to the point of severely hampering the Austrian administration of Holstein. And although he was out of harm's way as far as day to day politics were concerned, he was still called to crucial meetings of the Crown Council, such as those held on May 29 1865 and February 15 1866. It is surprising, therefore, that as the final crisis approached in 1866, Bismarck found it necessary to give him a sharp rebuke, writing to him reprovingly on June 9:

> I was acquainted with your conviction, expressed here when you had occasion, that for political, military and financial reasons we must take on the war quickly and wherever opportunity offers. I saw to it, therefore, that my telegram conveying your instructions should prompt you to act in that sense. I expected important news from you in the course of yesterday. Information about the friendly tone of the music on both sides of the military chassés – croirés does not harmonise with the feeling *here* which expects news from you of the first cannon shots ... If you don't do it, you will not only frustrate my European plan out of military courtesy but you will find no one, apart from the Württembergers, in the army who any longer understands your behaviour... Every three days costs us

2 millions which we shall not have in our possession to give much longer; for we do not, like Austria, live at the expense of our creditors. Every three days brings to Austria 5,000 more men of the Confederation. In all parts of Europe the wind lies in our favour. People *expect* us to act. *Today* they would find it natural, perhaps in a week's time they would not.[16]

Manteuffel had some 16,000 men in Schleswig, more than three times as many as Gablenz, his Austrian opposite number in Holstein. When the latter, in response to instructions from Vienna, summoned a meeting of the Holstein Estates at Itzehoe, it had been on Bismarck's orders that Manteuffel, after writing a letter to Gablenz which the Minister President would have seen as over friendly, ordered his troops to occupy those parts of Holstein not occupied by the Austrians, a move which did not produce the desired result. Bismarck was still grumbling about it after his letter of June 9, saying to the Italian Minister: 'If only there had been an exchange of shots.'[17] On June 11, the day fixed for the meeting of the Holstein Estates, Manteuffel raised the stakes by occupying Itzehoe and arresting the Austrian Commissioners; when next day Manteuffel moved on Altona, Gablenz realised that the time to depart had come, and during the night of June 11 loaded his troops, which consisted of the Brigade Kalik, on trains which rumbled across Germany to take them to join Benedek's army in Bohemia; the Prussian occupation of the Duchies was thus completed without a shot being fired, much to Bismarck's disappointment.

Following the departure of the Austrians, Manteuffel moved on Hamburg, from which city he prepared to march south of Hanover. His division was now part of the Prussian forces, commanded by General Vogel von Falckenstein, soon to be designated the Army of the Main. Although Manteuffel had disappointed his political master in the matter of provoking hostilities in the Duchies, he was to give complete satisfaction to Moltke in the campaign that was about to unfold in Western Germany.

17

From the Main to the Doubs

In the first phase of the campaign in Western Germany, Manteuffel himself played little part. It was, however, his advance guard under Major General Eduard von Flies that was to undertake the first significant operations of the campaign, having pressed on southward from Hamburg through Hanover in pursuit of the Hanoverian army. By the evening of June 25 Flies had reached Gotha. En route there had been a series of complex negotiations in the hope of a possible deal with the Hanoverians; when these broke down, the temporary armistice came to an end, and Flies moved towards Langensalza, where he encountered Hanoverian troops; his orders required him 'to remain close upon the enemy,' which he chose to interpret as an instruction to attack, perhaps fearing that the enemy might escape northwards.

Facing odds of two to one, Flies fought all day on June 27 in baking heat. His attack across the River Unstrut, at first successful, stalled, and the Hanoverian counter attack turned him back through Langensalza. The exhausted Hanoverians could do no more, and fresh Prussian units were closing in. A final attempt to escape to the north east failed, and on June 29 the Hanoverian army capitulated; at the King's suggestion it was to be left to Manteuffel to negotiate the terms. When he reached Langensalza he found that Vogel von Falckenstein and the Hanoverian commander, Arentschild, had agreed an unconditional surrender; but the milder terms brought by Manteuffel were added to the final capitulation agreement.[1]

The key objective assigned to the Army of the Main was the Bavarian army under Prince Charles. After a clash with the enemy on July 10 Manteuffel led his division to Kissingen, where it took part in the series of engagements which led Prince Charles to fall back on Schweinfurt, with Manteuffel in pursuit. He was next, however, required to concentrate on occupying all the territory north of the Main, while Goeben's 13th Division continued to press the enemy.

Moltke had in the meantime reached the conclusion that Falckenstein, after a series of misdemeanours, could not continue in command of the Army of the Main, and he was shunted off to Bohemia to take charge of the occupied territories there. As his successor, the choice fell on Manteuffel, who took up his duties on July 20. Moltke might himself have chosen Goeben on the basis of his proven ability; but it was no doubt due to Manteuffel's close relationship with the King that he was appointed. Flies took over command of the Combined Division.

The record of the instructions sent by Moltke to Falckenstein during his tenure as army commander compared to those during Manteuffel's time is informative. Once Manteuffel had taken over, the need for a constant flow of orders ceased, and he was left to get on with the job of disposing of the Federal Army. Although this enjoyed a substantial numerical advantage, Manteuffel won a series of victories, culminating in a vigorous engagement to the east of the Tauber. By July 27 he was moving forward on Würzburg. Prince Charles wrote to Manteuffel pleading with him to spare Würzburg as an open city, following this with copies of despatches announcing the armistice in Bohemia; he sought a week's truce. Manteuffel, without news, felt that by taking a hard line he could get Würzburg without a fight. His reply was that Würzburg could not be treated as an open city, since it was defended by the strongly held height of the Marienberg. That position must therefore be surrendered at once. On July 28 his Chief of Staff, Colonel von Kraatz-Koschlau, began negotiations with his opposite number, Lieutenant General von der Tann. Before these were concluded Manteuffel heard from Moltke that peace preliminaries had been signed with Austria on July 24, and that a truce with Bavaria was to begin on August 2. Manteuffel, on his own initiative, agreed with Charles on a temporary ceasefire, and on both sides the troops went into quarters.[2]

On July 30 Moltke confirmed to Manteuffel that he should in any case occupy as much territory as possible. Meanwhile the Federal army was beginning to disintegrate; that day Prince William of Baden asked Manteuffel for permission for his troops to go home, and this was readily agreed. Moltke told Manteuffel that he had freedom of action until August 2, so the latter gave notice to end the ceasefire at 6.00 am on August 1 unless Würzburg was given up at once. Charles had no choice but to agree, and, with this, Manteuffel's campaign with the Army of the Main ended after an almost unbroken run of success.[3]

With the Seven Weeks' War duly won, it was now Bismarck's concern to ensure that Prussia could keep her winnings without international complications. In addition to France, he had particularly to take reaction in Russia particularly into account. To make certain that Tsar Alexander remained sympathetic to Prussia's expansion, notwithstanding the probable hostility of Prince Gorchakov, Bismarck turned again to Manteuffel, who was sent off at once to St Petersburg. There, his diplomatic skills and his impeccable monarchical and anti-democratic credentials achieved Russian acquiescence in the annexation by Prussia of Schleswig-Holstein, Hanover, Nassau, Electoral Hesse and Frankfurt.

Thereafter Manteuffel returned for a time to the command of the Prussian troops in Schleswig-Holstein. Later, he took leave of absence from the army, retiring to Naumburg, where he had the benefit of a stipend as a member of the chapter of the cathedral there. His ecclesiastical commitment prompted a particularly bitter jibe about him: 'One leg in the army, the other in the church, his head in diplomacy, and his heart nowhere.'[4] In August 1868 Manteuffel returned to the army as commander of the I Corps, a position which he held on the outbreak of war in 1870.

The corps was assigned to the First Army, commanded by General Karl von Steinmetz, whose choleric disposition gave Moltke a lot of trouble, both in 1866 and again in 1870. The I Corps constituted the rear echelon of the First Army and as a result did not reach the front line until later than the other units, being finally concentrated on August 11. Next day it was ordered to move forward towards the French units which were believed to be on the left bank of the Nied. These had, however, fallen back to Metz, and Moltke ordered Steinmetz to remain on the Nied, and endeavour to clarify the French intentions. Steinmetz interpreted this as meaning that the First Army should remain strictly on the defensive.[5]

Although the French appeared still to have large bodies of troops east of Metz, cavalry patrols began to report on August 14 that the French were retreating through the city. When an engagement began to develop, Manteuffel ordered his corps to advance, reporting this to Steinmetz at 4.45 pm; Zastrow, commanding the VII Corps, also reported that he was in action. Steinmetz, shocked by the news, ordered both corps 'to break off the battle immediately,' riding forward to emphasise this personally.[6]

Manteuffel had ordered the advance because he judged that Zastrow needed support. By 6.00 pm his corps was heavily engaged, and as night fell, he ordered up fresh troops which threw back Ladmirault's Corps towards Metz.. At 8.00 pm Steinmetz arrived, and was far from pleased with what he heard about the exploits of Manteuffel's corps:

> Through he fully recognised the brilliant valour of the troops and the skilful leadership of the commanders, he could not but express disapprobation that so serious an action had been engaged in without orders from higher authority, and that it had been permitted to develop to such an extent, when the role of the First Army was essentially defensive, and the vicinity of a large fortified place must render any immediate useful result of victory impossible.[7]

No doubt the irascible Steinmetz expressed himself in very much more pungent terms than Schell's tactful account suggests. In fact, though, as Schell went on to point out, there was no time to get approval of an attack on the retreating enemy, and the vigour of Manteuffel's assault significantly delayed the retreat, so that 'the fruits of the victory on August 14 were to be gathered on the other side of Metz.'[8]

Manteuffel, writing to Steinmetz that night, made clear that he would remain on the battlefield, to recover his wounded, and 'to clinch the victory;' and although ordered to return to the position he held before the battle, he disobeyed. The victory, though important, had been dearly bought; total losses amounted to 2,903 officers and men.

During the battles of Mars La Tour on August 16 and Gravelotte two days later, the I Corps had the important but unenviable task of watching the Army of the Rhine from positions to the east of Metz. Later, during the siege of the city, the corps was reinforced by the 3rd Cavalry Division and later also the 3rd Reserve Division (von Kummer). Manteuffel had largely a free hand to conduct the operations on the right bank of the Moselle and to deal with any attempt by Bazaine to break out. An attempt on August 26 was aborted, apparently due to threatening weather; on August 31 Bazaine tried again, this time launching an assault on Manteuffel's corps which during a period of four hours beat off a series of attacks. That night Manteuffel reported the outcome of the day's fighting:

> Battle ceased at nightfall. The positions are retained, and the enemy has been repulsed everywhere. Supply of ammunition replenished; my troops will be under arms at 4.00 pm tomorrow.[9]

Next day Manteuffel counter attacked; after a day of fierce fighting the village of Noisseville, which had changed hands three times, was in the possession of the I Corps. Manteuffel had been outnumbered throughout, but had conducted the operation with great coolness and determination. Total German casualties were 2,972, of which 2,756 were sustained by the I Corps and the other units under his command; the French lost approximately 3,550 men.

On September 6 Manteuffel had a fall with his horse, fracturing a bone in his foot, which thereafter had to be bandaged daily for the rest of the war. Hermann von Wartensleben, his Quartermaster General and acting Chief of Staff, later wrote:

> To ease his weak foot, the General was obliged to use a walking stick, and could not mount his horse without assistance. Nevertheless, although sixty three years of age, he performed almost all marches on horseback, long and fatiguing as many of them were.[11]

On September 13 Moltke was finally able to get rid of Steinmetz, who was posted to be Governor General of Posen. For the moment he was not replaced; but on October 27, as the capitulation of Metz drew near, Manteuffel was appointed to the vacant command, Wartensleben continuing to act as his Chief of Staff. He remained in command of the I Corps. After the fall of Metz, the first objective of the First Army was to be the reduction of a number of key fortresses which threatened the German lines of communication, such as Verdun, Montmédy and Mézières. Thereafter Manteuffel was to march north to deal with the new French forces that were being put together there. His movement was, however, delayed by the unexpectedly large number of prisoners at Metz with which his army had to deal.[12]

Once the First Army was able to move north to carry out its primary mission, Moltke on November 18 sent Manteuffel orders as to how to achieve this. It was to march towards Rouen; the crucial point, however, was Amiens, which was to be occupied permanently with a substantial force.[13] On November 22 and 23 the army moved towards the Oise; Manteuffel now appointed Bentheim to the command of the I Corps. While the army was advancing Manteuffel had also been concerned with the progress of the sieges of La Fére, Thionville and Mézières, which were the responsibility of Zastrow's VII Corps. To the latter Manteuffel sent a reminder that he wanted Senden's detachment, currently before Mézières, to be forwarded to him as soon as possible.[14]

Manteuffel was conscious that the French success at Coulmiers on the Loire had not only strengthened their self confidence but had also impressed the neutral powers. A quick victory was desirable, and since Farre appeared to be standing in his position around Amiens, Manteuffel resolved to strike at once without waiting for all his troops to come up. He was, however, always inclined to seek support for his views from those around him, and particularly Goeben, as Wartensleben observed:

> At such moments General Manteuffel was wont to ask the opinions of those persons especially in his confidence. The commanding general of the VIII Army Corps, General Goeben, was at the moment in Montdidier: he, as well as the Chief of the Staff of the army *ad interim*, unanimously pronounced themselves in favour of an immediate advance upon Amiens.[15]

Manteuffel expected to fight the French around Amiens on November 28, and the orders he issued reflected this. However, Farre had concluded that if he merely held the line of the Somme he could not realistically hope to defend Amiens, and he pushed forward to the heights between the Somme and the Avre. As a result the leading units of the First Army ran into the French on November 27, and a major battle developed. In fact, it was two battles; Goeben's VIII Corps advanced on the left, with Bentheim's I Corps on the right. Between them, a gap opened, which Manteuffel had to plug by using the troops escorting his headquarters to display the maximum activity.[16] After a day of stiff fighting the First Army was successful in defeating the French in both sectors. Farre had it in mind to continue the battle on the following day. He learned that night, however, that a council of war held in Amiens in his absence had unanimously determined that the city must be abandoned.

Next day Manteuffel reviewed his options with Wartensleben. On the one hand, the obvious military decision would be to pursue the Army of the North and finish it off. On the other hand, Moltke had expressly given Rouen as the next objective once Amiens had been secured, and there were clear signs that the French forces on the Seine under Briand were capable of being a serious threat and the First Army was directed to march on Rouen. Von der Groeben, with the 3rd Cavalry Division (less two regiments, and with the 3rd Brigade, remained behind to hold Amiens.[17]

By December 5 the patrols of the First Army were pushing forward towards Rouen. Goeben, up with the leading troops of his corps, was soon reporting that he was seven miles from the city and proposed to ride in; this he did at 2.30 pm, in the face of an extremely hostile and resentful population. Manteuffel ordered him to pursue Briand, but the French moved too fast to be caught. While awaiting further instructions Manteuffel sent out strong columns to the north and west to ensure that the French were kept at a safe distance. The mission of the First Army was now, as its Chief of Staff observed, of a defensive nature.

One question which must immediately be resolved was the best way to defend Rouen. A report from his artillery and engineer commanders concluded that a defensive perimeter of at least thirteen miles in length, based on fifteen forts, would be needed; it would require a whole corps for its defence. Manteuffel could not afford to lock up half his strength in this way; it would be necessary to rely, therefore, on a flexible and mobile defence. Meanwhile Moltke was concerned that Briand's forces must be pursued, and he sent telegrams to Manteuffel to this effect on December 6 and 7, following these with a letter setting out detailed instruction for the further operations of the army.[18] These certainly did not contemplate a wholly defensive stance; the pursuit towards Le Havre was to be undertaken with a view to breaking up Briand's army rather than to occupy that city.

Moltke was not entirely happy with the operations of the First Army, and his concern deepened with the French capture of Ham on the night of December 9/10, a move which took its defenders completely by surprise. Von der Groeben, ordered by Manteuffel to do something about it, protested that he could not move before December 16. Moltke thought this not good enough, and ordered von der Groeben to intervene at once. On December 13 he wrote to Manteuffel to explain, again, what was needed. It was not his intention to occupy the whole of north western France; the role of the First Army must be to break up any French forces that could present a threat to the siege of Paris, and for this purpose its forces should be kept together.[19]

Partly complying with Moltke's instruction, Manteuffel ordered von der Groeben to move to Raye, leaving two battalions, a battery and a cavalry regiment to hold Amiens. He did not, however, take steps to reunite the I Corps with the rest of the army. On the night of December 16, though, Manteuffel was appalled to receive a letter from von der Groeben to the effect that he had decided to abandon Amiens, save for the garrison of the citadel, and to march to Montdidier for a junction with Kummer. Furious at this, Manteuffel at once sent off orders for the reoccupation of Amiens. On December 18 he was relieved to hear that Mirus, with the 3rd Brigade, had reoccupied the city It was just in time; that day Faidherbe had ridden forward to reconnoitre Amiens from the Noyau suburb.

Thwarted there, Faidherbe posted the Army of the North along the line of the River Hallue, with his left on the Somme, there to offer battle; he had a numerical advantage of two to one. On December 23 the First Army advanced against the French positions, and a fierce struggle began all along the front. The fiercest fighting was at Daours, on the French left, and Pont Noyelles in the centre. Manteuffel had hoped to outflank the French right, but Faidherbe's line was prolonged further north than was realised. By nightfall, the line of the Hallue was in German hands. A fierce French counter attack was beaten off by 6.00 pm; the German troops were able to dig in around the villages they had occupied, while the French bivouacked in the open.

Next day neither side made a move; during the night of December 24/25 the French retreated northwards. It had been, tactically, a drawn battle; Wartensleben, however, was entitled to claim it as a strategic victory, since Amiens had been secured and the French driven out of positions from which to threaten the city.[20]

Manteuffel had hoped that when Mézières capitulated, as it did on January 1, he would be able to add the 14th Division which had been besieging the place to the troops he had available to resist the inevitable further advance by Faidherbe. Moltke, however, was obliged to disappoint him; the 14th Division was required to make an immediate attack on Rocroi and thereafter to reinforce the troops investing Parris. He did, however, write encouragingly to Manteuffel:

> It is with a full heart that I send to Your Excellency not only my best wishes for the New Year, but also all my congratulations on the two important victories that you have won near Amiens. I believe that it will be extremely difficult for General Faidherbe again to get across the line of the Somme if you succeed in occupying Péronne.[21]

The denial of the 14th Division meant that Goeben would have to resist Faidherbe's next advance with what he had. He expected the French to attempt the relief of Péronne; and he told Manteuffel that he would not be strong enough to resist the advance with the prospect of success, since he must leave Barnekow, now commanding the troops around Péronne, with at least two brigades. He was inclined to expect that Faidherbe would advance from the direction of Cambrai; in fact, however, the Army of the North moved from Arras. On January 2 there was a sharp engagement at Sapignies: although Strubberg's 30th Brigade held its ground, by nightfall Kummer felt obliged to concentrate his division in and around Bapaume, upon which Faidherbe planned a concentric attack for the following day.

Throughout January 3 there was a bitter struggle lasting nine hours as the French attempted to get around the left flank of the German positions. Both sides suffered heavily; in the two days' fighting the total German casualties amounted to 1,066 killed, wounded and missing, of which about 200 were lost on January 2. Goeben reached the conclusion that a voluntary retreat was to be preferred to an unsuccessful defence of Bapaune on January 4, and he issued precautionary orders to Barnekow to be prepared to lift the siege of Péronne, while Kummer fell back to the south of Bapaume. Unknown to him, however, his adversary also took a pessimistic view of the situation. The Army of the North had failed to overcome the 10,000 troops defending Bapaume; shelling the town would cause heavy civilian casualties; and a further all out attack on the enemy positions must be costly. Many of the villages were encumbered with dead and wounded. With these thoughts in his mind, Faidherbe gave orders for a retreat northwards. The battle, although a tactical draw, was, as Wartensleben claimed, another strategical victory for the First Army, since the attempt to relieve Péronne had failed.[21]

Manteuffel demanded an immediate pursuit of the retreating French, telling Goeben that von der Groeben 'should complete the victory you have gained by pursuing the enemy energetically, especially with cavalry. I also now expect that the siege of Péronne will be continued with all available and procurable means.'[22]

It was obviously necessary to press on with the siege of Péronne as vigorously as possible before Faidherbe made another attempt to relieve the fortress. There were indications that this might occur very soon, and Manteuffel began shifting troops from Rouen to reinforce Goeben, who was prepared if necessary to meet any renewed French advance from behind the line of the Seine.

Moltke was watching these events from Versailles with some anxiety. He had, however, other problems on his mind as well, notably the situation in South East France, where he had decided to reinforce the XIV Corps under Werder, creating a new army command to be known as the South Army. On the morning of January 7 he decided that Manteuffel should command this, and ordered him to report to Versailles for instructions; Goeben would succeed him as commander of the First Army. Meanwhile throughout the day he sent a series of anxious telegrams to Manteuffel to ascertain whether sufficient reinforcements were being sent to Goeben, indicating that if necessary some troops could be spared from the Army of the Meuse.

Next day Manteuffel departed for Versailles, issuing a farewell order to his troops, announcing that Goeben would succeed him:

> Today, but today in my own name alone, and from my innermost heart and soul, I also express my deep felt thanks to the army, and most heartily wish it further laurels. I thank the Headquarters staff; I thank the generals, commanders of regiments, and officers; I thank each individual soldier of the army …And thus I say to all of you, farewell! And, in saying farewell I at the same time think with fervent gratitude of our fallen and wounded comrades, the shedding of whose blood has contributed so greatly to the glory of the army. May God be with your standards henceforth.[23]

Wartensleben, who was to be Chief of Staff of the South Army, together with part of the staff and some of the ADCs, accompanied Manteuffel in his new command. The latter arrived for his briefing at Versailles on January 10. On January 12 he reached Châtillon, where he formally assured command, announcing this to his troops:

> When his Majesty the King entrusted me with the command, he remarked that the task allotted to the Army was one of great difficulty, but that he knew his troops. Soldiers of the South Army, with God's help, we will justify the trust our Lord and Master puts in us.[24]

To an even greater extent than was usual, Manteuffel made frequent references to divine support in his public pronouncements.

The South Army would consist of Fransecky's II Corps, now marching from Paris to Montargis; Zastrow's VII Corps, at Châtillon and Montigny; and the XIV Corps, soon to be locked in combat along the Lisaine with the French Army of the East under Bourbaki. The need to bring support to Werder was so great that Manteuffel at once decided that it would not be possible to give the II Corps a rest day, nor await the complete assembly of the VII Corps.

Impressed by this main idea – the necessity of losing no time – General Manteuffel, immediately after his arrival at Châtillon, gave orders in the course of the same night to push forward the advanced guards of both corps as far as the line Montbard – St Marc – Lengley – Aubepierre, immediately. The great object in thus throwing forward the advanced guards, each of which was accompanied by a detachment of pioneers, was to gain possession of and, if necessary , repair, all the principal roads leading eastwards before the arrival of the main bodies of the corps. The direction of the subsequent operations of both corps was decided on the morning of January 13.[25]

For the moment Manteuffel would issue no direct orders to Werder who, until the arrival of the South Army, would remain accountable to Moltke.

The first, and crucially important, strategic decision that Manteuffel and Wartensleben must take was the line of march to be taken by the South Army. There were, as Wartensleben recorded, 'very weighty and tempting reasons' for marching on Dijon. The roads were better; the two corps could easily dispose of Garibaldi's isolated corps at Dijon; there would be considerable symbolic value in retaking the city; and it would provide a rail link which when repaired would be the best line of communication. The South Army's objective was, however, Bourbaki's army; and the sooner it could bring help to Werder the better. On January 13, therefore, Manteuffel chose the Vesoul route.[26] This would involve passing between strong enemy positions at Dijon and Langres, with no convenient lateral roads to enable his separated units easily to cooperate. The route of the II Corps would lead it through the Cote d'Or to Selongey; that of the VII Corps to Prauthoy and Longeau. To Fransecky and Zastrow Manteuffel gave special instructions to move as quickly as possible; the first to leave the mountains was to extend its front both right and left to assess whether the adjoining exits were free:

> Our present position is such that I shall for some days be unable to give many direct orders; all arrangements will therefore lie in the hands of the generals commanding the troops, and of the leaders of the different marching columns. If the enemy oppose our march he must be driven back.[27]

The march began on January 14 in mist and snow in a hard frost. The roads, otherwise good, were extremely slippery, which caused the cavalry, artillery and baggage trains particular difficulty. By January 17, when a thaw set in, both corps had reached the outlets of the Cote d'Or, finding no enemy before them. Manteuffel expected to be on the Saône by January 20. News having arrived of Werder's victory on the Lisaine, he ordered the latter to 'endeavour as much as possible to keep firm hold of the enemy, so as to gain time for my flank movements.'[28] By now Manteuffel was only two marches away from Werder, so was able to coordinate the movement of the two parts of his army. It seemed to Manteuffel and Wartensleben, however, that uniting the army would not produce a decisive result, since although no doubt Bourbaki would be defeated, he would merely fall back on his natural line of retreat. On the other hand, to move directly to cut Bourbaki's line of communications by marching down the Saône in the direction of Lyons would oblige Bourbaki either to fight a decisive battle near Besancon or retreat though the mountains of the Jura.

When Manteuffel reported to Moltke his intention to adopt this riskier policy, the latter entirely approved, remarking to William: 'General von Manteuffel's movement is extremely bold, but it may lead to the greatest results. Should he suffer a check he ought not to be blamed, for in order to gain great successes, something must be risked.' Moltke was always pleased to support those of his generals prepared to take vigorous action. Wartensleben described the risks involved in the plan:

> The fulfilment of such a task taxed to the very utmost the efficiency of the troops, the faculty on the part of their leaders of acting independently in cases of urgency, and the capability of the commissariat department to provide for a time the necessary means of subsistence without supplies from the rear, and yet to main-tain the army in a state of perfect readiness for action. General Manteuffel was inspired with full confidence on all these subjects; his trust was not deceived.[29]

During his briefing by Moltke at Versailles, Manteuffel had no doubt been told of the concern felt there at times about Werder's rather tentative approach, and he was soon spelling out to the commander of the XIV Corps what he expected. On January 21 he stressed that he depended on Werder 'keeping at close quarters with the enemy' and following his main body in whatever direction it took.[30] It is certainly true that Werder was moving rather slowly, reporting on the exhaustion of his troops and the lack of supplies. Manteuffel was impatient with this, ordering him to launch a vigorous attack on January 23 to head off any advance towards Gray. Meanwhile Fransecky and Zastrow had been making good progress; on January 20 the advanced guard of the II Corps had seized Dôle, with its vital bridge over the Doubs, and 230 railway trucks full of supplies.

On January 24 Manteuffel reviewed the options apparently open to Bourbaki in a set of general instructions for his corps commanders. There seemed to be six possibilities. First, he might try to go south between Villers Farley and Pontarlier, in which case the II Corps and VII Corps would attack his flank. Next, he might try to break through by Quingey and Dampierre; Zastrow would meet this assault, while Fransecky came up on his rear. Next he might head for Gray; in this case the 14th Division and Knesebeck's brigade would attack his left flank and the Baden Division the right. If he turned back on the XIV Corps, the II and VII Corps would come up from the south. If he retired towards the Swiss frontier he would be chased by the advanced guards of all three corps. Finally, he might stay put around Besancon, in which case he would be blockaded. To each of his three commanders he added that he was giving his views of the situation, so that they might 'at any time be able to initiate operations in keeping with their spirit, without waiting for orders from me, in case circumstances should make it necessary to take a sudden resolution.'[31]

Werder, who concluded that the French would not now attack towards Gray, and who did not fancy an advance directly on Besancon, decided that his mission should be to cover the South Army's rear against an attack from Dijon, and he reported this to Manteuffel on January 25. The latter was not pleased, replying that what was required was not to stop the enemy by standing in his way, but to attack him on both flanks. The endgame was now approaching; Bourbaki, analysing his options, had reduced them to two; either to break out to Auxonne or to retreat to Pontarlier. All save one of those who attended his council of war were for retreat; the exception was Billot, the commander of the 18th Corps, but he declined Bourbaki's suggestion that he take over the command for the breakout. The retreat was accordingly ordered; Cremer, with two divisions and the army reserve was to cover the flank.

However, Koblinski, with Fransecky's advanced guard, had pushed forward to Salins, and succeeded in capturing the town, shutting off one more escape route and finally destroying Bourbaki's morale when he heard of it. Bad news was reaching him from all quarters, while from far away Freycinet was sending a stream of impractical orders. On the night of January 26, he attempted suicide, shooting himself in the head; the bullet, however, only grazed his skull. The command pressed to Clinchant, who saw quite clearly that the only hope was a rapid retreat to Pontarlier, notwithstanding the appalling weather conditions. Manteuffel, however, was tightening his grip. Fransecky had at once grasped the French intention, and moved his main body to Arbois accordingly; when he heard this, Manteuffel ordered Zastrow to send troops south to Salins in support.

Although French morale was crumbling, the rearguards were still putting up a determined resistance as the Army of the East streamed along all the available roads to Pontarlier, followed by Fransecky's leading units which by nightfall on January 29 reached Censean and Les Planches. At 5.00 pm Manteuffel received the news of the armistice in Paris, which would come into force generally on January 31; the departments of the Cote d'Or, Doubs and Jura were for the moment excluded. Although Moltke's telegram correctly reported this, the information reaching Clinchant did not. As a result there was considerable confusion; Zastrow, on hearing from Clinchant of the armistice, released about 1,000 French soldiers that had voluntarily surrendered. Manteuffel, when he heard of this, issued a general order that the armistice did not apply to the South Army, and that the advance should be pressed forward. He was becoming increasingly frustrated by the confusion; to Clinchant, who asked for a ceasefire on the basis of his incorrect information, he wrote to refuse it, suggesting that Clinchant might put forward his own proposals 'as are in conformity with the military situation prevailing here at this moment.'[32]

In point of fact, both Manteuffel and Clinchant had separately reached the conclusion that the best thing for the Army of the East was to pass into Switzerland, the former pragmatically preferring not to have to send 100,000 more prisoners of war to Germany and the latter as a matter of honour.

By January 31 Pontarlier was in German hands, and the long lines of French troops were heading for the frontier at Verrieres. Clinchant signed a convention with the

Swiss General Herzog, and on February 1 the French began to cross the frontier. Next day Manteuffel issued a congratulatory order to his troops:

> Soldiers of the South Army! Your marches and combats amidst the snow and ice of the High Jura have not been fruitless. 2 eagles, 12 cannons, 7 mitrailleuses, 15,000 prisoners including two generals and many officers, several hundreds of provision wagons, several thousand chassepots are in your hands ... Bourbaki's army is hors de combat, and whatever still remains of it will soon succumb to your arms.[33]

With the fighting ended, the South Army was dissolved. Manteuffel was appointed to the command of the Second Army on March 30, and on June 20 as commander in chief of the army of occupation, a post he held until September 1871.

It was not without its difficulties, as it involved many quasi political decisions, not all of which received the approval of Bismarck or indeed of the Emperor. Manteuffel was joined by Albrecht von Stosch who served as his Chief of Staff, and who observed at first hand the bitter struggles with Bismarck that marked this period.

Returning to Germany, he was promoted to the rank of Field Marshal. GLM Strauss, in his hagiographical sketches of the leading personalities of the German Empire, commented on the fact that this promotion was

> most coldly received and most adversely commented upon, not alone by the general public, but also in high and low military circles. It is, indeed, difficult to account for the very large measure of apparently groundless popular dislike that seems to have fallen to the share of this man.[34]

In fact, it is not very difficult to account for. To the general public, or at least to the Liberal opposition and sections of the popular press, Manteuffel was the apotheosis of right wing reaction; while in military circles his ruthless weeding out of officers judged to be incompetent meant that he had plenty of enemies. Another factor in his unpopularity was the widespread suspicion that he had used his influence with the King to secure the removal of Vogel von Falckenstein from the Army of the Main and his own appointment to succeed him.

Moltke always enjoyed a warm personal relationship with Manteuffel. After the death of Mary von Moltke in 1869, Manteuffel shared the concerns of many about the effect of Moltke's loss; knowing that Moltke was fond of his nephew Henry, he suggested that the latter should be appointed as his personal aide de camp. The friendly relationship between Moltke and Manteuffel evidently continued for the rest of their lives; in 1880 Moltke was writing from Gastein to Henry to express the hope that he would be meeting Manteuffel and his family in Salzburg.

Many of those who saw in Manteuffel an arrogant extremist did not look beyond his actions to the driving motivation behind them. Some of them did, however; Bismarck said of him: 'Manteuffel is of noble metal. For him reason of state far transcends personal interest.'[35] Schweinitz, ambassador to St Petersburg, who was also strongly opposed to Manteuffel, wrote of him in similar terms:

> A burning love for his country, true piety, enthusiasm for the noble and sublime filled this true Prussian heart; Christian humility and classical greatness of soul united in this man and made him, to whom nature had given the bent to fanaticism, a model of those virtues upon which Prussia's greatness is founded.[36]

It was an epitaph which Manteuffel justly deserved.

18

Goeben

August Karl von Goeben was the ablest of all Moltke's subordinates. In him, Moltke reposed absolute trust, as indeed did the men whom Goeben led. There was no commander on either side who inspired such total confidence in his troops. Goeben possessed in the highest degree the ability to grasp a battlefield situation which is the mark of a successful commander.

He was, however, by no means a typical Prussian general either in his general appearance or in his personality, as Heinrich von Sybel graphically described:

> This talented officer was filled with a passion for daring adventure and venturesome undertakings, that had driven him in the time of peace into the uncertain fortunes of the great Carlist War, and which found a vent for itself in quiet times in the most foolhardy games of chance. At ordinary times, careless about his dress and manners as he was, with a heavy pair of spectacles before his eyes, he hardly gave the impression of being a soldier, but rather a pedagogue that had happened by chance to be dressed up in a uniform; especially since in conversation with strangers he was embarrassingly reserved, although among his friends he overflowed with wit, information and worldly wisdom. But so soon as a serious and dangerous task presented itself to him, he seemed to be utterly transformed. Erect and with a dignified demeanour, he considered the advantages and the obstacles, and held with an iron calmness a firm rein upon his inward impulses, until the right moment came and the ardour of his own enthusiasm led on the troops to an irresistible attack; and he was then again able at the right moment to command to himself and his men an inexorable halt![1]

Goeben was a personal friend of Moltke and his family, and was frequently mentioned in Moltke's letters to his wife, giving her news of Goeben's current and future postings. In February 1851, when Moltke and the rest of the Prussian army were still seething over the national humiliation at Olmütz, Goeben visited him at Magdeburg and shared a bowl of punch with him en route to a posting to Prince William's corps in Coblenz. There Moltke, taking up his duties as adjutant

Goeben.

to Prince Frederick William, found him in 1855 serving as Chief of Staff of the VI Corps.[2]

Goeben was born in the kingdom of Hanover in 1816, in the army of which his father had served as an officer. He joined the Prussian army shortly before his seventeenth birthday, and was made a lieutenant in 1835. He was a keen student of the intellectual aspect of his profession, but above all was eager to see active service. There seemed little prospect of this in the Prussian army, and in 1836 he resigned his commission, and travelled to Spain to enlist in the Carlist army fighting in the civil war there. He soon found the action he was looking for, taking part in a series of battles. Having reached the rank of Captain, he was seriously wounded at the battle of Sotoca in 1838. He served both in the engineers and the infantry, leading a company in the battles of 1839. In the following year, as a major, he was again seriously wounded at the battle of Teruel, following which, at the age of twenty four, he was promoted to lieutenant colonel in the engineers. However, the tide was turning against the Carlists and in 1840 Goeben found himself unemployed, and almost penniless, as he made his way home through France. He got back in September 1840 and next year published an account of his experiences in Spain, which attracted a good deal of attention.

Goeben was determined to resume his career in the Prussian army, which he rejoined in February 1842; he was assigned almost at once to the General Staff, a considerable tribute to the high regard in which he was held. This also led to his relatively rapid promotion to the rank of Captain, in which he served on the staff of Prince William's army in Baden in 1849. Following this, after a short spell in the infantry, Goeben rejoined the General Staff as a major, becoming a lieutenant colonel and Chief of Staff first of the VI Corps in 1855 and three years later of the VIII Corps. As a colonel, he went with the Prussian military mission to the Spanish army operating in Morocco in 1860, led by Leopoldo O'Donnell, a former Cristino commander in the Carlist War. Here, he encountered many of those against whom he had fought in 1836-1840.[3]

Returning from this assignment, he was promoted to major general and in 1863 was appointed to the command of the 26th Brigade. This, the following year, provided him with the opportunity for distinction at the head of his brigade as part of the Prussian forces in Jutland, and he seized it with both hands. The 26th Brigade formed part of Lieutenant General von Wintzingerode's 13th Division. Once the Danes had evacuated the Dannewerk it moved forward with the rest of the Prussian Combined I Corps under Prince Frederick Charles to take up a position in front of the lines of Düppel. Moving into the front line, Goeben launched a surprise raid on the outposts on the Danish right on March 13, taking 31 prisoners before withdrawing. He repeated the exercise three days later, pushing forward towards Lillemolle and Stavegarde, and taking the Danish advance posts before falling back.[4]

Next day the Danes took the initiative, advancing towards Rackebull with a view to driving back those Prussian troops which still occupied the wood north of the village. Goeben saw this as a major attack and applied to Roeder's 12th Brigade for support before advancing into the village. There followed a period of confused fighting, during which Roeder advanced to take the village of Düppel. A Danish counter attack put the 12th Brigade in jeopardy and in his turn Roeder called on Goeben for support; but his troops were now very extended, as a result of his pulling back his leading units in the mistaken belief that fighting had ended for the day.[5]

Goeben was convinced, as indeed was Moltke, that a frontal assault on the strong Düppel position would be a serious mistake, and strongly advocated a landing on Alsen. The successful assault on the island of Fehmarn on the night of March 14/15 encouraged those of similar views, as a result of which Blumenthal was instructed to prepare a plan for a seaborne attack on Alsen. This, as has been described in Chapter 5, had to be abandoned due to the adverse weather conditions on April 3. Writing to his nephew Henry, Moltke expressed his disappointment that a further attempt could not be made on the day of the assault on the Düppel position:

> I am grieved that your regiment has not been able to accomplish the daring enterprise which had been allotted to it on the day of the storming, and the successful issue of which would have been of the most decisive importance. Had it been possible, there is not the slightest doubt that General Goeben would have accomplished it.[6]

Since again the weather did not permit a seaborne assault on Alsen when the assault on the Düppel position was launched on April 18, Goeben's brigade was confined to a subsidiary role, launching some pontoons as if to attempt a crossing to Alsen and generally making a demonstration. When, following the ending of the armistice, the amphibious assault on Alsen took place on June 29, the 26th Brigade took a much more active part. Crossing with the second wave, the brigade was soon driving back the Danes defending Sonderburg, after first resisting a counter attack launched in an attempt to hold back the Prussian advance. Goeben occupied Sonderburg by 6.30 am. Moltke, who watched the operation throughout, gave his wife in a detailed account of the crossing and subsequent operations:

> Most admirable was the behaviour of our Westphalians belonging to Goeben's brigade, who had advanced against Sonderburg and took the Danes in the rear behind a quickset hedge, although they themselves were in imminent danger of being taken in like manner from the side of Sonderburg. Whole swarms of the enemy retreated in haste through the cornfields. One battery after another was silenced, while their occupants fled.[7]

After the end of the campaign Goeben was rewarded with the command first of the 10th Division and then the 13th Division, and was promoted to Lieutenant General. In 1866, his division formed part of the force assigned to deal with the Middle States in Western Germany initially under the command of General Vogel von Falckenstein. The first, and essential, mission was to move against Hanover and Electoral Hesse, the forces of which must be prevented from marching south to join the Bavarians and the Federal 8th Corps. Falckenstein's conduct of the campaign caused profound dissatisfaction in Berlin, particularly when he took his eye off the ball, ignored the Hanoverians for the time being and gave orders to march against the Federal 8th Corps. Moltke dealt with that, or at least attempted to, and Goeben with six battalions made a forced march to Kassel on June 25. On the following day he planned a flank attack on what he believed to be the Hanoverian position, but overnight the enemy withdrew. On June 27 Goeben found himself in temporary command, Falckenstein having gone to Kassel. Unknown to him, Flies had launched his attack on the main body of the Hanoverian Army at Langensalza; Goeben was more concerned with a threatened advance by the Bavarians, who in reality were miles away, than with the battle at Langensalza, whch he supposed to be a minor rearguard conflict. Schlieffen was critical of Goeben's failure, observing that it was not until the night of June 27/28 that Goeben 'was first awakened from his trance' by the explicit order from Moltke to Falckenstein to ignore the Bavarians and to deal at once with the Hanoverian army.[8] That, however, notwithstanding the victory at Langensalza, had had enough, and before the Prussians had advanced far the Hanoverian high command decided to capitulate.

As the campaign against the Bavarian army under Prince Charles and the Federel 8th Corps under Prince Alexander of Hesse got under way, Falckenstein's dispositions, based on inaccurate information, resulted in the 13th Division bearing the brunt of the fighting. At Kissingen on July 10 the Prussians were faced with the need to cross the deep flowing River Saale if they were to get at the Bavarians, who had retreated to the left bank and occupied the city. The stone bridge carrying the main road was heavily defended; a wooden bridge further up river had been almost completely destroyed and the iron footbridge had had all the planking removed. As Goeben's main body under Wrangel came up, it was able to seize the wooden bridge, and in spite of heavy fire from the Bavarian side of the river his engineers succeeded in repairing it sufficiently to render it passable, and an assault began on the southern part of the city. The Bavarians held out for several hours in bitter house to house fighting; then, as first the footbridge was crossed and then the stone bridge was taken, the resistance crumbled. An attempt was made by the Bavarians to stand on the Winkels heights overlooking the city; but Goeben swiftly followed up his taking of the city, and drove the defenders back. A subsequent Bavarian counter attack retook the heights; but although Goeben could spare no reinforcements, Wrangel, in command there, succeeded in regaining the lost heights, and the Bavarians fell back.

When Falckenstein switched the direction of his advance towards the 8th Corps, Goeben's division found itself once more in the leading position. Advancing in blistering heat over the Spessart on July 13 Goeben, riding with an advanced patrol of hussars from Wrangel's brigade, encountered troops from Frey's Hessian Brigade. A brisk battle ensued when Wrangel's infantry came up; it appeared to have ended when Perglas, commanding the Hesse-Darmstadt Division of the 8th Corps, launched a suicidal attack on Wrangel's brigade, which broke down with heavy casualties in the face of the needle gun.

Goeben pushed on towards Aschaffenburg, where he met Hahn's Austrian brigade, supported by Perglas. Launching both of his brigades into an immediate assault on July 14, Goeben took the town with the loss of 180 casualties after inflicting 2,469 on the enemy. Advancing towards Frankfurt, he entered the city on the evening of July 16. Falckenstein was removed from command of the Army of the Main on July 18 and replaced by Manteuffel.[9]

In the subsequent campaign of the Army of the Main Goeben's division was in the thick of it. On July 24, during the battle of Tauberbischofsheim, his troops took the town and beat off all the subsequent counter attacks. Next day, pressing on to Gerchsheim, Goeben bounced the units of the 8th Corps opposed to him out of their positions and forced them back to Kist; although exhausting both his troops and his ammunition in the process, he sustained only 60 casualties.[10]

It was unsurprising that in 1870 Goeben should have risen to the position of corps commander. At the age of 54, he was placed in command of the VIII Corps which, apart from the 29th Brigade (von Wedell), consisted largely of Rhinelanders. His divisional commanders were Lieutenant General von Weltzien (15th Division) and Lieutenant General von Barnekow (16th Division). His Chief of Staff was the able Colonel von Witzendorff. The corps formed part of Steinmetz's First Army. After mobilisation the direction of its advance was down the Nahe valley toward Saarlouis;

as it moved towards the Saar it soon became involved in Steinmetz's erratic handling of his army. On July 30 Goeben telegraphed Moltke to report that the token force at Saarbrücken had repulsed an attack by large forces, but was in great danger, and asked if it could be reinforced from the Second Army. Moltke immediately responded:

> Little band at Saarbrücken must not be sacrificed. Support by Second Army at present impossible, but it could come without inconvenience from a detachment coming from Wadern, following which it could fall back on Sulzbach or Neuenkirchen. Destruction of the railway is no longer necessary.[11]

Later in the evening Moltke instructed Lieutenant Colonel von Pestel, the commander at Saarbrücken, that he should pull back his infantry towards Sulzbach, while the cavalry maintained contact with the enemy. By August 3, not having heard the outcome of this, Moltke asked the commandant of Saarlouis what had happened at Saarbrücken ; Goeben had already sent a full report, but Moltke did not receive it until the middle of the afternoon. He replied that the possession of Saarbrücken was presently of no importance, and added that the First Army had been ordered to concentrate at Tholey, an instruction which was to annoy Steinmetz.

It was from Goeben that Moltke was to receive the first news of the Prussian victory at Spicheren on August 6; he at once asked by telegram to know the strength of French involvement in the battle, the numbers of the French regiments, and what prisoners had been taken.[12] Goeben had become involved with the movements which were to lead to the battle of Spicheren when on the morning of August 6 he had ridden forward to the Saar to reconnoitre the proposed crossing of his corps at Saarbrücken. Encountering Major General von Francois, commanding the advance guard of the energetic Lieutenant General von Kameke's 14th Division, he promised to support him if needed. Kameke had obtained from his corps commander, von Zastrow, leave to use his own judgment about crossing the river and occupying the heights. Meanwhile the III Corps from the Second Army was also moving forward, and its commander Konstantin von Alvensleben, hearing that his 9th Brigade (von Doering) had moved up to support Francois, ordered the rest of his corps to advance. All these advancing units were using a limited number of roads converging on Saarbrücken, and they inevitably became entangled. No one seems to have bothered to consult Steinmetz: as the attack developed Kameke controlled it at first, but Goeben assumed command at about 3.00 pm when his leading troops arrived on the heights. It was only at about 7.30 pm that Steinmetz arrived on the scene to find that his troops had won a hard fought victory without him.

Goeben's corps took no part in the battle of Borny-Colombey on August 14, having been expressly forbidden by Steinmetz to do so; his advance in support of the rest of the First Army was halted for the moment on the following day. With the battle of Mars la Tour-Vionville having been fought on August 16, which resulted in Bazaine's retreat towards Metz, the VII and VIII Corps were ordered across the Moselle, Steinmetz being instructed that his sole consideration was to enable them to reach the enemy as soon as possible. At 1.45 pm on August 17 Moltke issued his extremely concise orders for the battle that was expected to take place next day. For the VIII Corps, these prescribed that it should be attached to, and form the right wing of, the Second Army.[13] This enraged Steinmetz extremely, and he sent a violent protest to Royal Headquarters at thus being deprived of one of the corps under his command.

Although Moltke, by this decision, had in theory reduced Steinmetz's capacity for misconduct, the latter was to behave throughout the battle of Gravelotte-St Privat as though the order had not been given. And, as it happened, it was not Steinmetz who took the step which Moltke had sought to prevent. When Manstein's artillery opened fire at Verneville at noon, Moltke sent a message to Steinmetz to the effect that the gunfire he could hear was only a partial engagement, and was not to lead to a general attack by the First Army, which should not deploy large masses of troops, but which should prepare its artillery for an attack to be commenced later.[14] It was Goeben who, on hearing the sound of the guns, immediately pushed forward the 15th Division under Weltzien, with the 29th Brigade advancing along the road Gravelotte-Point du Jour, and the 30th Brigade (von Strubberg) towards the Bois des Génivaux. The divisional artillery opened fire at about 12.45 pm. It is not clear whether Goeben was aware of the restraining message which Moltke sent to Steinmetz; but Hönig takes the view that the decision to attack was not inconsistent with it.[15] The objective of the attack was the farm of St Hubert, and soon after 3 pm the farm and the adjacent quarries were in Prussian hands.

Hönig noted a curious feature of the command situation of the First Army and its component corps, and, even more notably, Goeben's demeanour as his troops went into action:

> Generals von Steinmetz, von Zastrow and von Goeben, with their staffs, were but a few hundred paces from each other. The whole behaviour of the latter was quiet and equable, and his appearance in accordance with his strength. He sat in the saddle with his tall figure bowed forward, with his shoulders a little drawn up, and with his head stretched forward, while through his spectacles showed two wise eyes, which shone at times, when a moment of tension arrived. The officers of the other staffs watched Goeben's actions, as if they felt that this was indeed the man. Hardly a word was spoken; with his glance steadily directed on the enemy, he sat there like a bronze statue, a sure support both in soul and in brains in any severe work. A word quietly spoken to this or that general, or to a staff officer as an adjutant, a calm nod when he received a report; in this manner, and without fuss, he did all that a general could do under the circumstances, with a degree of certainty, of sequence and of quiet that, in spite of the difficult situation of the struggle, gave all around him a feeling of security, which was transmitted, as if by electricity, to every private. We know well that this can be, but we do not know how it comes about! A general can inspire confidence where a fool may be the cause of a panic.[16]

Hönig records that, until he rode up to St Hubert, Goeben only once moved from where he sat his horse, which was when the King approached his right flank.

It is one of the curious features of the battle of Gravelotte that Goeben, whose corps was to constitute the right wing of the Second Army, received no orders from that army nor, more surprisingly, from Moltke, who had detached him from the First Army. On the other hand, Steinmetz issued a series of orders to him, behaving as if the VIII Corps remained part of his army. As to these latter, Goeben had in most cases anticipated them, although as the battle proceeded an order to commit his reserves was one with which he totally disagreed. Steinmetz entirely ignored his protests.

Once the battle was won, albeit at hideous cost, the VIII Corps, with the rest of the First Army, took part in the investment of Metz. It was an assignment which, like Frederick Charles, Goeben did not much enjoy. There was no realistic chance, he thought, that Bazaine could escape from Metz, the capture of which being only a matter of time. Better, he considered, to detach two of the corps investing the place and use them before Paris or on the Loire and on October 9 he wrote to Moltke to suggest this. His letter was delayed; but Moltke replied on October 20:

> Certainly, it would be extremely helpful for us to have another corps in front of Paris, for our line of investment is very thin. But if, up to now, we have not considered the possibility of reducing the Army of Metz, it is because, since Sedan, we calculate that it is at Metz that one must look for the decisive result of the whole campaign. A lucky break out by Bazaine would doubtless result in a partial rupture of our line of investment. The Army of Paris cannot take sword in hand without abandoning the capital. It would be very well from the military point of view but very dangerous from a political standpoint.[17]

Moltke was plainly going to take no chances. He went on to review for Goeben's benefit the overall situation as he saw it, setting out in detail the position around Paris. It was a mark of the confidence and cooperation between the two men that they should correspond in this way; it is doubtful whether any other subordinate corps commander would thus exchange views with Moltke.

It was not to be long, however, before Goeben was released from the drudgery of the investment. Metz capitulated on October 28, and Goeben's VIII Corps prepared to move north as part of the First Army, now commanded by Edwin von Manteuffel. Goeben seems to have had a good relationship with the latter, having of course served under him during the campaign of the Army of the Main in 1866. Certainly Manteuffel showed every confidence in Goeben, whom he allowed to conduct, to a considerable extent, the battles fought against the Army of the North.

Heavily outnumbered, the First Army was successful in the battles of Amiens and on the Hallue. However, it was soon after the latter that it was required to face perhaps its most difficult moment in the campaign, when Faidherbe moved south in an effort to relieve the besieged fortress of Péronne. Goeben, who had taken up a position at Bapaume to cover the siege, was reporting to Manteuffel as early as December

31 that there was increased French activity in his front. This, he correctly concluded, indicated an intention to advance to the relief of Péronne, and he was candid in his assessment of his ability to resist it:

> With regard to the enemy's army, a change has in so far taken place, as it now occupies the villages in the immediate neighbourhood of the fortresses, and displays, on the whole, a greater degree of activity … It seems, therefore, that an advance will be made for the purpose of relieving Péronne and I do not deceive myself as to the fact that, if such an attempt should be made on a large scale, I shall - as two infantry brigades must be left at Péronne – not remain strong enough to resist it with the prospect of success.[18]

The battle that ensued on January 2-3 was a very close run thing indeed. Goeben conducted it with immense skill, and at the end of the day still held the town and key positions around it. During the day he had taken the precaution of warning Barnekow, who was conducting the siege of Péronne, that he must prepare to retreat to the south side of the Somme. Now, as he reviewed his situation on the night of January 3, it seemed to him that it would be best to accept defeat and pull back all his troops to the line of the Somme. However, his adversary was also having serious doubts about his position. A fresh assault would cost heavy casualties; his troops were already exhausted by the two days' fighting, in which he had lost over 2,000 men. Accordingly, Faidherbe gave orders for a withdrawal, and the siege of Péronne continued.

On January 7 Manteuffel was appointed by Moltke to command the Army of the South, and Goeben took over the leadership of the First Army. The problem of Péronne was soon solved, when the fortress capitulated on January 10. There was a false alarm when, just before Barnekow occupied the fortress, reports arrived of a further southward advance by the Army of the North; when this was cleared up, Goeben was able to concentrate all his attention on Faidherbe's next move.

The enormously high regard in which Goeben was held by his officers and men was noted by the correspondent of the *Daily News* accompanying the First Army:

> Very many officers of this army attribute to Manteuffel's slowness the fact of Faidherbe not having been beaten in a more decided manner on previous occasions. The confidence of the ordinary soldier in Goeben's talent is striking. On the march through snow and mud, from morning till evening, you can often hear these tired fellows say, 'Well, Goeben knows all this is necessary,' and continue as jolly as ever.[19]

In the same report, the '*Daily News*' correspondent quoted the words of a friend of his who, as commander of a regiment, was considering the orders issued by Goeben for January 19, the battle of St Quentin:

'This is von Goeben,' said he; 'I know him well from 1866, when he was operating against the so called South Army. The peculiarity of his disposition is the
great exactness with which care is taken of all parts; none being neglected; each
working for itself for a certain time, and scarcely knowing it is connected with
a neighbour until the time comes when all act together as a whole. He cares
comparatively little how many men perish on the march so long as the march
is completed in the given time. And you will see today,' my friend added, 'the
results he obtains. You will particularly notice that everybody will be not only in
his right place, but also in due time.'[20]

The comment about Goeben's indifference to casualties on the march is certainly
unjust, and was no doubt added to emphasise the precision with which he ordered the
proceedings of his troops.

As Howard pointed out, the outcome of the decisive battle of St Quentin was by
no means a foregone conclusion. Faidherbe enjoyed a superiority of two to one in
infantry, and was defending a position that was difficult to attack.[21] But his troops
were tired and dispirited, while Goeben inspired his subordinate commanders, and
through them their troops, with the confidence of success. That confidence was not
misplaced; the outcome of the battle was a stunning victory. Goeben's total casualties were 2,376; Faidherbe lost over 15,000 men of whom some 12,000 were taken
prisoner. The Army of the North had been smashed, and in spite of Faidherbe's brave
words, was incapable of further effort.

After the war Faidherbe published a short account of the campaign, which seriously
annoyed Goeben, who wrote a refutation of many of the claims made by his opponent.
In it, he loftily offered an explanation for Faidherbe's misstatements:

> It causes me besides especial satisfaction to venture at once to declare, that,
> notwithstanding these facts, I have throughout no doubt that General Faidherbe
> on his part was at the time he wrote his brochure, thoroughly convinced of the
> accuracy of his statements, as well as the correctness of his conclusions. He
> certainly did not wittingly pen that which is an untruth. But he is a Frenchman
> and on French sources alone did he draw; necessarily, must self-delusion, that
> cause of so much woe to the French, play a great part. These can at no time
> attain to a calm and dispassionate contemplation, and for this impossibility we
> are compelled to make allowance when passing judgment.[22]

Faidherbe did not leave this unanswered, publishing a strident rebuttal, which in turn
brought forth a further article from Goeben in the *Allgemeine Militar Zeitung*. It seems
that the war of words may have continued still further after this.[23] But one thing is
clear; Goeben had, in his campaign against the Army of the North, demonstrated to
the full why it was that Moltke regarded him a perhaps the safest pair of hands which
he possessed.

19

Steinmetz

For Moltke, some of his most disagreeable command problems during the Wars of Unification came at the hands of General of Infantry Karl Friedrich von Steinmetz. These were caused by the latter's obstinate and self willed conviction that he knew best, and a pronounced reluctance to accept direction from anyone.

Steinmetz was born in 1796. At the age of sixteen he volunteered to join the army and, as a lieutenant, in 1814 won the Iron Cross for the courage he displayed during the Wars of Liberation. Thereafter, as usual in the Prussian army, progress was slow; by 1835 he had still only reached the rank of Captain. It took several more years before he was promoted to Major; by 1848, aged fifty one, he was a lieutenant colonel commanding the 2nd Infantry Regiment, based in Berlin. He led two battalions of the regiment during the street fighting in the March Days. Later, his regiment formed part of the Prussian contingent during the First Schleswig War in 1850, in the course of which he won the Pour le Mérite.

His character and his abilities had, during the course of his career, already become evident to his superiors. In 1848 his divisional commander described him as 'a really outstanding staff officer, who must, however, be handled firmly if he is to be kept under control.'[1] Promotion now came more rapidly; after the end of the war of 1850 he became a major general. Given the command of a division, he reached the rank of Lieutenant General before, finally, becoming General of Infantry and the commander of the V Corps based at Posen.

Steinmetz's personality was markedly affected by the tragedy of the death in 1854 of his only daughter. Grief stricken, he suffered hallucinations in which she came to his table. He became prone to moodiness and outbursts of rage and developed further his strong propensity to disputes with his superiors. All this suggests that, in the continued progress of his career, his good qualities were recognised to a remarkable extent, outweighing the defects of his character. Manteuffel justly prided himself on having made a major contribution to Prussian success by his ruthless weeding of the officer corps; that Steinmetz survived the process is a not inconsiderable tribute to his military abilities.

Steinmetz.

Command of the V Corps, forming part of the Second Army in 1866, meant that he would occupy a crucially important position as the army made its way through the passes of the Riesengebirge. Verdy, serving on the staff of the Second Army, described Steinmetz, then approaching the age of seventy, as he appeared at that time. He found him 'a small, energetic man with a sharply chiselled soldier's face, eyes that showed intelligence and energy, with full white hair.' He noted that his campaign cap was covered with black oil cloth, copying that which he had worn as a young lieutenant, although this was certainly contrary to uniform regulations.[2]

The V Corps constituted the most southerly of the units of the Second Army, advancing from the salient formed by the Silesian frontier. Steinmetz had been thoroughly discontented with the plans for the deployment, and after a conversation with the Crown Prince he wrote to Moltke on May 29 a long letter pointing out their defects. In particular he considered that removing the VI Corps from Upper Silesia, and posting his own corps at Waldenburg was tantamount to an invitation to the Austrians to invade Silesia and that insufficient provision had been made in Western Germany. Moltke wrote a patient reply:

We have only one really dangerous enemy; it is the soul of all the other armaments preparing in Germany against us. This enemy is there, fully armed and ready. It would be wrong to leave a whole corps on the Rhine inactive against an enemy that does not yet exist. We need all our forces against the 240,000 men of Austria, and we have called up nine corps, that is all our corps, except one division provisionally left at Minden. Austria had six weeks' start of us in her mobilisation. It was necessary to prepare to resist her with the least possible delay. The only way to do this was to use all our railway lines simultaneously but each could carry only one corps, and could not disembark them beyond the frontier. This being so, the points of disembarkation had to form a cordon along the frontier. No other deployment could change this nor change the geographical necessity that means that, in Bohemia, Austria is on the interior line between Silesia and the Mark ... For Silesia, we could assemble only two corps in the time available. It is not in Silesia that Silesia can be defended, but in Bohemia.[3]

The advance of the V Corps required in the first instance that the pass at Nachod be seized. Loewenfeld, commanding the advance guard of the corps, found it weakly held and occupied it with his leading troops on the morning of June 27. At this point the corps was echeloned back over nearly twenty miles; Schlieffen was critical of Steinmetz for failing to push the whole of the advance guard through the pass on the previous day and bringing up the rest of the corps to start crossing the Mettau bridge on June 27:

Steinmetz made the various echelons, maintaining their intervals, break camp at the usual hour of 6.00 am and after having made half of the march, halted for one half hour, according to custom. Consequently it was not surprising that both van and advance guards were opposed during several hours by a numerically superior enemy and exposed to a complete defeat.[4]

Steinmetz was, however, a commander capable of quick assessment, and not afraid of responsibility; and he threw himself energetically into the conduct of the battle. This resulted, ultimately, in the defeat of Ramming's corps which opposed Steinmetz, not least because of the pronounced superiority of the Prussian artillery as well as the effectiveness of the needle gun. At 2.00 pm the Austrians fell back to Skalitz; Schlieffen was scornful of the failure then to follow up the victory:

The troops were considered too exhausted and tired for pursuit, as if each victorious army were not exhausted and tired at the end of a victorious battle and as if, notwithstanding its condition, pursuit were not required as the only thing to make the victory complete. The pursuit, desisted from, may be excused by the fact that the Prussian army had only two thirds of its strength at the end of the combat on hand and that these two thirds were entirely scattered. The responsibility for this unfavourable situation lies entirely at the door of the Prussian commander.[5]

Steinmetz went on, on the following day, to fight the battle of Skalitz; the V Corps had three Austrian corps in front of it, but this did not disturb its aggressive commander. Nor did it worry his army commander or the Chief of Staff, who had accompanied Steinmetz at Nachod but who had moved to Kosteletz to enable them to be in touch with the rest of the army. 'What a shame we can't be with Steinmetz! I'd just like to watch how the old fellow finishes them off!' said Blumenthal.[6] Next day Steinmetz won another victory, this time over Festetics's Corps at Schweinschädel, inflicting heavy casualties in an unplanned encounter. On June 30 the two men rode to the V Corps to congratulate Steinmetz on another victory.

As the Second Army moved towards the decisive battle of Königgrätz, the V Corps brought up the rear of the marching columns, so that on July 3 it was able to take no effective part in the battle; its leading troops did not reach Chlum until 8.00 pm that evening. Although as the Second Army's reserve it could theoretically have been employed in taking up the pursuit of the retreating Austrians, there was in practice no way it could get forward far enough or fast enough to do so, due to the compression of the three Prussian armies by the end of the battle into a very narrow space.

Steinmetz ended the war of 1866 with all the public acclaim to be expected as a uniformly successful field commander and inspirational leader of his troops. He received a handsome grant from the appreciative government. By 1870, however, he was in his seventy fourth year, and the question of how to utilise him was not an easy one. To pass over such a determined fighting general as the 'Lion of Nachod' would certainly be controversial, and his undoubted qualities would be of value, if properly harnessed. On the other hand, his age might justify a decision not to employ him. His appointment to lead the First Army prompted considerable anxiety among well informed deservers such as Verdy, who noted:

> The nominations certainly aroused some misgivings. The universal and high appreciation of the merits of this gallant fighting general was merited in every respect. But however high his military capabilities were, his personal qualities and his independence of character were such as to make it difficult for his superiors to deal with him, and made friction probable if he, at the head of an army, was subordinate to a higher command.[7]

Waldersee commented in his diary on July 29 in blunter terms:

> I cannot understand the giving of the First Army to old Steinmetz. Even in 1866 he was three quarters cracked, and now he is four years older. He will not be at fault in the matter of energy and action, but these things are no good by themselves.[8]

Pondering the question a few days later, Waldersee saw what had probably led to the appointment:

> It was thought that the French might take the offensive early against the Lower Moselle, and it was felt that there was need here for an army leader of iron nerve who would hold out under any conditions; and Steinmetz was considered to be fitted for the part.[9]

It may perhaps have been hoped that Major General von Sperling, the Chief of Staff of the First Army, would be able to control his wayward commander, but from the outset Verdy had his doubts about this, which in due course were confirmed:

> The choice of a proper Chief of the Staff may in such cases do much to smooth matters, and the best possible was made in the person of General von Sperling, a clear-headed, circumspect, and resolute officer. But even his eminent military as well as personal qualities were not able to prevail with such a character as that of General von Steinmetz.[10]

Bronsart was another outspoken critic of Steinmetz's appointment, observing of him that 'his judgement and activity had been affected, only his obstinacy remains.'[11]

Blumenthal, usually so outspoken, made no comment on the appointment of Steinmetz; he did, though, reflect enviously on the task assigned to him, commenting that he 'appears to me to have the pleasantest and easiest task allotted, as long as the neutrality of Belgium and Luxembourg is respected by the French. He will, if God grants him health and life, have all the laurels.'[12] To carry out his task, Steinmetz had some strong individuals among his subordinate commanders. Goeben, commanding the VIII Corps, was possibly the most accomplished of the corps commanders in the Prussian army. Manteuffel, whose I Corps would not join the invasion of France until a couple of weeks had elapsed, had been the very successful commander of the Army of the Main in 1866, and was of course a powerful and influential individual in his own right. Zastrow, the commander of the VII Corps, was less outstanding, though a competent divisional commander in 1866. In Kameke, the commander of the 14th Division, Zastrow had a leader of considerable merit.

Almost as soon as the campaign began Steinmetz began to exhibit the signs of independence that the doubters had feared would appear. The First Army was edging further to its left than Moltke had intended, due to Steinmetz's eagerness to get to grips with the enemy. On August 3 Moltke ordered the First Army to concentrate on the following day around Tholey. Apprehensive that Steinmetz might move on from this position, Moltke sent a telegram at noon on August 4: 'Agree with the position which you have taken up; remain there until further orders.'[13] He followed this up with a letter which appears not to have reached Steinmetz during the course of the afternoon. In this letter he notified Steinmetz that he would receive further orders either to support the Second Army or to act against the enemy's left flank: 'It is not intended to cross the Saar before August 9. The enemy seems to intend remaining on the defensive behind this river.'[14] Moltke's original telegram of August 4 annoyed Steinmetz extremely, and at 3.00 pm he fired off an angry telegram to Moltke, which reached the latter only at 8.00 pm:

> I would have much preferred to remain in position on the Saar, where my army formed an offensive flank on the line of the Second Army. From there the First Army could take more effective action than from St Wendel or still more so Baumholder, where it merely prolongs the front of the Second Army … Accordingly, I do not understand the strategic conception of abandoning the Saar, which is not justified by the military situation. I would therefore ask for clarification if I am to play my part correctly …I am afraid the French will see in our new position an advantage won by them.[15]

Moltke replied at once by telegram to say that his letter was en route. Next morning, at 6.00 am, he thought that he had better make the position crystal clear, so he wrote again to Steinmetz; this letter seems not to have been despatched until noon, and not to have to reached Steinmetz until 2.30 am on August 6. In this Moltke patiently explained what was wanted of the First Army:

> As was already explained at Berlin, I believe to Your Excellency in person, but certainly to your Chief of Staff and Quartermaster General, the role intended for the First Army, apart from the protection of the Rhine provinces in the first instance, consists of making a decisive attack against the left flank of the enemy. This attack naturally cannot be made in isolation but only in conjunction with the Second Army … Not until the Second Army has approached the Saar will it be the time for the First Army to cross that river. A partial advance against an enemy who seems to have concentrated all his forces could lead only to a disaster. The cooperation of the three armies can be directed only by his Majesty, but their freedom of action to execute the orders issued will not be limited.[16]

In the meantime, before getting this letter, the increasingly choleric Steinmetz sent off a telegram over Moltke's head to the King, complaining about the orders that had been issued, which, he said, would mean that the Second Army would push itself forward in front of the First Army; 'As I have received no instructions for a further advance I have no basis for coming into action.' The King endorsed this with a note: 'Is it not a flank position that was intended'?[17]

The movement of the First Army to its left was by now causing considerable traffic problems on the St Wendel-Ottweiler road, where its troops had no business to be, and Moltke sharply ordered Steinmetz to remain where he was on August 5 and 6, and to clear off entirely from that road. On August 7 the First Army might be able to more up to the Saar, attracting as little attention as possible; but 'His Majesty expressly reserves to himself the orders for the execution of this operation, since the manner of undertaking it and the direction it is given, will depend upon the outcome of events with the Third Army.'[18] Moltke was becoming extremely concerned at Steinmetz's refusal to accept direction, but he still hoped to be able to launch an encirclement of the French south of the Saar, with Steinmetz coming down on the French left, crossing at Saarlouis and Völklingen, and Frederick Charles attacking between Saarbrücken and Sarreguemines. In this way the Army of the Rhine would be driven away from Metz and into the advancing Third Army. That was Moltke's plan; but Steinmetz's reaction to his instructions effectively wrecked it. On the evening of August 5 he ordered both his corps forward to the Saar, moving due south on Saarbrücken, thus again crossing the path of the Second Army, and heading straight for a frontal assault on the French army.

When he finally received Moltke's letter of August 5, Steinmetz wrote a lengthy explanation of his proceedings. Even Moltke's iron self restraint was seriously tested by this, as appears from the marginal notes he made on Steinmetz's letter, which began:

> I have the honour of replying that I had no doubt about the mission of the First Army so long as the Second Army sought to effect its strategic deployment towards the Saar. This mission could only consist of facilitating the advance of the Second Army by drawing the enemy troops away from that army on to the First Army, and to attack these vigorously if the Second Army was unable to advance without fighting.

To this Moltke noted: 'Would have exposed the First Army to defeat.' To a convoluted sentence apparently explaining why he had not cleared the St Wendel-Ottweiler-Neunkirchen road, an exasperated Moltke noted: '??' When Steinmetz went on to announce that he was now only one march away from the Saar, and had recovered the necessary freedom of movement and the equally necessary room for the deployment of its troops, Moltke wrote: 'Instead of taking the enemy in flank, it will itself be taken in flank by Boulay as soon as it advances from Saarbrücken-Völklingen.'[19]

Steinmetz concluded his insubordinate epistle with an impertinent demand that he should be 'furnished with the directives planned for the operations,' since, as he put it, the timely arrangement of his dispositions depended on his timely knowledge of the King's intentions. While he was writing his letter, however, events were overtaking both him and Moltke. The leading units of both the First and Second Armies had, in the early hours of August 6 advanced towards Saarbrücken, where cavalry patrols found the French positions to have been abandoned. Zastrow's VII Corps, inclining to its left, moved into the path of the Second Army. Kameke concluded that the abandonment of the heights meant that the French were in retreat, and asked Zastrow for leave to cross the Saar to occupy them; Zastrow raised no objection. Meanwhile Goeben, riding ahead of his corps, with which he had also intended to cross the river at Saarbrücken, found Kameke's advance guard under Francois already on the road to the town; letting them through, he promised support if necessary.

The stage was thus set for an encounter battle that was completely at odds with Moltke's strategic intentions, and was to be fought without any substantial input from either of the army commanders whose troops were involved. Frederick Charles, angered by the discovery that the First Army was again crossing his path, ordered Stülpnagel with the 5th Division to clear the trespassers off the road. By now, however, Kameke had begun to fight, and the sound of the guns attracted units from both the First and Second Armies which came forward pell mell to attack the French under Frossard. He had taken up on extremely strong position on the Spicheren heights, and which in spite of the arrival of units from Goeben's VIII Corps and Alvensleben's III Corps he held all day against Zastrow's attacks, before retreating southwards as night fell. These attacks cost the Prussians heavy casualties which might, as Howard points out, have been avoided if instead of frontal assaults they had edged round Frossard's left and thereby obliged him to pull back. However, as he goes on to observe, although this premature battle ruined Moltke's strategy, the outcome of the battle seriously damaged the equilibrium of the French High Command.[20]

Although he might have been enraged that his intentions had thus been set at nought, Moltke, years later, wrote rather more forgivingly about Spicheren, dealing with suggestions that it had been fought 'in an ill judged locality, and that it interfered with more important plans,' both of which statements were of course perfectly true:

> It had certainly not been anticipated, but, generally speaking, a tactical victory rarely fails to fit in with a strategic design. Success in battle has always been thankfully accepted, and turned to account. By the battle of Spicheren the 2nd French Corps was prevented from withdrawing unharmed; touch of the enemy's main force was obtained, and to the supreme direction of the armies was afforded a basis for further resolutions.[21]

In August 1870, however, Moltke was not taking such a relaxed view of Steinmetz's performance. Relations between them had reached a new low, and Steinmetz sulkily gave the Royal Headquarters the minimum of information. On the evening of August 7 Moltke ordered Steinmetz to remain where he was; further orders could only be issued when the cavalry had located the enemy's main body.[22] Meanwhile Steinmetz had also fallen out with Frederick Charles, to whom he complained that the Second Army was poaching on his requisition area and using his roads. With this sort of thing in mind, Moltke issued a general order on August 8 that all military messages and reports sent by army commands should be addressed in the first instance to him.

Contemplating the angry telegram from Steinmetz to Frederick Charles, Moltke drafted a suitable letter of which a copy in pencil in his handwriting appears among the official records, but which was not sent. It illustrates just how seriously Moltke took Steinmetz's behaviour. After pointing out precisely what had been the original direction assigned to the First Army, Moltke reminded Steinmetz that the First Army had been expressly ordered to use the roads to Völklingen and Saarlouis for its further advance:

Yet in spite of that order it went through Guichenbach and Fischbach towards Saarbrücken-Forbach, exposing itself in the event of the continuation of its movement to being taken in the flank by the enemy forces still assembled at Boulay. I must therefore inform you that I consider as unfounded the statements made by you in your telegram to the Second Army. On the contrary I must expressly state that the Second Army has been led in a manner absolutely conforming to my intentions and I have informed General of Cavalry Prince Frederick Charles of this.[23]

It no doubt did Moltke good to relieve his feelings in this way, but if not sent, this was perhaps just as well, since it would have caused a considerable further upset at the headquarters of the First Army.

Still in ignorance of the situation of the Army of the Rhine, Moltke ordered the First Army to remain a further day in its position. It was not until August 10 that cavalry patrols located the French in position along the Nied; Frederick Charles suggested that there was an opportunity there to encircle them, but Moltke preferred to wait until he could concentrate ten corps to deal with them, and in the event, before anything else could happen, the French pulled back towards Metz. He had occasion, however, to administer a further reproof to Steinmetz on August 10:

It is suggested that Your Excellency has moved your headquarters from Völklingen to Lauterbach. No official report of this has been received, nor of the movements carried out today by the First Army, nor of any projected changes in the position of this army for tomorrow; these reports are still awaited.[24]

That was sent during the evening; early next morning Moltke was writing again to the errant commander of the First Army. This followed yet another complaint by Steinmetz that troops of the Second Army had been found on the roads assigned to the First Army, together with a request that his trains should be allowed to go to St Avold. Moltke, in his reply, agreed that the 35th Regiment (part of Alvensleben's III Corps) was out of position; insisted that trains must move on the same roads as the corps to which they belonged; and pointed out that the assignment of the principal roads to each of the armies held good only until the position of the enemy was known.[25] A few hours later, Moltke was writing yet again to reproach Steinmetz:

During the whole of yesterday his Majesty, until 10.00 pm was without any information as to the position of your headquarters and of the corps of the First Army, today it is still not known what movements are intended. His Majesty reminds the commander in chief of the orders that each day reports are to be sent to him so that His Majesty can dispose the corps. It becomes increasingly important to take care to do this as the armies approach nearer to the enemy.[26]

With the French having withdrawn from the line of the Nied, Moltke gave orders on August 12 for an advance on a broad front. The Second Army pushed its cavalry far forward; Steinmetz was, however in Howard's words, 'conducting his army with a defiant timidity,' following the reproaches he had received. Ironically, it was as he halted his army on August 14 that events once more took the situation out of his hands. Major General von der Goltz, the commander of the 26th Brigade, the leading unit of Zastrow's corps, was among the commanders to whom it was reported that the French were retreating across the Moselle. Others had learned of this; Manteuffel asked permission of Steinmetz to attack, which was refused, so the I Corps stayed put. But von der Goltz, without obtaining any approval to do so, resolved to attack; once the battle began, Manteuffel's corps joined in. Steinmetz, when he learned of it, was furious, and ordered Manteuffel and Zastrow to break off the battle at once, while Goeben was told not to get involved. It was, however, too late; the I Corps and the VII Corps were heavily committed. The result of the battle was indecisive, and considerable casualties had been incurred on both sides. As it ended, Steinmetz reached the battle field at 8.00 pm, and ordered both Manteuffel and Zastrow to retreat to the Nied. Mindful of the importance of bivouacking on the battlefield, they refused to do so. The historian of the First Army recorded Steinmetz's reaction: 'He could not but express disapprobation that so serious an action had been engaged in without orders from higher authority, and that it had been permitted to develop to such an extent, when the role of the First Army was essentially defensive.'[27]

To Steinmetz's chagrin, Royal Headquarters endorsed the decision of his subordinates, and the King came up next day to congratulate von der Goltz, who had been somewhat apprehensive about whether his action would be approved. Verdy talked to him next day:

> I was in a position to reassure him on that point by telling him that his course of action had eminently furthered the objects aimed at; for the delay which the battle had caused to the French was favourable to our projected operations and would facilitate their execution.[28]

Following news of the battle of Vionville-Mars la Tour, Moltke was concerned to get the two available corps of the First Army over the Moselle as soon as possible (Manteuffel's I Corps was to remain on the east bank of the river), and he issued an order to Steinmetz to this effect at 5.00 pm on August 16. He added the stern injunction that Steinmetz was to direct the VIII and VII Corps in a manner solely to bring them in touch with the enemy as soon as possible.[29] He repeated the requirement at 2.00 am on the following morning, doubtless because he was conscious that Steinmetz was being deliberately awkward.

It was, however, Moltke's order of 1.45 pm on August 17, outlining the moves to be made on the following day, which drove Steinmetz into a special fury, since it not only gave directions as to the VII and VIII Corps, but also removed the latter from the First Army and attached it to the Second Army as its right wing. He denounced this treatment of him as 'wanting in consideration,' since he now effectively had only the VII Corps under his command, the I Corps being now outside his direct sphere of influence. What, then, was he there for? Moltke was unmoved, coldly replying to Steinmetz on the morning of August 18, before he left for Flavigny:

> There is no change in the arrangements for the command of the First Army. Direct orders of His Majesty will also be issued today on the battlefield. The VII Corps will at first observe a defensive attitude. Contact with the VIII Corps can only be towards the front. If the enemy retreats into Metz, it will result in a change of direction to the right on our part. The First Army will, if necessary be supported by the second echelon of the Second Army.[30]

Hönig, in his study of the battle of Gravelotte, regarded this order as of immense historical significance, indicating as it does that Moltke was already considering the possibility that Bazaine would retreat into Metz which, indeed, he did, albeit after the battle had been fought.[31] Steinmetz, meanwhile, was not mollified by the suggestion that he might be supported by the Second Army. It was his conviction that the VII Corps was in an exposed and dangerous position. That being his belief, albeit incorrect, Hönig suggested that he could have resolved it by occupying Gravelotte on the afternoon of August 17. He went on to dissect Steinmetz's instructions to the VII Corps throughout that and the following day, noting that the general only took up his position at 8.00 am on the morning of the battle.

It was however later in the battle that Fritz Hönig's narrative most vividly conveyed the extent to which Steinmetz had lost the plot. Perhaps due to the effect of his age, or his experiences thus far in the campaign, or to the acceleration of the mental illness that had afflicted him for so long, or a combination of these, Steinmetz was clearly no longer fitted to be an army commander. Hönig compared him very unfavourably to the calm and assured conduct by Goeben of the VIII Corps in the preceding chapter. Steinmetz's behaviour presented a complete contrast, as Hönig described:

> When gloomy depression rests upon the face of the leader, when he says nothing, but betrays the conflict in his soul by his gestures and restless behaviour, when he incessantly tugs at and turns his horse, and remains silent for a long time, and, when he does speak, shows the agitation which he suffers inwardly by the sharpness of his voice and accent, there can then be in those around him no quiet and no courtesy, no feeling of confidence and trust. Proof as he was against the advice of others, Steinmetz was as headstrong as he was vain. There was no harmony between him and his staff, and no cheerful spontaneity; military absolutism weighed like lead on the best dispositions, and prevented all from delighting in their duty … In this battle he failed to find, at the right time, either the strength or the decision to let orders be simply orders, or to come to a great and good resolve, and then to use all his might to forward it.[32]

Zastrow, with whom Steinmetz was not at all in harmony, was not a great deal better. With no agreement between the two men, the infantry of the VII Corps were never employed properly throughout the day: 'The leader of this corps simply frittered away his infantry, thus making himself tactically impotent.' Their response to Goeben's request for support for his 15th Division, and to the suggestion, plainly correct, to a report from von Wedell that a turning movement would result in the capture of the heights held by the French, was absolutely to ignore the opportunity offered. They held to a conviction that the French were retiring, which was obviously wrong. Both were, as Hönig put it, of 'that description of men who do not like forward inferiors to interfere with anything; moreover, since 1866, General von Steinmetz had regarded himself as infallible.'[33] Instead of reinforcing Goeben, Steinmetz and Zastrow gave orders for an advance which led to the catastrophe in the Mance Ravine, when infantry, artillery and cavalry suffered appalling losses.

By 5.00 pm Steinmetz's mistakes had led to some 43 companies from seven regiments being pinned down around St Hubert, unable to advance. He also wrongly, reported to the King that the heights had been taken. He now applied to the Royal Headquarters for permission to use the fresh troops of Fransecky's II Corps, which were moving forward. It was this that led to the incident described in Chapter 4, when the King overruled Moltke's opinion and at 5.30 pm ordered the II Corps to place itself under Steinmetz's orders. Steinmetz accordingly ordered Fransecky to advance on Point du Jour.[34]

Moltke remained tight lipped about the incident when he came to write his account of the war, simply taking upon himself a responsibility which was not his, when he wrote:

> It would have been better if the Chief of the Staff of the army, who was present on the spot, had not allowed this advance to take place at so late an hour of the evening. A nucleus of troops which was altogether intact might have been most desirable on the following day, but could scarcely on this evening bring about a decisive change.[35]

Hönig explains this by 'the character, the mode of thought and the feelings of Moltke,' who hoped thereby to put an end to controversy, and to protect the King from criticism: 'It is thus intelligible that Moltke should decline to say a depreciatory word with regard to General von Steinmetz,' who had effectively destroyed the prestige he had won in 1866. Phil Sheridan had heard of the disastrous casualties sustained as a result of Steinmetz's orders, and so great was the indignation expressed at the Royal Headquarters that he thought Steinmetz would be relieved on the spot. He described Steinmetz's reception by the King:

> Followed by a large staff, General Steinmetz appeared in the village presently, and approached the King. When near, he bowed with great respect, and I then saw that he was a very old man, though his soldierly figure, bronzed face, and

short cropped hair gave some evidence of vigour still. When the King spoke to him I was not close enough to learn what was said; but his Majesty's manner was expressive of kindly feeling, and the fact that in a few moments the veteran general returned to the command of his troops, indicated that, for the present at least, his fault had been overlooked.[37]

The Official History contained a number of comments on the battle which were critical of Steinmetz, a few of which Hönig found to be unjust. He also records that Steinmetz, after the war, sought to defend himself by writing a memorandum on the subject of his relationship with Moltke and with Frederick Charles, but which William refused to allow him to publish. Steinmetz, to his credit, therefore remained silent in the face of the criticisms made of his conduct.

Although the battle had undoubtedly been a strategic victory, the appalling casualties suffered by the Prussians caused general dismay. Bismarck spoke for many when he declared that 'people are fed up with Steinmetz's butchery.'[38] The fact of Steinmetz being placed under the command of Frederick Charles for the investment of Metz suggested that there might be trouble ahead, as the Crown Prince, who knew Steinmetz well, speculated in his diary on August 23:

I own I should be surprised to see this turn out well, for already the old lion of Skalitz would seem to have behaved so outrageously that only His Majesty's personal intervention prevailed to maintain the necessary authority. General von Steinmetz seems wishful to play at being a sort of little despot without there being any reason for it. It is a pity he is growing old, for, set on the right track, he does the right thing – that is how I read his character. But it is no light task to be set in authority over him.[39]

It was certainly only a matter of time before there was a further conflict, this time between Frederick Charles and Steinmetz. Moltke had made it clear to the former that he should put up with no more nonsense from the old man, and when the Prince reported that Steinmetz was 'withholding from him the customary civilities due to a superior officer,' the King was furious. On September 15 Steinmetz was transferred to the post of Governor of Posen, and Moltke's worst headache was cured.[40]

20

Werder

Of all his subordinates, Moltke was most inclined to underrate August von Werder, at least during the Franco-Prussian War. Perhaps he sensed in Werder a lack of self confidence, which prompted him sometimes unnecessarily to seek approval for a particular line of action. On occasion, in response to such communications, Moltke would reply somewhat tersely, in a manner which he would not use to those in whom he had absolute trust.

Werder was born in East Prussia on September 12 1808, the son of a Prussian officer who rose to the rank of Lieutenant General. At the age of 17 he joined the Garde du Corps, and in March 1826 he was commissioned as a sub lieutenant in the 1st Guard Regiment. From then on, as usual in the Prussian army, he worked his way up extremely slowly. In 1833 he attended the *Allgemeinekriegschule* before returning first to regimental service and then a spell with the engineers. Thereafter, he served as an instructor at the cadet school, followed by employment in the topographical bureau. It was not until 1842, at the age of thirty four, that he finally attained the rank of First Lieutenant.

It was following this promotion that Werder was sent abroad on a mission which was to give him a taste of combat for the first time. He was despatched to serve with the Russian army in the Caucasus, operating against the insurgent tribes that were proving such a thorn in the side of the Russians attempting to pacify the region. His military experiences there were many and varied, riding into action with the Cossacks, and visiting many of the Russian fortresses and coast defences. Seeing action at first hand, however, was not without its dangers. In June 1843, while serving with the Cossacks in an engagement with insurgent tribesman on the banks of the River Kefar, he was severely wounded in the lelt arm. The bone was smashed, and he only narrowly escaped amputation.[1]

Werder returned home to recuperate, and in March 1846 was promoted to captain, and five years later to major. His slow progress up the ladder continued with his promotion to lieutenant colonel in 1856. In the following year he took command of the fusilier battalion of the 2nd Guard Regiment. After two years in this post he became colonel, and in January 1863 received the command of the 8th Brigade.

Shortly after this he was promoted to Major General and in 1864 was transferred to the command of the 4th Guards Brigade. In May 1865 he was provisionally appointed to the command of the 3rd Division at Stettin; next year he was confirmed in this post with the rank of Lieutenant General. It had been a steady, rather than spectacular rise; what is noticeable is that since becoming a first lieutenant he appears to have served none of his time on the General Staff, which may well have meant that he did not become well acquainted with Moltke or some of his key collaborators. Just possibly this may have had some bearing on Moltke's relationship with him in 1870-1871. At any rate, apart from dining with Werder's father in 1849, Moltke makes no reference to him in his extensive correspondence.

It was as commander of the 3rd Division that Werder went off to war in 1866; the division formed part of the II Corps, in turn part of Frederick Charles' First Army. Unlike the other two corps which made up the army, the II Corps had a command structure, and was led by Lieutenant General Stefan von Schmidt. Major General Georg von Kameke was its Chief of Staff. In the early stages of the campaign in Bohemia the II Corps was in the second line of the advance of the First Army, and it was not until after the abortive strike at Münchengrätz that its troops first came into action.

On June 29 Werder's division marched from Sobotka and Podkost towards Gitschin, approaching the town from the west, while Tümpling's 5th Division advanced towards it from the north. The fighting did not begin until mid afternoon, with Tümpling's troops engaged in a fierce struggle around Diletz. Werder, meanwhile, advanced on the villages of Ober Lochow and Unter Lochow, taking the latter at 7.15 pm. A turning movement by the 5th Brigade forced the defences back; Werder's troops were completely exhausted after the battle, but, as there was no water available to refresh them, Schmidt, who had come up, led them forward into Gitschin itself, entering the town at 10.30 pm. They bivouacked for the night in the colonnaded arcades of the square. They remained in Gitschin throughout the following day, moving forward to a position five miles south of Kamenetz on July 1.

When, on July 3, the First Army advanced on the Austrian positions along the Bistritz, the 3rd Division was in the centre of the army's front. As the 4th Division advanced from Mzan in support of Horn's 8th Division it began to take heavy casualties from the Austrian gunners, and Schmidt ordered Werder forward, stressing the need for him to bring his artillery to the front. The pressure of the three divisions forced back the Austrian infantry and Werder was able to get his division over the Bistritz, and into the villages of Dohalitz and Moskrowitz. Although having crossed the river into a reasonable defensive position, the division was hampered in bringing up its artillery by the lack of crossings over the Bistritz. Unlike the 4th Division, which was exposed to heavy casualties when Schmidt ordered it back from the Holawald, Werder was able to limit casualties by taking advantage of the buildings which his men had occupied, and by eschewing any advance. By the end of the battle the 3rd Division had suffered far less than the 4th Division. For his part in the victory Werder was awarded the Pour le Mérite.

Werder.

On the outbreak of the Franco Prussian war Werder was placed in command of the Württemberg and Baden Divisions, assigned to the Third Army under the Crown Prince. During the battle of Wörth, on August 6 Werder's troops came up on the left of the Third Army through Reichshoffen. before becoming involved in the struggle around Elsasshausen. Thereafter, as Moltke put together his armies to deal both with the Army of the Rhine and what became the Army of Châlons, Moltke assigned Werder to the task of reducing the fortress of Strasbourg. The Württemberg Division was to remain with the Third Army; Werder was to have the Baden Division as the nucleus of a force that was to carry out a task that was by no means easy. Moltke was concerned that not a moment should be lost, and telegraphed Lieutenant General Gustav von Beyer, the commander of the Baden Division, on August 10:

> Make known to the commander of the troops before Strasbourg that His Majesty orders that all reinforcement of troops or materiel destined for that city, particularly from the south, is to be prevented. It would be best completely to invest the place; reinforcements for this are en route.[2]

In what was to become a familiar pattern, Moltke was quick to send a crisp reminder two days later: 'What measures have you taken to execute my telegram of August

10? Reply by telegram.'[3] Beyer dutifully responded that he had, in order to invest Strasbourg, established two brigades to the north and west, and cavalry to the south; a battalion was posted at Kehl.

On August 14 Moltke confirmed to Werder the forces that would be available to him. These were, in addition to the Baden Division, two Landwehr divisions (Guard and 1st) the 34th Fusilier Regiment, the 30th Regiment, the 2nd Reserve Dragoon Regiment and three reserve batteries. The siege train, fortress artillery and engineers would be sent by rail. Werder's task, Moltke told him laconically, was to take Strasbourg as soon as possible.[4] Werder was uncertain whether it would be justified to bombard the city from Kehl, the other side of the Rhine; certainly, replied Moltke, if that would bring about a capitulation. He added, however, that it was not possible to judge it from the Royal Headquarters. For the rest of the month Moltke had his hands full with the pursuit of the Army of Châlons, and he left Werder to get on with the business of the siege. Once the French army had capitulated at Sedan, Moltke informed Werder of the situation, and ordered him to summon Strasbourg to surrender.

Werder had commenced the bombardment of the city on August 23. Considerable damage had been done, and civilian morale was gravely affected. From the point of view of Werder's staff, however, who had been assessing the effect of the bombardment, it did not seem to be achieving much, and it was decided to embark on formal siege operations. By September the second parallel was completed; next day a major French sortie was thrown back with heavy loss. Once the news of Sedan had arrived, Werder carried out Moltke's instructions; Uhrich, the commandant, refused the summons. He wanted permission to send out two officers who could report back to him on the situation, and that there should in the meantime be an armistice. Werder sought further instructions:

> General Uhrich has broken off negotiations because I refused an armistice and because, on our side, we cannot accept as a basis for negotiations that the garrison should march out with their arms and equipment. Should I offer new terms in the light of the political situation? The siege works and in particular the reinforcement of the artillery have made excellent progress.[5]

Moltke replied that a rapid capitulation was certainly desirable; however, the garrison must become prisoners of war. If necessary, a French officer would be allowed to come to the Royal Headquarters, under escort.

Werder wrote on September 8 to suggest that a resumption of the bombardment would hasten a surrender; in reply, Moltke authorised this as a last resort, but it should be avoided if possible, and in any case Uhrich must be given due warning. Time passed without further news; on September 21 Moltke sent an irritable telegram from Ferrières to the effect that he had heard nothing for a week; daily reports by telegram were required. Werder, in a tone of injured innocence, replied that he had indeed been sending reports, and next day they turned up. Asked by Werder whether he had authority to negotiate a capitulation when the situation arose, Moltke confirmed that he did. As to the terms, the garrison must be made prisoners of war; the honours of war must be accorded them; the officers could return home on giving their parole on the same terms as had been granted at Sedan.[6]

By September 26 Uhrich was ready to accept that no further defence was practicable, and terms were agreed for a capitulation. Next day the garrison marched out, led by Uhrich and his senior commanders on foot. Werder and the Grand Duke of Baden dismounted to receive them. That same day Werder was rewarded with a well deserved promotion to the rank of General of Infantry.

On September 28 Moltke issued instructions for Werder's next mission. It was to move with his whole corps (less the Guard Landwehr Division, which had been sent off to join the investment of Paris) to the upper Seine, in the direction of Troyes and Châtillon sur Seine. On the way, Werder was to prevent the assembly of enemy forces in the departments of Vosges, Haute Marne and l'Aube, disarming the populations; he was also to attempt to get the railway from Blainville to Chaumont in running order. Since Langres presently barred the way to this, a coup de main against that fortress might be attempted. An emerging problem was the activity of the franc tireurs. Moltke had on August 24 issued a warning order about the establishment of bodies of these volunteers, describing their uniform and arms. He added that they were not to be treated as soldiers, and were liable to be shot. Werder was already very much aware of the threat that the franc tireurs posed, and asked and received permission to send a brigade to deal with a concentration of them at Raon L'Étape.

During the ensuing four months, as Werder endeavoured to carry out the various, complex and frequently changing tasks assigned to him, Moltke communicated with him on a regular basis. In this period he sent him no less than thirty two orders, many by telegram. What is even more remarkable however, is the tone of these instructions. Moltke addressed Werder in terms which he would not have thought of using to his other independent commanders at this stage of the war. The contrast, for instance, between the manner of Moltke's correspondence with Werder and that with, say, Goeben, is particularly striking. Moltke was not someone who could generally be accused of impatience; but where Werder was concerned he seems often to have given way to this.

Werder assigned the operation against Raon L'Étape to a column led by Major General Alfred von Degenfeld. It was successfully carried out after a bitter struggle on October 6 in the battle of Etival against the forces led by General Dupré. Meanwhile the main body of the XIV Corps had been advancing against the principal French force in the region commanded by General Cambriels. Werder found St Dié abandoned; his advance guard drove the French out of Rambervillers, and on October 10 the 1st Baden Brigade under Colonel Beyer attacked Cambriels at Bruyeres. He took the town, and advanced to Laval before encountering substantial French forces. These, however, were already in a state of moral collapse, and Cambriels retreated all the way to Besancon, where his arrival on October 14 caused public dismay.

Werder, meanwhile, had occupied Epinal. He was, however, unsure what he should do next, since as far as he knew Cambriels still represented a distinct threat. On October 14 he sent a telegram to Moltke suggesting that with the complete destruction of the railway, and the proximity of Cambriels' corps, the projected march through Jussey could not be carried out. Perhaps, he added, the best thing would be to march by Neufchâteau and Chaumont. He concluded: 'I may remark that on the departure of the Corps, hostile pressure will most likely be felt at Lunévile, and I therefore request further instructions.'[7] This was not at all well received at Versailles. It seemed to Moltke that the strength of the enemy was being exaggerated, and he responded sharply on October 15:

> His Majesty orders that the attack of the enemy be carried out without any other consideration. His forces can only consist of depot troops and gardes mobiles and, in particular, a maximum of 36 guns. A base and railway lines are not essential. Acknowledge.[8]

Before this arrived at Werder's headquarters, he reported that Cambriels had retreated to Rupt; he put his strength at 16-20,000 bad troops. Moltke's response was abrupt. Having had no reply to his previous telegram, he repeated it, saying that the views expressed still held good: 'Accordingly, do not take the town of Vesoul as the object of your advance, but only the position of the enemy'[9]

Werder sent a defensive response to Moltke's telegram of October 15:

> For eight days, I have directed all my efforts to attacking the enemy, but he has never stood. In accordance with your order I am going immediately to march on Luxeuil and Lure, points on which he must retire. I ask whether I should follow the enemy further to the south, or march again on my principal objective, the Upper Seine.[10]

To this Moltke replied that he might push his offensive against Cambriels as far as Besancon, but should then resume his march westward through Dijon on Bourges. This last point marked a distinct change in the general strategy which the XIV Corps was to pursue. It was, as Ludwig Löhlein, the historian of the Corps operations, observed, a distinct one 'which admitted of no modification.'

Werder troops duly occupied Vesoul without resistance; he was on the point of abandoning his pursuit of Cambriels when he learned that the latter had taken up a position along the Ognon. Although distinctly uneasy about moving to the assault of an enemy of unknown strength, close to a powerful fortress, Werder felt that in view of the emphatic instructions that he had been receiving, he had no choice but to advance to the attack notwithstanding all the difficulties. It would be necessary to leave behind the trains and other equipment. As Löhlein put it:

> Since the Vosges had been crossed the weather had been extremely bad. One may really say that there were only hours in which it did not rain; the clothes and

boots, the latter of which had suffered considerably in the trenches at Strasbourg, which were often very wet, were in very bad order. The task set to the corps contained many difficulties; it was hardly possible to weigh them all, the only thing to do was to resolve to advance firmly and as fast as possible, leaving behind as above stated all the train, and to carry out the distinct order from the Royal Army Chiefs without asking any more questions.[11]

The ensuing operations on the Ognon were only partially successful; although the enemy were driven back, the attempt to cut off a part of their forces failed. Examining the French positions around Besancon, Werder found them, as he expected, to be extremely strong, and he concluded that he should now march off towards Dijon. He began his westward move by marching on Gray; again, the French that he encountered eluded him by falling back through terrain that was extremely difficult.

This was the situation on October 29, when Werder received a detailed instruction from Moltke that had been delayed, having been written on October 23. Announcing that the fall of Metz was imminent, and that the Second Army would then march towards the Loire, Moltke went on:

> The task hitherto set your Excellency is (as was also stated in the telegram of this date) hereby changed, and the XIV Corps, to which are added the 1st and 4th Reserve Divisions, and from which the Guard Landwehr Division is removed, has to carry out the investment and immediate siege of Schlettstadt, Neu-Breisach and Belfort, to cover Alsace and the left flank of the Second Army, and to keep in check the enemy in its front, whose strength is equal to its own. The Army Corps will now, so long as the enemy is in great force near Besancon, stand for the most part in Vesoul, occupy Dijon in force, and secure itself against Langres, Besancon and Belfort.[12]

Moltke was not however, going to let Werder suppose that he was relenting in his insistence on attacking the enemy wherever that was practicable; he went on:

> Your Excellency will not hesitate to assume the offensive against any weak parties of the enemy; the fortress of Belfort, which is to be invested by the 1st Reserve Division which can scarcely arrive before November 6, is to be most strictly watched, and the organisation of a guerrilla war, based on it, in the Vosges and upper Alsace, to be prevented. Under these circumstances it may become requisite to turn considerable forces against Belfort.[13]

Pondering these instructions, Werder began to wonder whether it was altogether a good idea to attempt to occupy Dijon in present circumstances, with his forces so split up as would be necessary to do all the other things required of him. He decided that he would concentrate the bulk of the XIV Corps around Vesoul, watching Belfort, and hold Bray with two brigades to cover himself against any move from Besancon and the Ognon. The move on Dijon would, for the moment, be postponed. However, just as the orders were being written to give effect to these intentions, there came a report from a cavalry patrol that Dijon was unoccupied, and could be seized without difficulty; it would be a good deal harder to do so after the concentration around Vesoul. New orders were drafted for Beyer, with the columns of Prince William of Baden and Keller, to advance to Dijon, while those of Degenfeld and Krug von Nidda should make their way to Vesoul.

In the meantime, however, the municipal authorities in Dijon had been compelled by the population to reverse their intention of not defending the city, and it was only after a prolonged struggle that Beyer was able to march in on October 31; his losses were 268 killed and wounded. It was a prestigious success but meant that having captured the place, it should if possible be held, so that Werder's forces were stretched still further. It would be pleasant to be able to record that Werder was congratulated on an important achievement; but regrettably no such message was received by him from Versailles. What he did get, on November 3, was a telegram from Moltke to the effect that he could now pursue an offensive towards Dôle, as well as an advance from Dijon towards Chalon sur Saône, while continuing to observe Besancon. To do all these things was a tall order. However, that was the last he heard from Moltke for a period of three weeks, during which a good deal happened in the theatre of the XIV Corps.

What was soon clear to Werder was that the French forces opposed to him were rapidly growing in strength, which made the Dôle operation very hazardous; to carry it out might involve giving up Dijon, but he left it to Beyer to decide whether to pull out. The latter decided to take this step in order to cooperate in an advance on Auxonne; but when it appeared that this place was too strongly held, Werder concluded that it would be best to reoccupy Dijon, and this was done on November 14. That day Werder sent a report to Moltke reviewing his recent operations; he had reinforced Tresckow, who was now besieging Belfort, and was covering the communications over the wide front for which he was responsible. Mindful of Moltke's likely response, he added:

> The offensive against Chagny and Chalon, where the main body of the enemy is now, is possible, certainly, but not advisable until the mountains of the Côte d'Or can be swept by other troops. I, therefore, consider that I have for the present performed the tasks assigned to me; I remark, however, with emphasis, that I have no intention of entering upon a state of rest, but that I intend to constantly harass the enemy.[14]

By November 23, after most of his troops had enjoyed a well earned break, Werder had concentrated the bulk of his corps around Dijon, and reported to Moltke that he was now preparing for the advance to Chagny and Chalon, to deal in particular with Garibaldi's force. Moltke approved the plan, and wished Werder success in the operation. However, he also informed Werder that the formation of new French units at Le Mans and Tours meant that the Second Army would not be able to spare troops to cover its lines of communication:

As soon as your Excellency has succeeded in inflicting a decisive defeat on Garibaldi's bands, which will keep them quiet for a long while, the XIV Corps must detach flying columns between the Seine and the Loire to render it impossible for any significant enemy forces to operate from the south against the Second Army's lines of communication. This will thus indirectly provide the necessary support to this army.[15]

This further responsibility was not good news for the embattled Werder.

During the following fortnight there were a series of engagements with the forces of Garibaldi and Cremer, but Werder was anxious about his position in Dijon, and pulled back his forces to the city. On December 6 it started to snow very heavily indeed, rendering operations extremely difficult; Werder's troops, more comfortably situated in the city, suffered less than the French. Meanwhile Moltke sent on December 8 a further detailed letter of instructions, although it did not reach Werder until December 13. In it, he redefined Werder's task as being to cover the siege of Belfort, to isolate Langres, in conjunction with Zastrow's VII Corps to cover the communications of the Second and Third Armies, and to complete the pacification of the southern parts of the Governments-General of Lorraine and Reims. Moltke added that these tasks would 'not be best performed by long periods of inactivity; on the contrary, it is necessary with sufficient forces to undertake vigorous offensives against enemy concentrations.'[16] Werder was entitled to be more than a little offended by the implied criticism, but he dutifully rearranged his forces to comply. It was not long, however, before his responsibilities were again increased, Moltke writing on December 15 requiring him to take over part of Zastrow's duties of covering lines of communication in the Nuits-Semur area.

On December 18 Werder's forces won the hotly contested battle of Nuits, following which Werder planned to send a brigade to Semur; Moltke left this to his discretion, but required flying columns to move in that direction to cover the railway line Chaumont-Ravierés. Meanwhile enemy forces were gathering which threatened the whole area of Werder's operations; in particular, it was thought that an attempt would be made to raise the siege of Belfort, and it was clear that this must be where Werder should go. On December 21 Werder asked whether he could expect reinforcements; without them, Dijon could not be held, but Moltke could promise only one battalion. There was considerable uncertainty as to what the French were actually about; Moltke told Werder on December 30 that in his front at Besancon there were merely unorganised units; nothing more was known. That day, however, Werder's own reconnaissance told a different story, and he obtained full particulars of the French regiments that had been moved to Besancon.

With the need to move east to cover Belfort, it had been necessary to abandon Dijon; the evacuation began on December 27, but it was necessary to leave behind over 430 sick and wounded, with their medical attendants. Making good time in spite of the fearful conditions, the bulk of the XIV Corps had reached its planned position by December 30. Now came another red herring; on the basis of cavalry reports, it seemed to Moltke that perhaps Bourbaki's army was not after all moving east, and Werder should perhaps return to Dijon. This intelligence was, however, completely wrong. Bourbaki's leading units were in Besancon, and the rest of the Army of the East was heading that way, although Moltke remained sceptical. His prescription was for Werder to assume the offensive, and he clung to this idea, based on a belief that Bourbaki was still at Bourges, as late as January 5.[17] Others at Versailles took a graver view of Werder's situation; the Crown Prince recorded in his diary that Werder and Zastrow would have a heavy task before them.

As it was, Werder had to make up his own mind as to what to do. To make sure what Bourbaki really intended, he pushed forward a brigade under Keller, to make a reconnaissance in force. During the night of January 8/9 his patrols reported that indeed Bourbaki was heading for Belfort, and Werder at once ordered the whole of the XIV Corps to march eastwards. On January 9 his leading troops collided with the corps of Billot and, later, Clinchant at Villersexel, where a fierce struggle took place before Werder ordered his troops to break off the fight and continue the march eastwards towards Belfort.

On January 7 Moltke had written a very long letter to Werder, which was only received on the evening of January 10 as he was on his way to examine the positions along the Lisaine which he would occupy to cover the siege of Belfort. By the time he wrote it, Moltke had accepted the reality of Bourbaki's offensive, and had decided upon the formation of the Army of the South. Werder would continue to report to Versailles, until Manteuffel arrived to take over. The siege of Belfort was to remain Werder's priority; in addition, Moltke wrote:

> Your Excellency will not neglect to keep your eye on the enemy should he advance northwards on the west of the Vosges, and will therefore keep in communication with the Government-General of Lorraine … Should your Excellency be compelled to retire for a moment, you must do your best never to lose the touch of the enemy, in order, should he grow weaker in front of you, to be able to assume the offensive at once, and so prevent him from throwing himself with superior forces on the II and VII Corps as they advance towards you.[18]

Werder proceeded to meet with Tresckow to make the necessary arrangements for the defence of the line of the Lisaine. An immense amount of work was done to strengthen the position, which was naturally a strong one. By January 13 the French had moved forward, driving back the advanced pickets that Werder had posted to the west of his position. Werder expected an attack next day; it did not come, but a severe frost caused the rivers and canal to be frozen hard, so that they were passable not only by infantry but also by cavalry. That night, deeply concerned about his situation, he telegraphed Moltke to explain his fears:

> Fresh troops are advancing from the south and from the west against Lure and Belfort. Large forces are known to be at Port sur Saône. The enemy made a

fruitless attack on my outposts at Bart and Dung. I earnestly beg you to consider whether, thus surrounded and attacked by greatly superior forces, I am to continue to cling to Belfort. I think I can protect Alsace, but not Belfort as well, unless the very existence of the corps is to be risked. Having to cling to Belfort I am debarred from all freedom of movement – owing to the frost the rivers can be crossed.[19]

Moltke was never going to tolerate this sort of thing. His reaction to this telegram, received just after midnight on January 14/15, was graphically described by the Crown Prince:

One must have seen General Count Moltke's face and known him too as well as I do to form a conception of the look with which he communicated this telegram to me in the King's antechamber, then read it out at the report, and with what an air of imperturbable, icy calm he added: 'Your Majesty will, I trust, approve of this answer to General von Werder, that he has simply to stand firm and beat the enemy wherever he finds him.' I cannot say how admirable beyond all praise I thought General Moltke at this moment; any other man would have launched out with reflections and exclamations – he in one second relieved the whole strain of the situation and, thank heaven, restored General von Werder's steadiness.[20]

Moltke's response was remorseless: 'await the attack of the enemy in the fortified position covering Belfort, and accept battle. The possession of the Lure-Belfort road is of the highest importance.' He added that Manteuffel's advance would soon make itself felt.[21] By the time that this reached Werder at 6.00 pm on January 15, he had already fought the hardest of the three days of the battle on the Lisaine.

At Versailles, Moltke was apparently the only man to face the outcome of that battle with equanimity, as news was awaited. The Crown Prince on January 17, noting that Werder's right wing had been obliged to fall back, recorded the anxiety which prevailed at the Royal Headquarters:

It is in no little suspense we look for the arrival of the next news, for although the occurrence mentioned is in itself no real disadvantage, we have grounds for supposing that it is just at this point the enemy's main force will concentrate; thus even so small a success will no doubt duly set aflame the French spirit of enterprise. General von Moltke takes this information quietly, in fact all he said to it was: 'The good God will not allow us to suffer reverses,' but otherwise went on unshaken in his usual calm composure. The King's mood is already so depressed that he cannot be talked out of the conviction that at the very moment of his installation as Emperor we shall receive the very worst news from the Vosges.[22]

In fact, by the time he made this entry, in his diary the battle of the Lisaine had been won.

It had been a remarkable victory, for which Werder, for all his anxieties about the situation, deserved the greatest credit. Moltke's response was characteristically business like, and regrettably included no words of congratulation. He simply ordered that the siege of Belfort should be pursued with the utmost energy; and, as usual, urged that the XIV Corps should pursue the enemy.[23] As to that, Löhlein records that Werder, on a close consideration of the circumstances, concluded 'that it was absolutely necessary for him to stay where he was.' Löhlein pointed to the utter fatigue and exhaustion of Werder's men, the great superiority in numbers of Bourbaki's army, and the fact that an attack on a well posted enemy in strong positions must entail entirely disproportionate casualties.[24] All the surrounding circumstances indicated that Werder's decision was entirely correct, displeasing though it must be to Moltke.

The King, at least, displayed his appreciation of Werder's feat, conferring on him the Order of the Red Eagle with Swords, and writing to him that 'your heroic three days defence of your position with a besieged fortress in your rear, is one of the greatest feats of arms of all times.' It was praise which Werder, and his brave troops, entirely merited.[25]

For the rest of the campaign Werder was under the orders of Manteuffel. Sad to say, the latter also displayed some dissatisfaction with what he regarded as Werder's tardiness in getting into position. It is entirely probable that in his briefing by Moltke before he left to take command of the Army of the South, Manteuffel was told to keep Werder up to the mark. On January 25, for instance, Manteuffel wrote to Werder in terms very reminiscent of Moltke: 'The course to be adopted in case the enemy try to break through towards Gray is not to stop him by standing across his path, but to attack him on the march by both flanks.'[26] In the following days Manteuffel relentlessly tightened his grip on the Army of the East; the movements of the armies led ineluctably to the retreat of the French over the Swiss border, and with that the fighting in the Franco-Prussian War came to an end.

What Moltke wanted in his generals was initiative and an instinctive understanding of what he would expect them to do. In Werder, Moltke found a diffidence and uncertainty which weakened his confidence; it was a vicious circle, because the more that Werder sensed this, the more hesitant he became. But although Moltke may not have had the highest regard for him, the Crown Prince did, and so did his father, who later bestowed on Werder the Grand Cross of the Iron Cross, an honour shared with only six others of the victorious leaders – the Crown Prince, Frederick Charles, the Crown Prince of Saxony, Moltke, Manteuffel and Goeben. It was a company he was entitled to join.

21

Falckenstein

In one of the most curious and inexplicable perversions of military history ever written, Eduard Ernest Frederick Hannibal Vogel von Falckenstein was in 1875 described in these terms:

> Next to Moltke this is unquestionably the greatest strategist and the most accomplished staff officer of the Prussian and German armies, also the most consummate tactical leader in the field, and altogether the first of the great military captains of the age, though not yet a field marshal.[1]

He would more accurately have been described as being next to Steinmetz, the most obstinate, wrong-headed and disobedient of all Moltke's generals.

He was three years older than Moltke, a fact which may have contributed to his conviction of his own omniscience. Born at Breslau, he joined the army at the age of sixteen to take part in the Wars of Liberation. He took part in the battle of the Katzbach, after which he was made ensign; in December 1813 he was promoted to lieutenant. He took a distinguished part in the fighting in France in 1814, winning the Iron Cross and promotion to first lieutenant after the battle of Montmirail. By 1818 he was in command of a battalion; however, he remained a lieutenant colonel for no less than thirty years. He was wounded in the street fighting of the March Days; later in 1848 he took part in the Schleswig Holstein campaign, becoming chief of staff to Wrangel; he reached the rank of Colonel in 1851.

In his youth Falckenstein discovered that he had a considerable talent for design and for painting, in which he engaged all his life, working in various mediums but especially in oils. Later, he turned to painting on glass and porcelain. This work attracted the attention of the future King Frederick William IV, upon whose instructions Falckenstein established in due course the Royal Institute for Painting on Glass, of which he became the first head. He was responsible for a particularly fine stained glass window in the church of St Mary, near Danzig.[2]

His performance in Schleswig Holstein and his career thereafter appears to have given satisfaction; at all events, by 1858 he had reached the rank of Lieutenant General, and was given the command of the V Corps. In 1864, with the outbreak of the Second Schleswig War, he was appointed as Chief of Staff to the Allied army invading Denmark. Once again his commander was the aged Field Marshal Frederick von Wrangel, at eighty Falckenstein's senior by thirteen years. There had been a good deal of concern that the Austrians might insist on a Royal prince being appointed to the command; but Wrangel's seniority and his previous experience in the Duchies made him an acceptable choice. It was not, however, a wise one; Sybel noted that he 'had not as was soon to be seen, gained with age in breadth of view and keenness of insight, in sureness of judgment, nor in evenness of temper and will.'[3]

With the choleric and impetuous Wrangel in command, it was essential that his chief of staff be able to exercise a beneficial influence over him. Regrettably, this proved not to be the case. As the campaign progressed, all the indications were that far from restraining Wrangel, Falckenstein positively encouraged him. By the end of April Manteuffel had become convinced that the confusion at Wrangel's head-quarters was largely due to the chief of staff, and he urged Roon, as War Minister, to replace him by Moltke. Falckenstein was given command of an enlarged III Corps, awarded the Pour le Mérite and made governor of Jutland, while Moltke restored order at headquarters. This latter task was made a lot easier by Wrangel's replacement by Prince Frederick Charles.

Somewhat surprisingly, given the need for his replacement during the campaign, Falckenstein was after the war given command of the VII Corps. He still occupied that post at the outbreak of the Austro Prussian War in 1866. Although the 14th Division was detached from his corps to form part of the Army of the Elbe, it was his command of the VII Corps, based as it was in Western Germany, that led to Falckenstein's appointment to the command of all the forces that were to oppose first the Hanoverians and later the Federal 8th Corps and the Bavarian army. There were three divisions, the 13th Division under Goeben, and two Combined Divisions, one led by Beyer and the other, consisting of the forces in Holstein, by Manteuffel. All told, the force comprised 53 battalions, 29 squadrons and (at first) 12 guns. It would be heavily outnumbered by the opposition.

In a letter to Manteuffel on June 6 Moltke set out on June 16 the task facing the Prussian forces in the west, of which Manteuffell's division was a key element. Falckenstein, he wrote, had been instructed not to lose sight of the key objective, which was to disperse and disarm the Hanoverian Army; for this to succeed, speed was essential. Thereafter, it might be possible for the available forces to be employed in another theatre.[4] Moltke's first concern was for Manteuffel's division to get in touch with the rest of Falckenstein's forces.

On June 18 Moltke gave Falckenstein a comprehensive overview of the situation in Western Germany, and a clear statement of what was expected of him. He pointed out that Falckenstein's army was at least as strong as the forces opposed to it, and that these were not ready and in any case not yet under a unified command. In this calculation he excluded the Hanoverian Army, the situation of which was uncertain; as to this, Goeben's division had already begun to move on the city of Hanover itself.

Vogel von Falckenstein.

On the following day Moltke wrote again to Falckenstein to spell out once more the importance of moving swiftly. He was to act with all the forces available to him in a concentrated offensive against the South German contingents assembling on the line of the Main. Immediately, he was to concentrate his forces in the area Hersfeld-Hünfeld-Vacha, from which a rapid advance on Fulda should be undertaken.[5] The overriding objective must be the disposal of the South Germans.

However, on June 19, Falckenstein received a telegram from another quarter entirely. Bismarck had received a report from his minister in Karlsruhe, and he took the unwise step of forwarding it to Falckenstein's headquarters. In part, it read:

> The German confederative army is still fully disorganised. A speedy advance by Prussia against Frankfurt-am-Main would make any organisation impossible and would easily lead to a second Rossbach.[6]

This telegram seems to have had a most regrettable effect on Falckenstein's concept of the strategy he should pursue. It was only since the King's order of June 2 that all such communications should go through Moltke, but Bismarck was clearly at fault in sending it direct.

Three days later, having lost touch with the Hanoverian army, Falckenstein was seduced by Bismarck's telegram into making preparations for an advance on Frankfurt. This was in spite of a series of telegrams from Moltke identifying the whereabouts of the Hanoverians. On June 23 he sent Falckenstein a telegram with explicit instructions to send a strong detachment of all arms by rail to Eisenach, to prevent the retreat of the Hanoverians. The response was profoundly unsatisfactory, Falckenstein replying at noon on the same day that it was not possible to block the road taken by the Hanoverians nor to catch up with them. He went on to announce that next day he would march on Frankfurt. Moltke scribbled crossly in pencil on this telegram a note that the line between Göttingen and Northeim to Eisenach was practicable: 'Goeben's division has arrived at Göttingen. Why is it not being transported to Eisenach?'[7] A further despatch from Falckenstein in the late afternoon claimed that the move to Eisenach was impossible; when the King saw these messages he too scribbled on the margin:

> Since Falckenstein has made his u-turn, the Hanoverians have got away!! Fabeck must draw Beyer towards him, Falckenstein wants to have him with him to march on Frankfurt-am-Main. What is he going to do then?'[8]

Eisenach was of crucial importance. The only troops available to bar the way of the Hanoverians were some Landwehr and garrison troops which Moltke sent to join Fabeck's two battalions in Gotha, and two Guard battalions under Colonel von Osten-Sacken which he sent to Eisenach. Falckenstein, meanwhile, had grandiose schemes in mind to justify his advance on Frankfurt: 'It is my intention to annihilate the 8th Confederate Corps at Frankfurt and then cover the Rhine Province, disengage Baden, and draw away the Bavarians from Saxony and Bohemia.'[9]

Since Falckenstein's dispositions had left such a weak force to oppose the Hanoverians, Moltke endeavoured to slow down their progress by instructing Fabeck to call on them to surrender as they were surrounded on all sides.[10] The effect of this at the Hanoverian headquarters was considerable, reinforcing the views of the pessimists there, and there followed tortuous negotiations during an armistice to see whether terms could be agreed. With these, Falckenstein was not involved; direct instructions to the units under his command enabled Moltke to bring up sufficient troops to ensure that the Hanoverians could not break through to the south, but he was not satisfied that Falckenstein even now was carrying out his explicit instructions. A peremptory order to Falckenstein to use the Magdeburg line to reinforce Gotha, sent at 8.00 am on June 24, also appeared to have been ignored, and at 4.30 pm Moltke sent a further telegram which unmistakably showed his annoyance:

> An order of His Majesty was telegraphed this morning to Hanover by virtue of which troops were to have been sent to Gotha-Eisenach via Magdeburg. Negotiations with the Hanoverian army continue with a view to a capitulation: probably they will not end today and will be broken off tomorrow. It is of

the greatest importance to reinforce the weak detachments that up to now have prevented the enemy's passage in any force. From here it is not possible to reach General Glümer. What measures have you taken?[11]

This was in part prompted by a particularly cross note which the King wrote to Moltke during the morning, bewildered at Falckenstein's proceedings. Moltke wrote two notes in reply during the day to reassure his anxious master of the steps he was taking to bring Falckenstein's forces into position. By the end of the day Falckenstein was reporting that half of Goeben's division would go to Eisenach while Flies, with five battalions from Manteuffel's division, would proceed to Gotha; the latter did nor arrive until late on June 25.

Falckenstein himself reached Eisenach late that evening. He was not at all happy that his projected advance on Frankfurt had been thwarted, and coming late into the negotiations with the Hanoverians he was in no mood to be conciliatory. He knew nothing about the armistice terms; when the Hanoverian Colonel Rudorff arrived at Falckenstein's headquarters and asked for a train to take him to Berlin in order to discuss these, Falckenstein rudely told him to ask Alvensleben, who had the conduct of the negotiations. This treatment of his envoy seriously enraged King George, who thought Falckenstein was dishonestly ignoring the existing terms of the armistice. It also contributed to the ultimate breakdown of the armistice talks, and hence led directly to the totally unnecessary battle of Langensalza. Meanwhile Falckenstein had received an incorrect report that the Bavarians had got to Vacha, only eighteen miles from Eisenach; he must, he told Moltke, launch an attack next day to avoid being caught between two fires.

During the day Moltke, tiring of the nuisance of having to try to get Falckenstein to do as he was told, had been issuing orders direct to Goeben and Flies. In view of the threat from the Bavarians, he instructed Falckenstein late that night that on the following day, at 10.00 am, when the current armistice expired, he should attack the Hanoverians without further delay. Colonel von Doering would be arriving to continue the discussions on June 26 with King George and would keep Falckenstein informed of any extension of the truce. However, the discussions between Doering and King George were heated and, in the end, unproductive, and the armistice came to an end. During the night of June 25/26 a further complication had arisen when a report reached Bismarck that suggested that the Hanoverians, instead of standing still during the armistice, were marching northwards through Mülhausen. Moltke at once telegraphed Falckenstein and Flies to pursue the enemy, and to reinforce Manteuffel, still at Hanover. It was only when Doering arrived to find that it was entirely a false alarm that the armistice discussions had been able to proceed, albeit unsuccessfully.[12]

Thus in the absence of further information it was expected that Falckenstein, in pursuance of his instructions, had ordered an attack, whereas in fact, the Mülhausen report having proved false, he disposed his forces to take account not only of the Hanoverian army, but also the imagined approach of the Bavarians and a possible advance by the 8th Corps towards Giessen. To deal with all these threats, Falckenstein decided to move Goeben and Beyer west from Eisenach to face the Bavarians, while Manteuffel's division, and the detachment under Flies, should advance on the Hanoverians from the north and south respectively; Flies was told not to attack before June 29. This, however, was unknown in Berlin, where news of the attack on the Hanoverians was hourly awaited. In his anxiety, the King sent his own telegram to Falckenstein; 'I repeat the order sent through General Moltke, that you are to concentrate everything at our disposal per march and per railway, and force a capitulation, coûte que coûte. Bavarians are said to be in Meiningen.'[13]

Falckenstein had, of course, instead of concentrating, divided his force. His response to the King, based on his own idea of the situation, was sent at once: 'Your Majesty's commands will be executed. Whether a successful issue is possible cannot be foreseen.' Meanwhile, on the morning of June 27 Falckenstein received a message from the King, written the day before on the assumption that he had attacked the Hanoverians with all his force, appointing him provisional Governor of Hesse Cassel. As he was setting off for Cassel Falckenstein received news that Flies was now engaged with the Hanoverians at Langensalza. This did not persuade him that administrative functions in Cassel were a lot less important than the fierce fighting that had erupted along the River Werra.

Nor did a crucially important telegram that Lieutenant Colonel von Veith handed him. Veith had been sent by Moltke to impress, once again, on Falckenstein what it was that he was required to do, while keeping Moltke informed of what was going on. The telegram had been despatched by Moltke to Veith at 7.15 am on June 27, and read as follows:

> Hanoverians marching last night on Tennstedt. In order to revictual, they cannot go into billets. All the Bavarian and imperial troops are actually now secondary. His Majesty expects absolutely that the Hanoverians should be immediately attacked and disarmed. They can only march on Sondershausen or Soemmerda. The railway from Eisenach to Erfurt or Weimar is at General Falckenstein's disposal. Is there any movement of the weak detachments of Flies and Kummer? What dispositions has General Falckenstein made for today? Reply immediately.[14]

Falckenstein seems to have put this in his pocket and went off with it to Cassel, from where he sent a response with his account of the current situation, adding that the telegram to Veith had come into his hands too late but could be considered answered with this reply. His complacent satisfaction was rudely shaken when towards midnight he received a very angry telegram over the King's signature:

> General Flies, for want of sufficient support, was driven back by superior numbers, and stands now at Warza before Gotha. I command you to march with all the troops you can summon, directly and without delay, against the Hanoverians. For the present no attention is to be paid to Bavarians and South Germans; but

in accordance with my will, already expressed, the complete disarming of the Hanoverians is alone to be considered. The receipt of this command is to be acknowledged immediately, and the arrangements are to be announced at once.[15]

The vigorous and aggressive Flies, ordered to follow the Hanoverians, had on the morning of June 27 set off in pursuit. Early exchanges showed him that he was facing more than the rearguard of a retreating enemy; but chance intervened, as Sybel described:

It was at this point that he sent word that he did not intend to cross the river. Now would have been the time to have stopped the fighting; but, unfortunately, just at this moment the heat of the sun caused such a rush of blood to his head that he lay for more than an hour unconscious. The other officers did not venture to begin the retreat without orders.[16]

As a result, when Flies came to, he found that his small force was heavily engaged with a much superior enemy and was forced, yard by yard, to fall back to a point four or five miles from Gotha. Thanks to the chain of events leading up to the battle some 570 men had lost their lives to no purpose whatsoever, 170 on the Prussian side and 400 on the Hanoverian. Fortunately common sense was soon to prevail to avoid further needless loss of life when all King George's senior commanders signed a petition on June 28 to the effect that there was no point in fighting any further. The Prussians were closing in on all sides; the Hanoverians had barely enough ammunition for a single action nor provisions for a single day. Negotiations at once began for a capitulation. Falckenstein's terms required that the soldiers return home without arms, and the officers be sent on leave with the privilege of keeping their arms and on full pay. Arentschild, the Hanoverian commander, surrendered unconditionally. Meanwhile Moltke had sent a telegram appointing Manteuffel to conduct the negotiations; when he arrived, he was able to offer somewhat more favourable terms to take account of King William's wish to recognise the brave and honourable conduct of the Hanoverian army.[17]

Falckenstein's performance had occasioned severe displeasure in Berlin, where Moltke and the King were both furious with his disobedience. He had failed to send troops to Gotha on June 21, delayed the march to Eisenach on June 23, failed to obey the order to attack the Hanoverians on June 26 and by these omissions created the situation which led to the defeat at Langensalza. According to Sybel the decision to replace Falckenstein had already been taken, although for the moment he remained in command as his army set off to deal with the Bavarians and the 8th Federal Corps.[18] Schlieffen reviewed the lessons to be learned from these events:

The success obtained by the Prussians on June 28, after overcoming numberless difficulties, committing mistakes and misunderstandings, after numerous marches and counter marches, and after the loss of a bloody battle, could have been attained on June 24 smoothly, unhesitatingly, and without bloodshed, if Moltke's simple plans had been adopted. But the Prussian generals, notwithstanding their prominence and excellence, could not enter into the cycle of ideas of the grey haired theorist who had never commanded even a company ... Moltke endeavoured calmly and indefatigably to rebuild the broken cycle. In the beginning he limited himself to kindly persuasion. He was forced in the end to resort to royal commands of the most peremptory character. It is not the least of his achievements that he carried out his will, and brought everything to a fortunate conclusion.[19]

Falckenstein's army moved off on July 2 in two columns, Beyer on the right towards Hünfeld and Goeben on the left towards Markstuhl and Lengsfeld, with Manteuffel behind. Falckenstein's aim was to reach Fulda; Moltke had seen Schweinfurt as the better target, but revised his view when it appeared that Fulda could be reached before either the 8th Federal Corps or the Bavarians could get there. With the subsequent battles Falckenstein had at first little involvement. Beyer routed the Federal cavalry at Hünfeld on July 4 and Goeben won a brilliant victory on the same day over the Bavarians at Dermbach. Falckenstein, though, ordered him to pull back, and diverted Beyer from the advance on Fulda, in the belief that he was now in contact with the whole Bavarian Army. In fact, however, the Bavarians had retreated. As the Prussians pushed on Goeben reached the line of the Saar, and fought and won the battle of Kissingen without much intervention from Falckenstein.

By July 11 it was clear that the defeated Bavarians were marching towards Schweinfurt, which was the obvious next objective for Falckenstein's army; but at this point Bismarck, anxious to occupy all the territory north of the Main for political reasons with an eye to imminent peace negotiations, asked Moltke to give instructions accordingly to Falckenstein.[20] As a result the Prussians swung to their right, with Goeben leading the way over the Spessart. His advance was to lead to the battles of Frohnhofen and Asschaffenburg; when Prince Alexander's 8th Federal Corps retreated from Frankfurt and the Federal Diet also removed itself, the Senate on July 16 declared it an open city. Next day Falckenstein marched in, telegraphing to the King that 'all the territory north of the Main lies at the feet of Your Majesty.'[21]

Back in Berlin, however, Moltke had made up his mind to give effect to the decision to remove Falckenstein, who was appointed to the post of Governor General of Bohemia. His replacement by the unpopular Manteuffel, a court favourite who was suspected of having intrigued against Falckenstein, caused a storm of public protest. Perhaps it was an echo of this that led Strauss to make the observations that he did; at all events there was no public expression of any dissatisfaction with Falckenstein. Moltke was content to leave it at that; all that he wanted was to be rid of his insubordinate commander, and to get on with the rest of the campaign.

When the Franco-Prussian War broke out there could be no question of Falckenstein being given an operational command; but enough was thought of him for him to be appointed as *Generalgouverneur der deutschen Küstenlande*, with responsibility for the defence of the German coastline. Perhaps one reason for the appointment was that his seniority might help to overawe any local opposition to the measures that must be taken. The nucleus of the forces available to him was the 17th Division, later to be posted to the Loire; for the rest, he relied on Landwehr units. His headquarters were in Hanover. As the war proceeded he was effective in organising the defences of river mouths and harbours and a rapid system of communications to ensure that any French landing, if it came, would be promptly resisted. After the war he retired to his estate at Dolzig, with the Order of the Black Eagle as a reward for his endeavours. He seems to have remained on good terms personally with Moltke, in spite of the latter's professional disapproval; in 1875 Moltke paid a visit to Dolzig, which he described in a letter to his nephew Henry. In particular, Moltke was struck by the splendid view through a large plate glass window. The building itself he thought 'an irregular old place, not at all beautiful':

> The rooms are low, but there exists one loftier apartment in which the general has tastefully assembled glass paintings, old armour, flags, escutcheons, antlers, and all manner of curiosities.[21]

Schlieffen's comment on the Langensalza campaign sums up one aspect of Moltke's management from afar of his field commanders, Another was his use of trusted and experienced staff officers such as Doering and Veith to visit the headquarters of any formation seen to be giving trouble. It did not always work; Falckenstein was not the kind of leader to take kindly to junior officers telling him what to do; in a similar situation Steinmetz, for instance, would not have been cooperative. But the proof of the pudding is in the eating; and by one means or another Moltke got the results he sought.

22

Demigods

Reference has already been made to the crucially important role of the chiefs of staff of the major operational units. It was essential that Moltke be able to rely on their diligent execution of his directives. Thus it was an understatement for one biographer of Moltke to write:

> It must have been of considerable assistance to Moltke that the executive power of the various subordinate headquarters was in the hands of officers trained in one and the same school, and the school of which he was the head.[1]

In the passage quoted in Chapter 3, Moltke himself spelled out with great clarity the extent to which the chief of staff must be the sole adviser of the commander. Moltke used his extensive correspondence with the chiefs of staff to provide context for the carrying out of the objectives which he had directed. In 1866, as has been seen, he wrote frequently and in considerable detail to Blumenthal, as Chief of Staff of the Second Army, and likewise to Stülpnagel, the Quarter-Master General of the First Army, in his case because Moltke had a much closer and more comfortable relationship with him than with Voigts-Rhetz, the Chief of Staff. In 1870-1871 Moltke's correspondence with Blumenthal, with Schlotheim, the Chief of Staff of the Army of the Meuse and with Stiehle, the Chief of Staff of the Second Army, was central to his management of the Prussian armies in the field.

Moltke also depended on the hand picked team of General Staff officers who surrounded him. These he had selected from the General Staff officers who had grown up to absorb Moltke's personal work ethic, as Walter Görlitz, the historian of the General Staff, observed:

> Because he had confidence in himself, he had confidence in others, and because his own strong sense of responsibility communicated itself to his subordinates, there thus came into being under him a generation of General Staff officers distinguished by a very high standard of morals and great simplicity of life. These men held a common body of military doctrine, and represented a military

community of a very unusual kind; it was moreover one which had great influence on the Army, since nearly all the higher commanders passed through the school of the General Staff.[2]

The four members of his team closest to Moltke were the Quartermaster-General, Lieutenant General Theophil von Podbielski, and the three sections heads: Colonel Paul Bronsart von Schellendorff, responsible for operations, Colonel Karl von Brandenstein, in charge of rail transport and supply, and Colonel Julius von Verdy du Vernois, who headed the intelligence section.

Theophil Eugene Anton von Podbieleski was born in 1814, and joined a cavalry regiment in 1831. From 1836 to 1839 he attended the *Kriegsakademie* in Berlin. By 1855, having reached the rank of Major, he was serving on the General Staff. In 1858 he returned to regimental duties, being appointed to the command of the 12th Hussar Regiment. He was promoted to lieutenant colonel in the following year, and to colonel in 1861. In March 1863 he took command of the 16th Cavalry Brigade. With the imminent outbreak of the Schleswig Holstein War he was selected for the post of Quartermaster General in the headquarters of the allied army preparing for the invasion of the Duchies. In this capacity his immediate superior was Lieutenant General Vogel von Falckenstein, the Chief of Staff. He continued in the post when Moltke took over as Chief of Staff. In the following year he was promoted to major general, and in 1866 he was appointed to the post of Quartermaster-General, serving directly under Moltke. After the end of the Austro Prussian War he became Director General of the War Department in the Ministry of War, being promoted to lieutenant general in 1868. With the outbreak of the Franco-Prussian War he returned to the post of Moltke's Quartermaster-General, serving as Moltke's right hand throughout the war.

He had, therefore, for a long period been one of Moltke's closest collaborators. It was with Podbielski for instance, that Moltke had watched the Prussian descent on Alsen at the end of June 1864; and he worked closely with Moltke during the build-up to the Austro Prussian War. When the Royal Headquarters took the field in 1866, and again in 1870-1871, Podbielski was effectively Moltke's deputy. From the start of their collaboration Moltke held the highest opinion of Podbielski's ability, writing of him in 1864:

> Colonel von Podbielski is a perfect Quartermaster-General with or without the Chief of Staff; he manages affairs in the most orderly way. Equally, for operations I believe him to have a sound judgement and a strong will. The Prince values him highly. Von Podbielski fills his place admirably and will be very difficult to replace.[3]

Podbielski was never afraid to speak his mind. Colonel Hale described his personality:

Podbielski.

Verdy.

Bronsart.

Karl von Brandenstein.

A bluff, outspoken man, one of that invaluable class of men who, though they may see the darker side of affairs, express themselves in optimistic language and treat of difficulties with contemptuous speech.[4]

Podbielski's habit of expressing an optimistic view of any situation was apt seriously to annoy the king, for whom the glass was almost invariably half empty. This often manifested itself during the Franco Prussian war in the daily 10.00 am conferences with the King, attended by Moltke, Podbielski, Roon, Lieutenant General Hermann von Tresckow, the Chief of the Military Cabinet, and the Crown Prince. The latter's diary records a number of instances in which Podbielski's strong opinions contrasted with some of the others at Versailles. On October 27, for instance, the Crown Prince wrote:

> His Majesty during the military report of today was not a little excited, which may well be accounted for by the heavy exertions he has lately undergone. On the other side, present signs make it more than ever manifest that France is everywhere restlessly engaged in making preparations for the relief of Paris. Hitherto little weight was attached to the news, especially as Lieutenant General von Podbielski demonstrated with the utmost calm and confidence that the French were in no position to make the strenuous efforts that could be any sort of danger to us. Certainly we have no reason for any special alarm, still we should keep our eyes open and, just because so far we have won such successes, we must not venture to go to sleep on our laurels.[5]

Podbielski entirely supported Moltke's opinions throughout the war, not least during the prolonged and ill tempered dispute over the bombardment of Paris. He may also have been one of those who all along were particularly hostile to what was perceived as Bismarck's interference in wholly military questions. Bismarck himself claimed that, on his way to the front in 1870, he overheard Podbielski boasting that a military boycott would be imposed on him; but doubt has been cast on the truth of this.[6]

Moltke's high opinion of Podbielski was expressed in a passage which he wrote after the wars of unification, paying tribute to him for his effective management of the Royal Headquarters:

> Although as a rule the intended operations were kept secret, sometimes individuals sent home reports of what had happened or what they thought was supposed to happen. These reports frequently gained quite an importance because of their sources. The heavy demands already made on the telegraph by the most important orders were very substantial, and it is to the great credit of the Quartermaster General, General von Podbielski, that he maintained strict control over this without regard to individuals.[7]

Verdy, in his account of the Royal Headquarters, recorded that he had not known Podbielski intimately before the war:

> A certain decision in his manner made him appear somewhat abrupt to those who had not the opportunity of becoming better acquainted with him. But it was not long before I found out that this man of keen intellect and inflexible will possessed a heart that soon made us all his most faithful supporters. With his chivalrous feelings, his ideal conception of duty and true devotion to friendship, he bore a chief part in maintaining a cheerful spirit of cooperation and a healthy tone among the staff. I only mention this because the great influence of the general in this respect is not universally known. I need not enter further into his other merits, but as regards his capability as a soldier I may sum up by saying: Moltke could not have had a more faithful and more efficient assistant during the campaign than he was.[8]

This is high praise from a shrewd observer; and it is noteworthy that when consideration was being given to the need to replace Roon due to the critical condition of his asthma, Podbielski was one of those thought of as a possible successor.[9]

The three section heads were remarkably young for the responsibilities that they bore, none of them having reached the age of forty before the outbreak of the Franco-Prussian War. They had been friends ever since they played the war game together; another of the participants was Alfred von Waldersee. Verdy described how this had attracted the attention of their instructors:

> They encouraged our efforts at the game, which we had started on our own initiative. The year 1855 brought us into the same division at the staff college, where we passed the three years together. Here also what was at that time called the 'garrison game,' in which the officers of the whole garrison of Berlin were invited to take part, offered to us, beside our scientific pursuits at the college, a common point of interest which did much for our military education, the more so because the war game was very popular, being under the direction of very eminent generals, such as General Vogel von Falckenstein and Count Oriola. General von Moltke himself did not disdain to come from time to time during the last year of our course there and to follow it attentively.[10]

The three men maintained their close friendship, and would constantly exchange opinions on military questions, so much so that, as Verdy noted, their 'whole training in troop leading had been of so uniform a character as would have been difficult to find in any three others.'[11] Their friendship was further strengthened when all three joined the General Staff soon after leaving the college, and by their participation together in various staff tours. Their close and continued contact, both socially and at work, was of great importance in their professional functions, as Verdy explained:

One of us, for instance, might suddenly be called away from his work while writing down an order to one of the armies, to receive some fresh instruction, another would then go and finish the document which the first had begun, and yet the whole would be completed in the same spirit.[12]

The great influence of the three men was well understood throughout the army, and it did not enhance their popularity. They were known, sardonically, as the 'demigods.' Their responsibilities were enormous, but their support staff were surprisingly few in numbers. The total establishment consisted of eleven officers, ten draughtsmen, seven clerks and fifty nine other ranks which, as Howard remarked, was 'not an overlarge organisation for the control of armies which by the end of the war were to total some 850,000 men.' In spite of this they performed their duties with striking efficiency, as Howard observed: 'Thanks to Moltke's long training they did their work with a speed and economy which set a standard that staff officers have been aiming at, and not always achieving, ever since.'[13]

Paul Eduard Heinrich Anton Bronsart von Schellendorff was born in Danzig in 1832. He joined the Prussian Guard Corps in 1849. In 1861, with the rank of Captain, he joined the General Staff. In that capacity he formed part of the headquarters staff of the allied army in Denmark in 1864, and wrote a series of reports on the subject of the Düppel position and its bombardment. His final report dealt with the storming of the line of forts; Moltke wrote: 'Bronsart, whose reports are made with the greatest intelligence, has given me today an outline of the course of the battle.'[14] Later that year Bronsart returned to regimental duties. It was not long, however, before he rejoined the General Staff, lecturing at the *Kriegsakademie*. He was promoted to major in 1865 and lieutenant colonel four years later.

In his diary of the campaign of 1870-1871, Verdy wrote affectionate accounts of his two friends:

> Bronsart von Schellendorff was tall and slender, elastic in his movements, with a fresh healthy complexion and fair hair verging on brown; his countenance indicated both ability and good-humour, his conversation showed his ability, while the clear logic of his arguments was eminently convincing. His whole character and presence showed the knight *sans peur et sans reproche*. He possessed a thorough grasp of military affairs, and his forecasts were singularly shrewd; he was also active, indefatigable, and reliable in the highest possible degree. The instructions issued from the Royal Headquarters, which were models of their kind, were mostly his work.[15]

In the course of the war, Bronsart, like the other two 'demigods' was despatched on many missions to the headquarters of armies and corps, to see for himself the actual situation – Moltke could depend on the absolute reliability of his reports – or to convey Moltke's wishes in person to the unit concerned. It was from Bronsart, for instance, who had joined Alvensleben's III Corps, that Moltke learnt of the opening of the battle of

Mars la Tour.[16] The most famous mission on which Bronsart was sent, however, occurred at the battle of Sedan. As it became increasingly clear that the French resistance could not long continue, Moltke sent Bronsart, accompanied by Colonel von Winterfeldt, to summon the French commander to surrender. Riding down under a flag of truce to the Torcy gate, they entered the city among the masses of disorganised and dejected French troops. Bronsart was taken to the Sous-Préfecture, meeting, to his astonishment, not MacMahon but the Emperor Napoleon, who was engaged in writing a personal letter to King William. Napoleon explained to Bronsart that Wimpffen was now in command, and that he would be sending General Reille with his personal letter. Bronsart rode back out of the city and up the hill at Frénois to the Royal Headquarters. As he approached, he urged his horse into a gallop, pointing back to Sedan and shouting 'Der Kaiser ist da!' This brought cheers from those around the King, but not from Moltke, who severely admonished Bronsart for his improper conduct in the King's presence.[17]

Bronsart, who, like Verdy, was an accomplished writer, and like him kept a diary of his experiences during the war of 1870-1871, was another of Moltke's staff who shared his chief's views on the bombardment of Paris. He recorded a number of bitter comments on the subject of Bismarck, views which he and his immediate colleagues openly expressed in conversation. Like all the soldiers, Bronsart was insistent that all the resources of the nation should be applied to the winning of the war. In October 1870 he angrily wrote in his diary on the subject of requisitioning rolling stock in Germany:

> People seem generally to have forgotten in the victory celebrations that we are at war, and they must learn to put up with its exigencies, even if, as a result, private traffic in Germany is somewhat restricted.[18]

As disputes between Moltke and Roon developed over the demands for additional resources for the front line, Bronsart predictably took Moltke's part. When Roon protested about the scale of operations which resulted in these demands, Bronsart wrote:

> God protect us from our friends! … He (Roon) appears to stand as a strategist on about the same level as Count Bismarck; but as a comedian he anyhow ranks immeasurable higher.[19]

The extent to which Bronsart and the other demigods, were involved with Moltke's most intimate thinking was demonstrated by the fact that it was Bronsart who wrote the first daft of the memorandum to the King after the latter had effectively pronounced in favour of Bismarck to resolve the dispute between the Chancellor and Moltke. In the revised draft, Moltke toned down the more extreme passages of Bronsart's version.

After the war, promoted to colonel, Bronsart became Chief of Staff of the Guard Corps; he became major general in 1876 and a divisional commander with the rank of

Lieutenant General in 1881. In 1876 he published the first edition of his comprehensive work on the duties of the General Staff. In 1881 he became War Minister, and during his term of office oversaw many important army reforms. He was only appointed after agreeing to two conditions which limited the role of the War Minister; first, that the Chief of the General Staff should be entitled to direct access to the Emperor without the War Minister necessarily being present, and secondly that all personnel matters should be the responsibility of the Chief of the Military Cabinet.[20] As his term of office came to an end, however, Bronsart was engaged in a bitter dispute with Alfred von Waldersee, by then Chief of the General Staff.

Karl Hermann Bernard von Brandenstein, the second of the demigods, was born in 1831, and joined the Guard Grenadier Regiment in 1849. With his two friends, he attended the *Kriegsakademie* from 1855 to 1858, leaving for regimental duty first with a field artillery regiment, and then a pioneer battalion. He returned to the *Kriegsakademie* as a lecturer in 1862. During the Austro-Prussian war he was on the staff of the Army of the Elbe, and after the end of the war had a stint with the rank of Major as General Staff officer of the 21st (Hessian) Division before joining the General Staff in 1868. He was promoted to lieutenant colonel in July 1870, and served as a section head throughout the ensuing war. Verdy described him thus:

> Karl von Brandenstein, or, as we generally called him 'das Karlchen' (Little Charles), resembled Bronsart in many of his intellectual gifts. He too was modest, straightforward, and simple in his ways, Sincerity and trustfulness were written on his face. When thoroughly interested – and there were many things which interested him intensely – his eyes flashed fire and he would support what he considered right with an uncompromising tenacity. He also possessed an extraordinary capacity for work, and his mind was full of original ideas on the most varied subjects. The excellent plan for the transport of the troops to form the various armies was mostly his work. It was a feat the more to be admired because there was, up to that time, no practical experience in moving large bodies. In personal appearance he was, in contrast to Bronsart, short of stature, but well set, with fair curly hair and pale complexion.[21]

It was to Brandenstein that fell the difficult task of visiting the headquarters of Steinmetz's First Army, soon after the frontier battles. Moltke, having explained that the object of the visits to army headquarters by General Staff officers was for them to give verbal explanations of their assessment of the situation, described the background to this one:

> Thus, on the morning of August 14, Colonel von Brandenstein clearly explained to the First Army commander that Royal Headquarters considered the task of the First Army, which stood on the French Nied only ten miles from the enemy at Metz, as anything but passive, even though it had a directive to remain in its

positions on August 14. In vain did the representatives of Royal Headquarters urge General von Steinmetz to push his advance guards further out.[22]

Verdy concluded that von der Goltz's advance with his brigade, which precipitated the battle of Colombey-Nouilly, was in fact prompted by Brandenstein's presence. Von der Goltz believed, correctly, that it was important to delay the retreat of the French army as long as possible. During the battle of Gravelotte on August 18 Brandenstein spent a large part of the day with the army of Frederick Charles; reports, however, took time, as Verdy explained:

> He furnished us with intelligence as to what was taking place there, and as to the intentions of its Commander in Chief. It must not be forgotten, however, that the sending of reports from a distance takes time, and that, if the headquarters be posted in a suitable spot, many things will be known sooner than they can be by reports, which when they come from the foremost fighting line, have often to pass through several hands.[23]

Brandenstein served as section head throughout the war, continuing to share with the other two the duty of visiting army headquarters when necessary. Their work at the Royal Headquarters was very demanding; Verdy noted that both Bronsart and Brandenstein had become so ill with overwork that for a time it was feared that they could not go on.[24] With the coming of the armistice the three men were fascinated to go together to inspect the French fortifications which they had only seen from afar. Brandenstein continued after the war as head of the railway section. He was promoted to colonel in 1875 and in the following year to major general. He commanded a division with the rank of Lieutenant General until in 1884 becoming Inspector General of the Engineer and Pioneer Corps.

Julius Adrian Friedrich Wilhelm von Verdy du Vernois was just the youngest of the three demigods. Born in 1832, he entered the army in 1850, after completing his course at the Cadet School, joining the 14th Infantry Regiment before going to the *Kriegsakademie* in 1855. Thereafter he joined the General Staff, initially in the Topographical Branch. He was made a captain in 1861. In January 1863, during the Polish rebellion, he was sent to Poland, where he was attached until December 1865 to the headquarters of the Russian army there. He then returned to the General Staff in Berlin, where he worked in the section dealing with the Austrian Army; in 1866, promoted to major, he served on the staff of the Second Army. Shortly after the end of the war he was promoted to lieutenant colonel and in 1867 was appointed to head the intelligence section of the General Staff. Compared to many of the senior officers of the Prussian army, his rise through the ranks, like that of his two comrades, had been relatively fast; Moltke had no doubt earmarked them to play key roles on his staff.

Verdy's reminiscences of the Franco-Prussian War provide a fascinating account of life at the Royal Headquarters on campaign, with many penetrating assessments of the great and the good with whom he came into contact. As the war began, he very soon found himself on the particularly delicate mission to the headquarters of the Third Army previously described. Verdy's tactful and persuasive style achieved the result of clearing the air, while imparting Moltke's wishes that the advance be accelerated. Actually, he was pushing at an open door; Blumenthal was anxious to get forward as soon as he could. It was the first of many such instances recorded by Verdy in his account of the war.

In spite of his relatively junior status, Verdy was never afraid to express on opinion. During the battle of Gravelotte, he was riding with Moltke towards the King. As he dismounted, he was irresistibly provoked to speak out:

> Just then I heard a superior officer saying to the King in a very impressive manner: 'Now it is my humble opinion, sire, that we, considering our heavy losses today, should not continue the attack tomorrow, but await the attack of the French.' This idea seemed to me so monstrous, that I could not help blurting out: 'Then I don't know why we attacked at all today.' Of course I got my answer, which was not exactly spoken in a very gracious tone: 'What do you want here, Lieutenant Colonel?' But at this moment Moltke, who had heard what was said, stepped between us two towards the King, and said in his quiet and decided manner: 'Your Majesty has only to give the order for the continuation of the attack in case the enemy should make a further stand outside Metz tomorrow.' The orders were drawn up at once, also the despatch to be sent to Berlin.[25]

When, on August 25, news arrived that the army of Châlons had abandoned the great fortified camp there, evidently with a view to a flank march in an attempt to relieve Metz, it was Verdy who was sent to ride through the night to the headquarters of the Crown Prince of Saxony, commanding the Army of the Meuse. He took with him the revised orders necessary in the changed situation, but even more importantly was able to convey directly to the Crown Prince and Schlotheim, his Chief of Staff, what Moltke now had in mind.[26]

During the battle of Sedan Verdy was sent to the headquarters of the V Corps, commanded by Lieutenant General von Kirchbach; they knew each other well, Verdy having been a student of Kirchbach at the *Kriegsakademie*. From there, Verdy witnessed the progressive collapse of the French army, before making his way back to rejoin Moltke and the others. During the negotiations with Wimpffen at Donchery Verdy was present as Moltke and Bismarck made plain to the French commander that there must be a capitulation.

At Versailles, Verdy recorded the events at Royal Headquarters in graphic detail, During the period when the Grand Duke of Mecklenburg-Schwerin's Detachment was causing considerable anxiety, Verdy wrote home on November 26 to explain why he was not commenting on the situation there:

> The world need not know of the dark side of glorious times. There are too many people who love to gloat over, and who seek to diminish our pride in

the great things which have been done, and detract from their well merited acknowledgement.[27]

Ever since November 14 it had seemed likely that someone would have to go to the Detachment; Verdy thought it would be Bronsart, whose turn it was to be sent on such a mission, although in the end it was Stosch who went.

After the war Verdy assumed responsibility for the Military History Section of the General Staff. He also began to lecture at the *Kriegsakademie*, evolving a technique for instructing Prussian staff officers that became extremely influential. In 1876 he was promoted to major general, and from 1879 to 1883 worked in the War Ministry. In 1881 he was made a lieutenant general. He served as governor of Strasbourg from 1887, next year becoming General of Infantry; and in 1889 he succeeded his friend Bronsart as War Minister. Throughout this time he wrote extensively on military topics and continued to do so after he retired in 1890.

The three friends from cadet school had, in the course of their career as key collaborators of Moltke, particularly in 1870-1871, left their mark on the military history of Europe. Of course, they were by no means the only talented young officers who contributed to Moltke's success; there were many others, such as Wartensleben, Winterfeld, Doering and Veith, but it was the section heads upon whom Moltke counted most.

23

Conclusion

Although the Oxford English Dictionary traces the word 'leadership' in the English language only as far back as the nineteenth century, the qualities and principal characteristics of leaders have been the subject of philosophical enquiry for thousands of years. Sanskrit literature, for instance, is said to define ten types of leaders. Sun Tzu, the Chinese general who wrote *The Art of War* in about 500 BC, produced the oldest military treatise in the world, but one which is constantly quoted by management gurus. He wrote that leadership was a matter of wisdom, sincerity, benevolence, courage and strictness, adding that with the possession of these five virtues together, each appropriate to its function then one could be a leader.[1] It may perhaps be observed that the study of management is an extremely recent science, if that is what it is, but that it certainly has to be based on first principles.

In Western literature, Plato's *Republic* and Plutarch's *Lives* were among early works which considered the qualities which make a great leader. Thomas Carlyle made an examination of the defining characteristics of men who rose to power; it was central to his thesis that history resulted from the intervention of outstanding individuals, without whom it must have taken a different course. Karl Marx, of course, propounded the opposite view; that history was more than this and that it was the overriding circumstances of the time that shaped destiny. Bismarck, an outstanding pragmatist, on a number of occasions observed that one could not change the current of events; one could only float with it, and steer.

The terms 'leadership' and 'management' have sometimes been treated as being virtually synonymous. The huge body of literature that they have mushroomed into existence since the early part of the twentieth century has examined these concepts with minute attention, frequently producing conclusions based on extensive social science research which, looking back through the long view of history, are difficult to apply to individuals who might satisfy, for instance, Carlyle's criteria.

Certainly Moltke's contemporaries, aware that they were in the presence of a remarkable leader, would not have been considering his success in terms of the jargon of social science, since for them the modern concepts of leadership and management scarcely existed.

Leadership has, it is said, been one of the least understood concepts across all cultures and civilisations, giving rise to many mistaken assumptions about its nature. In their most extreme form these assumptions tend to produce disastrous results, especially in terms of politics. A dominant personality may not be the ablest of leaders, and nor must his influence on the organisation he leads necessarily be beneficial.

Like any top manager, Motlke had to make the most effective use of the human material that was available to him. He did so not only by the effectiveness of the selections which he made, and the thoroughness of the training which they received, but also by an instinctive insight into how to get the best out of them. Generally, his confidence in them enabled him to let his subordinates get on with the tasks which they were set, but he also knew when it was necessary to intervene.

Moltke's influence over the choice of his subordinate commanders was very much less at the start of his career as Chief of the Great General Staff than was later the case. On the other hand, his development of the role of the General Staff and its key personnel ensured that he was able to maintain his influence over the conduct of operations through the chiefs of staff and other staff officers. The appointment of the most senior commanders was a process that began at the very top, with the King and his immediate advisers, such as the War Minister, Adjutant General and Chief of the Military Cabinet. The relative influence of each varied according to the force of their personality and the interaction between them. The frequent necessity for the titular command of an army to be a Royal personage, or a general of great seniority, naturally reduced the number of possible candidates for any given appointment.

Moltke's intimate understanding of the close-knit brotherhood of the General Staff meant that he was able to match, in most instances, competent and authoritative chiefs of staff to the most refractory army commanders. This was not, however, invariably the case. One instance of this going seriously wrong was the pairing of the ineffectual Colonel von Krenski with an obstinate and not particularly intelligent commander in Francis Frederick, Grand Duke of Mecklenburg Schwerin in the Loire campaign of 1870.

The air of calm authority which Moltke naturally possessed was enormously enhanced by his success. His management style was firm, but never flamboyant or overstated. He was also, incidentally, pretty good at managing his nominal superior, King William, who generally accepted his advice without question. Moltke was able to manage through the form of general directives because most of those in key posts had come up through the General Staff system and hence could be trusted to act in the way he wished. Unfortunately this did not always apply to army commanders. In the cases of Steinmetz and Vogel von Falckenstein, for instance, Moltke was dealing with obstinate, self willed individuals who responded badly to direction. With them, reasoned explanations of what was required were useless; and even the clearest of direct orders were sometimes disobeyed. Both, in the end, had to be removed; the only surprise about this is why it took so long. Perhaps not the only surprise; it was remarkable that Falckenstein in 1866 or Steinmetz in 1870 were appointed to the positions they held when so much was already known about their leadership characteristics.

No doubt Royal support for their appointment had much to do with it. In theory the influence of their chiefs of staff should have moderated the conduct of these wayward commanders; in practice this was not always the case.

During the course of the wars of unification, Moltke endured many anxious movements. These he almost invariably met with an Olympian calm which amazed those around him. The vicissitudes of combat he could naturally accept as part of the job, but he was no doubt inwardly less philosophical about the problems sometimes caused him by subordinates. He did not, however, castigate these as he might have done when he came to write his own account of the Franco-Prussian War. Indeed, for a long time he refused to put pen to paper, saying to his nephew: 'Everything official that I have had occasion to write, or that is worth remembering, is to be seen in the archives of the General Staff. My personal experiences had better be buried with me.'[2]

And on another occasion he remarked: 'Whatever is published in military history is always dressed for effect: yet it is a duty of piety and patriotism never to impair the prestige which identifies the glory of the army with personages of lofty position.'[3] These words, of course, echoed those of Verdy du Vernois quoted above.

It was not until 1887 that he finally yielded to his nephew's urging, conceding that the Official History was too full of detail and too technical for the general reader, and that an abridgement should be made. The result was an extremely uncontroversial book that avoided expressing any adverse opinions about any of his subordinate commanders. Although his nephew described it as 'practically from beginning to end the expression of a private opinion of the war by the Field Marshal himself,' it is, sadly, precisely his personal opinions that are lacking, and which would have made much more interesting reading.

On the other hand, he was somewhat more forthright in comments which he made in various military writings published by the General Staff, and which were gathered together and edited by Daniel Hughes in his *Moltke on the Art of War*, published in 1993. Even here, though, the reader will seek in vain for anything in the way of comment on individuals. It is thus to the voluminous military correspondence written under the pressure of events that one must turn to distil the essential nature of Moltke's relationships with his commanders. Although couched in the stately prose required by the convention of the times, there are many instances in which it is possible to see just how Moltke saw the situation at any given time, as well as how he dealt with what was, when it came to it, a remarkable body of men.

That correspondence, both by telegram and field post, came about because Moltke was conducting enormous operations over great distances; but the fundamentals of leadership were unchanged, as Martin van Creveld reminds us:

> It is easy to forget (and it has in fact often been forgotten) that command, rather than being simply an assortment of technological marvels around which organisations and procedures are built, consists instead of a series of processes – each of them as old as war itself – by which the technological means at hand are pressed into service.[4]

Moltke stands out from his predecessors and his contemporaries because of the way in which he created systems that became the blueprint for the conduct and management of war in the twentieth century.

Nearly two and-a-half millennia after Sun Tzu defined them, Moltke's career demonstrated the five cardinal virtues of a leader. Unassuming, intellectually honest, consistent and clear sighted, he deservedly inspired absolute trust in those around him in his leadership and management of the Prussian army.

Epilogue

When Moltke took his place in the victory parade in Berlin on June 16 1871 he still was to have nearly two decades of service to his country as Chief of the Great General Staff. As the procession wound through the streets of the capital, with Moltke, Bismarck and Roon riding ahead of the Emperor William I.

One of the onlookers, observing Moltke's grave imperturbability, thought it more indicative of his planning for a battle rather than one receiving the tumultuous ovation of the huge crowd.[1]

Moltke carried with him the baton of a field marshal, the rank conferred on him that morning by the Emperor. It was an award to which he, above all others, was overwhelmingly entitled, but it was one which was only sparingly given. Prior to the Franco-Prussian War, the only officer of that rank was the aged Field Marshal Friedrich von Wrangel, who was appointed in 1856. During the war, the Crown Prince and Prince Frederick Charles were promoted to field marshal, immediately after the fall of Metz. After the conclusion of the war Moltke and Roon were duly appointed, and were followed not long after by Manteuffel, Steinmetz, and Herwarth von Bittenfeld. It was not until 1888 that the next appointment was made, with the promotion of Blumenthal. None of the other prominent commanders of 1870-1871 were so honoured, although no doubt Goeben at least would have been had he not died in 1880.

Still surrounded by the younger colleagues whom he had so carefully trained, Moltke continued to devote himself to the work of military organisation and to the development of the General Staff. He worked particularly closely with Verdy, the chief of military history, and Wartensleben, the next to hold that post; and also with Colonel Alfred Kessler, who headed the Railroad and Mobilisation sections.[2] He looked closely at the lessons which were to be learned from the wars of German unification, and applied them to the continuous work of preparation for any future war. He carefully supervised the preparation of the official account of the Franco-Prussian War, parts of which he wrote himself. In 1881, when decorations were conferred on a number of officers who had worked on the official account, William praised Moltke in a Cabinet Order for 'the possession of two merits rarely united in the same person – eminent services in the successful direction of war itself, and in the worthy historical representation of the same.'[3]

That year Moltke, now over eighty, felt that the time had come for a younger man to take his place, and he tendered his resignation. William, however, would have none of it, issuing a Cabinet Order to the effect that Moltke's services were so valuable that his resignation could never be accepted, and he continued in office until after the death of his imperial master.

Although working tirelessly at his duties, Moltke was able to relax during the summer months at his estate at Creisau in Silesia, which he and his wife had bought in 1868. There, he devoted himself to the simple pleasures of the country life, and to the development of the estate. After the death of his sister, his nephew Major Helmuth von Moltke and his family came to live at Creisau. The old Field Marshal had lost none of the pleasure that he took in reading, in music, and in sketching. It is recorded that he particularly enjoyed the novels of Charles Dickens. On the estate at Creisau he had built a chapel, where his wife was buried; while there not a day passed without his visiting her.

In addition to his duties as Chief of the Great General Staff, Moltke had always taken an active part in public affairs, representing in the Reichstag a constituency for which he had been elected in 1867 until his death. Spencer Wilkinson recorded a visit which he paid to the Reichstag during the winter of 1884-1885:

> At the first meeting, as soon as members were in their places, a tall officer in uniform walked up to the President's table and stood erect, in an easy attitude, behind it. The buzz of talk was suddenly hushed and the officer said 'The law requires that at the first meeting of a new Reichstag the oldest member should preside. I was born on the 26th of October, 1800. If no other member announces that he was born before that date I shall take the chair.' After a short pause he sat down at the table and opened the proceedings for the election of a President. That oldest member was Field Marshal Count Moltke, Chief of the Great General Staff of the army. A few days later I passed him in the corridor of the house, and saw a face that I shall never forget. The skin was wrinkled and tanned like leather, so that it seemed like the mask of a mummy, a suggestion not belied by the smooth-lying brown hair. The features were grandly sculptured. The firm chin and set lips had the strength of granite, and from under the high forehead looked out piercing grey eyes that seemed to sum me up in a glance, without interrupting the Olympian serenity of the mind that shone through them. I received the impression of having seen on that face the experience of infinite time combined with a power of which I had never met the like.[4]

Moltke's most important task, during his final years as Chief of the Great General Staff, was the preparation and revision of the war plans that required constant review in the light of changing international conditions. His first opinion, immediately following the war of 1870-1871, was that in the event of a war with France and Russia, Germany would be strong enough to launch an offensive on both fronts. He soon came to realise that, with France's strong military recovery, this was no longer possible; and he favoured an immediate offensive against France, while pursuing a defensive policy against Russia. This remained his view until 1880 when, following the alliance with Austria Hungary in 1879, he reconsidered his strategy, and suggested that the first offensive should be against Russia, while a holding operation was conducted in the west. He was, however, somewhat sceptical about the strength of the alliance, remarking: 'It is useless to stipulate common operations in advance, because in practice they will not be carried out.'[5]

In the west, he was prepared nonetheless to take a forward position to defeat the anticipated French offensive; 'I am of the opinion that even facing superior numbers, we must risk a battle in front of the Rhine before withdrawing behind it'.[6] As the years went by, he began to revert to the idea of making the initial effort principally against France; his final plan, effective from April 1 1888, was based on the repulse of the French offensive with a counter-attack with two thirds of the German army; only eighteen divisions would remain in the east to cooperate with Austria-Hungary.[7] Waldersee, who succeeded Moltke, was coming to the same view, although it was not until Schlieffen took office in 1891 that the concept of an all out offensive in the west took a final, and fatal, hold.

In 1888 Moltke again expressed his wish to retire, this time to the young Kaiser Wilhelm II; and this time his resignation was graciously accepted. He continued, however, to attend the Reichstag regularly; although his speeches were short, and to the point, they commanded profound attention from the other members. The work he had done in his closing years as Chief of the Great General Staff had shown him just how difficult of solution was Germany's strategic problem. It had also shown him the likely face of modern war; in his last speech to the Reichstag, he warned that due to the violence of popular feeling, future wars could last seven, or even thirty years, and could shatter the established social order.[8]

In spite of this, he still regarded war as an inevitable part of life. In 1889 he had set down his fundamental belief as to this:

> Perpetual peace is a dream, and it is not even a beautiful dream. War is an element in the order of the world ordained by God. In it the noblest virtues of mankind are developed; courage and the abnegation of self, faithfulness to duty, and the spirit of sacrifice; the soldier gives his life. Without war the world would stagnate and lose itself in materialism.'[9]

It is difficult to conceive of a twenty first century military commander publicly expressing such a sentiment. As Professor Arthur Marder has put it, however, 'to the pre-1914 generation war was the law of the civilised world as much as of the uncivilised.'[10]

Moltke outlived many of his generals. The first to go was Steinmetz. He formally retired from the army in April 1871. He kept his word, given to the King, that he would not challenge the official view of his military conduct during 1870, although he bitterly resented it. His loyalty was rewarded by promotion to the rank of Field Marshal, and by being made a member of the Upper House of the Prussian Landtag. He died at Bad-Landeck in Silesia on August 2 1877.

Podbielski was appointed as Inspector General of Artillery in 1872. In the following year he was promoted to the rank of General of Cavalry. He died on October 31 1879, and was survived by his wife and six children.

Goeben continued in command of the VIII Corps after the ending of the war, based in Coblenz, and remained in this post for the rest of his life. Like all the leaders of the German army during the wars of unification, he was laden with honours in his lifetime; a fort at Metz was named after him and, many years later, the battle cruiser *Goeben* was to have a major influence on world history. He died on November 13 1880.

Three others of Moltke's most prominent collaborators predeceased him. Falkenstein, after his successful stint as governor general of the German coastal lands during the war of 1870-1871, retired from the army with the rank of General of Infantry. He died at his home at Schloss Dolzig in Brandenburg on April 6 1885. That year also saw the death of Prince Frederick Charles. After the war he had been appointed as Inspector General of the Prussian army, a task to which he no doubt brought the painstaking thoroughness which was his characteristic. He, too, received a large number of awards and decorations, many of which were from foreign monarchs; he was made a Field Marshal of Russia by Tsar Alexander III, and in 1878 was made a Knight Grand Cross of the Order of the Bath by Queen Victoria. He died on January 15 1885, survived by his wife, Princess Maria Anna of Anhalt-Dessau and four of their five children. Werder, when the war ended in 1871 continued in command of the XIV Corps, based in Baden, a post he held until he retired from the service in 1879. His considerable services during the wars of unification were then further recognised when the Emperor made him a count. He died at Grüssow in Pomerania on September 12 1888.

Blumenthal continued to be an active member of the German army. In 1871 he was sent as an observer of the British army manoeuvres of that year, which took place at Chobham. Later in 1871 he was appointed to the command of the IV Corps at Magdeburg, and in 1873 was promoted to the rank of General of Infantry. In 1883 William conferred on him the title of count. Five years later he was made field marshal; he continued in service until he retired in 1896 to his estate at Quellendorf near Köthen, where he died on December 21 1900.

Of the three young 'demigods'. Bronsart and Verdy both survived Moltke, although in Bronsart's case only just; he died at his estate at Scheffnienen near Braunsberg on June 23 1891. Brandenstein, whose health had broken down in 1876, had returned to active service in 1883; however his health broke down again in 1886, and he died in Berlin in March of the year. Verdy, however, enjoyed a long retirement after resigning as War Minister. In 1894 the University of Königsberg recognised his literary activities with the award of Dr. Phil honoris causa. He died in 1910.

Moltke died on April 24 1891, taken ill suddenly while playing whist at home in Berlin:

> Without a struggle and without suffering he passed away, his last conscious act being to turn his face towards the wall where Marie von Moltke's portrait hung.

His countrymen gave him an imposing and solemn funeral in Berlin; and then they laid him to rest in the little chapel at Creisau, beside the wife whom he had so tenderly loved, and whose image, since her death, had never been absent from his heart.[11]

Notes

Chapter 1 Ein Ganz Seltener Mensch

1. Heinrich von Poschinger, *Fürst Bismarck*: *Neue tischgesprache und interviews* (Stuttgart 1899) II p.256; quoted Rudolf Stadelmann, *Moltke und der Staat* (Krefeld 1950) p.32
2. Helmuth von Moltke, *Letters to his Wife and Other Relatives*, trans. JR McIlwraith (London 1896) I p.68-69
3. Quoted FE Whitton, *Moltke* (London 1921) p.52
4. Quoted Sidney Whitman, *Conversations with Prince Bismarck* (London 1900) p.27
5. Gerhard Ritter, *The Sword and the Sceptre* (London 1972) I p.185
6. Arden Bucholz, *Moltke and the German Wars* (London 2001) p.27
7. Ibid., p.32
8. Ritter, I p.193
9. Eberhard Kessel, *Moltke* (Stuttgart 1957) pp.109-110
10. Ibid., p.145
11. Dennis Showalter, *Railroads and Rifles* (Hamden, Conn. 1975) pp.29-30
12. Ibid., I p.31
13. Ibid., I p.35
14. *Letters to his Wife*, I p.88
15. Ibid., I p.31
16. Ibid., I p.175
17. Ibid., I p.177
18. Ritter, I pp.187-188
19. Ibid., I p.189
20. Quoted, I p.189
21. Ritter, I p.191
22. *Letters to his Wife*, I p.211
23. Helmuth von Moltke, *Letters to his Mother and Brothers*, trans C Bell and H Fischer (New York 1892) pp.145-146; Whitton p.61
24. Bucholz, pp.44-46
25. *Letters to his Mother and Brothers*, p.146

26. Quoted Ritter, I p.193
27. Ibid.
28. *Letters to his Wife*, I p.232
29. *Letters to his Mother and Brothers*, pp.154-155
30. *Letters to his Wife*, I pp.262-296
31. Helmuth von Moltke, *Letters from Russia*, trans Robina Napier (London 1878) p.152
32. Ibid., p.124
33. Quoted Whitton, p.67
34. Ibid.,
35. *Letters to his Wife*, II p.82
36. Ritter, I p.194
37. Emperor Frederick III, *War Diary 1870-1871* (London 1927) p258 (cited as Crown Prince)

Chpater 2 Military Philosophy

1. Daniel Hughes, ed, *Moltke on the Art of War* (Novato, CA 1993) p.5
2. Ibid., p.47
3. Herbert Rosinski, *Scharnhorst to Schlieffen; The Rise and Decline of German Military Thought* (Naval War College Review 29, 1976) pp.83-103; quoted Antulio Echevarria II, *Borrowing from the Master* (War and History, 1996) p.274
4. Kessel, p.108
5. Gunther E Rothenberg, ' Moltke, Schlieffen, and the Doctrine of Strategic Envelopment' in *Makers of Modem Strategy*, ed Peter Paret (Oxford 1994) pp.297-298
6. Hughes, pp.35-36
7. Ritter, I p.303; Hughes pp.36-37
8. General von Caemmerer, *The Development of Strategical Science During the Nineteenth Century*, trans K von Donat (London 1905) pp.85-86
9. Quoted Ritter, I p.304
10. Hughes, p.37
11. Ritter, I p.305
12. Hughes, p.101
13. Ibid., p.108
14. Rothenberg, p.296
15. Field Marshal Count Alfred von Schlieffen, *Cannae* (Fort Leavenworth, Kan. 1931) p.128
16. Hughes, pp.263-264
17. Hajo Holborn, 'The Prusso-German School' in Paret, op.cit. pp.288-289
18. Hughes, p.45
19. Ibid.
20. Holborn, p.290
21. Caemmerer, pp.180-181

22. Field Marshal Count Karl Leonhard von Blumenthal, *Journals* (London 1903) p.39
23. Caemmerer, pp.182-183
24. Caemmerer p.188; Prussian General Staff, *Official Account of the Campaign of 1866* (London 1872) pp.239-242 (cited hereafter as Official Account 1866)
25. Schlieffen, pp.137-138
26. Hughes, p.63
27. Schlieffen, p.297
28. Fritz Hönig, *Twenty Four Hours of Moltke's Strategy* (Woolwich 1895) p.184
29. Hughes, p.76
30. Ibid.
31. Ibid. p.77
32. Field Marshal Count Helmuth von Moltke, *The Franco German War of 1870–1871* (London 1907) p.413
33. Hughes, p.171
34. Ibid., p.172
35. Ibid., pp.216-219
36. Caemmerer, p.219
37. Prussian General Staff, *The Franco German War 1870-1871*, trans Captain FCH Clarke (London 1874) I p.155 (cited hereafter as Official History)
38. Hughes, p.181
39. Ibid., p.133
40. Ibid., p.168
41. Rothenberg, p.310
42. Bucholz, p.185

Chapter 3 Organisation and Management

1. General Paul Bronsart von Schellendorff, *The Duties of the General Staff* (London 1905) pp.10-13
2. Quoted ibid., p.3
3. Ibid., p.18
4. Walter Görlitz, *The German General Staff* (London 1953) p.10
5. Colonel J D Hittle, *The Military Staff; Its History and Development* (Harrisburg, Pa. 1949) pp.15-16
6. Ibid., pp.58-59
7. Görlitz, pp.15-16
8. Ibid., p.19
9. Bronsart, pp.23-24
10. Ibid., p.24
11. Ibid., pp.26-27; Hittle, p.62
12. Bronsart, p.28
13. Hittle, p.64
14. Colonel Christian Millotat, *Understanding the Prussian-German General Staff System* (Carlisle, Pa. 1992) p.31

15. Bronsart, p.30
16. Ibid, pp.30-31
17. Görlitz, p.65
18. Görlitz, p.67
19. Colonel TN Dupuy, *A Genius for War* (London 1977) p.59
20. General Julius Verdy du Vernois, *With the Royal Headquarters in 1870-71* (London 1897) p.101
21. Bronsart, p.31
22. Ritter, I p.302
23. *Letters to his Mother and Brothers*, I pp.249-250
24. Bronsart, p.33
25. Hittle, p.66
26. Moltke, *Franco-German War*, p.418
27. Colonel Lonsdale Hale, *The People's War in France 1870-1871* (London 1904) pp.186-187
28. Friedrich von Holstein, *Memoirs,* ed Norman Rich and MH Fisher (Cambridge 1955) p.41
29. Quoted Gordon A Craig, *The Politics of the Prussian Army 1640-1945* (Oxford 1955) p.195
30. Bucholz, p.52
31. Ritter, I p.184
32. Herbert Rosinski, *The German Army* (London 1939) pp.127-128

Chapter 4 Moltke and the King
1.   Archibald Forbes, *William of Germany* (London 1888) p.75
2.   Ibid., p.91
3.   Paul Wiegler, *William the First: His Life and Times* (London 1929) p.227
4.   Ibid., p.91
5.   Ibid., p.154
6.   Ibid., p.227
7.   *Letters to his Wife,* I p.214
8.   Ibid., II p.155
9.   Ibid., III p.158
10. Wiegler, p.245
11. Ritter, I p.181
12. Gordon A Craig, *Königgrätz* (London 1965) pp.114-115
13. Ibid., p.115
14. *Letters to his Wife,* III p.299
15. Craig, *Königgrätz*, p.133
16. Hönig, p.149
17. Field Marshal Count Alfred von Waldersee, *A Field Marshal's Memoirs* (London 1924) p.65; Wiegler p.303
18. General Philip Sheridan, *Personal Memories* (London 1888) II p.371

19. Forbes, pp.240-241
20. Hönig, p.146
21. Quoted Spenser Wilkinson, *The Brain of the Navy* (London 1895) p.28
22. Helmuth von Moltke, *Correspondance Militaire* (Paris n.d) II p.524 (cited hereafter as MCM)
23. MCM, II pp.524-525
24. Ibid., II pp.526-527
25. Crown Prince, p.224
26. Ibid., p.251
27. Ibid., pp.259-260
28. MCM, II p.571
29. Blumenthal, pp.235-236
30. Crown Prince, p.255
31. Craig, *Politics*, p.213
32. Ibid., p.214

Chapter 5 Blumenthal

1. Blumenthal, p.344
2. Ibid., p.346
3. Ibid., p.347
4. *Letters to his Wife*, I p.211
5. Quoted Craig, *Politics* p.185
6. MCM, IV pp.117-119
7. Ibid., IV pp.119-121
8. Ibid., IV pp.124-125
9. Ibid., IV pp.126-127
10. Ibid., IV pp.130-133
11. Heinrich von Sybel, *The Founding of the German Empire by William I* (New York 1890) III p.309
12. Craig, *Politics*, p.189
13. MCM. IV p.135-138
14. Craig, Politics, p189
15. MCM, IV pp.150-154
16. Ibid., IV p.175
17. Ibid., IV pp.179
18. Ibid, IV pp.182-183
19. Ibid, IV p.183-184
20. Ibid, IV pp.189-191
21. Ibid, IV pp.205-210
22. Prince Kraft zu Hohenlohe-Ingelfingen, *Aus Meinem Leben* (Berlin 1897) III pp.168-169
23. MCM, IV pp.210-214

Chapter 6 The Campaign in Bohemia
1.   Blumenthal, p.11
2.   Ibid., p.13
3.   Ibid., p.15
4.   Hohenlohe-Ingelfingen, III pp.222-223
5.   Blumenthal, pp.16-17
6.   Ibid., p.21
7.   Ibid., p.25
8.   MCM, V pp.278-282
9.   Ibid., V p.282
10. Blumenthal, p.26
11. MCM, V pp.285-287
12. Ibid., V pp.288-290
13. Ibid., V pp.291-293
14. Blumenthal, p28
15. S Wilkinson: *Moltke's Correspondence during the Campaign of 1866 against Austria* (London 1915) p.43
16. MCM, V pp.326-327
17. Blumenthal, p.28
18. MCM, V pp.327-328
19. Ibid., V pp.326-327
20. Blumenthal, p.34
21. Quoted Craig, *Königgrätz* pp.80-81
22. Blumenthal, p.34
23. MCM, V p.332
24. Ibid., V p.333
25. Ibid., V p.334
26. Blumenthal, pp.38-39
27. Ibid., pp.39-40
28. MCM, V p.338
29. Blumenthal, p.40
30. Ibid.
31. Quoted Craig, *Königgrätz*, pp.126-127
32. Blumenthal, p.41
33. Ibid., p.42
34. Ibid.
35. Ibid., pp.44-45
36. Ibid., p.47
37. Ibid., pp.49-50
38. MCM, V pp.369-370
39. Blumenthal, p.53
40. MCM, V pp.378-387
41. Ibid., pp.386-387

42. Blumenthal, pp.57-58

Chapter 7 Sedan
1.   Blumenthal, p.76
2.   Ibid., pp.80-81
3.   Crown Prince, p.12
4.   Blumenthal, p.82
5.   MCM, I pp.228-229
6.   Verdy, p.46
7.   Ibid., pp.46-47
8.   Ibid., p.49
9.   Blumenthal, pp.85
10. MCM, I pp.243-325
11. Ibid., I p.255
12. William Howard Russell, *My Diary During the Last Great War* (London 1874) pp.74-75
13. MCM, I p.26
14. Blumenthal, pp.88-89
15. MCM I p.261
16. Blumenthal, p.91
17. Ibid., p.93
18. Ibid., p.96
19. Crown Prince, p.58
20. Blumenthal, pp.98-99
21. MCM I p.309
22. Blumenthal, p.102
23. Russell, p.148
24. Blumenthal, p.105
25. Ibid., p.107
26. Ibid.
27. MCM, I pp.333-334
28. Blumenthal, p.108
29. MCM, I p.334-336
30. Ibid., I p.336
31. Blumenthal p.110
32. MCM, I p.339
33. Blumenthal, p.111
34. MCM, I p.340
35. Blumenthal, p.113

Chapter 8 Versailles

1. Blumenthal, p.115
2. Ibid., p.120
3. Ibid., p.122
4. Ibid., p.124
5. Ibid., p.125
6. MCM, II p.385
7. Ibid., II pp.382-383
8. Blumenthal, pp.141-142
9. MCM, II p.409
10. Blumenthal, p.148
11. Crown Prince, p.148
12. Blumenthal, p.149
13. MCM, II pp.415-416
14. Blumenthal, p.159
15. Ibid., p.160
16. Ibid., p.163
17. Ibid.
18. Ibid., p.177
19. Crown Prince, p.174
20. Blumenthal, p.168
21. Ibid., pp.179-180
22. Ibid., pp.180-181
23. Ibid., p.182
24. Ibid., pp.184-185
25. Ibid., p.190
26. Ibid., p.192
27. Ibid., pp.197-198
28. MCM, II pp.573-575
29. Crown Prince, pp.202-203
30. Blumenthal, p.202
31. Ibid., pp.211-212
32. Ibid., p.219
33. Ibid., pp.225-226
34. MCM, II pp.570-571
35. Blumenthal, p.236
36. Ibid., p.240
37. Ibid., p.245
38. Ibid., p.257
39. MCM, II p.643
40. Blumenthal, p.268
41. Ibid., p.285
42. Ibid., p.286

43. Ibid., p.288
44. Ibid., p.339

Chapter 9 Stosch
1. Frederic BM Hollyday, *Bismarck's Rival* (Durham, NC 1960) p.4
2. Ibid., p.7
3. General and Admiral Albrecht von Stosch, *Denkwürdigkeiten* (Stuttgart 1904) p.16
4. Hollyday, pp.12-13
5. Stosch, p.20
6. Hollyday, p.13 quoting Kessel, p.194
7. Hollyday, p.16
8. Ibid., p.18
9. Ibid., p.28
10. Stosch, pp.72-73
11. Ibid., p.75
12. Ibid.
13. Verdy, quoted Hollyday, pp.32-33
14. Hollyday, p.34
15. Ibid., pp.36-37
16. Stosch, p.106
17. Hollyday, p.43
18. Ibid., p.46
19. Hollyday, p.43
20. Ibid., p.46
21. Stosch, pp.120-121
22. Quoted Hollyday, p.55
23. Stosch, pp.124-125
24. Quoted, Hollyday, p.59
25. Ibid.
26. Ibid., p.60
27. Ibid., p.62
28. Ibid.
29. Ibid., p.63
30. Ibid., p.65

Chapter 10   The Loire
1. Crown Prince, p.7
2. Stosch, p.186; Hollyday, p.69
3. Quoted Hollyday, p.69
4. Official History, p.75
5. Moltke, *Franco German War*, p.6
6. MCM, V pp.354-355
7. Martin van Creveld, *Supplying War* (Cambridge 1977) p.85

8. Hollyday, p.71
9. Van Creveld, pp.103-104
10. Ibid., p.108
11. Lieutenant Colonel GA Furse, *The Organisation and Administration of the Lines of Communication in War* (London 1894) p.205
12. Van Creveld, p.102
13. Verdy, p.211
14. Hollyday, pp.73-74
15. Quoted, Hollyday, p.74
16. Hale, p.186
17. Hale, p.198
18. Ibid., pp.222-223
19. Ibid., p.225
20. H Helvig, *Operations of the I Bavarian Corps under General von der Tann* (London 1874) p.279
21. MCM, II pp.539-540
22. Hale, p.249
23. Ibid., p.250
24. Quoted Hale p.262
25. Hale, p.263
26. General Ludwig von Wittich, *Journal de Guerre (*Paris 1902) p.234
27. Official History, III p.360
28. MCM, II p.564
29. Helvig, p.352
30. Hollyday, p.78
31. Verdy, p.225
32. Hollyday, p.76
33. Quoted Hollyday, p.8
34. Hollyday, p.84
35. Ibid., p.85
36. Ibid., p.101
37. Ibid., p.105
38. Ibid., p.217

Chapter 11 The Red Prince
1. Prince Frederick Charles, *A Military Memorial* (London 1866) p.32
2. Dupuy, p.116
3. Karl Demeter, *The German Officer Corps* (London 1965) p.79
4. *Letters to his Wife*, I p.224
5. Ibid, p.226
6. Ibid., II p.103
7. Craig, *Politics*, p.154
8. MCM, IV pp.22-30

9. Ibid., pp.73-74
10. Sybel, III pp.273-274
11. Craig, *Politics*, p.188
12. Quoted Craig, *Politics*, p.189
13. National Archives, FO 425/77 p.159
14. *Letters to his Wife*, II pp.117-180

Chapter 12 Königgrätz

1. MCM, V pp.295-298
2. Quoted Craig, *Königgrätz*, p56
3. Theodor Fontane, *Der Deutsche Krieg von 1866* (Frankfurt 1984) I p.139; quoted Craig, *Königgrätz,* p.62
4. Quoted Craig, *Königgrätz*, p.64
5. MCM, V p.331
6. Ibid., V p.333
7. Quoted Craig, *Königgrätz*, p.91
8. Ibid.
9. Wolfgang Foerster, *Prinz Friedrich Karl von Preussen* (Stuttgart 1910) II p7
10. Official History, pp.164-165
11. MCM, V p.339
12. Craig, *Königgrätz,* p.108
13. Ibid., pp.109 and 205n
14. *Letters to his Wife*, II p.299
15. Quoted Craig, *Königgrätz*, p.134
16. Ibid., pp.176 177
17. Foerster, III p.126; quoted Terence Zuber, *The Moltke Myth* (Lanham Md. 2008) p.147
18. Zuber, pp.vii-viii
19. Ibid., p.73
20. Wilson Blythe, Michigan War Studies Review, October 1 2009

Chapter 13 Metz

1. Crown Prince, p.7
2. Waldersee, p.p60
3. MCM, I pp.271-272
4. Ibid., I pp.271-272
5. Ibid., I pp.290-291
6. Ibid., I p.294
7. Hönig, p.37
8. MCM, I p.297; Hönig, pp.48-49
9. Hönig, p.58
10. Hönig, p.184
11. MCM, I pp.302-303

12. Ibid., I pp.307-308
13. Crown Prince, p.156
14. Quoted Craig, *Politics*, pp.207-208
15. MCM, II p.131

Chapter 14 Le Mans
1. Hale, p.18
2. Ibid., p.21
3. Ibid., p.5
4. Ibid., p.124
5. Crown Prince, p.182
6. MCM, II p.456; quoted Hale p.7
7. MCM, II p.480
8. Waldersee, p.81
9. Ibid., p.82
10. Ibid.
11. Hale, pp.181-182
12. Ibid., pp.188-189
13. Ibid., p.190
14. Waldersee, p.84; Hale, p.209
15. Hale, p.212
16. MCM, II pp.512-515
17. Hale, p.225
18. MCM, II 539-540
19. Hale, pp.242-243
20. Blumenthal, p.; Hale pp.241-242
21. Hale, pp.247-248
22. Ibid., p.280
23. Ibid., p.251
24. MCM, pp.594-596
25. Ibid., II pp.637
26. Waldersee, pp.83-84

Chapter 15 Crown Prince Frederick William
1. Crown Prince, p.199
2. Ibid., p.210
3. Hale, p.60
4. Ibid., p.61
5. Ibid., p.61-62
6. Blumenthal, pp.211-212
7. Waldersee, pp.59-60
8. *Letters to his Wife* II pp.87-88
9. John van der Kiste, *Emperor Frederick III* (Gloucester 1981) p.80

10. Blumenthal, p.15
11. Margaret von Poschinger, ed, *Diaries of the Emperor Frederick during the Campaigns of 1866 and 1870-71* (London 1902) p.9
12. Ibid., p.44
13. Ibid., p.49
14. Ibid., 48
15. Craig, *Politics*, p.203
16. Crown Prince, pp.5-6
17. Ibid., p15
18. Ibid., p.20
19. Ibid., pp.37-38
20. Ibid., p.45
21. Ibid., p.65
22. Ibid., p.81
23. Blumenthal, p.111
24. Crown Prince, p.92
25. Ibid., p.157
26. Blumenthal, p.154
27. Crown Prince, pp.253-254
28. Ibid., 241
29. Ibid., p.161
30. Ibid., p.190
31. Van der Kiste, p.208

Chapter 16 Manteuffel
1. Craig, *Politics,* pp.99-100
2. Demeter, p.18
3. Gordon A Craig, *War, Politics and Diplomacy*, (London 1966) p.102
4. Ibid., p.101
5. Ibid., p106
6. Ibid., p.104
7. Ibid., p.105
8. Quoted Demeter, p.18
9. MCM, IV p.191
10. Ibid., IV p.193
11. Craig, *Politics*, p.186
12. Ibid., p.187
13. Ibid., p.173
14. Lothar Gall, *Bismarck: The White Revolutionary* (London 1986)I p.157
15. Craig, *War, Politics, and Diplomacy*, p.111
16. Quoted H Böhme, *The Foundation of the German Empire* (Oxford 1971) p.166
17. Heinrich Friedjung, *The Struggle for Supremacy in Germany 1859-1866* (London 1935) p.190

Chapter 17 From the Main to the Doubs

1. Official Account 1866 p.58
2. Ibid., p.477
3. Ibid., p.482
4. GLM Strauss, *Men who have made the New German Empire* (London) II p.175
5. A von Schell, *Operations of the First Army under General von Steinmetz* (London 1873) p.86
6. Ibid., p.71
7. Ibid., p.80
8. Ibid.
9. Ibid., p.203
10. Ibid., p.215
11. H von Wartensleben, *Operations of the First Army under General von Manteuffel* (London 1873) p11
12. Ibid., p.17
13. MCM, II p.407
14. Wartensleben, *Manteuffel* p.47
15. Ibid., 57
16. Ibid., 62
17. Ibid., p.73
18. MCM, II p.640
19. Ibid., II 579-551
20. Wartensleben, *Manteuffel,* p.199 n
21. MCM, II p.640
22. Wartensleben, *Manteuffel,* p.199n
23. A von Schell, *Operations of the First Army under General von Goeben* (London 1873) pp.59-60
24. Wartensleben, *Manteuffel,* pp.205-206
25. H von Wartensleben, *Operations of the South Army* (London 1872) p.6
26. Ibid., pp.8-9
27. Ibid., pp.9-11
28. Ibid., p.15
29. Ibid., 30
30. Official History 1870-1871, V p.10
31. Wartensleben, *South Army,* p.30
32. Ibid., p.34
33. Ibid., 49-50
34. Ibid., p.80
35. Ibid., p.95
36. Strauss, II p.163
37. Quoted Craig, *War, Politics, and Diplomacy,* p.93
38. Ibid.

Chapter 18 Goeben
1. Sybel, V p.354
2. *Letters to his Wife*, I pp.195, 213 and 247
3. Strauss, II pp.192-196
4. Michael Embree, *Bismarck's First War* (Solihull 2006) pp.169-174
5. Ibid., p.180
6. *Letters to his Wife*, II p.127
7. Ibid., III p.140
8. Schlieffen, *Cannae* p.82
9. Official History, 1866 p.346
10. Ibid., p.464
11. MCM, I p.227
12. Ibid., p.256
13. Ibid., p.295
14. Ibid., p.298
15. Hönig, p.88
16. Ibid., p.102
17. MCM, II pp.423-424; Schell, *Goeben*, p.15
18. Schell, *Goeben*, p.15
19. Daily News, *Correspondence of the War between Germany and France 1870-71* (London 1871) pp.503-504
20. Ibid.
21. Michael Howard, *The Franco Prussion War* (London 1962) pp.404-405
22. August von Goeben, *Contributions to the History of the Campaign in the North East of France*, trans. Capt. JL Seton (London 1873) p.6
23. Howard, p.406

Chapter 19 Steinmetz
1. Craig, *Königgrätz*, pp.71-72
2. Ibid., p.72; J von Verdy du Vernois, *Im Hauptquartier der Zweiten Armee 1866* (Berlin 1900) p.42
3. MCM, V pp.260-261
4. Schleiffen, p.96
5. Ibid., p.100
6. Quoted Craig, *Königgrätz*, p.80
7. Verdy, *Royal Headquarters*, p22
8. Waldersee, p.60
9. Ibid., pp.61-62
10. Verdy, *Royal Headquarters*, p.22
11. Quoted Howard, p.61
12. Blumenthal, pp.26-27
13. MCM, I p.246
14. Ibid, I p.246

15. Ibid., I pp.246-247
16. Ibid., I pp.247-248
17. Ibid., I p.249
18. Ibid., I p.250
19. Ibid., I pp.252-253
20. Howard, p.99
21. Moltke, *Franco German War*, p.25
22. MCM, I pp.259-260
23. Ibid., I p.262
24. Ibid., I p.267
25. Ibid., ip 269
26. Ibid., I pp.269-270
27. Schell, *Steinmetz,* p.86
28. Verdy *Royal Headquarters*, pp.67-68
29. MCM, I p.292
30. Ibid., I p.296
31. Hönig, *24 Hours*, p.42
32. Ibid., pp.102-103
33. Ibid., p.109
34. Howard, p.178
35. Moltke, *Franco German War*, p.58
36. Hönig, *24 Hours*, p.149
37. Sheridan II p.373
38. Howard, p.180
39. Crown Prince, p.70
40. Howard, p.190

Chapter 20 Werder

1. Strauss, II pp.203-206
2. MCM, I pp.264-265
3. Ibid., p.277
4. Ibid., I pp.282-283
5. MCM, II p.359
6. Ibid., II p.389
7. Ludwig Löhlein, *The Operations of the Corps of General von Werder*
8. (Chatham n.d) p.19
9. MCM, II p.419
10. Ibid. II p.420
11. Ibid.
12. Löhlein, p.23
13. Löhlein, pp.37-38; MCM, II pp.434-436
14. Ibid.
15. Löhlein pp.54-55

16. MCM, II p.504
17. Ibid., II pp.557-558
18. Ibid., III p.649
19. Löhlein, pp.117-118;MCM, II pp.657-660
20. MCM, II p.669
21. Crown Prince, p.259
22. MCM, II p.669
23. Crown Prince, pp.264-265
24. MCM, II p.680
25. Lohlein, pp.145-146
26. Ibid., p.148
27. Ibid., p.162

Chapter 21 Falckenstein
1.   Strauss, II p.181
2.   Ibid. II p.183
3.   Sybel, III p.261
4.   MCM, V p.392
5.   Ibid., V pp.400-401
6.   Quoted Craig, *Politics*, p.197
7.   MCM, V pp.413-414
8.   Ibid., V p.414
9.   Sybel, V p.48
10. MCM, V p.409
11. Ibid., V p.421
12. Sybel,V pp.62-64
13. Ibid., p.67
14. MCM, V pp.435-436
15. Sybel, V p.69
16. Ibid., V p.72
17. MCM, V p.444
18. Sybel, V p.75
19. Schlieffen, pp.83-84
20. MCM, V p.448
21. Sybel, V p.373
22. Moltke, *Letters to his Wife* II p.259

Chapter 22 The Demigods
1.   Whitton, p.76
2.   Görlitz, p.76
3.   MCM, V p.292
4.   Hale, p.31
5.   Crown Prince, p.171

6. Craig, *Politics*, p.205n
7. Hughes, p.88
8. Verdy, Royal Headquarters pp.23-24
9. Crown Prince, p.254
10. Verdy, *Royal Headquarters*, pp.24-25
11. Ibid., p.25
12. Ibid.
13. Howard, p.62
14. MCM, V p.189
15. Verdy, *Royal Headquarters*, p.26
16. Hughes, p.83
17. Archibald Forbes, *Memories and Studies of War and Peace* (London 1895) p.77
18. Paul Bronsart von Schellendorff, *Geheimes Kriegstagebuchs* 1870-1871 ed Peter Rassow (Bonn 1954) pp.279-280; quoted Howard p.351
19. Ibid., p.241; quoted Howard, p.349
20. Craig, *Politics,* p.229
21. Verdy, *Royal Headquarters*, p.26
22. Hughes, p.82
23. Verdy, *Royal Headquarters* p.83
24. Ibid., p.235
25. Ibid., p.92
26. Ibid., p.112; Hughes , p.85
27. Verdy, *Royal Headquarters*, p.215

Chapter 23 Conclusion

1. Sun Tzu, 'On the Art of War' in *Roots of Strategy*, ed Brig Gen. TR Phillips (Harrisburg Pa.) 1940 p.21
2. Moltke, *Franco German War*, p.V
3. Ibid.
4. Martin van Creveld, *Command in War* (Cambridge, Mass.1985) p.103
5. Bucholz, p.187

Epilogue

1. Whitton, p.301
2. Bucholz, p.65
3. Whitton, p.303
4. Spenser Wilkinson, *The Early Life of Moltke* (Oxford 1913) pp.3-4
5. Rothenburg, p.308
6. Ibid.
7. Ibid., p.309
8. Ibid.
9. Whitton, p.308
10. Arthur J Marder, *From the Dreadnought to Scapa Flow* (Oxford 1961) I p.3
11. Whitton, p.309

Bibliography

BLUMENTHAL, Field Marshal Count Karl Leonhard von, *Journals* (London 1903)

BRONSART VON SCHELLENDORFF, General Paul von, *The Duties of the General Staff* (London 1905)

BRONSART VON SCHELLENDORFF, General Paul von, *Geheimes Kriegstagebuchs*, ed.. Peter Rassow (Bonn 1954)

BÖHME, H, *The Foundation of the German Empire* (Oxford 1971)

BUCHOLZ, Arden, *Moltke, Schlieffen and Prussian War Planning* (New York 1991)

BUCHOLZ, Arden, *Moltke and the German Wars* (London 2001)

CAEMMMERER, General von, *The Development of Strategical Science during the Nineteenth Century* trans.. K von Donat (London 1905)

CRAIG, Gordon A, *The Politics of the Prussian Army* (Oxford 1955)

CRAIG, Gordon A, *Königgrätz* (London 1965)

CRAIG, Gordon A, *War, Politics, and Diplomacy* (London 1966)

CREVELD, Martin van, *Supplying War* (Cambridge 1977)

CREVELD, Martin van, *Command in War* (Cambridge, Mass. 1985)

DAILY NEWS, *Correspondence of the War between Germany and France 1870-71* (London 1871)

DEMETER, Karl, *The German Officer Corps* (London 1965)

DUPUY, Colonel TN *A Genius for War* (London 1977)

EMBREE. Michael, *Bismarck's First War* (Solihull 2006)

FOERSTER, Wolfgang, *Prinz Friedrich Karl von Preussen* (Stuttgart 1910)

FONTANE, Theodor, *Der Deutsche Krieg von 1866* (Frankfurt 1984)

FORBES, Archibald, *William of Germany* (London 1888)

FORBES, Archibald, *Memories and Studies of War and Peace* (London 1895)

FREDERICK III, Emperor of Germany, *War Diary 1870-1871* (London 1926)

FREDERICK CHARLES, Prince, *A Military Memorial* (London 1866)

FRIEDJUNG, Heinrich, *The Struggle for Supremacy in Germany 1859-1866* (London 1935)

FURSE, Lieutenant Colonel GA, *The Organisation and Administration of Lines of Communication in War* (London 1894)

GALL, Lothar, *Bismarck: The White Revolutionary* (London 1986)

GOEBEN, General August von, *Contributions to the History of the Campaign in the North East of France*, trans. Capt. JL Seton (London 1873)

GÖRLITZ, Walter, *The German General Staff* (London 1953)

HALE Colonel Lonsdale, *The People's War in France* (London 1873)

HELMS, M, *Moltke, his Life and Character* (London 1982)

HELVIG, H *Operations of the I Bavarian Corps under General von der Tann* (London 1874)

HITTLE, Colonel JD, *The Military Staff: Its History and Development* (Harrisburg Pa. 1949)

HOHENLOHE INGELFNGEN, Prince Kraft zu, *Aus Meinem Leben* (Berlin 1897)

HOLBORN, Hajo, 'The Prusso-German School' in *Makers of Modern Strategy*, ed. Peter Paret (Oxford 1994)

HOLLYDAY, Frederick BM. *Bismarck's Rival* (Durham, NC 1960)

HOLSTEIN, Friedrich von, *Memoirs*, ed. Norman Rich and MH Fisher (Cambridge 1955)

HÖNIG, Fritz, *Twenty Four Hours of Moltke's Strategy* (Woolwich 1895)

HOWARD, Michael, *The Franco-Prussian War* (London 1962)

HUGHES, Daniel, ed. *Moltke on the Art of War* (Novato Ca. 1993)

KESSEL, Eberhard, *Moltke* (Stuttgart 1957)

KISTE, John van der, *Emperor Frederick III* (Gloucester 1981)

LÖHLEIN, Ludwig, *The Operations of the Corps of General von Werder* (Chatham n.d)

MALET, Sir Alexander, *The Overthrow of the Germanic Confederation by Prussia in 1866* (London 1870)

MILLOTAT, Colonel Christian, *Understanding the Prusso-German General Staff System* (Carlisle Pa. 1992)

MOLTKE, Field Marshal Count Helmuth von, *Correspondance Militaire* (Paris, n.d.)

MOLTKE, Field Marshal Count Helmuth von, *Letters from Russia*, trans. Robina Napier (London 1878)

MOLTKE, Field Marshal Count Helmuth von, *Letters to his Mother and Brothers*, trans. C Bell and H Fischer (New York 1892)

MOLTKE, Field Marshal Count Helmuth von, *Letters to his Wife and other Relatives*, trans. JR McIlwraith (London 1896)

MOLTKE, Field Marshal Count Helmuth von, *The Franco German War of 1870-1871* (London 1907)

NASO, E von, *Moltke*, (Hamburg 1937)

POSCHINGER, Margaret von, ed.., *Diaries of the Emperor Frederick during the Campaigns of 1866 and 1870-71* (London 1902)

PRUSSIAN GENERAL STAFF, *Official Account of the Campaign of 1866* (London 1871)

PRUSSIAN GENERAL STAFF, *The Franco-German War 1870-1871* trans. Capt. FCH Clarke (London 1874)

RITTER, Gerhard, *The Sword and the Sceptre* (London 1972)

ROSINSK, Herbert, *The German Army* (London 1939)

ROTHENBERG, Gunther E, 'Moltke, Schlieffen and the Doctrine of Strategic Envelopment' in *Makers of Modern Strategy*, ed. Peter Paret (Oxford 1994)

RUSSELL, William Howard, *My Diary during the Last Great War* (London 1872)
SCHELL, A von, *Operations of the First Army under General von Goeben* (London 1873)
SCHELL, A von, *Operations of the First Army under General von Steinmetz* (London 1873)
SCHLIEFFEN, Field Marshal Count Alfred von, *Cannae* (Fort Leavenworth Kan 1931)
SHEREIDAN, General Philip, *Personal Memories* (London 1888)
SHOWALTER, Dennis, *Railroads and Rifles* (Hamden Conn. 1975)
STADELMANN, Rudolf, *Moltke und der Staat* (Krefeld 1950)
STOSCH, General and Admiral Albrecht von, *Denkwürdigkeiten* (Stuttgart 1904)
STRAUSS, GLM *Men who have made the New German Empire* (London 1875)
SUN TZU, 'On the Art of War' in *Roots of Strategy* ed. Brig. Gen. TR Phillips (Harrisburg Pa. 1940)
SYBEL, Heinrich von, *The Founding of the German Empire by William I* (New York190)
VERDY DU VERNOIS, General J von, *With the Royal Headquarters 1870-1871* (London 1897)
VERDY DU VERNOIS, General J von, *Im Hauptquartier der Zweiten Armee 1866* (Berlin 1900)
WALDERSEE, Field Marshal Count Alfred von, *A Field Marshal's Memoirs* (London 1924)
WARTENSLEBEN, H von, *Operations of the South Army* (London 1872)
WARTENSLEBEN, H von, *Operations of the First Army under General von Manteuffel* (London 1873)
WHITMAN, Sidney, *Conversations with Prince Bismarck* (London 1900)
WHITTON, FE, *Moltke* (London 1921)
WIEGLER, Paul, *William the First: His Life and Times* (London 1929)
WILKINSON, Spenser, *The Brain of an Army* (London 1895)
WILKINSON, Spenser, ed., *Moltke's Correspondence during the Campaign of 1866 against Austria* (London 1915)
WILKINSON, Spenser, *The Brain of the Navy* (London 1929)
WITTICH, General Ludwig von, *Journal de Guerre* (Paris 1902)
ZUBER, Terence, *The Moltke Myth* (Lanham Md. 2008)

Index

Lightning Source UK Ltd.
Milton Keynes UK
UKHW021226300721
387998UK00002B/10/J